CASES IN
FINANCIAL ACCOUNTING

DAVID E. MIELKE Ph.D.
Marquette University
Milwaukee, Wisconsin

DONALD E. KIESO Ph.D., C.P.A.
Northern Illinois University
DeKalb, Illinois

JERRY J. WEYGANDT Ph.D., C.P.A.
University of Wisconsin
Madison, Wisconsin

JOHN WILEY & SONS

New York Chichester Brisbane
Toronto Singapore

The authors wish to acknowledge the following source for Case 19-7:

THE WALL STREET JOURNAL, May 8, 1985, Vol. CCV #90 p.34

ISBN: 0-471-83194-8
Printed in the United States of America
10 9 8 7 6 5 4 3 2 1

PREFACE

The case method is a teaching method that has been in existence for some time. It differs from traditional teaching methods in that it does not involve the memorization of facts and an instructor lecturing the students on his thoughts. The emphasis is on the development of thinking, problem solving skills, and technical knowledge through discussion. The lecture method has learning through listening with an emphasis on the acquisition of facts as its primary goal. In contrast, the case method has learning through discussion with an emphasis on thinking as its primary goal.

To some extent the degree of success in reaching the primary goal of the case method is dependent on the availability of a collection of cases which pertains to a variety of issues with varying degrees of difficulty and requiring different levels of student expertise and involvement. This book attempts to satisfy those needs by providing over 238 cases with a variety of formats, solution approaches, and degrees of difficulty. The topics covered include almost all those covered in an Intermediate Accounting textbook and additional topics which might only be studied in advanced accounting courses.

We have attempted to develop a set of cases which will permit different pedagogical approaches to be used. The book may be used alone in the classroom or as a supplement to a more conventional accounting text. Sufficient cases are available in this textbook on which an entire course could be developed; for example as the text for an advanced theory course in financial reporting. It might also be used in connection with outside readings to study many topical and sometimes controversial issues in accounting and financial reporting. The solutions manual presents recommended readings for each chapter which might be used in this respect.

Some instructors might wish to use the text as a supplement and assign only a limited number of cases for classroom discussion in Intermediate Accounting. Others might wish to expand the intermediate accounting sequence as some schools have done (such as three semesters) and integrate the case method into this expanded time allotment.

The cases are aimed at students who have some exposure to basic accounting concepts and methods. However, because of the variation of degrees of difficulty involved in the cases the students might be at the intermediate or advanced level. Master's students and business executives would also find ample materials appropriate at their levels.

The cases themselves are of many different types. Some of the cases are similar to AICPA or CMA type questions. They are relatively short and require a solution that can be considered right or wrong. Others are technically oriented. The issue to be resolved is fairly obvious, the facts are given relative to the issue, some numerical calculations may be required, basic judgments might be made about the relative importance of various considerations, and a technical accounting solution is reached.

Other cases are more of the armchair variety that are not subject to precise definition or a single solution. One armchair approach might require the identification of a particular accounting issue and the evaluation of potential alternative treatments of the issue. Another approach may be to assess the economic implications of the accounting treatment and to speculate as to the motivations of the preparers of the financial statements. The students could also be placed in the role of a decision maker and asked to respond. Although the majority of the armchair cases are conceptual in nature, a number may also require computations and journal entries.

Another type of case may require the consideration and discussion of accounting theory. An excerpt from a speech, editorial comment, magazine article, or other published source may serve as the focus of an accounting theory controversy. Varying degrees of research are required to prepare these solutions.

Finally, certain cases attempt to bring the study of accounting and the real world together. The materials explore and analyse the application of financial accounting in the context of actual annual reports.

The student's role in this course can be easily stated: preparation and participation. It is important that students realize that the case method may require new methods of preparation relative to previous lecture oriented courses and that the first attempts at case solutions may lead to frustration. Students may want closure. They want the "right" answer. They may think that, as in other accounting courses, there are sets of rules or methods of solution that if memorized and followed, will lead to the correct answers. This is not usually the situation with case analysis. There may be no single correct solution, but a variety of solutions. Actual real world situations as depicted in the cases may involve exceptions, little well-defined guidance, and uncertainties.

A generalized procedure is offered as a model to aid the student in approaching most cases. First, scan the case to obtain a fast, accurate overview of the primary issues or problems involved, the type of information provided, type of information required, and whether or not quantitative analysis will be necessary.

Second, the student should read the case carefully. Underline key facts and write notes in the margin.

The next step required may be an examination of the underlined material and margin notes to identify the problems faced by the manager or accountant and if not stated in the case instructions, state the problem as succinctly as possible. By writing down the problems the student may better clarify the issues in their minds.

Fourth, the student should think about the information required for the analysis and solutions. There may be a need to examine accounting textbooks, professional pronouncements, or other literature to search for solutions. This research and investigation process is a valuable bonus of the case method.

The next step is the accumulation of the required information from both within the case, and, if necessary from outside sources and to outline a solution.

Sixth, since communication is important in practice, the student should prepare a case write-up--whether or not it is to be turned in. The write-up should answer the questions logically and if necessary build an argument from an introduction at the beginning to the conclusions and recommendations at the end.

Finally the student should participate in class discussion. The student should be willing both to express and support his or her work and to listen to and objectively analyze the work of others. The key is to relax, learn, and help others learn through your participation.

A basic premise of the case method is that one learns by doing. It follows that the best way to learn about the case method is to use it. It can be a stimulating, rewarding experience for both the student and for the instructor.

Special thanks are extended to the primary reviewers of our manuscript:

Robert Bartlett
California State
University-Sacramento

George C. Holdren
University of Nebraska

David Finley
University of Houston

Thomas Nunamaker
Washington State University

We would also like to extend our thanks to the students who, over the past years, participated in the development of some of the case materials, Kathleen Hawkins for her tireless efforts in typing the manuscript, and to Christine Mielke for her constant encouragement and patience during the writing process. While we are pleased to credit all those who assisted us, the responsibility for any errors rests solely with us.

CONTENTS

CHAPTER 1 – THE ENVIRONMENT OF FINANCIAL ACCOUNTING AND THE
DEVELOPMENT OF ACCOUNTING STANDARDS   1

Savings and Loan Dilemma   1
"Generally Accepted Accounting Principles"   2
The Role of the SEC and FASB   3
Economic Consequences   3
Accounting Standard Setting   4
Models for Setting Accounting Standards   5
The Role of Research   6
The Accounting Environment   7
Operating Efficiencies at the FASB   8
The Accounting Profession   9

CHAPTER 2 – THEORY FORMULATION AND THE CONCEPTUAL FRAMEWORK   11

Examination of the Conceptual Framework   11
Theoretical Framework   12
Major Problems of Accounting Theory   13
Social Welfare   13
Insurance Industry   14
Harbott, Inc.   15
Approaches to Constructing Accounting Theory   16
Users of Accounting Information   16
Information Characteristics   17
FASB Concepts Statement No. 2   18

CHAPTER 3 – STATEMENT OF INCOME AND RETAINED EARNINGS   21

The Definition of Income   21
Vulcan, Inc. Income Statement Presentation   22
Tooey vs. Percival   24
Mecklin Inc.: Extraordinary Losses?   25
Unusual Events   26
Holmes, Inc.   27
Current Operating vs. All Inclusive Income   28
Classification of Irregular Items   29
"Life is Not Smooth"   31
Income and Capital   31
Discontinued Operations   32

CHAPTER 4 – THE BALANCE SHEET AND STATEMENT OF CHANGES
IN FINANCIAL POSITION   35

The Historical Cost Balance Sheet?   35
Hillery, Inc.   36
Allied Communications Co.   39
Balance Sheet Presentation   40
Balance Sheet Disclosures   42
Lockstep Corp   43
Yoho Plumbing, Inc.   44
The Volkswagen Group   45
Relationship Between the Balance Sheet and Income Statement   47
Jemco, Inc.   48
Weston, Inc.   49

CHAPTER 5 – CASH AND RECEIVABLES   51

Handy Man, Inc.   51
Cold, Hard Cash   52
Northwest Lumber Co.   53
Floating Deposits   62
Marshall Chemical Co.   62
Smalley Supply, Inc.   63
Double Default   64
Largo Company   65
Rice Co.   66
Horsing Around   67

CHAPTER 6 – VALUATION OF INVENTORIES   69

Inventory is Inventory   69
Harnischfeger Corporation   70
"Profitable" Obsolete Inventory Losses   72
Cost of Goods Sold and Inventory   73
Liquid LIFO Inventory   74
Standard Costs for Inventory?   75
Lower of Cost or Market   77
Sutro Company   78
The Munz Company   79
Manor Nylons, Incorporated   79

**CHAPTER 7 – ACQUISITION AND DISPOSITION, DEPRECIATION, AND
DEPLETION OF PROPERTY, PLANT, AND EQUIPMENT   81**

Useful Arbitrary Allocations   81
The Nature of Property, Plant, and Equipment   82
Electricpower's Audit Program   83
The High Sierra Real Estate Co.   84
Depreciaton Disclosure   86
Roadway Transport Co.   88
Standard, Inc.   89
Warren Manufacturing, Inc.   91
Capitalize or Expense?   91
Depreciation Problems   93

CHAPTER 8 – INTANGIBLE ASSETS   97

HAL Corporation   97
C.W. Dean   99
The Value of Professional Athletes   101
Spartan Corporation   102
Rent-A-Tech   104
Equine Enterprises   106
Hubert Inc.   107
Motor Carrier Industry   109
Simpson Photo   110
Amortization of Development Costs   113

CHAPTER 9 – CURRENT LIABILITIES AND CONTINGENCIES   115

Red Inc.   115
Zoe Corporation   116
Marchael Manufacturing, Inc.   117
Fresno Airlines   118
The Changing Liability   118
Fountain, Inc.   119
The Greyhound Corporation   120
Contingencies   121

American Fidelity Corporation   122
RCA Corporation   123

CHAPTER 10 - LONG-TERM LIABILITIES   125

Consolidated Foods Company   125
Adventure Manufacturing Company   126
Chavez Company   128
Goodwealth Tire Company   129
Restructuring of Debt   130
WLTA Bank   132
Ross Steel Company   133
The Formerly Troubled Company Inc. (FTC)   134
Acme Restaurants, Inc.   137
Chrysis Corporation   138
In-Substance Defeasance   140
Cooperation for Off-Balance Sheet Financing   141

CHAPTER 11 - STOCKHOLDERS' EQUITY   143

"Secret Reserves"   143
Bush Terminal   144
Ford Motor Company   147
Hawkeye Chemical   148
City Utility   149
Financial Press Statement   150
Hock Pencil Company   151
Growing Shares of Stock   152
The Value of Treasury Stock   153
Microsoft Corporation   155

CHAPTER 12 - DILUTIVE SECURITIES AND EARNINGS PER SHARE   157

Summary Indicator   157
Noreen Enterprises   158
Steel City Gem   160
Epson Company   161
Beam-O-Light Corporation   163
Smother Co.   164
Earnings Per Share   165
Hargrove Manufacturing Company   166
Satellite Services, Inc.   168
Fast Grow Corporation   169

CHAPTER 13 - INVESTMENTS   171

Business Combinations   171
City Builders Corporation   172
Acquisitions, Inc.   173
Tanzania Refining Company   174
Real Data Systems   176
Land and Building Planning, Inc.   177
Badger Company 178
Maniott Corporation   179
Sharp, Inc.   180
Purchase Versus Pooling   182
Boston Corporation   186
Temporary Investments   187
Leather Luggage Company   188

CHAPTER 14 - REVENUE RECOGNITION   191

Gerscke Enterprises   191

Real Estate Development, Inc.   192
Today's Youth   194
Chief Burger 195
Southern Fried Shrimp   196
Samson, Inc.   198
Video Station   200
Modern Investment Services, Inc.   201
Inexco Oil Company   203
Satellite Systems Corporation   205

CHAPTER 15 – ACCOUNTING FOR INCOME TAXES   207

Let the Tax Follow the Income   207
Personal Financial Statements 208
Aetna Life and Casualty   216
Omaha Corp.   218
Subsidy or Stimulant?   220
American Electric Power Co.   223
Menlow Engineering 228
Beck Company   229
Death and Taxes   230
Crop-Keep Corp.   231

CHAPTER 16 – ACCOUNTING FOR PENSION COSTS   233

The Pension Obligation   233
Pretentious Packaging, Inc.   238
Champion Motors   242
Benevolent Corporation   243
Buying a Pension Plan   245
Bethlehem Steel Corporation 248
Delta & Sigma Phototype, Inc.   254
Scott Steel Co., Inc.   256
Pension Terms   257
Actuarial Services   259

CHAPTER 17 – ACCOUNTING FOR LEASES   261

A Lease is a Lease is a Lease ...   261
Auto-Lube, Inc.   262
Community Hospital   263
Amco Company   265
Betty Young's Bakery   266
The Davids Corporation   268
Lease Agreement 270
First City Bank   271
Leveraged Leasing   272
St. Francis Hospital   273
BankAmerica Corp.   275

CHAPTER 18 – ACCOUNTING CHANGES AND ERROR ANALYSIS   277

The AT&T Divestiture   277
Norbert Electrostatics, Inc.   280
Quick-Wash Services, Inc.   282
FIFO to LIFO to FIFO   283
Harnett, Inc.   284
Interlaken, Inc.   286
Monte Corp.   287
Restatement for Comparison?   288
The Errors of Naples   290
Sturm, Inc.   291

CHAPTER 19 - INTERNATIONAL ACCOUNTING 295

"THE" Accounting Change – 1982   295
Functional Currency   297
Foreign Inflation   298
International Consolidation 299
One or Two Transactions?   301
Hedging   302
International Accounting Standards?   304
Comparative Systems of Accounting   307
Adjust to GAAP   308
Foreign Disclosure   310

CHAPTER 20 - FINANCIAL REPORTING AND CHANGING PRICES   313

Accounting for Inflation   313
Enterprise Building Contractors   315
Hershey Foods Corporation   316
Allen, Inc.   318
Valueland Investment Trust   320
The Fallacies of General Price Level Accounting   321
Inflation Accounting for Nonmonetary Assets   323
San-Tan, Inc.   324
The SEC and ASR190   325
Wild Enterprises   326

CHAPTER 21 - BASIC FINANCIAL STATEMENT ANALYSIS 329

"Picking Winners"   329
Financial Statement Analysis   330
Earnings Analysis   331
Loan Evaluation   333
Fundamental Investment Analysis   334
Schaefer Retailers 336
Dividend Policy   337
The Value of Book Value   338
Acquisition Analysis   340
Trading on Equity   342

CHAPTER 22 - FULL DISCLOSURE IN FINANCIAL REPORTING   345

The Penn Central   345
Management's Responsibilities   346
Social Responsibilities   348
Comparable Segmental Information?   351
Big Sky Ski Company   352
Atlantic, Inc.   354
"Safe Harbor" Forecasts   355
Harness Corporation 356
State Utility   358
T.A. Properties   359

CHAPTER 23 - EMERGING ISSUES   361

ADC Loans   361
Sale of Securities with a "Put"   363
Recognition of Purchased Losses   364
Accounting for Section 83 Stock Purchase/Option Plans   365
Temporary Control Income 367
Contingent Stock Purchase Warrants   368
Purchased Lease Residuals 369
Debt or Equity?   370
Creative Financing   371
The Problem of Duplicate Facilities   372

THE ENVIRONMENT OF FINANCIAL ACCOUNTING AND THE DEVELOPMENT OF ACCOUNTING STANDARDS

1-1 Savings and Loan Dilemma

In the early 1980's, hardly a day went by in which the problems of the savings and loan (S&L) industry were not discussed in the financial press. The cause of the S&L's problems was that the rates paid on the monies they borrowed had substantially increased, whereas the return on their assets (mostly long-term fixed rate mortgages) had risen slowly. For example, in the first part of 1981, S&Ls paid 10.31% for their money and received only 9.72% on their mortgages. Such a situation causes two problems financially for the industry namely, capital adequacy and liquidity. Capital adequacy problems arise because if the loan portfolio were written down to its market value, many S&L's net worth would be eliminated. Such a treatment might lead to a total loss of confidence in the industry. Liquidity problems develop because some S&Ls are paying out more than they receive, and therefore may not have enough to pay their bills and to allow depositors to withdraw their monies.

One solution proposed would be to allow the S&Ls to sell mortgage loans at a loss (increase liquidity) but allow them to charge the loss to capital over the life of the loan (maintain capital). The savings and loan industry lobbied hard for such a treatment. The government through the Federal Home Loan Bank Board recommended that such an approach be permitted. Others disagreed. Many accountants argued that the sale of an asset (in this case, mortgage loans) should generate a gain or loss on sale. In addition, it was noted that to defer this loss has the effect of burying this item in the balance sheet such that an investor would not be aware of the transaction. Others argue that a deferred loss account cannot be an asset because no future benefits will be received from it.

You have a Savings and Loan Company as a client who has recently been experiencing a severe liquidity problem. The S&L sold some of its mortgages, but is now concerned with how to account for this transaction. Since this is a relatively new or emerging issue you explain that some research may be necessary to determine a method of accounting for the transaction.

Without addressing the specific financial accounting problem described, what is a general research approach that an accountant might take to investigate emerging issues such as the one described in this case? Include a listing of reference materials that might be helpful in your research.

1–2 "Generally Accepted Accounting Principles"

Following is the report of the independent certified public accountants for Anheuser-Busch Companies, Inc:

To the Shareholders and   February 6, 1985
Board of Directors of
Anheuser-Busch Companies, Inc.

In our opinion, the accompanying Consolidated Balance Sheet and the related Consolidated Statements of Income, Shareholders' Equity and Convertible Redeemable Preferred Stock, and of Changes in Financial Position present fairly the financial position of Anheuser-Busch Companies, Inc. and its subsidiaries at December 31, 1984 and 1983, and the results of their operations and the changes in their financial position for each of the three years in the period ended December 31, 1984, in conformity with generally accepted accounting principles consistently applied. Our examinations of these statements were made in accordance with generally accepted auditing standards and accordingly included such tests of the accounting records and such other auditing procedures as we considered necessary in the circumstances.

Price Waterhouse

INSTRUCTIONS:

    1. Explain the meaning of the term "accounting principles" as used in the audit report. (Do not discuss the significance of "generally accepted" in this part of the case.)
    2. How do you determine whether or not an accounting principle is

generally accepted? Discuss the sources of evidence for determining whether an accounting principle has substantial authoritative support. Do not merely list the titles of publications.

3. Do generally accepted accounting principles allow for diversity in accounting practice? Would you expect diversity of accounting practice to exist in an environment in which the accounting profession continually attempts to improve comparability? Why?

1-3 The Role of the SEC and FASB

A press release announcing the appointment of the trustees of the new Financial Accounting Foundation stated that the Financial Accounting Standards Board (to be appointed by the trustees) "...will become the established authority for setting accounting principles under which corporations report to the shareholders and others" (AICPA news release, July 20, 1972).

INSTRUCTIONS:

1. No mention is made of the SEC in the press release. What role does the SEC play in setting accounting principles?

2. How have accounting principles been set in the past ten years? In your answer identify the body performing this function, the sponsoring organization, and the method by which the body arrives at its decisions.

3. What methods have management and management accountants used to influence the development of accounting principles in the past ten years?

(CMA adapted)

1-4 Economic Consequences

The prospect of revised pension accounting standards continues to cause controversy. The long revision process started formally in the mid-1970's with an FASB research project concerned with employers' accounting for pension plans. The FASB Discussion Memorandum sought to identify all of the issues relevant to pension plan accounting. A significant period of time was allowed for public comment and in November 1982 the FASB published its "Preliminary Views: Employers' Accounting for Pensions and Other Postemployment Benefits."

Substantial criticism was directed at the FASB. A primary concern was the recognition of previously unrecorded pension liabilities. Opponents of the Preliminary Views fear severe economic consequences. For example, debt to equity ratios may deteriorate to the extent that companies may be in violation of existing debt covenants. This could cause massive loan defaults--and even bankrupcy. The higher debt to equity ratios may make it more difficult to raise capital and would surely raise the firm's interest expense. Besides, said many opponents, these liabilities do not represent legal liabilities and will never have to be paid. Employers might become reluctant to improve pension plan benefits. This could have severe economic (and social) consequences for future retired workers and even for the social security system.

Proponents of the liability recognition cite a consistent line of reasoning flowing from the conceptual framework and pension theory as a basis for the recognition of the pension liability. After all, neutrality in accounting is an important criterion for the establishment of accounting principles and information that is not neutral loses credibility. Slanting accounting information to favor one group or another is not consistent with the accountant's responsibility to "fairly present" the financial statements.

The criticisms continue: "The proposals do not portray economic reality," "the proposals will have severe economic consequences on capital markets, firms, and plan participants." "The FASB's problem is that it uses accounting theory to explain the world solely in terms of faith and reason and without direct observation of the economic consequences."

INSTRUCTIONS:

1. What is meant by the term "economic consequences" in regards to financial reporting standards? Present your discussion without specific reference to the pension accounting issue.
2. What role should economic consequences play in the development of financial reporting standards?
3. What has been the response of the FASB to the important issue of economic consequences?

1-5 Accounting Standard Setting

Mark Hauser, a new staff accountant, is confused in his first few months on the job because of the complexities involving accounting standard setting. Specifically, he is confused by the number of bodies issuing financial reporting standards of one kind or another and the level of authoritative support that can be attached to these reporting standards. Mark decides that he must review the environment in which accounting standards are set, if he is to increase his understanding of the accounting profession.

Mark recalls that during his accounting education there was a chapter or two in his accounting textbook regarding the environment of financial accounting and the development of accounting standards. However, he remembers that little emphasis was placed on these chapters by his instructor.

INSTRUCTIONS:

1. Help Mark (and yourself) by identifying key organizations involved in accounting standard setting.
2. In what ways is accounting involved in the environment as Mark refers to it? That is, what environmental factors influence accounting and how does accounting influence its environment?
3. Mark asks for guidance regarding authoritative support. Please assist him by defining, explaining, and noting the diversity of GAAP.
4. Give Mark a historical overview as regards to how standard setting has evolved so he will not feel as if he is the first one to be confused.
5. What authority for compliance with GAAP has existed throughout the period of standard setting?

1-6 Models for Setting Accounting Standards

Presented below are three models for setting accounting standards:

1. The purely political approach, where national legislative action decrees accounting standards.
2. The private, professional approach, where financial accounting standards are set and enforced by private professional actions only.
3. The public/private mixed approach, where standards are basically set by private sector bodies that behave as though they were public agencies and whose standards to a great extent are enforced through governmental agencies.

INSTRUCTIONS:

1. Which of these three models best describes standard setting in the United States? Comment on your answer.
2. Why do companies, financial analysts, labor unions, industry trade associations, and others take such an active interest in standard setting?

3. Cite an example of a group other than the FASB that attempts to establish accounting standards. Speculate as to why another group might wish to set its own standards.

1-7 The Role of Research

Recently, much attention has been directed toward the role of research in the accounting standard setting process. Alvin Jennings in a speech that led to formation of the Accounting Principles Board said, "Development of accounting principles should be regarded as in the nature of pure research." An examination of a number of journal articles indicates that there is disagreement with his position.

For example one writer noted, "Although the techniques of accounting research excel in systematic analysis of explicit information, accounting rulemakers must go beyond knowledge obtained from research and consider also knowledge largely intuitive, and of a high logical order amenable to systematic analysis. If the FASB should want no more than a recommendation as regards which course to follow, it would look to the wrong place if it looked to research. It would be better to consult a man of wide experience and demonstrated understanding, and to rely on his intuition."

Another writer notes that the choice among financial reporting alternatives is a political process. He states that "there is a misconception that the critical issues of accounting inquiry are essentially technical when they are actually political." Another author suggests that we have various possibilities available to use to attack the problem from a political angle. One approach is the confrontation mode in which the profession decides to take a firm stand on a given issue regardless of the consequences. A second approach is referred to as the incremental approach, in which the profession attempts to slowly change the financial reporting environment. Finally, there is simple abdication, where the FASB simply permits the public sector to legislate accounting standards.

INSTRUCTIONS:

1. What do you believe to be the roles of research and intuition in the accounting standard setting process? Are the roles complementary or opposing?
2. What do you believe to be the roles of research and politics in the accounting standard setting process? Are the roles complementary or opposing?
3. What type of approach confrontation, incrementation or abdication do you believe the accounting profession presently pursues? What approach do you believe the profession should follow?

A student of accounting history was amazed at the changes that have occurred in accounting theory and practice over the past fifty years. In general, accounting has experienced a shift of objectives from one of stewardship, to the determination of economic income, to more of an informational perspective. Under the stewardship viewpoint, management is the caretaker of capital supplied by investors and creditors. The capital suppliers entrust management with a portion of their resources and expect financial statements to provide a report to facilitate their evaluation of managements' stewardship. Under the economic income approach, accounting alternatives are evaluated in terms of their proximity to a "real" or "ideal" income measurement. Economic income is traditionally defined as the change in the present value of future cash flows. In the late 1960's the perspective shifted from economic income measurement to an informational approach. The current primary objective of accounting is to supply useful information.

Specific issues have come and gone that were the center of attention of accounting research, practice, and standard setting. Leases, human asset recognition, inflation, income taxes and investment tax credits, foreign currency translation, social responsibility, business combinations, the exploration and drilling costs in the petroleum industry, and pension plans are all examples of topics that have occupied the center of the accounting arena.

The student is at a loss to explain the change in objectives over the recent past. In addition, it is difficult to understand why specific issues were considered important at various times and how they fit in the general scheme in the development of accounting standards. Someone suggests that accounting is a product of its environment and that accounting has evolved to meet changing demands and influences.

INSTRUCTIONS:

1. Identify environmental factors that influence accounting principles.
2. What problems do environmental differences raise for the prospect of uniform international accounting principles (International GAAP)?

1-9 Operating Efficiencies at the FASB

In August 1982, the Structure Committee of the Financial Accounting Foundation released a report entitled Operating Efficiency of the FASB. The report states that "The Board's (that is, the FASB's) present due process procedures are appropriate, ...the Board is dealing with the right issues (though more timely guidance on implementation questions and emerging issues is needed), the degree of specificity in FASB standards has been about right, and the Board and its staff operate efficiently."

The FASB, however, recognized that a problem still exists concerning how to provide more timely guidance on implementation questions and emerging issues. As a consequence, a Task Force on Timely Financial Reporting Guidance was appointed.

Recently, the FASB's Task Force issued an Invitation to Comment entitled "Timely Guidance on Emerging Issues and Implementation of FASB Standards."

The FASB's Task Force has concluded that it needs input on the following major questions:

1. Is the FASB currently providing enough, too much, or too little accounting guidance on a sufficiently timely basis (a) for implementation of its standards and (b) in response to emerging issues, such as new business transactions or new tax legislation, that are not covered by existing standards?

2. If additional accounting guidance or more timely guidance is needed, should the FASB rely on another organization to develop such guidance in some circumstances? If so, what mechanism would ensure that the FASB remains the sole accounting setting body in the private sector?

INSTRUCTIONS:

1. Discuss the present reporting environment, identifying the relationship of various standard-setting bodies to one another.
2. Where does the ultimate power for establishing accounting standards reside?
3. Should the mission of the FASB be to address only concepts and pervasive major issues, or should it include providing guidance on implementation and emerging issues?
4. Do you believe only one body should establish accounting principles or should a number of groups be permitted to do so?
5. If you were given complete authority in the matter how would you propose that accounting principles or standards should be developed and enforced?

1-10 The Accounting Profession

Three freshmen business students, Tom, Ron and Linda, were discussing the courses that were required as part of their curriculum and the possible majors that were available to them. Tom and Ron were concerned about two required courses entitled, "Financial Accounting" and "Managerial Accounting". They did not understand why these courses were necessary as they had already completed Bookkeeping I and II while in high school. In fact, they wondered how there could be enough diversity in accounting courses to enable a student to major in this subject. At any rate, they were sure that accounting was not a major that they would consider. After all, everyone is acquainted with the stereotype of accountants as "bean counters" who wear green eyeshades and do nothing but post numbers in a ledger.

Linda announced that she was going to major in accounting. Her father was a CPA and he seemed to be involved in a diverse and exciting profession. He talked about preparing financial statements and financial reporting and it seemed very interesting to her. However, she was not quite sure what it was all about.

Tom and Ron asked her what kind of jobs might be available and just what the role of an accountant was in business. Linda was unsure. As a result, the three decided to talk to an accounting professor to get some answers.

INSTRUCTIONS:

1. In general what is the role of accountants in business?
2. Differentiate broadly between financial accounting and managerial accounting.
3. Differentiate between financial statements and financial reporting.
4. Briefly describe the general categories of accounting positions available in both public and internal accounting.

CHAPTER 2

THEORY FORMULATION AND THE CONCEPTUAL FRAMEWORK

2-1 Examination of the Conceptual Framework

At a FASB Conceptual Framework Symposium, a former member of the FASB discussed his views of a conceptual framework. Some excerpts:

Standard Setting in the Private Sector

A framework of concepts comprises ideas that coordinate to form the fabric of a system: they determine its bounds. In a system like financial reporting that serves a broad public purpose, the first plank in the framework identifies the public role. The decision of the public sector in the 1930's to look at the private sector for the principal thrust to standard setting was sound and extraordinarily enlightened. The credence given financial reporting will determine whether the private sector's role in standard setting will grow or shrink. An operable conceptual framework will go a long way in providing the necessary level of credibility. Without an operable conceptual framework, continuation of standard setting in the private sector would stand in considerable jeopardy.

Essence of the Conceptual Framework

The conceptual formulation starts with the broad role of financial reporting in society. It:

- Identifies its unique competence, that is, its bounds.
- States the objectives of the reporting.
- Defines the things admissible to financial statements.
- Identifies the circumstances triggering admission and qualities to be met for admission to financial statements.
- Selects useful measurements of things admitted.
- Furnishes criteria for display.

Those are major pieces of the framework. There are others, of course. The various parts are in a hierarchy ranging from highly abstract to reasonably concrete. They lend guidance -- they do not provide simple, no-think answers. They leave open a significant range for hard thinking and deliberation about reporting standards. They furnish the reference point for the thinking.

1. What are the basic components of the conceptual framework?
2. Have other conceptual frameworks been useful?
3. What are your views about the success of the conceptual framework?

2-2 Theoretical Framework

Mark Houser has managed to reduce his confusion about accounting standard setting, but he has some additional questions regarding the theoretical framework in which standards are set (see Case 1-6). He knows that the FASB and other predecessor organizations have attempted to develop a conceptual frmework for accounting theory formulation. Yet, his supervisors have indicated that these theoretical frameworks have little value in the practical sense (i.e., the real world). Mrk did notice that accounting standards seem to be established after the fact rather than before. He thought this indicated a loack of theory structure but never really questioned the processs at school because he was too busy doing the homework.

Mark feels that some of his anxiety about accounting theory and accounting semantics could be alleviated by identifying the basic concepts and definitions accepted by the profession, and considering them in light of his current work. By doing this, he hopes to develop an appropriate connection between theory and practice.

INSTRUCTIONS:

1. Having helped Mark identify and understand the environment and the process of standard setting, please help him recognize the purpose of and benefit of a conceptual framework.
2. Identify any <u>Statement</u> <u>of</u> <u>Financial</u> <u>Accounting</u> <u>Concepts</u> issued by the FASB that may be helpful to Mark in developing his theoretical background.

2-3 Major Problems of Accounting Theory

One of the leading academics in the United States has recently become very pessimistic with respect to the efforts of the FASB to develop a conceptual framework for accounting. The academic has just finished reading the monograph, <u>Statement on Accounting Theory and Theory Acceptance</u>. She is now convinced that there does not seem to be any appropriate way to resolving accounting controversies. She is afraid that no matter what type of approach the Financial Accounting Standards Board takes in a conceptual framework, there is going to be endless argumentation about the implementation of the eventual objectives. She notes that any type of an accounting theory is going to have problems, and that these problems simply seem insurmountable. She notes in particular that the above document, in effect, is a pessimistic one. The document does not seem to provide any solutions to the problems, but rather simply outlines why accounting theories have problems.

<u>INSTRUCTIONS:</u>

1. What do you believe are some of the major problems related to accounting theories?
2. What might be the benefit of a document, such as the <u>Statement of Accounting Theory and Theory Acceptance</u>, if it does not provide resolution of accounting issues?
3. Does it appear that the FASB has considered the problems that you have identified with respect to its conceptual framework project?

2-4 Social Welfare

One of the students in Accounting Theory has recently had a course in social welfare economics. He is extremely upset by the discussion which is presently taking place in class, because he feels that the issues that are being discussed really need to be addressed in a social welfare kind of situation. The issue at hand is how to account for the investment credit. One student has argued that what we should attempt to do is to determine or set up some normative criteria such as prediction of cash flow, then determine the type of reporting method for the investment credit that best predicts cash flow. The method that best predicts cash flow should then be the one selected.

A second student says that this is entirely incorrect. A better approach is to go out and ask users of financial statement information just exactly what kind of approach they would prefer. After all, they are the individuals that have to use the information in their decision-making function, and therefore they should be the ones who decide what should be reported for financial reporting purposes.

The student who has taken the social welfare course is outraged at the entire discussion. His remarks become quite heated as he states that the reporting of alternatives as far as accounting is concerned is really a social welfare kind of decision. As a consequence, we have to be concerned with matters such as externalities in the marketplace, and the indirect effects on other segments of the economy as well. He is extremely pessimistic about the entire approach to accounting policy formulation and where it is eventually going to lead. He is pessimistic because he just doesn't believe that there is any answer to the types of questions that are being developed. For example, he notes that any type of approach to setting up some sort of well-defined objective function is largely illusory. Secondly, he notes that the whole problem of whether one should produce more information or less information is an unsettled one that we simply do not know what types of physiological and psychological effects are developed when financial information is presented.

INSTRUCTIONS:

1. What type of an approach is a user approach such as that suggested by the second student? What type of an approach is that suggested by the first student?
2. What type of approach is advocated by the individual who has taken the social welfare course?
3. What does the student mean when he says that the employing of some well-defined objective function is largely illusory?
4. Do you believe that the appropriate way of resolving accounting controversies must be concerned with social welfare events? Discuss.

2-5 Insurance Industry

The insurance industry has always been quite concerned about the standard related to marketable securities. They note that if market value is used to value their marketable securities, income will be much more volatile, and, as a consequence, stock prices will be much more volatile as well. It should be noted that the market value of equity securities is presently disclosed in the financial statements of insurance companies. Some leading academicians dismiss completely the arguments made by the insurance industry in this regard. Much of their reason for disagreement centers around the theory of efficient markets, sometimes referred to as the decision usefulness aggregate approach.

Essentially, the efficient markets theory has developed a whole new body of thought and has had many implications so far as accounting theory is concerned. Such concepts as fair game, random walk, handling of the naive investor, are all issues which are handled very nicely within the confines of the efficient market theory.

INSTRUCTIONS:

1. What is meant when the security is said to be efficient with respect
to financial statement information?
2. What are the implications for the FASB if the market is efficient?
3. What do you believe are the main criticisms of the efficient market?

2-6 Harbott, Inc.

Harbott, Inc. has a stock option plan under which shares of treasury stock have been
sold to officers and key employees of the company. The company has no paid-in
capital and the excess of the proceeds over the average cost of the shares issued
each year was included in income.

The amounts were as follows:

	Excess of Proceeds Over Cost of Treasury Shares	Income Before Extraordinary Items
1980	$71,000	$18,400,000
1981	88,000	20,918,000
1982	310,000	24,900,000
1983	51,000	30,151,000

As auditors on this engagement, you have told the company that this excess should
not be credited to income, but rather should be a credit to paid-in capital. However,
the company prefers to report these amounts in income and you have permitted this
treatment and not qualified your opinion because the transactions were not
considered material.

In 1984, the excess totaled $997,000 with no tax payable. Net income for the year was
$35,250,000, excluding the gain on the treasury stock.

INSTRUCTIONS:

1. What criterion(a) should the auditor use in determining materiality?
2. Would you agree that the transaction was not material in 1984?
Comment.

2-7 Approaches to Constructing Accounting Theory

Recently, the Committee on Concepts and Standards for External Financial Reports developed a monograph entitled <u>Statement</u> <u>on</u> <u>Accounting</u> <u>Theory</u> <u>and</u> <u>Theory</u> <u>Acceptance</u>. In this statement, it was noted that there exists in the financial accounting literature, not a theory of financial accounting, but a collection of theories which can be arrayed over the differences in user environment specifications.

It was the view of the Committee that a universally accepted accounting theory did not exist at that time. Without a single accepted theory it is not possible to develop a conceptual framework. A multiplicity of theories has been proposed that has caused endless argumentation and an inability to resolve issues that are raised. The Committee felt that because of the complex nature of theory acceptance an imposed selection from the proposed theories would not provide sound theoretical closure.

One such theory that was developed in the monograph was the true income theory. A student taking accounting theory is confused by the underlying premises that develop using the true income theory, but feels that the theory makes sense. Another approach, a variant of the first, was referred to as the inductive theory or (the more popular term that is sometimes used), accounting Darwinism. This also seems logical to the student, but the student is uncertain as to the basic premises or foundations upon which the accounting Darwinism approach to accounting theory formulation is founded.

The student is finding the acceptance of a single theory very difficult. He decides to go back to the basics and study the alternative theories.

INSTRUCTIONS:

1. What are three dominant approaches to accounting theory?
2. Describe the various branches that exist as part of each dominant approach. Indicate the basic premises, if any, upon which each is developed.
3. What is accounting Darwinism and the true income approach?
4. What are some reasons why the profession has been unable to achieve consensus on a "general theory" of financial accounting?

2-8 Users of Accounting Information

Jim Blacksmith is a student in Intermediate Accounting. Jim experienced no difficulty with Beginning Accounting as he found the bookkeeping cycle quite easy to handle. However, he has become troubled as he enters Intermediate Accounting because of the various alternatives that are available for reporting on assets and liabilities. Jim is particularly perplexed because, in looking at the asset side of the balance sheet, he finds that accounts receivable is stated at current value, inventories are at the lower of cost or market, investments and marketable securities can be stated at the lower of cost or market, or under the equity method, or at cost in different types of situations, and that intangibles are sometimes expensed immediately, yet at other times are amortized over a legal life, and yet at other times are amortized over a useful life.

In short, Jim is having a great deal of difficulty with Intermediate Accounting. He asked his instructor why all of the differences in valuation. The instructor replied that one of the reasons for the differences that develop in accounting relates to the problem of identification of users. An additional problem, he notes, relates to the question of the environment in which accounting practices are formulated.

INSTRUCTIONS:

1. Specify what you consider to be the problems related to the identification of the user, and the processes that the user develops in assessing accounting data. Discuss the implications related to the environment in which accounting practice is developed.
2. Identify various users of financial accounting information and their primary reasons for using accounting information.
3. How does the variety of users relate to "general purpose financial statements"?

2-9 Information Characteristics

Accounting information provides useful information about business transactions and events. Whoever provides and uses financial reports must often select and evaluate accounting alternatives. FASB Statement of Financial Accounting Concepts No. 2, "Qualitative Characteristics of Accounting Information", examines the characteristics of accounting information that make it useful for decision making. It also points out that various limitations inherent in the measurement and reporting process may necessitate trade-offs or sacrifices among the characteristics of useful information.

INSTRUCTIONS:

1. Describe briefly the following characteristics of useful accounting information:

a. Relevance.

b. Reliability.
c. Understandability.
d. Comparability.
e. Consistency.

2. For each of the following pairs of information characteristics, give an example of a situation in which one of the characteristics may be sacrificed in return for a gain in the other:

   a. Relevance and reliability.
   b. Relevance and consistency.
   c. Comparability and consistency.
   d. Relevance and understandability.

3. What criterion(a) should be used to evaluate trade-offs between information characteristics?

2-10 FASB Concepts Statement No. 2

FASB Concepts Statement No. 2 identifies the qualitative characteristics that make accounting information useful. Presented below are a number of questions related to these qualitative characteristics and underlying constraints.

1. Rochester switches from FIFO to LIFO to FIFO over a two-year period. Which qualitative characteristic of accounting information is not followed?

2. Assume that the profession permits the savings and loan industry to defer losses on investments it sells because immediate recognition of the loss may have adverse economic consequences on the industry. Which qualitative characteristic of accounting information is not followed? (Do not use reliability.)

3. What are the two primary qualities that make accounting information useful for decision making?

4. Cross, Inc. does not issue its second quarter report until after the third quarter's results are reported. Which qualitative characteristic of accounting is not followed? (Do not use relevance.)

5. Predictive value is an ingredient of which of the two primary qualities that make accounting information useful for decision-making purposes?

6. Leggett, Inc. is the only company in its industry to depreciate its plant assets on a straight-line basis. Which qualitative characteristic of accounting information may not be

followed? (Do not use industry practices.)

7. Laclede Company has attempted to determine the replacement cost of its inventory. Three different appraisers arrive at substantially different amounts for this value. The president, nevertheless, decides to report the middle value for external reporting purposes. Which qualitative characteristics of information are lacking in this data? (Do not use reliability or representational faithfulness.)

8. What is the quality of information that enables users to confirm or correct prior expectations?

9. Identify the two overall or pervasive constraints developed in Statement of Financial Accounting Concepts No. 2

10. The chairman of the SEC at one time noted that "if it becomes accepted or expected that accounting principles are determined or modified in order to secure purposes other than economic measurement we assume a grave risk that confidence in the credibility of our financial information system will be undermined." Which qualitative characteristic of accounting information should ensure that such a situation will not occur? (Do not use reliability.)

CHAPTER 3

STATEMENT OF INCOME AND RETAINED EARNINGS

3-1 The Definition of Income

There have been a number of attacks on the entity income concept in recent years. In fact the problems have existed for at least forty years. Vatter pointed out in his 1947 book The Fund Theory of Accounting and its Implications for Financial Reports that "the measurement of income is not the sole, or even most important, aim of accounting" and that "it is impossible to meet all the demands which will be made upon it.... It may well be that accountants should avoid the complications, confusions and disappointments which arise from overemphasis on 'net income'".

The complications, confusions, and disappointments may result from a fundamental problem: the definition of income. The Committee on Terminology in 1955 defined it as follows: "Income and profit... refer to amounts resulting from the deduction from revenues, or from operating revenues, of cost of goods sold, other expenses, and losses...."

The APB in 1970 defined net income (net loss) as "... the excess (deficit) of revenue over expenses for an accounting period...."

The FASB as part of its Conceptual Framework Project defined income in 1980 as: "Comprehensive income is the change in equity (net assets) of an entity during a period of transactions and other events and circumstances from nonowner sources."

INSTRUCTIONS:

1. What are two approaches to the determination of and definition of accounting income that are expressed in these three definitions?
2. How might the two approaches cause differences in income determination and perhaps lead to Vatter's frustration with the net income concept?
3. Why is the FASB's definition especially significant?

3-2 Vulcan, Inc. Income Statement Presentation

Sam Worthy and Sally Hardke are discussing the merits of income statement presentation. Sam Worthy has decided to show Sally how he would present the information for Vulcan, Inc. His presentation is as follows:

Vulcan, Inc.
Income Statement

Sales		$225,693
Dividend Revenue		1,912
		227,605

Costs and Expenses		
Raw materials	$64,979	
Labor	35,245	
Depreciation of plant	24,791	
Other production expenses	27,018	
Administrative expenses	9,126	
Selling expenses	16,228	
Amortization of deferred expenses	3,372	
Research and development	3,748	
Valuation allowance for marketable securities	2,090	
Interest expense	4,740	
Federal income tax expense	13,600	
Other income tax expense	1,093	206,030
Net Income		$ 21,575

Sally Hardke disagrees completely with this approach and suggests that the income statement be presented in the following manner.

Vulcan, Inc.
Income Statement

Sales		$225,693
Deduct Cost of Products Sold:		
Raw materials	$64,979	
Labor	35,245	
Depreciation of plant	24,791	
Other manufacturing expenses	27,018	152,033
Gross Margin		73,660

```
Deduct Other Operating Expenses:
     Administrative                                        9,126
     Selling                                              16,228
     Amortization of deferred expenses                     3,372          28,726
Operating Income                                                          44,934

Add Dividend Revenue                                                       1,912
                                                                          46,846

Deduct Nonoperating Expenses
     Research and development                              3,748
     Valuation allowance for marketable securities         2,090           5,838
Income Before Interest and Taxes                                          41,008

Deduct:
     Interest expense                                      4,740
     Federal income tax expense                           13,600
     Other income tax expense                              1,093          19,433

Net Income                                                              $ 21,575
```

INSTRUCTIONS:

1. What method of income statement presentation does Sam Worthy prefer? Why might Sam Worthy prefer such an approach?
2. What method of income statement presentation does Sally Hardke prefer? Why might Sally Hardke prefer such an approach?
3. William Jones, controller for Vulcan, Inc., has been listening with much interest to the discussion between Sam and Sally. He has never been happy with the presentation of the income statement that is required under generally accepted accounting principles, and decides to ask Sam and Sally what they think of the following presentation:

Vulcan, Inc.
Income Statement

```
Sales                                                                  $225,693

Variable Costs and Expenses
     Raw materials                                       $64,979
     Labor                                                35,245
     Other manufacturing expenses                         16,192
     Administrative expenses                               1,183
     Selling expenses                                     12,545         130,144
Contribution Margin                                                       95,549

Nonvariable Costs and Expenses
     Depreciation of plant                                24,791
     Other manufacturing expenses                         10,826
     Administrative expenses                               7,943
     Selling expenses                                      3,683
     Amortization of deferred expenses                     3,372          50,615

Operating Earnings                                                     $ 44,934
```

What type of approach is William Jones advocating? What might be the advantages of this method to Vulcan, Inc.?

4. What other types of approaches might be followed as far as income statement presentation is concerned?

5. Assuming that the theory of market efficiency holds, which presentation method would be better for the users of financial statements?

3-3 Tooey vs. Percival[*]

An interesting court case was tried in the early 1900's in which the key issue was the legal definition of income. The case concerns itself with the construction of a written contract between T. A. Tooey (plaintiff) and C. L. Percival Company (Defendant), and involves the definition of net income as used in that contract. Tooey was engaged as manager of the paper and woodenware department of Percival Company, and was to receive a salary of $150 per month "and 25 percent of the net income of this department up to December 31, 1916." Eight percent on the amount of capital invested in this department was to be deducted before income division was made. The contract became effective July 29, 1915. The stipulated salary was paid and also the net profits were paid, on sales made and delivered to defendant's customers "up to December 31, 1916", when the contract was terminated.

However, a dispute arose concerning the nature of what is net income. Percival reported net income for 1916 of $51,708.16, of which Tooey's percentage was $12,927.04. However, Tooey argued that the following items should also increase net income:

1. Net income of $1,403.18, being the difference between the selling price and the cost price and carrying charges on shipments of merchandise from the paper and woodenware department after December 31, 1916, on bonafide orders received and approved by Percival prior to December 31, 1916.

2. Net income of $18,781.16, being the difference between the cost price and the market value of merchandise on hand in the department on December 31, 1916.

3. Net income of $8,788.69, being the difference between the total cost price and carrying charges of merchandise for the paper and woodenware department during 1916, but not delivered to Percival until after December 31, 1916, and the market value of the same merchandise on December 31, 1916.

4. Net income of $492, being for shelving and flooring in the department, which Tooey claims to be fixtures and, therefore, assets, but which amount was deducted by Percival as an expense item.

---

* Case rewritten and taken from Tooey vs. Percival Co.

Comment on the validity of Tooey's claim that net income should be increased for each of these items.

3-4 Mecklin Inc.: Extraordinary Losses?

Mecklin, Inc. is a subsidiary of Horton Controls and is engaged in, among other things, the manufacture of parts for the aircraft industry and in the production of heavy gauge pipe for the power generating industry. In 1977/78 the subsidiary suffered a serious curtailment of business following the generally depressed state of the economy and in the above industries specifically. The financial collapse of one of its major customers compounded this curtailment. In the view of the parent, certain production facilities owned by the Mecklin, Inc. were carried at a cost in excess of their future economic benefit. The major production facilities affected were: (a) Melting and cogging shop assets on which no future recovery was estimated. 100% of book amounts were written off. (b) Steel forging sections on which 50% of existing plant costs were written down. The write offs and write downs (amounting to $8,420,000) were determined by the management of the company after considering costs involved and future earnings potential.

In addition the company identified the following expenses and credits relating to these write offs and write downs:

1. Interest on long term debt: The company identified the portion of the long term debt which financed the purchase of the fixed assets. The future interest payable on this debt of $580,000 at its present value, was written off to expense.

2. Government grants: The company had received investment cash grants given by the Government as a contribution towards the cost of plant facilities.

As the company policy had been to amortize these grants received to income over the lives of the related assets, the unamortized portion of investment grants relating to the assets written off or written down ($1,200,000) was set against the book amount of the related assets written off or written down.

3. Deferred tax: There was approximately $250,000 of deferred tax liability before consideration of the write-off and write-down of assets. The constituent parts of the extraordinary write-off and write-down were all reversals of timing differences, which give rise to utilization of this $250,000 as the available deferred tax credits to be credited against the extraordinary write-off. In addition, $470,000 of

unamortized investment credit allowances were also credited
against the extraordinary write-off. (These investment
allowances were not cash grants but represented the unamortized
investment credit related to these assets.)

INSTRUCTIONS:

Comment on the accounting treatment related to these costs; that is, should the
write-off be extraordinary or not and what items should comprise the write-off?

3-5 Unusual Events

Explain the proper classification of the following items:

1. Trucking companies have in the past bought operating rights
   which represent the right to handle commodities between two
   points with very limited competition. Such rights have been
   classified as intangible assets. In 1980, the U.S. Congress
   passed the Motor Carrier Act allowing easier entry into the
   trucking industry and easier expansion by existing carriers.
   The legislation has caused a drop in the value of the intangible
   assets.

2. A paper products distributor disposes of one of its two
   divisions. One division sells paper products to wholesale
   grocery distributors and the other division sells paper products
   to fast food restaurants.

3. A company sells a block of common stock listed on the New
   York Stock Exchange. The block of stock is the only security
   investment the company has ever owned.

4. A shoe manufacturer discontinues all of its operations in
   France. The operations in France were composed of designing,
   manufacturing and selling shoes for the French market.

5. In 1985 Dynamic Co. exchanged $30 million of its 6%
   convertible debentures due in 1990 for $25 million of 12%
   convertible debentures.

6. Westview Lake Company borrowed $14,000,000 from Central City
   Bank to build and sell condominiums. The company cannot meet
   its loan obligations and the Bank agreed to accept real estate
   with a fair market value of $10,000,000 in full settlement of
   the loan obligation.

7. Roberts Corp. was forced to sell a plant located on company property located at the site of a new state park. The state had sought to purchase the land for many years but the company resisted. The state finally exercised its right of eminent domain and was upheld by the courts. In settlement Roberts received $1,200,000 for the plant and the land, which had a book value of $800,000.

8. Augur Corporation suffered a $400,000 net operating loss in 1984, its first year of operations. Realization of future tax savings was not assured beyond a reasonable doubt. Augur had $800,000 pretax accounting income in 1985.

9. The same facts in the previous case except that Augur Corporation was acquired by Spike Corporation in January 1985.

10. The Specialty Motors Corporation experienced a large loss in 1985 due to a strike at its Canadian operations.

3-6 Holmes, Inc.

Holmes, Inc. is a real estate firm which derives approximately 30% of its income from the Executive Management Division, which manages apartment complexes. As auditor for Holmes, Inc. you have recently overheard the following discussion between the controller and financial vice-president.

Vice-President:
If we sold the Executive Management Division, it seems ridiculous to segregate the results of the sale in the income statement. Separate categories tend to be absurd and confusing to the stockholders. I believe that we should simply report a gain or loss on the sale as other income or expenses.

Controller:
Professional pronouncements would require that we disclose this information separately in the income statement. If a sale of this type is considered unusual and infrequent, it must be reported as an extraordinary item.

Vice-President:
What about the walkout we had last month when our employees were upset about their commission income? Would this situation not also be an extraordinary item?

Controller:
I am not sure whether this item would be reported as extraordinary or not.

Vice-President:
Oh well, it doesn't make any difference because the net effect of all these items is immaterial, so no disclosure is necessary.

INSTRUCTIONS:

1. Based on the foregoing discussion, answer the following questions: Who is correct about handling the sale? What would be the income statement presentation for sale of the Executive Management Division?
2. How should the walkout by the employees be reported?
3. What do you think about the controller's observation on materiality?
4. What facts can you give the group about the earnings per share implications of these topics?

3-7 Current Operating vs. All Inclusive Income

Robert Pair, controller for W & M, Inc., has recently prepared an income statement for 1985. Mr. Pair admits that he has not examined any recent professional pronouncement, but believes that the following presentation represents fairly the financial progress of this company during the current period.

W & M, Inc.
Income Statement
For the Year Ended December 31, 1985

Sales		$347,852
Less: Sales Returns and Allowances		6,320
Net Sales		341,532
Cost of Goods Sold:		
Inventory, January 1, 1985	$ 50,235	
Purchases	$182,143	
Less: Purchase discounts	3,142	179,001
Cost of goods available for sale	229,236	
Inventory, December 31, 1985	37,124	
Cost of goods sold		192,112
Gross Profit		149,420
Selling Expenses	41,850	
Administrative Expenses	32,142	73,992
Income Before Taxes		75,428
Other Income		
Dividends received		31,000
		106,428
Income Taxes		41,342
Net Income		$ 65,086

W & M, Inc.
Statement of Retained Earnings
For the Year Ended December 31, 1985

Retained Earnings, January 1, 1985			$176,000
Add			
Net income for 1985	$65,086		
Gain from casualty (net of tax)	10,000		
Gain on sale of plant assets	21,400	$ 96,486	
Deduct			
Loss on expropriation (net of tax)	8,000		
Cash dividends on common stock	30,000		
Correction of mathematical error in depreciating plant assets in 1983 (net of tax)	7,186	(45,186)	51,300
Retained Earnings, December 31, 1985			$227,300

INSTRUCTIONS:

1. Determine whether these statements are prepared under the "current operating" or "all-inclusive" concept of income. Cite specific details.
2. Which method do you favor and why?
3. Which method must be used, and how should the information be presented? Common shares outstanding for the year are 100,000 shares.

For questionable items, use the classification that ordinarily would be appropriate.

3-8 Classification of Irregular Items

As audit partner for Check and Doublecheck, you are in charge of reviewing the classification of some particular items of interest that have occurred during the current year. The following items have come to your attention:

1. A construction company, at great expense, prepares a major proposal for a government loan. The loan is not approved.

2. A water pump manufacturer has had large losses resulting from a strike by its employees early in the year.

3. Depreciation for a prior period was incorrectly understated by $47,000. The error was discovered in the current year.

4. A large cattle rancher suffered a major loss because the state required that all cattle in the state be killed to halt the spread of a rare disease. Such a situation has not occurred in the state for twenty years.

5. A food distributor that sells wholesale to supermarket chains and to fast-food restaurants (two major classes of customers) decides to discontinue the division that sells to one of the two classes of customers.

6. An automobile dealer sells an extremely rare 1926 Type 37 Bugatti for $86,000, which it purchased for $15,000 ten years ago. The Bugatti is the only display item the dealer owns.

7. A drilling company during the current year extended the estimated useful life of certain drilling equipment from 9 to 14 years. As a result, depreciation for the current year was materially lowered.

8. A food-processing company incorrectly overstated its ending inventory two years ago by a material amount. Inventory for all other periods is correctly computed.

9. A retail outlet changed its computation for bad debt expense from 1% to 1/2% of sales because of changes in their customer clientele.

10. A mining concern sells a foreign subsidiary engaged in gold mining, although it (the seller) continues to engage in gold mining in other countries.

11. A steel company changes from accelerated depreciation to straight-line depreciation in accounting for plant assets.

INSTRUCTIONS:

From the foregoing information, indicate in what section of the income statement or retained earnings statement those items should be classified. Provide a brief rationale for your position.

3-9 "Life is Not Smooth"

A $10 billion a year conglomerate managed to report consistently rising earnings through the 1973–1983 period in face of high interest rates, high inflation, and recession. The company runs a specialty steel division, a consumer products company, and a property and casualty insurance subsidiary. At their annual meeting in 1983 the chairman of the board was describing their modest 10% earnings increase as part of a "nice, smooth, predictable earnings trajectory for the company."

A young financial analyst raised his hand to ask a question. "Mr. Chairman, why is it that you have such a curious mixture of items that seem to impact your earnings each year. In 1973, you lengthened your depreciation periods for the steel division and switched to taking your investment tax credits in the year they arose instead of spreading the credits over time. In 1975, you increased your reserves in the property and casualty insurance company, then decreased the reserves in 1980. In 1977, you prepaid and expensed your entire 1977 and 1978 advertising budgets for the consumer products division. In 1982, you retired some debt prior to maturity even though the company was experiencing some liquidity problems. All in all, I have identified 13 special items over the past 10 years that make your reported earnings soft. My adjusted earnings figures show a significantly different picture than you portray. The earnings are volatile and in general declining over the 10 year period. How can you explain the differences?"

The chairman was obviously upset. He replied that the reported earnings had been audited by a "Big Eight" accounting firm and that the company had received a clean opinion on all their financial statements. As far as he was concerned there were no differences; only a nice, steady, increase in earnings.

INSTRUCTIONS:

    1. What is the cause of the controversy? Why does the company adopt their particular reported earnings strategy?
    2. What are three general classes of techniques that may be used to manage earnings?
    3. Evaluate the chairman's strategy with respect to the efficient markets hypothesis.

3-10 Income and Capital

According to Kenneth Most, "Income is a flow of wealth: capital is a stock of wealth. The wealth represented as a flow is capital at any point in time. There can thus be no fundamental difference between income and capital."

However, looking at the economic and accounting literature there seems to be a misunderstanding on this point.

An often quoted version of the definition of Sir John Hicks of an individual's income is:

"The purpose of income calculations in practical affairs is to give people an indication of the amount which they can consume without improverishing themselves. Following out this idea, it would seem that we ought to define a man's income as the maximum value which he can consume during a week, and still expect to be as well off at the end of the week as he was at the beginning. Thus, when a person saves, he plans to be better off in the future; when he lives beyond his income, he plans to be worse off. Remembering the practical purpose of income is to serve as a guide for prudent conduct, I think it is fairly clear that this is what the central meaning must be."

INSTRUCTIONS:

    1. How does Hick's definition of income relate to capital?
    2. Explain the definition of capital maintenance.
    3. What are some alternative definitions of capital maintenance?
    4. How does the concept of capital maintenance relate to the FASB's definition of income?

3-11 Discontinued Operations

The Whirlpool Corporation provided the following information in their annual report for the year ending December 31, 1983:

	Year Ended December 31,		
	1983	1982	1981
	thousands of dollars		
Net Sales - Notes B and K	$2,667,682	$2,271,305	$2,437,091
Equity in net earnings of affiliated companies - Notes D and E	17,495	25,652	22,120
Other	49,113	43,274	45,549
	2,734,290	2,340,231	2,504,830
Cost of products sold	2,102,740	1,827,326	1,979,176
Selling and administrative expenses	309,384	271,749	280,677
Interest on long-term debt	5,287	5,497	5,497
Other interest expense	885	634	145
Provision for plant closings - Note B	23,156	--	--
Income taxes - Note J	129,800	98,800	104,100
	2,571,252	2,204,006	2,369,595
Earnings from continuing operations	163,038	136,225	135,235

Gain (loss) from discontinued operations - Note B	4,000	2,790	(9,675)
Net Earnings	$ 167,038	$ 139,015	$ 125,560
Per share of common stock:			
Earnings from continuing operations	$ 4.47	$ 3.75	$ 3.73
Gain (loss) from discontinued operations	0.11	0.08	(0.27)
Net earnings	$ 4.58	$ 3.83	$ 3.46
Average number of common shares outstanding	36,495,995	36,315,108	36,255,187

Note B - Provision for Plant Closings and Discontinued Operations

In 1983, the Company determined to close some of its manufacturing facilities in St. Paul, Minnesota and Evansville, Indiana and to relocate to other Company manufacturing operations the production of vacuum cleaners, room air conditioners and dehumidifiers. The provision for the estimated cost of this restructuring consisted principally of employee severance and relocation expenses, provisions for loss on the disposal of equipment and facilities and the preparation cost to transfer equipment to other locations.

In 1981, the Company discontinued the electronic organ business of its Thomas International Division. The loss from operations and provision for estimated loss on disposal of the electronic organ business have been presented as discontinued operations (after related tax benefit) in the consolidated statement of operations. The 1983 and 1982 gains from discontinued operations resulted from adjustments to the estimated provisions for such loss on disposal recorded in previous years.

INSTRUCTIONS:

1. Explain why Whirlpool has two separate line items on their income statement relating to Note B. Distinguish between plant closings and discontinued operations. Has Whirlpool correctly recorded these events?
2. How is the gain or loss from discontinued operations calculated?
3. How can Whirlpool report gains in 1982 and 1983 from operations that they discontinued in 1981?
4. What information, if any, would you expect to find on Whirlpool's balance sheet regarding the discontinued operations?
5. Should these irregular events be separately disclosed on the income statement? Why or why not?

CHAPTER 4

THE BALANCE SHEET AND STATEMENT OF CHANGES IN FINANCIAL POSITION

4-1 The Historical Cost Balance Sheet?

Yuji Ijiri is a notable defender of historical cost accounting. He has written numerous articles and books which advocate its use. In one of his articles he states,

> "It is truly remarkable that historical cost accounting has been the principal methodology of accounting over several centuries. Unfortunately, however, familiarity often breeds contempt, and attacks on historical cost accounting have been launched from various corners of business and accounting, especially since the beginning of the second half of this century.... I, myself, do not consider historical cost accounting to have all the answers for the whole field of accounting. Nevertheless, I do, believe that the contribution made by historical cost accounting is really significant and that it will continue to make significant contributions to business in the future as well.
>
> It is difficult to recognize the value of something to which we are very much accustomed. However, if the best way to recognize the value of the air is to try to stop breathing or to move into a highly polluted area, perhaps we can apply the same principle and imagine what the business world might look like without historical cost accounting."

The argument continues as to the appropriate valuation method to be used for accounting. Is it to be historical cost, some form of current cost, or some combination?

1. What are some of the advantages of using historical cost accounting? The disadvantages?
2. The items on the current balance sheet are valued at historical cost. Discuss.

4-2 Hillery, Inc.

Presented below is an income statement for Hillery, Inc. for the year 1985.

Hillery, Inc.
Income Statement
For the Year Ended 1985

Sales Revenues		$616,000
Cost of Products Sold		
Raw materials	$180,360	
Labor	129,800	
Depreciation expense	77,400	
Other operating expenses	62,000	
	449,560	
Administrative Expenses	50,000	
Selling Expenses	40,000	
Amortization of Deferred Advertising	20,000	559,560
Operating Income		56,440
Dividend Revenue		3,000
Change in Valuation Allowance on Marketable Securities		20,000
Interest on Long-term Debt		(24,000)
Income Tax Expense		(26,000)
Net Income		$ 29,440

The controller for Hillery, Inc. has decided that this year, cash flow information will also be provided with the income statement. He has recently read FASB Concepts Statement No. 1 "Objectives of Financial Reporting" which indicates that a basic objective of financial reporting is to provide a basis for assessments of the amounts, timing, and uncertainty of future cash flows. Reading further it was indicated that the assessment of future cash flows was basically a two-step process. First was an assessment of future earnings, and second adjustments were made to obtain assessments of future cash flows. Because little in the way of practical guidance has been provided concerning the presentation of cash flow data, the controller has developed a number of alternatives.

One alternative is as follows:

Hillery, Inc.
Statement of Cash Receipts and Payments
For the Year Ended 1985

Collections from Accounts Receivable		$600,400
Cash Outlays for Costs of Production		
Raw materials	$186,190	
Labor	134,400	
Other operating expenses	62,000	382,590
		$217,810
Administrative Expenses	$ 50,000	
Selling Expenses	40,000	90,000
Gross Cash Generated by Operations		$127,810
Dividends Received		3,000
Interest Paid on Long-term Debt		(24,000)
Income Tax Expense		(21,420)
Net Cash Generated by Operations		$ 85,390
Dividends Paid		(10,000)
Increase in Long-term Debt		
Issued during year	$150,000	
Redeemed during year	100,000	50,000
Purchase of Plant		(120,000)
Increase in Cash During Year		$ 5,390
Cash Balance at Start of Year		15,000
Cash Balance at End of Year		$ 20,390

A second approach is as follows:

Hillery, Inc.
Reconciliation of Earnings with Cash Flows
For the Year Ended 1985

Net Income		$ 29,440
Less Dividends Paid		10,000
		$ 19,440
Add: Increase in liabilities		
Income tax payable	$ 2,600	
Accounts payable	5,910	
Long-term debt	50,000	
Deferred taxation	1,980	60,490
Add: Decreases in noncash assets		
Deferred advertising expense		20,000
		$ 99,930

```
Less: Increase in noncash assets
         Plant                                    $  38,000
         Finished goods inventory                    17,000
         Raw materials inventory                       3,940
         Accounts receivable                          15,600
         Marketable securities                        20,000     94,540
      Increase in Cash During Year                            $   5,390
      Cash Balance at Start of Year                              15,000
      Cash Balance at End of Year                             $ 20,390
```

And a third alternative is as follows:

Hillery, Inc.
Reconciliation of Earnings and Cash Flows
For the Year Ended 1985

```
Operating Income                                               $ 56,440

Adjustments for Allocations
      Depreciation                               $ 77,400
      Amortization of deferred advertising expense  20,000       97,400
                                                               $153,840

Increase in Working Capital
      Finished goods inventory (materials and labor)  $ 12,400
      Raw materials inventory                          3,940
      Accounts receivable                             15,600
      Accounts payable                               (5,910)     26,030
                                                               $127,810

Financing Charges and Taxes
      Interest on long-term debt                  $ 24,000
      Dividends on common stock                     10,000
      Dividend income                              (3,000)
      Income taxes payable on income               24,020
      Increase in income taxes payable             (2,600)       52,420
Cash Available from Internal Sources                           $ 75,390

Increase in Long-term Debt
      Issued during year                         $150,000
      Redeemed during year                        100,000        50,000
                                                               $125,390
Purchase of Plant                                              120,000
Increase in Cash During Year                                  $   5,390
Cash Balance at Start of Year                                   15,000
Cash Balance at End of Year                                   $ 20,390
```

1. The controller recognizes the presentation of this material is controversial, and will have to defend whichever cash flow statement is prepared to the president and the chairman of the board. Could you help him by indicating reasons why a cash flow statement might be useful?

2. Why do accountants presently not require that a cash flow statement be presented?

3. Based on the three alternatives presented for cash flow data, which of these alternatives would you select? Discuss.

4-3 Allied Communications Co.

In August, 1983, the Allied Communications Co. received a contract from the Mexican Post Office for the purchase of mechanized letter sorting equipment for the largest post office in Mexico City. The equipment was manufactured by an affiliated company of Allied in England.

In November 1983, Allied bid successfully on a contract with the Mexican Post Office for postal mechanization equipment for twenty additional major post offices, to be delivered during the period February, 1985 to April, 1987. The value of this contract, depending on the quantity ordered, will range between $70 million and $90 million.

Start-Up Costs

In relation to this contract, the company anticipated spending in excess of $1,600,000 in start-up costs. These costs include:

1) The cost of preparing the contract bid and answering government queries.

2) The cost of engineering drawings purchased from their affiliated company in England.

3) The salaries and expenses of an engineering task force sent to London, England to learn the engineering requirements of the equipment.

4) The salaries and expenses of the manufacturing support personnel who also traveled to London to evaluate purchasing and suppliers.

5) The cost of moving two Divisions occupying the premises adjacent to the Allied Division into a new plant. Also incurred

were postal mechanization's occupancy costs such as taxes and utilities.

6) Salaries and expenses for administrative employees working exclusively for postal mechanization.

7) Electronic data processing postal mechanization work.

INSTRUCTIONS:

What is the appropriate accounting treatment for these costs? How are they classified for financial statement purposes?

4-4 Balance Sheet Presentation

Two students are discussing a FASB Concepts exposure draft on "Reporting Income, Cash Flows, and Financial Position of Business Enterprises." In examining this exposure draft, they find that the following guides provide a basis for decisions on the optimal number of asset and liability items to be reported.

> 1. Assets that differ in their type or expected function in the central operations or other activities of the enterprise should be reported as separate items. For example, merchandise inventories should be reported separately from property, plant, and equipment.
> 2. Assets and liabilities with different implications for the financial flexibility of the enterprise should be reported as separate items; for example, assets used in operations, assets held for investment, and assets subject to restrictions such as leased equipment.
> 3. Assets and liabilities with different general liquidity characteristics should be reported as separate items. For example, cash should be separately reported from inventories.
> 4. Assets and liabilities with different measurement bases should be reported in separate categories; for example, inventories measured at historical cost and inventories measured at net realizable value.

The students, however, are a bit confused regarding the above guides in the exposure draft, because they are not sure how they might be implemented. Does this mean that the present method of presenting balance sheet information should change, and if so, how should it change? Specifically, the two students examine the balance sheet of IBM Corporation (provided below) in an attempt to answer their question.

International Business Machines Corporation
and Subsidiary Companies
Consolidated Statement of Financial Position
December 31, 1982
(Dollars in Millions)

Assets
Current Assets:

Cash	$ 405	
Marketable securities, at lower of cost or market	2,895	
Notes and accounts receivable - trade, less allowance: $216	4,976	
Other accounts receivable	457	
Inventories	3,492	
Prepaid expenses	789	
		$ 13,014
Rental Machines and Parts	16,527	
Less: Accumulated depreciation	7,410	
		9,117
Plant and Other Property	14,240	
Less: Accumulated depreciation	5,794	
		8,446
Deferred Charges and Other Assets		1,964
		$ 32,541

Liabilities and Stockholders' Equity
Current Liabilities:

Taxes	$ 2,854	
Loans payable	529	
Accounts payable	983	
Compensation and benefits	1,959	
Deferred income	402	
Other accrued expenses and liabilities	1,482	
		$ 8,209
Deferred Investment Tax Credits		323
Reserves for Employees' Indemnities and Retirement Plans		1,198
Long-Term Debt		2,851

Stockholders' Equity:

Capital Stock, par value $1.25 per share	5,008	
Shares authorized: 750,000,000		
Issued: 602,406,128		
Retained earnings	16,259	
Translation adjustments	(1,307)	
		19,960
		$ 32,541

1. What is the present practice for classifying assets and liabilities on the balance sheet? Discuss.
2. What other possibilities might exist for classifying assets and liabilities on a balance sheet? Discuss.
3. Two terms have often been used in discussing balance sheet presentation: liquidity and financial flexibility. What are liquidity and financial flexibility and what are their importance?

4-5 Balance Sheet Disclosures

The following items were brought to your attention during the course of the year-end audit:

1. The client expects to recover a substantial amount in connection with a pending refund claim for prior year's taxes. Although the claim is being contested, counsel for the company has confirmed this expectation.
2. Your client is a defendant in a patent infringement suit involving a material amount. You have received from the client's counsel a statement that the loss can be reasonably estimated and that a reasonable possibility of a loss exists.
3. Cash includes a substantial sum specifically set aside for immediate reconstruction of plant and renewal of machinery.
4. Because of a general increase in the number of labor disputes and strikes, both within and outside the industry, it is very likely that the client will suffer a costly strike in the near future.
5. Trade accounts receivable include a large number of customer notes, many of which had been renewed several times and may have to be renewed continually for some time in the future. The interest is settled on each maturity date and the makers are in good credit standing.
6. At the beginning of the year the client entered into a ten-year nonrenewable lease agreement. Provisions in the lease require the client to make substantial reconditioning and restoration expenditures at the termination of the lease.
7. Inventory includes retired equipment, some at regularly depreciated book value, and some at scrap or sale value.

INSTRUCTIONS:

For each of the situations above describe the accounting treatment you recommend for the current year. Justify your recommended treatment for each situation.

4-6 Lockstep Corp.

Presented below is the balance sheet for Lockstep Corporation:

Lockstep Corporation
Balance Sheet
December 31, 1985

Assets

Current Assets:		
Cash	$ 10,000	
Marketable securities	8,000	
Accounts receivable	25,000	
Merchandise inventory	20,000	
Supplies inventory	4,000	
Stock investment in Subsidiary Company	20,000	$ 87,000
Investments:		
Treasury stock		26,000
Property, Plant, and Equipment:		
Buildings and land	71,000	
Less: Reserve for depreciation	20,000	51,000
Deferred Charges:		
Unamortized discount on bonds payable		1,000
Other Assets:		
Cash surrender value of life insurance		17,000
		$182,000

Liabilities and Capital

Current Liabilities:		
Accounts payable	$ 12,000	
Reserve for income taxes	14,000	
Customers' accounts with credit balances	1	$ 26,001
Deferred Credits:		
Unamortized premium on bonds payable		2,000
Long-term Liabilities:		
Bonds payable		46,000
Total liabilities		74,001
Capital Stock:		
Capital stock, par $5	75,000	
Earned surplus	24,999	
Cash dividends declared	8,000	107,999
		$182,000

INSTRUCTIONS:

Indicate your criticism of the balance sheet presented above. State briefly the proper treatment of the item criticized.

4-7 Yoho Plumbing, Inc.

Bill and Terri Yoho are in the process of expanding their business and have been negotiating with the Batavia Bank and Trust regarding a $25,000 loan. They have provided a balance sheet and income statement for each of the last three years, but now the bank wants more information. The bank wants a statement of changes in financial position prepared on a cash basis in order to get a better idea of their cash flow.

Terri has taken a couple of accounting courses and can't understand why this statement is necessary. "After all," she comments, "the statement of changes in financial position is not really necessary when we provide comparative balance sheets and our income statement. The information the bank requires is contained in these statements."

Following are the comparative statements for the past two years.

Yoho Plumbing, Inc.
Comparative Balance Sheets
December 31, 1984 and 1985

	1985	1984
Assets		
Cash	$ 5,000	$ 8,000
Accounts Receivable	23,000	16,000
Inventory	15,000	10,000
Prepaid Expenses	1,000	2,000
Total Current Assets	44,000	36,000
Machinery	25,000	27,000
Accumulated Depreciation	(12,000)	(11,000)
Buildings	75,000	50,000
Accumulated Depreciation	(15,000)	(10,000)
Land	14,000	22,000
Goodwill	18,000	20,000
Long-Term Investments (at cost)	31,000	31,000
Total Assets	$180,000	$165,000
Liabilities and Stockholders' Equity		
Accounts Payable	$ 3,000	$ 23,000
Notes Payable - Current	5,000	5,000
Wages Payable	2,000	1,000
Dividends Payable	20,000	5,000
Bonds Payable	25,000	30,000
Mortgage Payable	35,000	40,000
Preferred Stock $10 Par 8% Cum.	23,000	20,000
Common Stock $1 Par	15,000	10,000
Additional Paid in Capital	30,000	15,000
Retained Earnings	22,000	16,000
Total Liabilities and Stockholders' Equity	$180,000	$165,000

Statement of Income
For the Years Ending December 31, 1984 and 1985

Sales	$220,000	$237,000
Cost of Goods Sold	120,000	130,000
Gross Margin	100,000	107,000
Selling Expenses	43,000	49,000
Administrative Expenses	20,000	18,000
Depreciation and Amortization	12,000	13,000
Operating Income	25,000	27,000
Gain on Sale of Assets	9,000	5,000
Other Income	2,000	3,000
Gross Income	36,000	35,000
Income Tax Expense	10,000	7,000
Net Income	$ 26,000	$ 28,000

INSTRUCTIONS:

1. Identify the investment and financing activities of Yoho Plumbing for 1985. What assumptions are necessary regarding these events that appear to have occurred in 1985?

2. What portions of the statement of changes in financial position on a cash basis can be prepared directly from the information given above? Prepare as much of the statement as possible with the available information.

3. What information that should be disclosed may not be evident in the above information?

4-8 The Volkswagen Group

The balance sheet summarizes information regarding the resources, commitments, and equities of a firm. It delineates the firm's resource structure into major classes and amounts of assets and its financing structure into major classes and amounts of liabilities and equity.

Various theories have been proposed to suggest the classification and arrangement of the balance sheet as well as the items to be included. In fact, disagreement exists as to the name of this financial statement. Is it a balance sheet or is it a statement of financial position?

The following balance sheet of the Volkswagen Group suggests additional differences in format and content that exist on an international basis.

Consolidated Balance Sheet of the Volkswagen Group
December 31, 1983

Thousand DM

Assets

	Jan. 1, 1983	Amounts brought forward³⁾	Additions	Disposals	Transfers	Depreciation	Dec. 31, 1983	Dec. 31, 1982
Fixed Assets and Investments								
A. Property, Plant, Equipment and Intangible Assets								
Real estate and land rights								
with office, factory and other buildings	3,693,565	—	242,946	40,847	172,262	310,943	3,756,983	3,693,565
with residential buildings	373,770	—	5,442	5,063	(1,522)	16,302	356,325	373,770
Buildings on leased real estate without buildings	168,000	—	12,605	6,173	(4,739)	2,981	156,712	168,000
Machinery and fixtures	64,724	—	3,880	274	1483	9,114	58,733	64,724
Plant and office equipment	2,047,465	22,392	841,847	21,810	206,454	1,063,048	2,010,308	2,047,465
Construction in progress and advance payments on fixed assets	3,534,880		2,688,112	466,130	427,497	1,989,644	4,217,107	3,534,880
Trademarks and the like	1,589,140		972,096	472,773	(790,286)	57,548	1,240,629	1,589,140
	2,530		1,805		817	1,090	4,062	2,530
	11,474,074	22,392	4,768,733	1,013,070		3,451,270	11,800,859	11,474,074
B. Investments								
Investments in subsidiaries and affiliates	75,296	—	9,983	2,383		5,230	77,666	75,296
Other investment securities	27,473	—	222	7,281	4,715	832	24,297	27,473
Loans receivable with an initial term of four years or longer	209,004		46,516	20,043²⁾		9,442	226,035	209,004
Par value at Dec. 31, 1983 304,034								
of which secured by mortgages 99,527								
loans in accordance with § 89 AktG 4,187								
loans in accordance with § 115 AktG 182								
Other investments	17,336		9,468	70	(4,715)	4,802	17,217	17,336
	329,109		66,189	29,777		20,306	345,215	329,109
	11,803,183	22,392	4,834,922	1,042,847		3,471,576	12,146,074	11,803,183
C. Adjustment Items Arising from Initial Consolidation							119,170	120,049
							12,265,244	11,923,232
Current Assets								
A. Inventories							5,845,491	5,649,243
B. Other Current Assets								
Advance payments to suppliers							32,372	14,525
Trade accounts receivable							1,734,318	1,419,485
of which amounts due in more than one year 67,570								
Trade acceptances		1,101					145,144	137,328
of which acceptances discountable at German Federal Bank								
Cash on hand, deposits at the German Federal Bank and in postal checking accounts							20,955	22,947
Cash in banks							6,098	7,349
Securities							1,043,150	1,785,049
Treasury stock (par value at Dec. 31, 1983: 15,060)							2,507,204	1,269,084
Receivables from subsidiaries and affiliates		5,368					21,235	21,235
of which amounts in accordance with § 89 AktG								
Miscellaneous other current assets							10,237	1,655
							4,251,797	3,333,733
							10,372,510	8,013,107
							16,218,001	13,662,350
Prepaid and Deferred Expenses							316,790	343,455
Less after Change in Reserves and Minority Interest							58,762	
							28,858,797	25,929,037

Stockholders' Equity and Liabilities

	Dec. 31, 1983	Dec. 31, 1982
Capital Stock of Volkswagenwerk AG	1,200,000	1,200,000
Consolidated Reserves		
Reserve from capital stock surplus¹⁾	190,809	571,798
Reserve of the Group arising from earnings¹⁾	4,826,678	4,144,869
Adjustment items arising from initial consolidation	37,880	37,367
	5,055,367	4,754,034
Minority Interest in Consolidated Subsidiaries		
in net earnings	2,921	
in loss	87,632	
	283,759	225,469
Reserves for Special Purposes		
Reserve in accordance with § 52 subsection 5 of the Income Tax Act	181,411	199,574
Reserve for investment in developing countries in accordance with § 1 of the Developing Countries Tax Act		
Reserve in accordance with section 34 of the Income Tax Guidelines	115,308	137,512
Reserve in accordance with French legislation	65,102	2,131
	48,126	
Reserve in accordance with § 3 of the Foreign Investment Act	8,509	
Reserve in accordance with § 1 of the Foreign Investment Act	5,789	7,236
Reserve in accordance with § 6b of the Income Tax Act	2,870	3,240
	427,115	349,693
Allowance for Doubtful Trade Acceptances and Accounts	45,005	35,884
Undetermined Liabilities		
Old-age pensions	4,235,067	3,625,851
Other undetermined liabilities		
Maintenance not performed during current year	16,543	10,940
Warranties without legal obligation	15,154	14,476
Other	5,368,312	4,352,650
	9,635,076	8,003,917
Liabilities with an initial Term of Four Years or Longer		
Loans	728,570	506,475
Due to banks	120,000	
of which secured by mortgages	1,010,728	702,730
Other liabilities	242,322	
of which secured by mortgages	271,940	241,397
Of which amounts due within four years	77,637	
	2,011,238	1,450,602
Other Liabilities		
Trade accounts payable	2,680,693	2,672,237
Liabilities resulting from the acceptance of bills drawn and the issuing of promissory notes	778,537	786,169
Due to banks	4,839,521	4,608,492
Advance payments from customers	81,530	63,467
Accounts payable to subsidiaries and affiliates	62	96
of which trade accounts payable 20		
Miscellaneous other liabilities	1,641,156	1,673,848
	10,021,499	9,804,309
Deferred Income	179,738	66,812
Net Earnings Available for Distribution	—	38,327
	28,858,797	25,929,037

Contingent liabilities with respect to trade acceptances	616,549	
Contingent liabilities with respect to guaranty obligations	173,675	
Contingent liabilities with respect to warranties	2,906	
Other contingent liabilities	47,399	

1) These items include the legal reserve of the Volkswagenwerk AG in the amount of 843,387 thousand DM.
2) Offset with foreign exchange adjustments in the amount of 8,533 thousand DM.
3) Amounts brought forward of companies consolidated for the first time

Compare and contrast the German balance sheet with the United States balance sheet. Note differences and similarities in form and content and with any accounting principles that appear evident from the balance sheet itself.

4-9 Relationship Between the Balance Sheet and Income Statement

Is it a Balance Sheet or a Statement of Financial Position? In either case, the intention of the statement is to have assets equal liabilities plus stockholders' equity: the accounts balance. But is it necessary to have these accounts balance or to have the income statement "articulate" with the balance sheet? In 1969 the American Accounting Association Committee on External Reporting produced a report evaluating external reporting practices. Excerpts from that report follow:

> "We find no logical reason why external financial reports
> should be expected to 'balance' or articulate with each other.
> In fact, we find that forced balancing and articulation have
> frequently restricted the presentation of relevant information."

The committee goes on to suggest an alternative statement called the "Statement of Resources and Commitments." The committee reports that:

> "Unlike the conventional balance sheet, the statement of
> resources and commitments is not intended to 'balance.'... In
> brief, the statement of resources and commitments is a summary
> statement of resources likely to contribute to future cash flows
> and commitments that represent probable future outflows."

INSTRUCTIONS:

1. What are the definitions of articulation and nonarticulation?
2. What are some advantages of each method?
3. What are two alternative orientations to defining accounting elements within the articulated approach? Briefly describe the two orientations.
4. What is the viewpoint of the FASB concerning articulation as expressed in the Conceptual Framework?

4-10 Jemco, Inc.

At December 31, 1985, Jemco, Inc. has assets of $9,000,000, liabilities of $6,000,000, common stock of $2,000,000 (representing 2,000,000 shares of $1.00 par common stock), and retained earnings of $1,000,000. Net sales for the year 1985 were $18,000,000 and net income was $800,000. As auditors of this company, you are making a review of subsequent events of this company on February 13, 1986 and find the following.

1. On February 3, 1986, one of Jemco's customers declared bankruptcy. At December 31, 1985, this company owed Jemco $200,000, of which $20,000 was paid in January, 1986.
2. On January 18, 1986, one of the three major plants of the client burned.
3. On January 23, 1986, a strike was called at one of Jemco's largest plants which halted 30% of its production. As of today (February 13) the strike has not been settled.
4. A major electronics enterprise has introduced a line of products that would compete directly with Jemco's primary line, now being produced in a specially designed new plant. Because of manufacturing innovations, the competitor has been able to achieve quality similar to that of Jemco's products, but at a price 50% lower. Jemco officials say they will meet the lower prices, which are high enough to cover variable manufacturing and selling costs but which permit recovery of only a portion of fixed costs.
5. Merchandise traded in the open market is recorded in the company's records at $1.40 per unit on December 31, 1985. This price had prevailed for two weeks, after release of an official market report that predicted vastly enlarged supplies; however, no purchases were made at $1.40. The price throughout the preceding year had been about $2.00, which was the level experienced over several years. On January 18, 1986, the price returned to $2.00, after public disclosure of an error in the official calculations of the prior December; correction of which destroyed the expectations of excessive supplies. Inventory at December 31, 1985 was on a cost or market basis.
6. On February 1, 1986, the board of directors adopted a resolution accepting the offer of an investment banker to guarantee the marketing of $1,000,000 of preferred stock.

INSTRUCTIONS:

State in each case what notice, if any, you would make in your report affecting the year 1985.

4-11 Weston, Inc.

Weston, Inc. had the following condensed balance sheet at the end of operations for 1984:

Weston, Inc.
Balance Sheet
December 31, 1984

Current Assets	$ 75,000	Current Liabilities	$ 30,000
Investments	40,000	Long-Term Notes Payable	33,000
Plant Assets (Net)	135,000	Bonds Payable	40,000
Land	62,000	Capital Stock	150,000
		Retained Earnings	49,000
	$312,000		$312,000

During 1985 the following occurred:

1. Weston, Inc. sold part of its investment portfolio for $20,600. This transaction resulted in a gain of $600 for the firm. The company often buys and sells securities of this nature.

2. A tract of land was purchased for $12,000

3. Bonds payable in the amount of $10,000 were retired at par.

4. An additional $20,000 in capital stock was issued at par.

5. Dividends totalling $15,000 were declared and paid to stockholders.

6. Net income for 1985 was $42,000 after allowing for depreciation of $18,000.

7. Land was purchased through the issuance of $36,000 in bonds.

INSTRUCTIONS:

1. Prepare a statement of changes in financial position (working capital approach) for 1985. (A supporting schedule of working capital changes need not be prepared).
2. Prepare the condensed balance sheet for Weston, Inc. as it would appear at December 31, 1985. Assume that current liabilities remain at $30,000.
3. How might the statement of changes in financial position help the user of financial statements?

CHAPTER 5

CASH AND RECEIVABLES

5-1 Handy Man, Inc.

Handy Man, Inc. operates a chain of hardware and building products stores in the central United States. The chain has been expanding rapidly and has started to experience some cash flow problems. The cash flow problems are due to the opening of a number of new stores and the requirement for rather extensive inventories. One reason for the company's growth is their use of credit terms for their customers. They build their volume by offering credit terms and somewhat lower prices to builders. They then do most of their retail sales on a cash basis.

The company is a closely held corporation and has made extensive use of short and long term bank credit. The possibility for further bank credit does not look promising.

A local bank with which the company has recently affiliated has presented the company with a good idea to increase cash flow. They feel that the company is sacrificing a good amount of retail business by operating on a cash and carry basis. The bank suggests that the company participate in a credit card plan. Under the plan the bank will mail credit card applications to persons in the company's marketing area. If the recipients wish to receive a credit card, they complete, sign, and return the application and installment credit agreement. Holders of such cards may charge merchandise at any participating establishment in the marketing area.

The bank guarantees to pay the company on all properly validated charge sales. The company will immediately receive 96% of the face value of the invoices. Any interest charges paid by the customers go directly to the bank. The bank presented this plan as the only and best alternative for the company to improve its cash flow.

The controller of the company is skeptical. He feels that the 4% cost of sales for the credit card service is high. The company has been exploring its own credit program and feels that the cost for their internal service would be about 1% of sales. They already are dealing with accounts receivable for the wholesale business.

The president is concerned and asks how increasing accounts receivable is going to increase cash flow? He feels this will only tie up more cash and merely aggravate their situation. He wants to set up a meeting with the banker as soon as possible to start up the credit card program.

1. What are (a) the positive and (b) the negative financial and accounting related factors that Handy Man, Inc. should consider in deciding whether to participate in the described credit card plan? Explain.
2. Suggest and explain some alternatives that the company might use to increase their cash flow by utilizing their existing or newly created accounts receivable.

(AICPA adapted)

5-2 Cold, Hard Cash

Although cash is generally regarded as the simplest of all assets to account for, certain complexities can arise for both domestic and multinational companies.

Following are some footnotes taken from the Multinational Manufacturing Corporation's annual report. The First International Bank is evaluating the liquidity of M & M Corporation as the first step in considering a loan.

a. The company has a revolving credit agreement with various banks for $5,000,000 at the prime rate. As part of the provisions of the agreement the company is required to maintain a 5% compensating balance.

b. During this year the company issued $50,000,000 of sinking fund debentures with an 8% coupon due January 1, 1995. The sinking fund requires payments of 2% of the principal each year until maturity.

c. The company utilizes the short term credit markets and from time to time purchases certificates of deposit and commercial paper for the investment of excess cash balances. These investments may be for as short a time as one day.

d. Due to the nature of the export and import business the company both issues and receives sight letters of credit. As of December 31st, the company has received sight letters of credit for $1,000,000.

e. The company maintains a bank account in London, England, the headquarters for their European sales operation.

f. Due to the recent devaluation of the peso and the restrictions on the outflow of dollars, the company's wholly owned subsidiary in Mexico was unable to pay the last three quarters' dividends that were declared.

g. Continuing inflation has: reduced the dollar's purchasing power; increased price levels; and has had the effect of distorting the operating results and financial position based on historical dollars, by matching revenues and costs originating in different time periods and expressed in dollars of varying values.

INSTRUCTIONS:

1. What are the normal components of cash?
2. Under what circumstances, if any, do valuation problems arise in connection with cash?
3. How might the footnotes impact the bank's evaluation of the Multinational Manufacturing Corporation's liquidity?

5-3 Northwest Lumber Co.*

Following is some correspondence between the Northwest Lumber Co. and the accounting firm of Haskins, Young, Waterhouse and Andersen.

HASKINS, YOUNG, WATERHOUSE AND ANDERSEN

MEMO   June 18, 1970

To: Bob Brown, Seattle

From: John Wilbur, Portland

Re: Northwest Lumber Co., Stumpage cost as a current asset.

We have a problem in connection with the financial statements of Northwest Lumber Co., on which we would like to have your advice. This problem will arise in connection

---

*Copyright, 1982 by Lloyd C. Heath. We would like to extend our thanks to Lloyd C. Heath at the University of Washington for granting us permission to use this case.

with the treatment of stumpage costs during the coming fiscal year of this client; it does not affect the audit report as of April 30, 1970 which is now being issued.

As you may remember, Northwest has not in the past owned any fee timber, but has operated exclusively on cutting contracts with the Forestry & Indian Service. The timber deposits and prepaid stumpage applicable to these contracts covering timber which will be cut during the next year have been considered as a current asset in Northwest's balance sheet. In May 1970, the company purchased approximately 500,000,000 feet of standing timber in northern Oregon. This timber purchase was financed principally by a loan from an insurance company, and the loan agreement contains stringent provisions with respect to working capital, dividend payments, etc.

The problem we have is the treatment in the company's balance sheet of the cost of timber to be cut during the next fiscal year. The company has proposed, and the insurance company has agreed subject to our approval, that the stumpage cost on timber which is to be cut during the coming fiscal year be classified as a current asset. This amount can be estimated with reasonable certainty. The company argues that such stumpage cost is, in fact, inventory which will be converted into receivables and cash during the next year and accordingly should be treated as a current asset. The amount of each stumpage will probably be significant in relation to the financial position of the company at the end of its fiscal year. Stumpage costs on the new timber acquisition will range from $12 to $14 per MBF, and the company expects that each year's cut will amount to approximately 30,000,000 feet. On this basis, we would be talking of an amount of from $350,000 to $500,000. At April 30, 1970, current assets were $5,700,000 and net working capital was $3,550,000.

When Buck Saw, the company's treasurer, discussed this point with us in Portland two weeks ago, we told him that we knew of no other lumber company which treated stumpage on timber to be cut during the next fiscal year as a current asset, and accordingly we were reluctant to agree with this presentation although we would appreciate his argument that this portion of timber owned would be converted into cash or receivables during the coming fiscal year. The company was quite anxious to allow this item in current assets since they are convinced that this proposed treatment presents properly the current financial position of the company, and, of course, they want the added protection under the working capital requirements of the loan agreement.

I told Buck that I would discuss this matter with you and advise him in the near future what position we would take. Although I have never heard of a lumber company following this method, it seems to me that there is considerable merit in recognizing that a portion of the timber cost will be liquidated each year and that, as long as the cutting estimates were reasonable, I see no objection to the company's proposed treatment. Would you please let me know if you have had any experience on this problem and what your opinion would be. I am sending a copy of this letter to Dan Murphy in New York as I would also like to have his opinion on this company's proposal. If there is any additional information I could furnish you, please let me know.

cc: Dan Murphy New York

HASKINS, YOUNG, WATERHOUSE AND ANDERSEN

<u>MEMO</u>   June 25, 1970

To: John Wilbur, Portland

From: Dan Murphy, New York

Re: Northwest Lumber Co., Stumpage cost as a current asset

I read with interest your letter of June 18, 1970 to Bob Brown. The problem presented by Northwest Lumber Co. is an interesting one and I can see where they would be intrigued with its possibilities. However, the question is not new, and in different variations is raised repeatedly. The most recent variation is the situation of a utility having bonds secured by property wishing to classify as a current asset the estimated depreciation expected to be realized during the following year, since such depreciation would offset the portion of the bonds due within one year and expected to be retired from the funds made available by depreciation.

We have steadfastly taken the position that there is no justification for classifying a portion of fixed assets expected to be realized through depreciation as a current asset, since this in fact represents no more than the anticipation of a portion of the succeeding year's operations. Not only does this violate the accounting principle of anticipating no profits, but there seems to be no more justification for anticipating a portion of the following year's operations than anticipating the following year's operations completely. I can find no examples in the case of any wasting asset where this procedure is followed.

I have reviewed our files for information on this subject, as I presume you did, and found nothing of interest.

cc: Mr. Bob Brown, Seattle

HASKINS, YOUNG, WATERHOUSE AND ANDERSEN

<u>MEMO</u>   June 30, 1970

To: Dan Murphy, New York

From: John Wilbur, Portland

Re: Northwest Lumber Co., Stumpage cost as a current asset

Thank you very much for your comments regarding this problem. Although I do not agree with the company's arguments, I find it hard to persuade them of the differences between down timber (a current asset) and standing timber (a fixed asset).

Their belief is that the definition of a current asset – one which will be realized in cash within one operating cycle – should apply to that portion of the standing timber which will in fact be so realized.

HASKINS, YOUNG, WATERHOUSE AND ANDERSEN

<u>MEMO</u>   July 5, 1970

To: John Wilbur, Portland

From: Bob Brown, Seattle

Re: Northwest Lumber Co., Stumpage as a current asset

Although on the face of it there appears to be some merit in the Company's contention that stumpage on timber to be cut during the next fiscal year be treated as a current asset, I frankly do not see any accounting justification for this position. Standing timber is a fixed, although wasting, asset by definition and by convention. I know of no lumber company that carries any part of its standing timber as a current asset.

When I received your letter I had the same thoughts expressed by Mr. Murphy with respect to carrying a portion of fixed assets expected to be realized through depreciation as a current asset. There just isn't any accounting logic that justifies classifying fixed assets or a portion of them as current assets.

From an auditing point of view we can verify with reasonable certainty the existence of cash, accounts receivable and inventories, but I am afraid that we would be on rather tenuous grounds in verifying X number of feet of standing timber that would be cut in the following year. Let's assume the company has a strike lasting two or three months shortly after our certificate is issued. It can collect on the receivables and realize on the inventories, but the standing timber just stays there. In that case, there just isn't anything current about it by realization, definition or convention.

A suggested solution to the company's problem with the insurance company could be worked out along the following lines.

The agreement could provide in computing current ratios that the current installment of long-term debt be excluded from current liabilities in making the computation.

We have had that situation here in Seattle with a lumber client and we handled it as follows:

Total, exclusive of current portion of long-term debt (Note 1)	$xxxxxxxxxx
Current portion of long-term debt	$xxxxxxxxxx
Total current liabilities	$xxxxxxxxxx

Note 1. Bank Loan Restrictions:
The bank loan agreement provides, among other things,
that (a) the Corporation shall maintain current assets
at least equal to current liabilities, exclusive of current
installments of long-term debt, and (b) shall not declare or
pay any dividends, except in stock, on any outstanding shares.

I hope I have been helpful and if there is anything further I can do, please let me know.

HASKINS, YOUNG, WATERHOUSE AND ANDERSEN

MEMO   July 10, 1970

To: John Wilbur, Portland

From: Gerry White, Atlanta

Re: Northwest Lumber Co., Stumpage cost as a current asset

Bob Brown sent me a copy of your letter to him of June 18 on the possibility of handling a part of stumpage cost as current assets. I am very much interested in this in connection with one of our clients.

Timber companies, I believe, have a better basis for argument than the public utiity example cited by Mr. Murphy. The particular part of the timber companies' argument which makes sense to me is that their real commodity (and their only important inventory) is timber. In the cotton industry, many clients buy a full year's supply of cotton ahead of time to assure themselves of a proper and ample supply. In the timber business, a company cannot buy simply one year's supply but must buy five to ten years' worth if it is to make a reasonable purchase in today's market. Banks recognize the fact that this is, in effect, an inventory item and will loan them on a payout – which is hitched largely to the expected timber to be cut.

Another difference is that depreciation is more or less an involuntary expense each year, but in timber depletion it is only an expense if it is decided to cut the timber and convert it into lumber. Still another important difference between timber companies and other natural resources is that the asset is subject to inspection and measurement on a reasonably accurate basis.

In a sense, the acquisition of a timber tract in many of these cases is simply the purchase of a number of years' inventory. The companies get themselves into a tremendous problem when they have to classify the current part of the bank loan coming up in the next year, which is very definitely tied to the timber cut, as a current liability but then they cannot show the timber to be cut to pay off that loan.

This seems to me to be the type of problem that our committee on accounting principles should research carefully.

Frankly, because of the many important clients we have in the timber industry and because many of them are financing their timber by purchases, can't this problem be researched by our forest products industry and all phases of it carefully studied?

cc: Dan Murphy – New York
    Bob Brown – Seattle

HASKINS, YOUNG, WATERHOUSE AND ANDERSEN

July 24, 1970

Mr. Buck Saw, Treasurer
Northwest Lumber Co.
808 Fir Street
Portland, Oregon 87002

Dear Buck:

I tried to telephone you today but was informed that you would not be back at your desk until the middle of next week. Accordingly, I am writing to you on the question of including part of stumpage costs as a current asset. I have given considerable thought to this matter and have discussed it with my partners. I wanted to give you our thinking on your problem.

It is my understanding that, in connection with determining net working capital under Northwest's loan agreement with an insurance company, you wish to include in current assets the stumpage cost on timber which would be cut during the next fiscal year subsequent to the balance sheet date. It is your argument that this stumpage cost is, in fact, inventory which would be converted into receivables and then cash during the coming year and accordingly should be treated as a current asset. It is your further contention that the amount of timber to be cut during a given 12-month period could be estimated with a reasonable certainty, and that the working capital of the company should include the cost of this timber. You stated that the insurance company would be willing to allow some stumpage costs as a current asset if this presentation is in accordance with generally accepted accounting principles and would be acceptable to us as the company's auditors.

This matter of classifying a portion of fixed assets as working capital is one which comes up frequently in a variety of situations. In a recent case a public utility having bonds secured by property wished to classify as a current asset the estimated depreciation expected to be realized during the following year, since such depreciation would offset the portion of the bonds due within one year and expected to be retired from the funds made available by depreciation. In another case, the operator of a large fleet of rental trucks and cars wished to classify as a current asset the portion of this rental fleet which would be sold during the coming year. I agree that there is some difference between timber or other wasting assets and the usual types of fixed assets. However, there is still no accounting justification for a lumber company classifying a portion of its standing timber as a current asset. We know of no lumber company which treats its standing timber in this manner, and we are not able to find any accounting logic that would justify this treatment at the present time. Mining companies, oil companies, quarries and other similar companies would conceivably have the same arguments as lumber companies for this treatment of a portion of their depletable assets.

We can well appreciate the problem which your company and other timber companies have in financing the acquisition of timber tracts, since the purchase of such timber is usually the purchase of inventory for a number of years to come. It creates a practical financing problem for these companies when they have to classify the current portion of the loan made to finance the timber purchase as a current liability but cannot show the timber to be cut to make this payment as a current asset. In these cases, we have generally come to a sub-total of current liabilities exclusive of the current portion of the timber-purchase loan and then added the current portion of the loan in order to arrive at total current liabilities. It has also been possible in some cases to exclude from the definition of working capital under the loan agreement the current installments of the long-term debt incurred to acquire the timber. In this manner, the companies involved have not been penalized with a working capital requirement which includes the current portion of the long-term debt but excludes the timber which must be cut to finance the current payment on such debt. Perhaps something along this line can be worked out in your case.

After you have returned to your desk and have an opportunity to review this letter, I hope that you will call me to discuss this problem further, if you wish. I assure you that we are most sympathetic to your problem and will be pleased to work out an acceptable solution with you, but we do not believe that classifying stumpage costs as a current asset can be justified.

Yours very truly,

John Wilbur

cc: Mr. B. Brown, Seattle
Mr. D. Murphy, New York
Mr. G. White, Atlanta

NORTHWEST LUMBER CO.
808 Fir Street
Portland, Oregon 87002

Mr. John Wilbur
Haskins, Young, Waterhouse and Andersen
404 Debit Avenue
Portland, Oregon 87005

Dear John:

I finally got my desk cleared away after being in Texas all last week, and have given your letter of July 24th some considered thought.

First of all, our desire to include in current assets the stumpage cost on timber which will be cut during the next fiscal year subsequent to the balance sheet date is not only motivated by our working capital requirements under our loan agreement, but also our working capital presentation in general. We find it hard to distinguish between including a deposit on a government current contract for timber as a current asset and then on the other hand, just because we own the timber, not to include this deposit. After all, the money we have paid for this timber is money expended for raw materials and these raw materials are, in effect, part of our inventory, to the extent that they will be consumed within the next year. In fact, I believe you mentioned on the phone the other day that in the case of a redwood company, their inventory of green lumber takes sometimes as much as eighteen months to dry and be marketable. Therefore, I believe you must make some deviation from the old fixed one-year principle.

It appears to me that you hesitate to call the stumpage cost of timber to be cut in the next year a current asset merely because past practices of other companies and also the technical wording. Right now I'm wondering what you would do if we sold this timber to another company and then put up a deposit equivalent to the next year's stumpage costs. This would be similar to our present government cutting contracts where we put the money up for security and you classify that as a current asset.

In rereading the American Institute bulletin on working capital, I find that in paragraph 4 they use a more or less broad concept of current assets and definitely include inventories of merchandise, raw materials, goods in process, finished goods, operating supplies and ordinary maintenance materials and parts. Then later on, in the same paragraph, they include prepaid expenses with the additional explanation as follows: "Prepaid expenses are not current assets in the sense that they will be converted into cash, but in the sense that if not paid in advance, they would require the use of current assets during the operating cycle." It seems to me that this same sentence could be applied to stumpage that we expect to cut during the ensuing year. Reading further on, Paragraph 5 in the same bulletin says that the operating cycle is more or less the determining factor as to what should be classified as current assets and what should be excluded.

I find it hard to believe that your firm would turn us down on a request strictly on the basis that no other companies do it. It seems to me that there is good logic in reclassifying a portion of this asset as a current asset, just as much as there is logic in splitting prepaid insurance between the current and long-term portions, similar to the way we do on our books.

I have considered the other alternative presentation you submitted, and my only question to the proposal you made is – what would you certify to as net working capital? It's too late to change our mortgage loan agreement now, in view of the fact that when I first brought up the subject, I thought we would receive general acceptance from you on the principle of classifying the ensuing year's cut as a current asset.

I expect to be in New York on business next month and if it is acceptable to you, I would like to discuss this matter with some of the partners from your home office who are on your firm's committee on accounting principles. I feel that if generally accepted accounting principles are what you say they are, they are discriminatory against our industry and would like to appeal to the Accounting Principles Board to have them changed.

I will look forward to hearing from you.

Yours very truly,

NORTHWEST LUMBER CO., INC.
B. Saw, Treasurer

INSTRUCTIONS:

1. How are current assets and current liabilities defined in authoritative accounting principles?
2. Does the cost of the stumpage as described in John Wilbur's memo dated June 18 fit the authoritative definition of a current asset? Why or why not? Defend your position.
3. Summarize and evaluate critically the arguments used by Haskins, Young, Waterhouse and Andersen for not classifying Northwest's stumpage as current.
4. Summarize and evaluate critically the arguments used by Northwest Lumber for classifying its stumpage as current.
5. If you were a member of the FASB would you vote for allowing companies to classify stumpage as a current asset? Why or why not? Explain fully.

5-4 Floating Deposits

Following are some exerpts from a recent article in Forbes magazine:

"At issue is the way banks account for deposits during the days while they wait for checks to clear. Traditionally, such funds -- technically uncollected -- show up on the books as cash assets and deposit liabilities. But several big banks recently commissioned a study by Coopers & Lybrand that recommends changing all that. It proposes taking this deposit float figure right off the balance sheet.

Citicorp, no laggard when it comes to accounting innovations, adopted the controversial, new method in the fourth quarter of 1983. 'This treatment... more properly reflects the substance of the check collection process,' it told shareholders, pointing out that the reclassification reduced total assets by about $600 million. Compared with other institutions, however, that figure may be on the low side. Chase Manhattan, a somewhat smaller bank, noted that a similar accounting change would reduce its assets by $2 billion.

...By arguing that this bookkeeping change is not material -- a term the accountants have yet to define clearly -- banks are free to make the switch on their own. For the moment, nearly all institutions still include deposit float in their reported assets. But First Chicago has already joined Citicorp in making the switch. Chase and others may soon follow."

INSTRUCTIONS:

1. Discuss the circumstances that cause the above accounting issue to arise.
2. Why would banks want to decrease their assets?
3. What do you feel is the appropriate accounting treatment for deposit float? Why?
4. What are the accounting implications for the corporate depositors if the banks adopt this new accounting method?

5-5 Marshall Chemical Company

Marshall Chemical Company has decided to sell a large portion of its receivables to Forth Financing Association. Marshall decided to sell these receivables because it has been experiencing cash flow problems; therefore, the sale would provide added cash resources to the enterprise. The terms of the sale are as follows:

The receivables are sold on a with recourse basis. The terms indicate that this transaction is considered a full recourse arrangement. In a full recourse arrangement, the transferor of the receivable with recourse must reimburse the acquirer in full regardless of whether the property is recovered from the debtor.

The planned sale has hit a snag. The auditor for Marshall Chemical has indicated that perhaps this transaction should be reported as a borrowing rather than a sale. The controller for Marshall Chemical has become quite irritated with the auditor, noting that he knows of no GAAP requirements that indicates this transactions should be reported as a borrowing. Furthermore, if the transaction is treated as a borrowing, the company will be in violation of one of its debt to equity covenants.

INSTRUCTIONS:

What are the arguments for treating this transaction as a borrowing? As a sale?

5-6 Smalley Supply, Inc.

Smalley Supply, Inc. conducts a wholesale merchandising business that sells approximately 5,000 items per month with a total monthly average sales value of $150,000. Its annual bad debt ratio has been approximately 1 1/2% of sales. In recent discussions with his bookkeeper, Mr. Smalley has become confused by all the alternatives apparently available in handling the Allowance for Doubtful Accounts balance. The following information has been shown.

1. An allowance can be set up (a) on the basis of a percentage of sales or (b) on the basis of a valuation of all past due or otherwise questionable accounts receivable -- those considered uncollectible are charged to the allowance account at the close of the accounting period; or specific items are charged off directly against (c) gross sales, or to (d) bad debt expense in the year in which they are determined to be uncollectible.

2. Collection agency and legal fees, and so on, incurred in connection with the attempted recovery of bad debts can be charged to (a) bad debt expense, (b) allowance for doubtful accounts, (c) legal expense, or (d) general expense.

3. Debts previously written off in whole or in part but currently recovered can be credited to (a) other income, (b) bad debt expense, or (c) allowance for doubtful accounts.

Which of the foregoing methods would you recommend to Mr. Smalley in regard to (1) allowances and charge-offs, (2) collection expenses, and (3) recoveries? State briefly and clearly the reasons supporting your recommendations.

5-7 Double Default

The Wall Street Journal reported in October, 1985 that the Supreme Court agreed to decide whether standby letters of credit issued by banks are equivalent to deposits issued by the Federal Deposit Insurance Corporation.

The case arose from the collapse of the Penn Square Bank in Oklahoma City in 1982. A federal appeals court in Denver ruled in December 1984 that a $145,200 standby letter of credit was like an insured deposit, on which the FDIC must pay as much as $100,000 in insurance proceeds.

The FDIC, backed by the Justice Department, appealed to the Supreme Court. The Justice Department is supporting the appeal since the administration feels that if the appeals court ruling is upheld, the FDIC may be required to insure $120 billion of standby letters of credit for banks nationwide. In addition, the FDIC said, banks would be required to pay as much as $100 million in insurance premiums to cover the additional deposit liabilities.

In 1981, the Philadelphia Gear Corp. sold parts to Orion Manufacturing Corp. for oil pumps produced by Orion for drilling in Oklahoma and Texas. Because of the risk involved regarding payment, Philadelphia Gear required additional security. Orion arranged with the Penn Square Bank to issue a standby letter of credit to Philadelphia Gear. The letter promised to pay Philadelphia Gear for its equipment if Orion defaulted.

Orion defaulted on its contract and Philadelphia Gear tried to collect on the letter of credit. But Penn Square collapsed in one of the largest U.S. bank failures. As a result, Philadelphia Gear sought the money from the FDIC. The FDIC refused to cover the letter of credit.

Philadelphia Gear sued and was successful. The basis of the 10th Circuit Court's ruling was that a letter of credit amounts to a deposit under federal law. The FDIC then appealed to the Supreme Court.

INSTRUCTIONS:

1. What is a standby letter of credit?
2. How would Philadelphia Gear Corp. have recorded the initial

transaction with Orion? Would you expect them to have established a provision for bad debts with respect to this sale?

3. How would you suggest Philadelphia Gear record the default by Orion?

4. How would you suggest Philadelphia Gear record the default by Penn Square?

5-8 Largo Company

Largo Company, a wholly owned subsidiary of Rightway, Inc., helps finance service station construction and product sales to certain customers. The Company grants this financial assistance on the basis of the results of its return on investment studies: the loans granted have a payback period of from two to ten years, depending on such ROI studies. All loans are repayable in equal monthly installments and bear interest at the rate of 12% per year, which is substantially below the prevailing cost of money (closer to 19%). However, 12% should be considered the legal limit. This legal limit does not have the practical effect of an interest ceiling since it is not generally enforced and since the rate of remuneration of such financing could legally be increased by charging inspection fees, commissions, etc. The Company has not charged these items because it feels that the increases would jeopardize the Company's competitive position.

Interest income is included in the Company's revenues annually as it is earned.

As an auditor of Largo Company, you raised the question of whether or not the notes receivable should be discounted to reflect the market rate of interest. The Company pointed out that since the legal limit on interest rates for such transactions is 12%, it would be inappropriate to discount the notes to reflect a 19% rate.

An overall estimate indicated that the Company would have to discount the long-term receivables by $3,500,000. The effect on the balance sheet is not considered to be material, but materiality in relation to income ($1,300,000 for 1985) depended on whether the required discount should be immediately recognized as a charge to current income or whether it should be amortized over future periods.

INSTRUCTIONS:

1. Why does the company charge a rate of 12% when the correct rate is 19%?

2 What are three alternatives that might be used to record these transactions?

3. Prepare the entries that would be presented for each alternative.

4. Which alternative would you suggest? Why?

5-9 Rice Co.

Soon after beginning the year-end audit work on March 10 at the Rice Company, the auditor has the following conversation with the controller.

Controller: The year ending March 31st should be our most profitable in history, and, as a consequence, the Board of Directors has just awarded the officers generous bonuses.

Auditor: I thought profits were down this year in the industry, according to your latest interim report.

Controller: Well, they were down but 10 days ago we closed a deal which will give us a substantial increase for the year.

Auditor: Oh, what was it?

Controller: Well, you remember a few years ago our former president bought stock in Hart Enterprises because he had those grandiose ideas about becoming a conglomerate. For six years we have not been able to sell this stock which cost us $1,500,000 and has not paid a nickel in dividends. Thursday we sold this stock to Casino, Inc. for $2,000,000. So, we will have a gain of $350,000 ($500,000 pretax) which will increase our net income for the year to $2,000,000, compared with last year's $1,900,000, As far as I know, we'll be the only company in the industry to register an increase in net income this year. That should help the market value of the stock!

Auditor: Do you expect to receive the $2,000,000 in cash by March 31st, your fiscal year-end?

Controller: No. Although Casino, Inc. is an excellent company, they are a little tight for cash because of their rapid growth. Consequently, they are going to give us a $2,000,000 noninterest-bearing note due $200,000 per year for the next 10 years. The first payment is due on March 31 of next year.

Auditor: Why are the notes noninterest-bearing?

Controller: Because everybody agreed to that plan. Since we don't have any interest bearing debt, the funds invested in the note do not cost us anything. We also were not getting any dividends on the Hart Enterprise stock.

INSTRUCTIONS:

Do you agree with the way the controller has accounted for the transaction? If not, how should the transaction be accounted for?

5-10 Horsing Around

Blue Haven Stables had grown from a hobby farm into an extensive horse training, breeding, and riding stable. With this growth came the need for tighter controls and a full time bookkeeper.

Christine, the owner and manager of the operation had always controlled the checkbook, but with a rather haphazard method. All checks written were rounded off to the next highest dollar and the bank statements were thrown into a shoebox until year end.

The new bookkeeper was trying to explain to Christine that a monthly bank reconciliation should be done. Christine commented that "the bank should know what they are doing and if we just wait until year end it will be a lot simpler to figure out our balance. Besides it was always confusing to determine whether outstanding checks should be added or subtracted and then there are service charges -- I would rather train horses!"

The bookkeeper was determined to change that perspective. The problem for the bookkeeper was to determine which bank reconciliation method to use. He knew he had only one chance to present the monthly reconciliation and it had to be in a format that Christine could easily understand.

Following is some data for the most recent month's activities for the Blue Haven Stables:

a. October 31 bank balance $16,939

a.	October 31 bank balance		$16,939
	November 30 bank balance		22,365
	Bank service charges		8
	Outstanding Checks:		
	October 31	#301	700
		#412	1,850
		#420	1,150
	Nov. 30	#301	700
		#454	4,201
		#461	100
	Deposits in Transit		
	October 31		4,200
	November 30		3,680
	Receipts		96,450
	Dispursements, actual		91,605
	Dispursements, per bank		91,024
	Dispursements, per books		91,650
	NSF check returned		215

b. Included with the bank statement was a debit memorandum dated November 30th for $360 interest on a floating rate note.

c. The bank deducted a check for $352 written on the Blue Sky account from the Blue Haven account.

INSTRUCTIONS:

1. Suggest to the bookkeeper the three possible bank reconciliation formats that could be used. What are the differences between them?
2. Prepare the bank reconciliation for Blue Haven Stables which you feel would be the most appropriate in this situation.

CHAPTER 6

VALUATION OF INVENTORIES

6-1 Inventory is Inventory

In spite of the theoretical difficulties with and criticisms of historical costs, they continue to be used almost exclusively in preparing financial statements in the United States and are widely used throughout the world. During any fiscal period it is very likely that merchandise will be purchased or produced at different prices. So although historical costs are used, the question arises as to which of the various cost prices should be associated with cost of goods sold and ending inventory.

Theoretical support for any of the possible cost flow allocations relies on certain basic assumptions and objectives. Conceptually, a specific identification of the given items sold and unsold seems optimal, but this measure is not only difficult but often impossible to achieve. Consequently, for practical reasons and in the interests of reliable financial reporting, the accountant must turn to the consistent application of one of several cost selection methods that are based on differing but systematic inventory cost flow assumptions. Therefore, the actual physical flow of goods and the cost flow assumption are often quite different. Some of the proposed cost flow methods are: specific identification; average cost; FIFO; LIFO; and, base stock.

The main objectives of cost identification for inventories have been the matching of costs with revenues and the association of costs with inventories for balance sheet valuation purposes. The objectives may be imprecise and so accountants have looked to more basic objectives.

One objective endorsed by the 1964 AAA Committee on Concepts and Standards stated: "Ideally, the measurement of accounting profit involves the matching precisely of the identified costs of specific units of product with the sales revenue derived therefrom." The emphasis here is on the physical flow of inventory.

The AICPA seemed to adopt a second objective in Accounting Research Bulletin No. 43, that is "the major objective in selecting the method should be to choose the one which under the circumstances, most clearly reflects periodic income". The emphasis here is not so much on physical flow as it is on income determination.

A third objective places the emphasis on the need for a current valuation for the ending inventory which is then assumed to permit better economic interpretation.

Another objective is to identify the gains and losses from price changes and measure separately the income which arises from buying and holding inventory. This objective necessitates the introduction of current cost information.

INSTRUCTIONS:

1. Define "cost" as applied to the valuation of inventories.
2. How well do each of the above mentioned cost flow assumptions meet the objectives outlined?
3. What are other arguments for and against the use of these five cost flow assumptions?

6-2 Harnischfeger Corporation

The Harnischfeger Corporation is an international firm involved principally in the manufacture, sale, and distribution of heavy equipment. Their three main operating divisions are: construction equipment; mining and, electrical equipment; and, material handling equipment and systems. The company's sales are affected by the world-wide economic activity in the capital goods market. Some interesting changes have occurred with the accounting for their inventory between 1980 and 1983.

Following are footnotes from their 1981 and 1983 annual reports:

October 31, 1981

Note 2 Inventories
The consolidated inventories consisted of the following:

| Year Ended October 31, | Thousands of Dollars | |
	1981	1980
At lower of cost or market (FIFO method)		
Raw materials	$ 18,081	$ 23,018
Work in process and purchased parts	139,392	147,438
Finished goods	114,421	106,524
	271,894	276,980
Allowance to reduce inventories to cost on the LIFO method	(35,272)	(18,352)
	$236,622	$258,628

Effective at the beginning of fiscal 1980, the Corporation changed its method of determining cost for U.S. inventories from the FIFO method to the LIFO method. The

Corporation believes the LIFO method more closely relates current costs with current revenues in inflationary periods. The change reduced fiscal 1980 net income by approximately $10,200,000 or $1.14 per share of common stock.

Inventories valued on the LIFO method represented approximately 85% and 83% of total inventories at October 31, 1981 and 1980, respectively.

During fiscal 1981, certain LIFO inventory quantities carried at lower costs prevailing at the beginning of fiscal 1980 as compared with the costs of 1981 purchases were liquidated, the effect of which was to increase fiscal 1981 net income by approximately $1,008,000 or $.10 per common share and common equivalent share.

October 31, 1983

Note 6 Inventories
Consolidated inventories consisted of the following:

	Thousands of Dollars	
Year Ended October 31,	1983	1982
At lower of cost or market (FIFO method)		
Raw materials	$ 11,904	$ 16,676
Work in process and purchased parts	72,956	110,239
Finished goods	105,923	126,728
	190,783	253,643
Allowance to reduce inventories to cost on the LIFO method	(37,189)	(43,145)
	$153,594	$210,498

Inventories valued on the LIFO method represented approximately 82% and 79% of total inventories at October 31, 1983 and 1982 respectively.

Inventory reductions in 1983, 1982, and 1981 resulted in a liquidation of LIFO inventory quantities carried at lower costs compared with the current cost of their acquisitions. The effect of these liquidations was to reduce the net loss by approximately $15,600,000 or $1.54 per common share in 1983, and by $6,700,000 or $.66 per share in 1982, and to increase net income by $1,008,000 or $.10 per share in 1981; in 1983 no income tax effect applied to the adjustment.

INSTRUCTIONS:

1. Explain how LIFO inventory valuation affects income.
2. Why did Harnischfeger Corporation adopt LIFO? Do you agree that this was their primary motive for adopting the change?
3. What kind of accounting change is a change from FIFO to LIFO?
4. What is the usual treatment for reporting an accounting change?

5. Is the accounting for a change to LIFO consistent with the general principle adopted for reporting changes in accounting principles?

6. What is the practical reason for the procedure followed for handling changes to the LIFO method?

7. Considering the reason given by Harnischfeger for the change from FIFO to LIFO, speculate as to why they did not convert all inventory valuation to this method.

8. Why is the difference between the valuation of inventory using FIFO and LIFO especially significant for a company like Harnischfeger? (versus a company like Wendys or McDonalds?)

9. Both footnotes mention LIFO liquidations. What does this mean?

10. What was the entry made in 1981 to adjust the allowance account? The entry made in 1983? Explain how both years resulted in LIFO liquidation gains in spite of the entries you just recorded.

11. What are the reasons that LIFO gains might occur?

6-3 "Profitable" Obsolete Inventory Losses

Speiss Company has a dilemma. 1985 was not only a poor year for the company, but also they have a large amount of obsolete inventory. They are reluctant to take any more losses, since the company can still report earnings per share of $.25 (down from $2.50). However, the accounting firm of Wise and Company has examined the inventory and has been asking questions. The final inventory valuation has not been agreed upon, but it is very apparent that the auditors will want a write down. The write down is material and will cause the company to report a per share loss of $.10, the first loss in its 20 year history.

Al Underly, the president, was sitting in his office when his sales vice president called. "Al, I have great news. You know that obsolete inventory we have? Well, I just got a purchase order signed to sell all of it next year. The order is for $1,000,000 and our cost is $1,500,000, but at least we got something for it."

Al greets the news as a mixed blessing. The inventory will be sold, but it will force a loss to be recognized. Al asks his controller to come into his office and explain the situation to him in more detail. The controller thinks the transaction is just what the company needs to avoid the inventory loss in 1985 and to defer it until 1986. Since the company has only a purchase order, the company will not have to report a sale until next year. In addition, since matching should be followed, it is only good accounting to maintain the inventory at its recorded cost and to recognize the loss when the sale is recorded.

Al breathes a sign of relief. The company will report a profit and the inventory problem is over.

Do you agree or disagree with the proposed handling of the inventory and purchase order transaction?

6-4 Cost of Goods Sold and Inventory

Williams Furniture Company has been growing rapidly. Unfortunately, their accounting system has not kept pace with the expansion. You were hired to correct the accounting records and to assist in the preparation of the financial statements for the fiscal year ending March 31, 1986. One of the first accounts that you review is the one entitled "Merchandise." The account summary and related information that you have accumulated follows. The letters in parentheses correspond to the additional information.

Merchandise

Balance April 1, 1985	(a)	Merchandise sold	(e)
Purchases	(b)	Consigned merchandise	(f)
Freight In	(c)		
Insurance	(d)		
Freight-out on consignment	(g)		
Freight-out on merchandise sold	(h)		

a. Williams employs the FIFO method of accounting. You have examined their records and are satisfied that the beginning balance is correct. The company maintains its inventory records on a perpetual inventory system.

b. The merchandise purchased was recorded in the account at the manufacturers' list price which is the price appearing on each invoice. However, all furniture purchased is subject to a 10-20% discount. These trade discounts are recorded as revenue when the invoices are paid.

In addition, all merchandise purchased has terms of 2%/10 net 30 days. Williams discounts only some of their invoices and has recorded $2,500 of discounts as revenue. Included in this account is some special order furniture which has been delivered to Williams Co., but as of year end has not been delivered to their customer. Williams rarely deals in special orders, but normally buys and sells only standard merchandise.

c. Most merchandise is purchased FOB shipping point. The freight in amount is the cost of transporting the merchandise from the manufactuers' warehouse to the Williams Co.

d. The insurance charge is for an all-risk policy to cover merchandise in transit to Williams Co.

e. The credit to this account for merchandise sold represents the manufacturers' list price of merchandise sold plus the cost of beginning inventory. The debit side of any entries made to this account is made to cost of goods sold.

f. Consigned merchandise represents goods that were shipped to Marcie's Furniture Boutique during December 1985. The furniture was billed at the manufacturers' suggested list prices. The offsetting entry to this transaction was made to the accounts receivable account. Williams does not separately account for consigned and nonconsigned merchandise.

On February 28, 1986 Williams received a payment from Marcie for one-fourth of the consigned merchandise, representing the amount sold to date. The payment was recorded as a reduction of accounts payable. The payment was the net amount of the invoiced furniture sold after Marcie had deducted its 15% selling commission and 2% TV advertising allowance.

g. The freight-out on consigned goods is the cost of trucking the consigned furniture to Marcie.

h. Freight-out on merchandise sold is the amount paid trucking companies to deliver merchandise sold to Williams customers.

INSTRUCTIONS:

1. What is the nature of the "Merchandise" account used by the Williams Furniture Company?
2. Review each of the items of information given above independently and discuss the appropriateness of including the item in the merchandise account, the impact of each item on cost of goods sold, and the impact of each item on any other account in Williams' March 31, 1986 financial statements.

(AICPA adapted)

6-5 Liquid LIFO Inventory

The Packard Sugar Co. is a medium sized, privately held company, engaged in the sale and distribution of liquid sugar and artificial sweeteners. Packard is on the LIFO inventory method and at the beginning of the year had LIFO layers of 2,000,000 gallons of sweeteners at an average LIFO price of 18¢ per gallon.

The company requires approximately 800,000 to 1,000,000 gallons of sweeteners to service its customers for a month. Candy and soft drink sales have been unexpectedly high approaching year end. Consequently, at year end, December 31st, the company anticipates having an inventory of 1,000,000 gallons of sweetner. This is especially alarming to the company since they wanted to increase their year end inventory above the current LIFO layer level.

To avoid the liquidation of LIFO layers and the payment of substantial taxes, the company has entered into a transaction with C and D Sugar, a major sugar refining company. The agreement calls for Packard to purchase 1,200,000 gallons of sweetener during the month of December. The company will pay 70¢ per gallon, the current wholesale price, and give C and D Sugar the option to repurchase the sweetener for a 30-day period at 71¢

The tax partner has told you that the transaction is good for tax purposes, because: 1. the client will have legal title to the sweetener, 2. there is a profit motive to the client because it will make $12,000 if the repurchase option is exercised; and, 3. there is risk because if the price falls, the repurchase option would not be exercised and the client would take delivery of the sweetener. He goes on to say that although the IRS would understand that a prime motive of the client in entering this transaction would be to avoid the liquidation of LIFO layers, the presence of profit potential and risk make the transaction good for tax purposes.

The partner in charge of the audit agrees with the tax partner for similar reasons. He believes Packard should be permitted to record the transaction as the purchase of inventory. However, the reviewing partner thinks the transaction lacks substance. He thinks that due to the volatility of the sugar market that the sweetener will almost certainly be repurchased. He believes the transaction is an accommodation between the two companies and that the $12,000 price differential is really interest on the $840,000 (70 x 1,200,000) which C and D will have the use of for the 30 day period before exercising the repurchase option. He points out that the $12,000 represents about an 18% interest rate which is not unreasonable in today's market. He feels the transaction is a sham and that the transaction should not be recorded as a purchase of inventory.

INSTRUCTIONS:

Which partner is correct, i.e. should this transaction be recorded as a purchase of inventory by the Packard Sugar Co.?

6-6 Standard Costs for Inventory?

The Robertson Corporation has a standard cost system for determining inventory and product costs. Its financial statements show the following data for the past four calendar years:

	1985	1984	1983	1982
Sales	$3,150,000	$3,200,000	$3,100,000	$3,000,000
Cost of sales	2,550,000	2,500,000	2,425,000	2,280,000
Gross profits	600,000	700,000	675,000	720,000
% Cost of sales	81%	78%	78%	76%

Costs of sales includes:

Costs at standard	2,447,000	2,437,500	2,365,500	2,222,500
Variance from standard:				
Unfavorable	(38,000)	(38,500)	(36,250)	(35,000)

Other Information:

a. Sales do not vary seasonally.

b. Inventory levels are constant throughout the year and have increased in the last four years in proportion to total sales.

c. The company takes its annual physical inventory at the end of the year.

d. During the first quarter of 1986, Robertson Company's trial balance included:

Sales	$850,000
Cost	662,500
Variances from standard:	
Favorable	10,000

INSTRUCTIONS:

1. What are standard costs? Are standard costs acceptable for financial reporting purposes? Why or why not?

2. What are the advantages of a standard cost system?

3. Present arguments in support of each of the following three methods of treating standard cost variance for purposes of financing reporting:

a. They may be carried as deferred charges or credits on the balance sheet.

b. They may appear as charges or credits on the income statement.

c. They may be allocated between inventories and cost of goods sold.

4. How would you suggest Robertson account for the favorable variance on the interim report for the first quarter of 1986?

6-7 Lower of Cost or Market

Popeye, Inc. (a German firm), acquired by ETT as of April 30, 1985, is engaged in the production and sale of canned and frozen food. The year-end physical inventory was taken as of January 1, 1986. Applying a net realizable test on an individual product basis to that inventory would have resulted in a write-down of approximately $340,000 (translated from German marks) as follows:

	Cans	Frozen	Total
Spinach	$ 8,000	$183,000	$191,000
Cut Beans	25,000	-	25,000
Peas	45,000	-	45,000
Mixed Vegetables	15,000	-	15,000
Parisienne Carrots	5,000	13,000	18,000
Carrots	3,000	-	3,000
Asparagus	4,000	-	4,000
Plums	14,000	-	14,000
All Other	25,000	-	25,000
	$144,000	$196,000	$340,000

This write down would approximate 10% of total inventory value and would increase the loss for the eight months ended December 31, 1985 by a corresponding amount, which was material.

The Company argued that inasmuch as the products are sold on a line basis (frozen or canned), with customers taking all varieties and only rarely are sold on an individual product basis, the application of the lower of cost or market rule to the total product line would result in the more proper determination of income (loss). A pricing of the inventory on this basis would result in the following $69,000 (translated from German marks) write-down:

	Cans	Frozen	Total
	$ 29,000	$ 40,000	$ 69,000

INSTRUCTIONS:

1. Explain the application and the restrictions of the lower of cost or market rule.
2. How should the inventory write-down be recorded and how should it be presented on the financial statements?
3. Do the Professional Standards substantiate your answer to Question Number 1?
4. Give arguments for and against the use of the lower of cost or market rule
5. Can you suggest an alternative existing method to account for losses in inventory value other than the use of the lower of cost or market rule?

6-8 Sutro Company

Sutro Company is a medium-sized manufacturing company with two divisions and three subsidiaries, all located in the United States. The Gunn Division manufactures metal castings for the automotive industry, and the Dunn Division produces small plastic items for electrical products and other uses. The three subsidiaries manufacture various products for other industrial users.

Sutro Company plans to change from the lower of first-in, first-out (FIFO) cost or market method of inventory valuation to the last-in, first-out (LIFO) method of inventory valuation to obtain tax benefits. To make the method acceptable for tax purposes, the change also will be made for its annual financial statements.

INSTRUCTIONS:

1. Describe the establishment of and subsequent pricing procedures for each of the following LIFO inventory methods:

   a. LIFO applied to units of product when the periodic inventory system is used.

   b. Application of the dollar-value method to LIFO units of product.

2. Discuss the specific advantages and disadvantages of using the dollar-value LIFO application as compared to traditional LIFO methods. Ignore income tax considerations.

3. Discuss the general advantages and disadvantages claimed for LIFO methods.

6-9 The Munz Company

The Munz Company, your client, manufactures paint. The company's president, Mr. Munz, has decided to open a retail store to sell Munz paint as well as wallpaper and other supplies that would be purchased from other suppliers. He has asked you for information about the retail method of pricing inventories at the retail store.

INSTRUCTIONS:

Prepare a report to the president explaining the retail method of pricing inventories. Your report should include these points:

a. Description and accounting features of the method.

b. The conditions that may distort the results under the method.

c. A comparison of the advantages of using the retail method with those of using cost methods of inventory pricing.

d. The accounting theory underlying the treatment of net markdowns and net markups under this method.

6-10 Manor Nylons, Incorporated

You are in charge of the audit of Manor Nylons, Incorporated. The following items were in Manor's inventory at November 30, 1985 (fiscal year end):

Product Number	075936	078310	079104	081111
Selling price per unit November 30, 1985	$15.00	$23.00	$28.00	$13.00
Standard cost, per unit, as included in inventory on November 30, 1985	$ 7.90	$11.25	$14.26	$ 7.40

In discussions with Manor's marketing and sales personnel, you were told that there will be a general 7% (rounded to the next highest five cents) increase in selling prices, effective December 1, 1985. This increase will affect all garments except those that have 081 as the first three digits of the product code. The 081 codes are assigned to new apparel introduction, and for product code 081111, the selling price will be $8.00 effective December 1, 1985.

In addition, you were told by the controller that Manor attempts to earn a 50% gross profit in selling price on all their nylons.

From the cost department you obtained the following standards, which will be used for fiscal 1986:

Product Number	1986 Standard
075936	$ 8.25
078310	$10.75
079104	$14.71
081111	$ 7.51

Sales commissions and estimates of other costs of disposal approximate 25% of standard costs to manufacture. Assume that standard costs provide an accurate assessment of the replacement cost of the product.

INSTRUCTIONS:

1. Compute the value at which each of the items should be reported in the November 30, 1985 inventory.
2. Why should inventories be reported at market?
3. Does the literal interpretation of the rule of lower of cost or market always apply? Could you cite in this case where a possible exception to the lower of cost or market might be employed?

CHAPTER 7

ACQUISITION AND DISPOSITION, DEPRECIATION, AND DEPLETION OF PROPERTY, PLANT, AND EQUIPMENT

7-1 Useful Arbitrary Allocations

Lutz and Lutz observed in their 1951 book, The Theory of Investment of the Firm, that:

"For the past hundred years accountants have been searching for the 'true' depreciation method which would allocate the cost of the machine over its lifetime in accordance with the rate at which it is actually being 'used up'."

This search had led to a variety of definitions of depreciation, such as:

1. A decrease in value with the lapse of time.

2. Impaired serviceability.

3. The value difference from an appraisal standpoint.

4. Amortized cost.

5. Fall in market price.

6. Physical deterioration.

7. Fall in value.

8. Allocation of cost.

9. The exhaustion of service-units embodied in fixed assets.

10. The loss in value due to wear and tear, deterioration and obsolescence.

11. The means to keep real capital intact.

12. The systematic amortization of cost without regard to value during life.

13. Arbitrary allocations.

The critical problem regardless of the definition of depreciation of plant and equipment is to assign some amount as an expense in the determination of the net income of each period.

INSTRUCTIONS:

1. What is the "true" definition of depreciation?
2. What is the accounting definition of depreciation?
3. What is the theoretically "best" method of depreciation to use to determine the amount to expense each period for the determination of net income?
4. What is the accounting rule by which an amount is expensed each period for the determination of net income?
5. What are the major factors considered by a firm in determining what depreciation method to use?

7-2 The Nature of Property, Plant, and Equipment

Almost every business enterprise of any size or activity uses assets of a durable nature in its operations. Such assets, commonly referred to as property, plant, and equipment; plant assets; or fixed assets include land, building structures, equipment, and vehicles.

The accounting for property, plant, and equipment is a measurement or valuation process that supplies information of interest to financial statement users in assessing the reporting entity's earnings power, solvency, and financial flexibility.

One accounting theorist sees the main objective in the accounting for plant and equipment as "the computation of the current depreciation amount to be charged to expense in the determination of the net income of the period." He also feels that the measurement process should have as one of its goals "the economic description of the capital resources of the firm." A third objective of measuring fixed assets is to "present information that will permit the prediction of future cash inflows and outflows."

These are all worthy objectives, but it seems that they are difficult to meet in a historical cost world.

Once equipment has been installed and placed in operation, subsequent expenditures relating to this equipment are frequently thought of as being in the nature of repairs or general maintenance and, hence, chargeable to operations in the period in which the expenditure is made. Actually, determination of whether such an expenditure should be charged to operations or capitalized involves a much more careful analysis of the character of the expenditure.

INSTRUCTIONS:

1. What are the major characteristics of plant assets?
2. How well are the accounting theorist's objectives met with the current accepted accounting for fixed assets?
3. Why is historical cost currently used by the accounting profession?
4. What are the factors that should be considered in making the decision to expense or capitalize costs incurred after assets have been acquired and placed in operation? Discuss fully.

7-3 Electricpower's Audit Program

The Electricpower's audit program calls for examining all records concerning all property additions over $100,000. In executing this audit step, you examined the following section of the property ledgers for project 830-10. This project is part of the expansion of the Custom Power division's productive capacity.

PROJECT 830-10

LAND

Date	Explanation	Ref.	Debit	Credit	Balance
2/ 1	Purchase for cash	CD	$200,000		$ 200,000
3/ 1	Purchase for cash	CD	55,000		255,000

BUILDINGS

Date	Explanation	Ref.	Debit	Credit	Balance
2/ 1	Purchase for cash	CD	$800,000		$ 800,000
3/ 1	Purchase for cash	CD	45,000		845,000
4/ 1	Building razed	GJ		$45,000	800,000
8/31	Transfer from con-struction in progress	GJ	500,000		1,300,000

Further examination of the records and inquiries of the executives of the corporation result in the following factual determinations:

As of February 1, land and a building located near the Custom Power division's current plant were purchased for cash of $1,000,000. The building was about 10 years old and was deemed to have a remaining useful life of 25 years. The aggregate price was allocated by the management at $200,000 to the land and $800,000 to the building.

On March 1, property adjoining this plant site was acquired for a purchase price of $100,000. There was a building in good condition on the property. Based on the relationship of assessed valuations for local property tax purposes, the purchase price was allocated $55,000 to the land and $45,000 to the building.

Since Electricpower could not use the building economically it was demolished on April 1 at a cost of $5,000. This amount was charged to operating expenses. The $45,000 allocated cost of the building was charged to operations.

During the period from April 1 to August 28, Electricpower's maintenance department constructed a building on the newly acquired property at a cost of $500,000.

The monthly cost of $25,000 for direct labor and $75,000 for materials was paid on the first day following each of the five months of construction (first payment was made on May 1). The maintenance department had an overhead rate of 40% of direct labor dollars. The building was placed in service on August 30.

On February 1, Electricpower borrowed $400,000 at 12% annual interest to finance this construction. Interest earned on these funds until they were used totalled $10,000.

The building was appraised at $650,000 for insurance purposes. Assume that Electricpower has no other debt.

INSTRUCTIONS:

1. What evidence might be examined to determine that properties are properly classified?
2. Prepare any adjusting journal entries which you would propose as of December 31. Explain the basis for each of the entries and show your computations.
3. The supervisor of property accounting mentioned to you that he believes that the company has been too "conservative" in capitalizing only the direct costs of the building constructed by company employees and believes that the building cost should be recorded at $650,000, the amount of the lowest bid received from outside contractors. How would you respond?

7-4 The High Sierra Real Estate Co.

The High Sierra Real Estate Development Co. owns and operates a chain of motel/hotel chalet units on the ski slopes of the Western United States. Their original units were built twenty years ago and were estimated to have a fifteen year life for depreciation purposes. As the business grew and prospered the company continued to build new motel/ hotel chalet units. In fact, they were able to complete one new project in each of the last ten years. They were consistent in their accounting for these units as they used the straight line depreciation method, a fifteen year life and no salvage value for their depreciation expense calculations.

Due to the changing real estate market and the high cost of maintaining and operating these seasonal recreation units, the company decided to renovate, remodel and sell all of their chalets as condominiums. As they close each unit, they will begin to sell the units to individuals. It will require approximately 12 months to renovate and subdivide the buildings. They estimate that it will take five years to totally convert and sell all of the ski chalet condominium properties.

The management is concerned with the potential accounting problems that might arise during the transition period. The first concern was the negative impact on income of continuing to depreciate the properties that were being renovated. During renovation they will not be generating revenue and the lower income due to lower revenue and continued straight line depreciation will make it more difficult for the company to obtain financing for their renovation projects.

The controller suggests that continued depreciation may be advantageous for tax purposes and that the extra tax deductions would increase cash flow. However, the controller was not sure of the correct basis for depreciation. Was it the current book values which were well below current appraisal values? Would it include costs of renovation incurred until the units were sold? And what was to be the new useful life?

The final problem involved the accounting treatment adopted for fully depreciated assets. The company had the policy of removing fully depreciated assets from its balance sheet. The controller was unsure as to how or if the assets should now be returned to the balance sheet on the basis of their sales value or fully depreciated value. Also, since no assets appeared on the balance sheet should the renovation costs be capitalized (and perhaps depreciated until the units are sold) as assets separate from the buildings, or should they be expensed as incurred?

INSTRUCTIONS:

1. Explain and contrast the asset-liability and revenue-expense theories relating to operating assets.
2. Discuss the issue raised by High Sierra's management regarding the depreciation of the units during the renovation period.
3. Discuss the issue raised for the treatment of the company's fully depreciated chalet units.
4. Discuss whether the use of current value accounting would have avoided the consideration of these issues.

7-5 Depreciation Disclosure

Depreciation continues to be one of the most difficult conceptual issues in practice. Because of companies' potential large investment in depreciable assets, the periodic expense allocation can have a significant impact on the income of a firm. The selection of the useful lives, salvage values, depreciable basis, and depreciation method can all impact the income from operations. Consequently, information related to a firm's depreciation policy can be very useful to financial statement users. Following is some of the information provided in the 1983 annual reports of General Motors Corporation and Caterpillar Corporation regarding their fixed assets and depreciation policies:

General Motors Corp.
Depreciation is provided on groups of property using, with minor exceptions, an accelerated method which accumulates depreciation of approximately two-thirds of the depreciable cost during the first half of the estimated lives of the property.

Expenditures for special tools are amortized, with the amortization applied directly to the asset account, over short periods of time because the utility value of the tools is radically affected by frequent changes in the design of the functional components and appearance of the product. Replacement of special tools for reasons other than changes in products is charged directly to costs of sales.

NOTE 9. Real Estate, Plant and Equipment and
Accumulated Depreciation

(Dollars in Millions)	1983	1982
Real estate, plant and equipment (Note 11):		
Land	$ 347.2	$ 361.8
Land improvements	1,145.1	1,136.8
Leasehold improvements-less amortization	47.1	41.8
Buildings	8,010.2	7,921.3
Machinery and equipment	25,669.1	24,802.1
Furniture and office equipment	469.0	403.6
Capitalized leases	754.7	711.7
Construction in progress	1,335.4	2,308.1
Total	$37,777.8	$37,687.2
Accumulated depreciation:		
Land improvements	$ 628.3	$ 576.5
Buildings	3,937.0	3,650.6
Machinery and equipment	15,057.8	13,505.9
Furniture and office equipment	196.4	160.9
Capitalized leases	297.3	255.0
Total	$20,116.8	$18,148.9

Caterpillar Corp.
Depreciation is computed principally using accelerated methods
for both income tax and financial reporting purposes. These
methods result in a larger allocation of the cost of buildings,
machinery, and equipment to operations in the early years of the
lives of assets than does the straight-line method. If the
straight-line method had always been in use, "Buildings,
machinery, and equipment -- net" would have been $733, $681, and
$594 higher than reported at December 31, 1983, 1982, and 1981,
respectively, and depreciation expense for 1983, 1982, and 1981
would have been, respectively, $70, $88, and $91 less.

For financial reporting purposes the depreciation rates
used worldwide are principally based on the "guideline" lives
established by the U.S. Internal Revenue Service. For income
tax purposes the depreciation rates used are principally based
on the "guideline" lives for assets acquired prior to 1971, on
the Class Life ADR System for 1971-1980 additions, and on the
Accelerated Cost Recovery System for additions after 1980.

When an asset becomes fully depreciated, its cost is
eliminated from both the asset and the accumulated depreciation
accounts.

Buildings, machinery, and equipment -- net

Buildings, machinery and equipment -- net at December 31, by major classification,
were as follows:

	1983	1982	1981
Buildings	$1,961	$1,875	$1,713
Machinery and equipment	3,777	3,553	3,249
Construction-in-process	334	437	494
	6,072	5,865	5,455
Deduct: Accumulated depreciation	2,915	2,526	2,155
	$3,157	$3,339	$3,300

The company has commitments for the purchase or construction of capital assets
amounting to approximately $230 at December 31, 1983. Capital expenditure plans
are subject to continuous monitoring and changes in such plans could reduce the
amount committed.

Maintenance and repair expense for 1983, 1982, and 1981 was $237, $336, and $437,
respectively.

1. What information regarding property, plant, and equipment and the depreciation policies must be disclosed by a corporation in their financial statements issued to stockholders? Consider both the body of the statements and the notes.
2. In general, how useful is the information to financial statement users?
3. Which of the two companies presents more "useful" information? Discuss.

7-6 Roadway Transport Co.

Roadway Transport Company invests substantial sums in trucking equipment to serve its clientele. In reviewing its competitors' balance sheets and income statements recently, the executive vice-president of finance noted that companies appeared to use various ways to account for their trade-ins. His review disclosed that trade-ins of revenue equipment of motor carriers are accounted for in one of the following ways:

1. By recognition of gain/loss on the asset traded in and recording of newly acquired assets at cost (the predominant practice).

2. By recording the newly acquired assets at the sum of the net book value of the assets traded in plus the cash (or other) consideration given, i.e., the income tax method.

The executive vice-president has come to you as controller and asked for an explanation for the diversity in the industry. Furthermore, she is interested in Roadway's present practice. The company this year is in need of some earnings, and perhaps it might make sense to sell off some of its trucking equipment.

INSTRUCTIONS:

1. Present arguments for both sides.
2. What is the present GAAP requirement? Does it differ from the income tax method?

7-7 Standard, Inc.*

Standard, Inc. is a small, independent, gas and oil producer (incorporated in 1971). Since inception, Standard has maintained a policy of aggressive exploration, which is financed with short-term and long-term debt. During the seventies, Standard made several sizable discoveries of reserves in Canada and the Middle East. Standard's aggressive policy accounts for its high percentage of exploration costs in relation to their total cost structure. Standard is unconcerned with the high percentage as it believes that its success in the industry is dependent on a large number of gas and oil wells owned.

The Industry

The gas and oil industry is under the close scrutiny of the public. After the 1973 oil embargo, the Justice Department considered anti-trust legislation and increased regulation of the gas and oil industry -- hence, accounting policy and national energy policy became inextricably bound. To circumvent economic, political, and regulatory risks, major oil and gas companies are diversifying into unrelated fields. Since the oil embargo U.S., energy dependence on foreign sources has increased, although the public appears to consider it essential that the U.S. lessen its dependence on foreign oil markets.

Problem

Roy Holten, is president of Standard Co. and is troubled by Accounting Series Release (ASR) No. 253. ASR 253 requires the supplemental use of reserve recognition accounting (RRA) for 1979-1981. RRA will then be evaluated to determine whether it should be adopted as the primary method. Until then, the full cost method (FC) or the successful efforts method (SE) may be used in the body of the financial statements. Roy is also troubled by the fact that the FASB has just released FASB Statement 19, "Financial Accounting and Reporting by Oil and Gas Companies" which requires the use of successful efforts. Standard currently uses full costing. Holten decided to call in his advisors for a meeting on whether Standard should continue to use full costing and whether Standard should join a coalition of gas and oil producers who are lobbying against RRA and successful efforts.

Discussion

Paul Marks, Vice-President of Management, believes that smoother earnings and greater asset and equity accounts result if full costing is used. Such an accounting approach makes it easier for Standard to obtain debt and equity financing. Under the successful efforts method, he believes Standard would have to cut back on exploration expenditures to balance out the loss of earnings even though Standard was having good success with its exploration program. The cutback on exploration fees would hurt Standard since exploration is vital to its livelihood.

James Sundem, Vice President of Finance, is against RRA. RRA does not correlate with cash flows. Also, Sundem believes the timing between discovery and production is

---

*Adapted from a case prepared by Thomas McHugh.

James Sundem, Vice President of Finance, is against RRA. RRA does not correlate with cash flows. Also, Sundem believes the timing between discovery and production is often inaccurate. For example, a Price Waterhouse study found delays of up to 2 years from the estimated production date. Since RRA uses the net present value of the reserves, the disparity in production date will affect the financial statements.

Other problems with RRA include the difficulty of estimating offshore reserves and foreign reserves. Sundem's analysis therefore led him to believe that investors would be unable to form trend lines under RRA or effectively evaluate business conditions or management efficiency. Sundem also felt that subjectivity of RRA would render the statements useless.

Sundem was also concerned about two recent studies. One study revealed an average decline of 4.5 percent in the stock prices of full cost companies who switched to the successful efforts method. These results were surprising in light of efficient market evidence. Sundem noted that the changeover would require an investment write-off which would decrease Standard's equity and increase the debt to equity ratio. Accordingly, the company might have difficulty obtaining new financing.

Roy Holten mulled the alternatives. SE accounting would probably render it more difficult for Standard to raise capital. Also, a manager's ability to gain bonuses or be promoted depend partly on reported earings. Management may change their strategy to alter the impact of the change in accounting methods, which would be detrimental to the company as a whole. Mr. Holton decided to maintain full costing.

INSTRUCTIONS:

1. Explain the history of GAAP in the oil and gas industry.
2. Define successful efforts and full costing.
3. Why are small oil producers generally opposed to successful efforts accounting?
4. Describe RRA. What are some of the criticisms of RRA?
5. What are some lessons that might be learned from the controversy concerning the proper accounting for oil and gas properties?
6. Which accounting method would you propose to Holton and why?

7-8 Warren Manufacturing, Inc.

Warren Manufacturing, Inc. began operations five years ago producing stetrics, a new type of instrument it hoped to sell to doctors, dentists, and hospitals. The demand for stetrics far exceeded initial expectations, and the company was unable to produce enough stetrics to meet demand.

The company was manufacturing its product on equipment that it built at the start of its operations. To meet demand, more efficient equipment was needed. The company decided to design and build the equipment since the equipment currently available on the market was unsuitable for producing stetrics.

In 1980 a section of the plant was devoted to development of the new equipment and a special staff of personnel was hired. Within six months a machine was developed at a cost of $210,000 which successfully increased production and reduced labor costs substantially. Sparked by the success of the new machine, the company built three more machines of the same type at a cost of $130,000 each.

INSTRUCTIONS:

1. In general, what costs should be capitalized for self-constructed assets?

2. Discuss the propriety of including in the capitalized cost of self-constructed assets:

   a. The increase in overhead caused by the self-construction of fixed assets.
   b. A proportionate share of overhead on the same basis as that applied to goods manufactured for sale.

3. Discuss the proper accounting treatment of the $80,000 ($210,000-$130,000) by which the cost of the first machine exceeded the cost of the subsequent machines. This additional cost should not be considered research and development costs.

7-9 Capitalize or Expense?

You have recently been hired as a junior accountant in the firm of Hargrove, Tick, and Check. Mr. Hargrove is an alumnus of the same school from which you graduated and, therefore, is quite interested in your accounting training. He therefore presents the following situations and asks for your response.

SITUATION I

Recently a construction company agreed to construct a new hospital for its client at the construction company's cost; that is, the contractor was to realize no profit. The construction company was interested in performing this service because it had substantial interests in the community and wanted to make the community more attractive. The building was completed in 1985, and the costs of the hospital were $7,000,000. An appraisal firm indicated, however, that the fair market value of the properties was $8,500,000, the difference due to the $1,500,000 that the company did not charge the hospital.

INSTRUCTIONS:

At what amount should the hospital value the asset? A related question is whether the donated property should be reported as income or as a capital contribution. What is your answer to this question?

SITUATION II

Recently, one of our clients asked whether it would be appropriate to capitalize a portion of the salaries of the corporate officers for time spent on construction activities. During construction, one of the officers devotes full time to the supervision of construction projects. His activities are similar to those of a construction superintendent for a general contractor. During periods of heavy construction activity, this officer also employs several assistants to help with administrative matters related to construction. All other officers are general corporate officers.

The compensation and other costs related to the construction officer are not dependent on the level of construction activity in a particular period (except to the extent that additional assistants are employed on a short-term basis). These expenses would continue to be incurred even if there was no construction activity unless the company decided to discontinue permanently, or for the foreseeable future, all construction activity. In that case, it could well reach the decision to terminate the construction officer. The company has, however, aggressive expansion plans which anticipate continuing construction of shopping center properties.

INSTRUCTIONS:

What salary cost, if any, should be capitalized to the cost of properties?

Every few years one of our client publishes a new catalog for distribution to its sales outlets and customers. The latest catalog was published in 1984. Periodically, current price lists and new product brochures are issued. The company is now contemplating the issue of a new catalog during the latter part of 1986. The cost of the new catalog has been accounted for as follows:

(a) Estimated total cost of the catalog is accounted for over a period beginning with the initial planning (1985) and is expected to end at time of publication.

(b) Estimated costs are accumulated in an accrued liability account through monthly charges to selling expenses.

(c) Monthly charges were based on the estimated total cost of the guide and the estimated number of months remaining before publication; periodic revisions were made to the estimates as current information became available.

(d) Actual costs were recorded as charges to the accrued liability account as they were accrued.

In summary, the company accrues the entire estimated cost (including anticipated costs to be incurred) of a contemplated catalog through charges to operations prior to the expected publication date.

INSTRUCTIONS:

Comment on the propriety of this treatment.

7-10 Depreciation Problems

Presented below are three different and unrelated situations involving depreciation accounting. Answer the question(s) at the end of each case situation.

SITUATION I

Morgan Paper Company, a subsidiary of Scott Paper Company, operates a 300-ton-per-day kraft pulp mill and four sawmills in Wisconsin. The company is in the process of expanding its pulp mill facilities to a capacity of 1,000 tons per day and plans to replace three of its older, less efficient sawmills with an expanded facility. One of the mills to be replaced did not operate for most of 1985 (current year), and there are no plans to reopen it before the new sawmill facility becomes operational.

In reviewing the depreciation rates and in discussing the residual values of the sawmills that were to be replaced, it was noted that if present depreciation rates were not adjusted, substantial amounts of plant costs on these three mills would not be depreciated by the time the new mill came on stream.

INSTRUCTIONS:

What is the proper accounting for the four sawmills at the end of 1985?

SITUATION II

Recently, Arkansas Company experienced a strike that affected a number of its operating plants. The controller of this company indicated that it was not appropriate to report depreciation expense during this period because the equipment did not depreciate and an improper matching of costs and revenues would result. He based his position on the following points:

a. It is inappropriate to charge the period with costs for which there are no related revenues arising from production.

b. The basic factor of depreciation in this instance is wear and tear, and because equipment was idle no wear and tear occurred.

INSTRUCTIONS:

Comment on the appropriateness of the controller's comments.

SITUATION III

The Norvell Company manufactures electrical appliances, most of which are used in homes. Company engineers have designed a new type of blender which, through the use of a few attachments, will perform more functions than any blender currently on the market. Demand for the new blender can be projected with reasonable probability. In order to make the blenders, Norvell needs a specialized machine that is not available from outside sources. It has been decided to make such a machine in Norvell's own plant.

INSTRUCTIONS:

1. Discuss the effect of projected demand in units for the new blenders (which may be steady, decreasing, or increasing) on the determination of a depreciation method for the machine.
2. What other matters should be considered in determining the depreciation method? Ignore income tax considerations.

CHAPTER 8

INTANGIBLE ASSETS

8-1 HAL Corporation[*]

HAL Corporation is a leader in the computer industry with diversified interests in various areas of the market. Below is the summarized balance sheet of fiscal year 1985:

Assets	(In Millions)
Current assets	$4,000
Long-term assets	4,900
Intangible assets	100
Total Assets	$9,000
Liabilities	
Bonds payable (short-term)	1,800
Long-term liabilities	2,700
Total Liabilities	$4,500
Stockholders' Equity	
Common stock ($10 par)	1,500
Retained earnings	3,000
Total Stockholders' Equity	4,500
Total Liabilities and Stockholders' Equity	$9,000

Technology in the electronics industry has changed rapidly in the past decade. Many small-sized companies have established a place in the market by developing expertise in specialized segments of the market. For example, the word processing equipment market is now dominated by Lang Lab of Massachusetts, which captured

---

* Adapted from a case prepared by Goldwyn K. Ling.

two thirds of the sales in this area in 1984. These small companies have lured away a considerable portion of HAL Corporation's clients and are making it difficult for HAL to maintain its leading position in the industry. Top management decided to restore its leadership by implementing a long-range master plan consisting of research projects, financing arrangements, and personnel recruitment. Following is a discussion of some of the steps taken in 1985:

(1) Research and development of $20,000,000 was spent on the development of three-dimensional silicon chips. The chips will have the capability of holding up to 8 million bits of memory and would provide a much faster operation than any existing two-dimensional chips. The project is still in its preliminary stage of planning and development.

(2) HAL Corp. has entered into a contract with the U.S. postal service to develop a central communication system that will allow audio-visual-textual communications via home television terminals across the country. Development costs were 4 million dollars in 1985.

(3) Management decided to challenge the word processing equipment market dominated by Lang Lab. It signed a contract with Digital Equipment Corp. to purchase certain technology of Ditigals' "four-phase office system," the counterpart of Lang's product. HAL Corp. agreed to pay 19 million dollars in cash in 1985.

All patents and patent applications generated by Digital Equipment Corp. in the course of developing the technology, including blueprints and notes, were acquired by HAL Corp.

(4) There was also a provision in the contract to pay royalties to Digital Equipment Corp. based on 5% of future sales of word processing equipment.

(5) A project has been conducted since 1980 to design a mode converter called "Minimax." It is essentially a minicomputer which will serve as a link between products of different computer companies. One of the biggest fears of potential users these days is that once their systems start with one company's products, it will be incompatible with software innovations available to other firms' computers. The minimax will eliminate such incompatability by interpreting and converting signals received from one machine and transmit them to another machine with different signal codes. It will be extremely easy to install and requires a minimum level of maintenance.

The industry has been watching the development of this product with favorable expectations. HAL Corp. is the only company with the financial resources and expertise to develop such sophisticated equipment. The sales department has already received 1,500 orders for delivery of Minimax by the end of 1988. Cost of development in 1985 was $600,000.

(6) A legal fee of $150,000 was incurred on litigation regarding patent protection.

(7) A building worth 1 million dollars was purchased as the site of the research and development department. The building was made up of the east wing and west wing. The east wing was used by the team developing the 3-D silicon chip technology. Development of the U.S. postal service communication system was underway in the west wing.

(8) HAL Corp. successfully persuaded the chief engineer of Control Data Corp. to join HAL Corp. as the project manager of the 3-D silicon chip development project. Salary in 1985 was $100,000.

(9) Costs of software improvement in HAL Corporation's management information system (MIS) incurred in 1985 were 2 million dollars. The MIS was designed for internal reporting of inventory control and other information needed for decision making, such as vouchers payable due for the month.

INSTRUCTIONS:

1. How should the transactions above be recorded for 1985 under FASB Statement No. 2?
2. What are the advantages and disadvantages of accounting for R&D costs under FASB Statement No. 2?

8-2 C. W. Dean*

C. W. Dean is a large mail-order manufacturer of leather goods located in Freeport, Maine. The company has experienced a rapid rate of growth over the past several years as more and more consumers are "shopping by mail". As a result of this growth, C. W., the Company president, has become more concerned about bottlenecks that are starting to occur in the order-entry system. For example, in the last quarter of 1985, a total of 12 customer orders were never received by the warehouse and consequently were never filled. At the 1985 year-end convention of mail-order manufacturers, C. W. found that many other companies had similar problems and were interested in finding a solution to this problem. Since C. W. Dean was considered the leader in the industry, it agreed to research the problem and try to come up with

---

*Adapted from a case prepared by Charles Whitaker.

an adequate order-entry computer software package that would alleviate the problem. It agreed to research this problem, however, only if the other companies agreed to buy the software package from C. W. Dean if it proved to be adequate.

In the following two weeks, 15 firms sent letters to C. W. indicating that if C. W. Dean could develop an adequate order-entry software package, they would buy the package at a price which would reimburse C. W. Dean for the money spent on research and development of the package. This assurance was good enough for C. W. and so the research department starting working on the project.

Eight months later, two elaborate computer software packages were presented to C. W. as follows:

(1) "The Researcher". This software package has the capabilities to test and experiment with new information systems that may be developed in the future. The research analyst told C. W. that, although the package was expensive to develop ($350,000), it could be used for many other research projects in the future. As he indicated, "it will pay for itself in five years."

(2) "O. E. Magnifique". This software package has the capabilities to handle a large volume of orders in a short period of time, all of which will appear on a T.V. screen (CRT) placed directly on the warehouse floor. It should eliminate all bottlenecks and lost orders. The full cost to develop this package was $650,000.

As the 1986 year-end was approaching, C. W. was anxious to get these amounts recorded properly so all 15 firms were contacted and told the good news of "O. E. Magnifique." A price was set at $40,625 plus the cost to reproduce the package. This amount was calculated using the $650,000 figure divided by the 16 firms who would use the package. The $350,000 was not included because C. W. decided to keep that package and use it in future research and development projects. All firms were agreeable to this proposal.

After consultation with the firm's controller, the following journal entry was made:

```
Accounts Receivable              609,375
"Researcher" asset (5 yr. life)  350,000
R&D Expense (C. W. Dean's share)  40,625
       Cash                                  1,000,000
```

For the year C. W. Dean reported a net income of $400,000.

During the year end audit, the senior on the job informed C. W. that all $1,000,000 of the order entry project had to be classified as R&D costs and be expensed. Thus C. W. Dean would show a net loss for the first time in several years. C. W. was hopping mad and called the controller and research analyst into the room. The analyst presented concrete evidence of a future life for the "Researcher" and even identified several future research projects where the "Researcher" would be used. The controller pointed out that the agreement with the other firms constituted a contract and C. W. would be reimbursed for its R&D costs. Thus, according to GAAP, it should be recorded as a receivable. The auditors stood firm saying that according to FASB 2 all the expenditures qualified as R&D costs and should be expensed as incurred. They were at an impasse.

INSTRUCTIONS:

1. How would you record these expenditures?
2. How would you record the subsequent receipt of cash from the 15 firms?

8-3 The Value of Professional Athletes [*]

In 1974 the Atlanta Falcons professional football team was engaged in an income tax refund suit which had the potential of affecting the market value of professional teams in all sports. The lawsuit pertained to the tax shelters available to owners of professional athletic teams. In 1966 the Falcons paid $8,500,000 to join the National Football League, and the resulting litigation was to determine if the amount paid could be written off for tax purposes. A victory for the government could have far reaching effects on professional sports since it would make league expansion and development riskier and potentially less lucrative.

Among the witnesses involved in the trial were experts testifying as to the dollar value of "superstars" and average football players. The main issue in dispute was the basis for allocating the $8.5 million between the franchise itself and the portion applicable to the 42 players who were selected from other teams in the league's expansion draft. Five Smiths Inc., the team's corporate owner, treated $50,000 as the franchise payment, and most of the remainder, approximately $7.875 million, as payment for the players' contracts.

The key issue was "allocation" since the franchise right could not be depreciated because of its indefinite useful life. "Depreciating" players' contracts has begun in baseball where such contracts are bought and sold for cash, a practice that now pervades all professional team sports.

Five Smiths assigned a useful life of 5 1/4 years, resulting in a $1.5 million deduction in each tax year. The first two years' resulting losses were $506,000 and $581,000

---

*Adapted from a case prepared by Robert Godin.

respectively. "Cash flow" was about $1,000,000 each year. The owners of Five Smiths were able to use these losses to offset profits from their other interests.

The Internal Revenue Service had determined the value of the player contracts to be $1,000,000, thus disallowing $1,300,000 of the $1,500,000 yearly deduction. However, the government subsequently decided that none of the $8.5 million was depreciable. The government argued that Five Smiths joined an exclusive class acquiring a number of substantial and valuable monopoly rights forming a single mass asset with an indefinite life. It pointed out that only 23 of the 42 players eventually played for the team, and that many of the 19 unsuccessful players' contracts were sold for the nominal $100 waiver price. Furthermore, it argued that the $50,000 value for the franchise was unreasonable if only because the Falcon's share of the league's network television revenue would be $1,200,000 per year. The franchise fee was originally $50,000 and the television contract is to run for four years.

The defendant, in turn, claimed that $1.4 million of the $8.5 million should be allocated to television rights, and that it be depreciated on that basis. The government countered that television rights have an indefinite life and are therefore not depreciable.

INSTRUCTIONS:

1. What service-potential benefits did the owners of the Falcons acquire via the franchise purchase?

2. What is the basic argument of the government relating to the valuation and amortization of those rights?

3. Even though this is a tax case, you should be mainly concerned with the underlying accounting theory questions. From this perspective consider the following questions:

   (a) How should the purchase price be allocated to the various assets acquired?

   (b) Should they be amortized and if so, over what time period?

8-4 Spartan Corporation*

The Spartan Corporation had sales and earnings for 1985 of $25,000,000 and $700,000, respectively. For the ten years ending with 1985, Spartan's sales grew at a 20 percent compounded annual rate while earnings increased at a 21.5 percent rate.

*Adapted from a case prepared by John Tilley.

Spartan produced and marketed a broad line of sports equipment. Its markets were characterized by intense price competition, which dictated that management have good internal controls. As part of its controls, Spartan introduced a "human asset accounting" system in 1984.

The president's letter in the 1984 annual report stated under the subtitle, "Organizational Assets":

> As managers we are entrusted with the care of two types of assets -- physical assets and human assets. Each manager is responsible for the effective utilization of these assets to create a profit while maintaining the financial soundness of the company.
>
> Managers now work with accounting data which reflect the condition of physical assets and changes in those assets over a period of time. The assets of human resources do not appear in dollar terms on the balance sheet. To employ effectively the two types of assets and realize the objectives of Spartan, equally reliable accounting instruments are required to reflect the condition of human assets and changes in these assets over time.
>
> To fulfill these objectives, we are now in the process of developing and installing a Human Resource Accounting System to measure in dollar terms the human assets and changes in these assets over time.

Spartan's commitment to human asset accounting was further articulated in its 1985 annual report:

> We set ambitious goals for profitable growth in 1985. We achieved these goals through the effective use of our resources. These resources are: (1) the financial resources available to the corporation; (2) the physical resources such as buildings, equipment, and production technology; (3) the human resources in terms of the skills and abilities possessed by the people who comprise the organization; (4) the intangible resources such as corporate name, brand names, copyrights, and patents; and (5) the information resources of the business which provide reliable data upon which to make decisions.

Spartan clearly noted that the human resource accounting system was a pioneering step and that it lacked refinement. Additionally, Spartan stressed that the human resource capital accounts are used for internal information purposes and are unaudited.

The 1985 Spartan annual report devoted two of its 25 pages to human resource accounting. The approach used by Spartan is to account for investments in securing and developing the organization's human resources. Outlay costs for recruiting, acquiring, training, familiarizing, and developing management personnel are accumulated and capitalized. In accordance with the approach conventional accounting employs for classification of an expenditure as an asset, only those outlays which have an expected value beyond the current accounting period deserve consideration as investments. Those outlays which are likely to be consumed within a twelve-month period are properly classified as expense items. The investments in human resources are amortized over the expected useful period of the investment. The basic outlays in connection with acquiring and integrating new management people are amortized over their expected tenure with the company. The system now covers all management personnel at all locations of the corporation.

INSTRUCTIONS:

1. What are the objectives of a human resource accounting system?
2. What are some of the applications of human resource accounting?
3. Comment on the following statement: A favorite cliche for any president's letter in the corporate annual report is, "our employees are our most important -- our most valuable -- asset," but when one turns from the president's letter to the financial statements, there is, typically, never any other indication or acknowledgement of human resources.
4. What are the criteria for determining whether an expenditure is an asset, and do "people" fit these criteria?
5. What are some alternative methods for valuing human assets besides acquisition costs that Spartan might use?

8-5 Rent-A-Tech[*]

Rent-A-Tech Corporation is a small service firm which specializes in supplying technically trained professionals to firms in the chemical and petrochemical industry for work in specialized short-term (six months or less) projects. Rent-A-Tech supplies either individuals or small teams up to three people to these firms. Currently, R-A-T employs 24 professionals and four clerical people in addition to Ms. Daisy Jones, the president and founder of the company.

---

[*]Adapted from a case prepared by Carol Becker.

Each new employee, typically a recent graduate with a B.S. or M.S. in chemistry, chemical engineering, or a related field, takes part in a one-week introductory training program. This program concentrates on developing the skills needed to work both individually and in small groups on these short-term projects. Typically, one or two senior consultants along with Daisy herself will conduct the training program. In addition, at least twice a year all employees take part in a week-end seminar in order to update their training themselves as to the most recent theoretical and technological innovations in fields directly related to their consulting work.

R-A-T pays a beginning B.S. graduate in chemical engineering approximately $20,000, while a typical petrochemical firm will pay from $20,000 to $30,000 for an equivalent graduate. On consulting her records for the eight years the firm has been in existence, Daisy has calculated that 10% of the professionals hired leave R-A-T by the end of their first year. Another 20% leave after two years. 95% of the professionals leave the firm within the first five years. Only two people have been with Daisy over six years.

Rent-A-Tech rents office space in a convenient downtown office building. The company owns some of the office furniture but leases the technical equipment it needs. The balance sheet for Rent-A-Tech follows:

ASSETS		LIABILITIES	
Cash	$ 7,000	Accounts Payable	$ 5,000
Accounts Receivable	22,000	Notes Payable	10,000
Office Furniture (net.)	3,000	STOCKHOLDERS' EQUITY	
		Common Stock	1,000
		Retained Earnings	16,000
	$32,000		$32,000

Ms. Jones is certain that the firm's most important asset are the people who make up the organization. She feels that the balance sheet does not reflect the true value of the firm.

INSTRUCTIONS:

1. Do you think that Rent-A-Tech's employees represent the main assets of the firm? What factors are important here in determining if Rent-A-Tech's employees should be considered assets?
2. Assuming the employees are assets, how should these assets be reported on Rent-A-Tech's books?
3. If Rent-A-Tech's employees do not represent assets that can be quantified and placed on the balance sheet, in what way can a measure of their value be helpful to Daisy and the firm?

8-6 Equine Enterprises*

Equine Enterprises, breeders and trainers of Standardbred horses (trotters), is experiencing severe cash flow problems. Having decided against either additional debt or equity financing, Equine's small group of stockholders is eager to sell out to the right buyer.

Hi-Grow, Inc., a grass and grain seed company, is seeking to diversify and sees the acquisition of Equine Enterprises as a profitable investment. There is a strong market for good trotters and advertising potential for Hi-Grow's pasture seed mix and feed grains (picture contented mares, frolicking foals, and feisty stallions).

Equine Enterprises has a net asset value of $20,000,000 with the major assets being several national champion Standardbred studs and superior broodmare stock (all carried as long-term, depreciable assets) and an inventory of promising colts and fillies. In addition to servicing Equine Enterprises own broodmares, the studs are also booked every year to several hundred mares from outside, with stud fees ranging from $2,000 to $5,000.

During the last breeding season, a viral infection rendered the studs temporarily infertile. Although the infection has been treated successfully with no permanent sterility, an entire crop of Equine foals as well as an entire breeding season's stud fees are lost. Annual stud fees total approximately $2,000,000.

Hi-grow's offer of $18,000,000 has been accepted by Equine Enterprises. Hi-Grow's controller (a former veterinarian) advocates accounting for the difference between the $18,000,000 purchase price and the $20,000,000 net asset value of Equine Enterprises as a bargain purchase (negative goodwill). He believes that Equine Enterprises has simply failed to produce sufficient earnings to maintain the value of the business. He does not believe that the net assets are overstated, and therefore the excess of equity in net assets acquired over the purchase price should be reported in a deferred credit account. This negative goodwill would be amortized through the income statement over a three-or four-year period. He feels that this would represent a fair accounting for the bargain purchase and taking the negative goodwill income over the three-or four-year period will allocate it evenly over the periods until a new crop of foals are trained and ready for sale (remember a year's foals have been lost).

However, the assistant controller feels the net assets are overstated. As regards horse breeding, he's convinced that if anything can go wrong it will. He thinks no horse can be worth the current book value placed on some of the studs and broodmares. It seems obvious to him that the net assets must be written down by the $2,000,000 overstatement.

---

* Adapted from a case prepared by Jo-Anna Featherman.

1. What is negative goodwill?
2. Which accounting treatment, the controller's or assistant controller's, is in accordance with GAAP?
3. Do you think application of GAAP in this case results in a fair presentation of the transaction?

8-7 Hubert Inc.

On February 10, 1983 Hubert, Inc. acquired 100% of the stock of Rostat for $4,000,000 plus an additional amount not to exceed $1,500,000 payable after five years depending upon the level of pretax income of Rostat during that period. In essence, the negotiated total price of Rostat (including contingent amount) was based on 10 times estimated net income over the next five years of $550,000 per year. Rostat was willing to accept part ($1,500,000) of the purchase price contingent on earnings in excess of $300,000. At the date of acquisition, the $4,000,000 purchase price exceeded the net worth of Rostat by $2,450,000; this amount was considered to be goodwill by Hubert.

Rostat assembles exterior lights (plus a minor amount of interior lights) for foreign cars of all types. The company sells directly to manufacturers and through distributors. Subsequent to the purchase of Rostat in 1983, the economic outlook for Rostat's business changed significantly; accordingly as of December 31, 1983, Hubert wrote off $1,000,000 of the goodwill related to Rostat. Some background information is as follows:

From 1979 (year Rostat was formed) through 1982, Rostat had significant sales increases, with 1982 sales increasing approximately 40% over 1981 sales. The increase in Rostat sales resulted because of the rapid growth during that period in foreign car sales versus American made automobiles. It should be noted that Rostat covered three primary markets, small foreign automobiles, large foreign automobiles, and luxury foreign automobiles. Approximately 50% of the sales were related to small cars, 5-10% to large foreign cars, and 40-50% to luxury foreign cars.

During 1983, the sales of small foreign cars leveled off after several years of rapid growth. During the latter part of 1983, the luxury foreign cars in fact experienced substantial sales declines and problems mainly because of the high cost associated with the purchase of these automobiles. The substantial decline in sales for Rostat could be attributable primarily to a decrease in sales in the luxury foreign car market.

With the decline in sales of small and luxury foreign cars, Robstat's sales began to decline in May 1983, from the comparable month of 1982. The following is a summary of monthly sales for 1982 and 1983:

		(000's omitted)	
	1982	1983	1983 Increase (Decrease)
First Quarter			
January	238	292	54
February	275	278	3
March	370	406	36
	883	976	93
Second Quarter			
April	346	383	37
May	428	379	(49)
June	345	306	(39)
	1,119	1,068	(51)
Third Quarter			
July	279	242	(37)
August	329	207	(122)
September	253	178	(75)
	861	627	(234)
Fourth Quarter			
October	280	188	(92)
November	222	142	(80)
December	196	79	(117)
	698	409	(289)
Total for Year	$3,561	$3,080	$(481)

In January 1984, sales were only $84,000 compared with January 1983, sales of $292,000, or a decrease of $208,000. Rostat management anticipated that sales would be at depressed levels during the first six-to-nine months of 1984, and that any pick up in sales would not come until the latter part of 1984. The company anticipated that sales in 1984 would be less than 1983 sales. Rostat management estimated 1984 sales to be between $2,000,000 and $2,500,000 (compared with $3,080,000 in 1983 and $3,561,000 in 1982) and that the 1984 sales would be made up as follows:

a) 75% of 1983 volume of existing products.
b) New products.

The following is a comparison of estimated 1984 and actual 1983 and 1982 sales.

	1982	1983	Est. 1984
Sales	$3,561,000	$3,080,000	$2,000,000 to $2,500,000
Net Income	$ 450,000	$ 328,000	$ 100,000 to $ 125,000

1. What are the general guidelines followed in recording goodwill?
2. Is it normal to write-off a substantial amount of goodwill immediately after a purchase?
3. How might a company such as Hubert go about determining the amount to write-off for goodwill?
4. How would you classify the write-off for goodwill?

8-8 Motor Carrier Industry

In the past, intangible assets in the motor carrier industry have been significant to many carriers and to the industry as a whole. Individual carriers have had the amount of intangibles in the financial statements range from zero to nearly 100% or more of shareholders' equity. On an industry-wide basis the amount of recorded intangibles is equivalent to about 15% of shareholders' equity. Most companies in the industry describe these intangibles in their financial statement as being "operating rights" or "operating authorities."

Historically, the motor carrier industry has always had a significant amount of activity in the area of mergers and acquisitions. Beginning in the late 1960s, this activity increased significantly and paralleled the growth of many of the companies that are the leaders in the industry today. While there are exceptions to this generalization, many of the largest motor carriers in the industry were quite small twenty or thirty years ago and had significant growth due to merger and acquisition activities.

Under pre-July 1, 1980 Commission regulations, common carriers had to obtain certificates of authority (operating rights) to handle specific types of freight over specific routes or within specific territories. In the early formation of the industry these authorities were granted freely by the Commission to those carriers who applied for them and could demonstrate that they could serve the shippers in those routes or territories.

As the industry grew and the number of carriers serving various territories expanded, the Commission gradually placed limitations on the freedom with which they dispensed these authorities and by the 1960's there was very little new authority being issued by the Commission except in cases where a particular segment of traffic was not being well served. As a result, the carriers who wished to expand their operation either had to increase their share of the market within those territories in which they operated or look to the acquisition of operating authorities contiguous to existing routes from other carriers.

During this period of heavy merger and acquisition activity, many of the carriers acquired were those experiencing significant financial or operating difficulty. Although the operations of the target carriers may not have been healthy, significant prices were often paid to obtain these companies or their operating authorities. As a result, in most of these acquisitions, it was commonly believed that the only significant asset being purchased was the operating authority. Substantially all of the costs in excess of the current market value of the tangible property were assigned as a cost of the operating authority. In some cases there have been amounts identified as relating to goodwill, going concern or other types of intangibles. In addition to mergers and acquisitions, there have been numerous direct purchases involving only operating authority. Thus, the operating authorities had substantial value themselves.

The Motor Carrier Act of 1980 was signed into law July 1. Key provisions include: easier entry into the trucking industry for new carriers and easier route expansion for existing carriers; removal of most route restrictions and a broadening of the classifications of commodities carriers are permitted to haul; eventual freedom for trucking firms to boost or cut freight rates without the Commission's permission; and limitations on the scope of collective rate making permitted under an antitrust exemption. The new legislation contains many provisions which will affect the operation of the trucking industry, including the impact on the carrying value of operating rights contained in the financial statements.

The basic issue facing the motor carrier industry and accounting profession today relates to the need for a common set of guidelines regarding the appropriate accounting and financial disclosures due to the recent legislation. Recent legislation lessening regulation over entry into the common carrier industry has given rise to significant concerns as to the continuing values of operating authorities. The validity of these concerns must be addressed more specifically and some form of agreement reached as to the proper method of accounting for the cost of these authorities.

INSTRUCTIONS:

1. What issues should be considered in determining the accounting for these operating rights?
2. What approaches might be utilized to account for these operating rights?
3. Is there a GAAP answer to how operating rights should be reported?

8-9 Simpson Photo

Simpson Photo is a manufacturer of commercial and industrial photography equipment. Sales have increased steadily over the last six years; however, net income has been erratic. Simpson Photo has always expensed internal research and development costs as incurred.

During the last two years, Simpson Photo has entered into two agreements whereby technological know-how and experience was purchased from other companies.

In late 1985, Simpson purchased from Harbor, Inc. technology relating to a photoprocess application which became the basis of Simpson's new product, the "Photo-Star." The following is a discussion of this transaction:

1. The purchase price was $300,000 in cash. There was also a provision to pay an additional $300,000 no later than December 31, 1986 (or, in the alternative, pay royalties to Harbor, Inc. based on 6% of future sales), or simply return all patent rights to Harbor, Inc.

2. Some portion of the technology and know-how acquired was encompassed by certain patents which must be returned to Harbor, Inc. should Simpson decide to abandon this project. Simpson believes these patents are of limited value.

3. Certain stock and test equipment was purchased for use in the research project.

4. A prototype was also purchased.

5. During 1986, Simpson Photo has expended an additional $50,000 to develop the "Photo-Star" and approximately $70,000 in determining its marketability.

6. Simpson Photo accounted for this acquisition as the purchase of "products rights" during 1985 and proposed to expense this amount in future years on a unit-of-production basis as units are sold.

7. The tax treatment of this item is identical to its financial statement reporting.

During 1986, Simpson Photo entered into a similar transaction with Eller Corporation for the purchase of certain technology of a "Laser Beam Photo." The facts surrounding this transaction are as follows:

1. The purchased price was $500,000 in cash. No contingencies or additional payments are required by this agreement.

2. Tangible assets as set forth in a schedule (subsequently valued at $291,000 on the basis of cost data supplied by Eller Corporation) were acquired.

3. A warranty on the part of Eller Corporation not to license or otherwise permit any other party or parties to use such assets was included. Additionally, Eller warranted that it had agreements with its employees not to disclose the propriety information which was purchased by Simpson Photo.

4. All patents and patent applications, as well as invention disclosures which were generated by Eller in the course of developing the technology, which includes notebook pages, engineering drawings, documents and other recorded information which may be directly or solely applicable to the laser application were acquired.

5. Eller agreed to assist Simpson in identifying and hiring their personnel familiar with the technology (no such personnel have been employed by Simpson however).

6. Until November 3, 1986, Simpson was permitted to have any of Eller's personnel consult with Simpson in Texas provided that Simpson reimbursed Eller for the salary and travel expenses of the personnel. Until August 31, 1987, Simpson will be able to consult with these personnel at Eller's location (California), again at Simpson's expense.

7. A four-year noncompete agreement from Eller and its subsidiaries was included.

8. Simpson may use on a royalty-free basis any other patents which may be applicable, but which have not been included in the transaction.

9. Eller agreed that, if it develops, within three years, any material invention which would be useful in connection with this technology, Eller will negotiate a license with Simpson or allow them to use this invention on a royalty-free basis.

10. Some laboratory testing equipment and other stock was acquired.

11. An additional $140,000 has been expended "in-house" on this research project thus far in 1986.

12. The accounting to date has been to record the $500,000 purchase price in two elements.

    a. Covenant not to compete – $208,714.

    b. Equipment and instrumentation – $291,286.

13. Simpson has proposed to charge to expense the covenant not to compete over its useful life, i.e. five years. In addition, Simpson has determined that the laboratory and testing equipment has a useful life of five years, and thus proposes to expense it over that period. Thus, the entire $500,000 will be expensed over the next five years beginning June 1, 1985 or $58,500 in 1986, $100,000 in 1987 through 1990, and the $41,500 balance in 1991.

INSTRUCTIONS:

1. What factors should be considered in whether a cost is classified as research and development costs?
2. How should the purchase price of $300,000 paid to Harbor, Inc. be recorded?
3. How should the provision to pay an additional $300,000 or the alternatives to pay 6% of future sales, or simply to return all patent rights be recorded?
4. How should the purchase price of $500,000 paid to Eller, Inc. be recorded?

8-10 Amortization of Development Costs

Cardamom, Inc. is a produce supplier with 1985 revenues in excess of $36 million. The company's primary commodities are lettuce and celery which account for over 95% of total revenues.

In 1983 the company began development work in preparing land for an asparagus crop. An asparagus field requires about 2-3 years of preparation to bring to full productivity and the product life runs between 10-12 years. A summary of financial information at December 31, 1985 is:

Deferred asparagus costs	$ 186,000
Other growing crop costs	1,845,000
Other current assets	9,756,000
Total current assets	11,787,000
Other assets (primarily property and equipment), net	4,768,000
Total assets	$16,555,000
Net income for 1985	$ 1,890,000

Costs incurred from the initial planting through the first partial harvest in the Spring of 1985 were capitalized. The revenues from the first harvest, net of current year farming and harvesting costs, were applied as a reduction of the capitalized costs and future net revenues will be credited to capitalized costs until the investment is fully amortized. In other words, no profits will be realized until the development costs are fully recovered.

The auditor's initial reaction to the above treatment was that it would result in a mismatching of revenues and expenses and that a more acceptable approach would be to amortize the development costs over the estimated productive life of the fields.

The Company's main argument in support of their accounting was the uncertainty that future revenues from asparagus sales would cover the ongoing farming and harvesting costs, i.e. there was no assurance that the development costs would be recoverable. The Company had not previously farmed asparagus and, considering their lack of experience with this new type of commodity, believed the conservative approach was warranted.

INSTRUCTIONS:

Do you agree with this method for amortizing the capitalized development costs?

CHAPTER 9

CURRENT LIABILIITES AND CONTINGENCIES

9-1 Red Inc.*

In 1984 Red Inc. became the first manufacturer to market a magnetic television antenna that has the capability of pulling in 150 different television stations from all over the world. Red Inc. is selling the antenna to retailers at a price of $1,000. Red Inc. requires larger retailers to enter into contracts that call for the delivery of at least 50 antennae at $1,000 during each of the first two years of the contract and a delivery of 100 antennae at $1,100 in the third year of the contract.

American TV signed a noncancelable contract with Red in July 1984. During the ensuing two years, sales of magnetic antennae have skyrocketed. Competition (six other manufacturers are now marketing similar products) plus economies of scale resulting from increased sales have enabled Red to sell the antenna at $700 as of June 1986. The decreased cost means that American is required to pay $40,000 more than the current market price for the 100 antennae it will be receiving from Red during the third year of the contract.

American's auditors inform the company that they must record a $40,000 loss. American agrees to record the loss but asks "what is the other half of the journal entry." The auditors tell them that the credit should be to "accrued loss on purchase commitments," and it will appear as a liability on American's balance sheet.

INSTRUCTIONS:

1. Is the accrued loss on purchase commitments a liability?
2. Does the original purchase contract create a liability?
3. What is the rationale behind the current method of accounting for these types of transactions?

---

*Adapted from a case prepared by Owen Hoitomt.

9-2 Zoe Corporation[*]

The accountant for Zoe Corporation, Joseph Lands, has compiled financial statements for the quarter ended June 30, 1985. Timothy, a promising summer intern, questioned the validity of the placement of "Estimated Sales Returns and Allowances" on the balance sheet as a contra to accounts receivable.

Zoe Corporation generated sales on account for this period of $1,000,000, and sales returns and allowances were estimated at $50,000. This transaction was originally recorded as follows:

```
Accounts Receivable                  1,000,000
    Sales                                         1,000,000
Sales Returns and Allowances            50,000
    Estimated Sales Returns and Allowances           50,000
```

Timothy argues that a study of the prior history of the company reveals that of the total estimated sales returns and allowances, 10% is usually paid out as cash refunds to customers, 5% is settled by the issuance of new merchandise, and the other 85% reduces the amount to be collected from customers.

Timothy believes that Joe's classification of estimated sales returns and allowances as a contra asset is misleading to potential investors and creditors. Due to the past history of this account, asserts Timothy, a portion of the "estimated sales returns and allowances" should be shown on the balance sheet as a liability.

Joe, on the other hand, declares that this account (estimated sales returns and allowances) is and always has traditionally been handled as a contra account. "This whole new concept of economic substance over form can in itself be misleading when accounts "jump" from one area of the financial statements to another, " replied Joe.

INSTRUCTIONS:

1. What is a liability? What is a contra account?
2. Whose viewpoint is correct? Explain.
3. Record the transactions after considering your response to questions 1 and 2.
4. How would your decision be affected if all sales were made for cash?

---

* Adapted from a case prepared by Sandra Johnson.

9-3 Marchael Manufacturing, Inc.

Marchael Manufacturing, Inc. is a small-sized manufacturer of industrial, electrical and mechanical products. The company has approximately 1,000 shareholders and is traded over the counter.

Marchael Manufacturing, Inc. entered into a revolving and term credit agreement with a major Houston bank on June 23, 1984. This agreement provided that a revolving credit not to exceed $2 million shall be extended to the company to be used at its discretion until May 31, 1987, at which time the company has the option to convert to a term loan payable in quarterly installments over a five-year period. The loan agreement provides, among other things, that "The obligation of the bank to make any loan pursuant hereto, whether under the revolving credit or the term credit, shall also be subject to the following conditions precedent: ... Since the date of the most recently issued certified consolidated financial statements ... there have been no material adverse changes in the condition, financial or otherwise, of the company or its subsidiaries."

A question was raised regarding terminology in the loan agreement, notably the term "material adverse change." Several meetings were held with company officials, legal counsel for the company, the bank's loan officer and the bank's legal counsel to discuss this situation. In these discussions, the loan officer indicated the bank had not yet developed its position relative to amending or further clarifying the terminology "material adverse change" contained in its standard revolving and term credit agreements. Therefore, it was not willing either to issue a letter clarifying the term "material adverse change," nor to delete this phrase from its loan agreement. However, management felt confident that the company would be in a position at May 31, 1987, to convert the revolving credit balance to the term portion, and legal counsel for the company was willing to issue an opinion that the revolving and term credit agreement was a "noncancelable binding agreement."

Examination of the consolidated balance sheet as of May 31, 1986 indicates that the financial position of Marchael Manufacturing is good. During the current year, the company experienced a 22% increase in sales and a 25% increase in net income. The growth in sales and net income over the past five years amounted to 340% and 314% respectively. The company has maintained a very good relationship with the bank.

INSTRUCTIONS:

Where should this possible loan borrowing be classified in the balance sheet and what type of disclosure is appropriate?

9-4 Fresno Airlines

Your accounting firm is auditing Fresno Airlines. Fresno's business is to transport freight to numerous locations across the United States. It owns eighty planes for this purpose. Until last year, Fresno insured these planes with an insurance company. Fresno has decided that the premiums are too high, and that it should self-insure. The amount of losses due to damages of Fresno's planes can be reasonably estimated from past experience.

You are the partner in charge of this audit, and the senior has called you from Fresno's office. The company's controller and the audit senior disagree about how the self-insurance should be handled in the financial statements. Although Fresno has experienced no losses for the year, the controller believes that a liability should be set up for the estimated amount for self-insurance. The senior believes that no such liability should appear on the balance sheet. Tomorrow you will visit Fresno's office. Both the controller and the senior are anxious to hear your opinion.

INSTRUCTIONS:

1. What reasons do you expect the controller to give for liability treatment?
2. What reasons do you expect the senior to give for not treating self-insurance as a liability?
3. What is your answer to the controller and the senior?

9-5 The Changing Liability

Accounting definitions have evolved over time, the Committee on Terminology, APB, and FASB have all defined liabilities as part of accounting theory formulation. Following are their definitions of liabilities:

ACCOUNTING TERMINOLOGY BULLETIN I

Something represented by a credit balance that is or would be properly carried forward upon a closing of books of account according to the rules or principles of accounting, provided such credit balance is not in effect a negative balance applicable to an asset. Thus, the word is used broadly to comprise not only items which constitute liabilities in the popular sense of debts or obligations (including provision for those that are unascertained), but also credit balances to be accounted for which do not involve a debtor and creditor relation. For example, capital stock and related or similar elements of proprietorship are balance sheet liabilities in that they represent balances to be accounted for, though these are not liabilities in the ordinary sense of debts owed to legal creditors.

ACCOUNTING PRINCIPLES BOARD STATEMENT 4

Economic obligations of an enterprise that are recognized and measured in conformity with generally accepted accounting principles. Liabilities also include certain deferred credits that are not obligations but that are recognized and measured in conformity with generally accepted accounting principles.

STATEMENT OF FINANCIAL ACCOUNTING CONCEPTS NO. 3

Liabilities are probable future sacrifices of economic benefits arising from present obligations of a particular entity to transfer assets or provide services to other entities in the future as a result of past transactions or events.

INSTRUCTIONS:

1. Discuss the different viewpoints of the definitions with respect to:

   a. The proprietary versus entity theory viewpoints.
   b. The concept of what constitutes a liability.

2. Distinguish between contractual liabilities, constructive obligations, equitable obligations, contingent liabilities, and deferred credit. Give an example of each.

3. Are the items mentioned in (2) all included as liabilities on the balance sheet? Are they consistent with the definition of liabilities according to SFAC 3?

9-6 Fountain, Inc.

The concern over environmental issues has fostered the establishment of many companies. One current issue is the pollution of our nation's ground water. Frank Augur established a company, Fountain Inc. in 1980 to deal with this problem. The company franchised local dealers across the United States to treat water. The dealerships were equipped to deal with polluted wells for individual residences and cities by supplying interim fresh water supplies. In addition, the polluted wells were treated in an attempt to provide a long-term solution to the problem.

The company expanded rapidly in the early 1980's, but never did enjoy growth in profits to match the growth in dealerships.

In 1985 Fountain Inc. declared bankruptcy. Frank revised his expectations and aspirations and felt his company could continue in operation and regain profitability under a greatly modified organization. Under an agreement worked out by the company, the creditors, and the court, accounts payable totaling $1.7 million will be paid out by the company on the following terms, without interest.

1985 (current year)	-0-
1986	10%
1987	20%
1988	30
1989	40
	100%

In discussing the proper presentation of the liability, some believe that the obligation of $1.7 million should be discounted. Others disagree.

INSTRUCTIONS:

    1. Conceptually, should the liability of $1.7 million be discounted?
    2. If the liability were discounted, what impact would occur on the financial statements (balance sheet and income statement) for the current and subsequent years?
    3. What is GAAP in this area?

9-7 The Greyhound Corporation

Following is a footnote from the Greyhound Corporation's 1984 Annual Report:

Note 7 - Other Matters:
Other operating costs–leasing and financial include $1,996,000
representing provisions for losses on dispositions of affiliates
in 1984. In 1982, premiums earned and losses and settlement
expenses were reduced by $25,400,000 and $42,000,000,
respectively, as a result of a reinsurance contract entered into
that year.

The property and casualty insurance subsidiaries have ceded insurance to other insurance companies in order to limit their maximum loss through risk diversification. Certain insurance accounts, primarily premiums earned, losses and settle- ment expenses and the liability for insurance losses and claims of the special risk and reinsurance business, are stated net of amounts ceded under reinsurance policies. Insurance ceded by the subsidiaries does not relieve liability in the event of a failure by a reinsurance company to pay claims. Premiums ceded during 1984, 1983 and 1982 were $32,145,000, $50,009,000 and $71,262,000 respectively, and net contingent liability for insurance ceded was $58,487,000 at December 31, 1984.

INSTRUCTIONS:

1. What is the meaning of the term "contingent liability" as disclosed by Greyhound Corporation?
2. Distinguish between accounting for a "gain contingency" and accounting for a "loss contingency."
3. What are the two basic requirements for the accrual of a loss contingency?
4. Did Greyhound Corp. accrue a loss contingency for the $58,487,000 associated with the ceded insurance? Why or why not?
5. Discuss how the two basic requirements for the accrual of a loss contingency relate to the three basic concepts of accounting: periodicity (time periods), measurement, and objectivity.

9-8 Contingencies

For each of the situations described below determine whether accrual for loss should be made and/or what financial statement disclosure, if any, is required.

1. XYZ Company experienced a three-fold increase in its cost of fire insurance. To decrease this cost, the controller increased the deductible on the policy from $10,000 to $1,000,000. He also established a $125,000 contingent liability to cover the future losses should a fire occur.

2. Western Company was notified in late November that the government of Chile planned to nationalize the Company's wholly-owned subsidiary by June 30. Discussions with several U.S. government officials and other corporate presidents who have had property in Chile expropriated indicated that Western will probably receive less than fair market value. However, at this time, no discussions on price have yet taken place. No

provision has been made for any loss which may result from this contingency. The company's book value for the operation is $4,800,000 and the fair market value is estimated at $6,500,000.

3. Your client, Tigertail Incorporated, is the defendant in litigation pending before the courts at June 30, 1985 (date of the financial statements). The issues before the court are substantive matters regarding patent infringement.

    a. Discussions on July 27, 1985 (prior to issuance of financial statements) with Tigertail's attorneys, with management and the independent auditors reveal that a court settlement unfavorable to Tigertail is likely to occur. The attorneys say that a reasonable estimate of the amount of loss is $3,500,000 (material to Tigertail). This estimate appears reasonable based on the facts of the case.

    b. Discussions on July 27, 1985 (prior to issuance of financial statements) reveal that it is reasonably possible (more than remote but less than likely) that a court settlement unfavorable to Tigertail will result. A reasonable estimate of the amount of the loss is not possible.

4. On December 28, 1985 the Food and Drug Administration banned the company's new diet product. After reviewing its alternatives, the company decided not to fight the decision. As a part of the FDA ruling, the company agreed to repurchase, as a part of its warranty policy, all packages of the product. The controller established a liability of $200,000 to cover these returns.

9-9 American Fidelity Corporation

American Fidelity Corporation is a retailer of television and stereo equipment. Significant financial data as of September 30, 1985 is as follows:

Current assets	$2,068,776
Total assets	$2,399,062
Current liabilities (as reported)	$1,601,671
Long-term debt (as reported)	$ 554,115
Stockholders' equity	$ 243,276

The company entered into a revolving loan and security agreement with Merchants Credit Corporation in 1985. This agreement provided for interest payments only. No principal payments were required unless: (1) the company was in default under certain convenants, (2) inventory balances dropped below certain specified levels, or (3) either party canceled the agreement. The loan is secured by all inventory and accounts receivable. The interest rate on the loan is 5% above the prime rate in effect, and interest is payable monthly.

The company refused to classify the debt as current, even though the agreement could be canceled on thirty days notice. The company took the position that this debt would continue to be revolved or would be converted into some other form of long-term debt.

INSTRUCTIONS:

1. What is the appropriate accounting treatment for this loan agreement?
2. Why is the firm so adamantly opposed to classifying the debt as current?

9-10 RCA Corporation

RCA Corporation reflects in the current liability section of its balance sheet at December 31, 1980 (its year-end), short-term obligations of $6,000,000, which includes the current portion of 8% long-term debt in the amount of $4,000,000 (matures in March 1981). Management has stated its intention to refinance the 8% debt in the following footnote.

Footnote 10. Other Long-Term Debt

...Commercial paper (with a weighted average of 12.8 percent at December 31, 1980) is backed by revolving-credit agreements in the aggregate amount of $500 million with a group of domestic and foreign banks. The $500 million commitment, which expires September 1985, declines semi-annually in amounts of $50 million beginning in March 1983 and by the amount of $150 million in March 1985. These credit agreements permit domestic borrowings at the prime rate through September 2, 1982, and at increasing premiums above prime rate thereafter, or alternatively, Euro dollar borrowings at the London Inter Bank Offering Rate (LIBOR) plus 3/8 of 1 percent through February 1981 and at increasing premiums above such LIBOR thereafter. There are no outstanding borrowings under the revolving-credit agreements. RCA intends to replace these commercial paper borrowings by new long-term borrowings or by borrowing under the revolving-credit agreements, and this commercial paper is classified as long-term.

INSTRUCTIONS:

1. Is management's intent enough to support long-term classification of the obligation in this situation?

2. Assume the RCA Corporation issues $5,000,000 of 10-year debentures to the public in January 1981 and that management intends to use the proceeds to liquidate the $4,000,000 debt

maturing in March 1981. Furthermore, assume that the debt maturing in March 1981 is paid from these proceeds prior to the issuance of the financial statements. Will this have any impact on the balance sheet classification at December 31, 1980? Explain your answer.

3. Assume that RCA Corporation issues common stock to the public in January and that management intends to entirely liquidate the $4,000,000 debt maturing in March 1981 with the proceeds of this equity securities issue. In light of these events, should the $4,000,000 debt maturing in March 1981 be included in current liabilities at December 31, 1980?

4. Assume that RCA Corporation, on February 15, 1981, entered into a financing agreement with a commercial bank that permits RCA Corporation to borrow at any time through 1982 up to $6,000,000 at the bank's prime rate of interest. Borrowings under the financing agreement mature three years after the date of the loan. The agreement is not cancelable except for violation of a provision with which compliance is objectively determinable. No violation of any provision exists at the date of issuance of the financial statements. Assume further that $4,000,000 representing the current portion of long-term debt does not mature until August 1981. In addition, management intends to refinance the $4,000,000 obligation under the terms of the financial agreement with the bank, which is expected to be financially capable of honoring the agreement.

   a. Given these facts, should the $4,000,000 be classified as current on the balance sheet at December 31, 1980?

   b. Is disclosure of the refinancing method required?

CHAPTER 10

LONG-TERM LIABILITIES

10-1 Consolidated Foods Company[*]

Consolidated Foods Company operates eleven divisions on a nationwide scale. Its operations consist of convenience stores, hot pretzel shops, production of meat and dairy products, bakery products, frozen foods, salt products, leather goods, and tourist facilities. As of December 29, 1985, the end of the Company's fiscal year, Consolidated Foods had as part of its debt structure $47,204,000 of 5% convertible subordinated debentures due June 15, 1998. These debentures were convertible at any time into an aggregate of 1,748,297 shares of the Company's common stock at a rate of $27 per share. The Company had the option to prepay the debentures in whole or in part upon payment of a premium of 4% prior to June 15, 1986 and at reduced amounts thereafter.

During 1985, Consolidated Foods made an exchange offer of new 11% convertible debentures due June 15, 2008 for the 5% debentures. The new debentures were convertible into common shares at a rate of $16 per share. Due to the higher interest payments and more advantageous conversion terms, 73% of the outstanding 5% debentures were tendered. In all, the Company issued $20,330,000 principal amount of 11% convertible subordinated debentures in exchange for $33,883,000 principal amount of its outstanding 5% convertible subordinated debentures. Despite the increase in annual interest expense from $1.7 million to $2.2 million, Consolidated Foods had removed nearly $13.6 million in debt. After taking into account the discount on the original issue of the 11% debentures, the Company realized a "profit" of $16,112,000. In addition to this refunding, Consolidated Foods repurchased an aggregate of $1,883,000 principal amount of its outstanding debentures for cash, realizing another $751,000 "profit" after deducting the original issue discount.

As a result of these transactions, the Company's debt to equity ratio was substantially reduced and book value per share increased significantly. Management believed the success of the exchange offer would improve the Company's ability to obtain future financing on reasonable terms and increase the probability that the convertible debentures will ultimately be converted into common stock. This exchange helped offset an otherwise mediocre year for Consolidated Foods in which its pretax income from operations dropped 25%. This was blamed mostly on wide fluctuations in commodity prices, which affected the profitability of its two largest divisions.

---

[*] Adapted from a case prepared by Neal Barry.

Some controversy arose in accounting for the refunding transactions. The Company's controller, who had been with Consolidated Foods over thirty years, proposed amortizing the $16.1 million difference between the reacquisition price and the net carrying amount over the remaining life of the extinguished debentures. The president desired to report the entire amount of the difference in the current year's income statement as a gain.

The financial vice-president believes that the difference should be divided into two components, one related to the debt retirement and the other to equity retirement. The company's auditors were called in to resolve the problem.

INSTRUCTIONS:

1. What is the rationale for the alternative methods of accounting for the difference between the reacquisition price and the net carrying value?
2. Which of the alternative methods should be applied in the case of Consolidated Foods?
3. What should be the presentation for Consolidated Foods in their 1985 financial statements?

10-2 Adventure Manufacturing Company[*]

Adventure Manufacturing Company had been a highly successful company in the 1970's. However, due to the recent recession, the company's sales and net income have fallen behind their projected goals. Because of the past success of the company, and its current financial difficulties, a large manufacturing firm, Frontier, Inc. has shown an interest in acquiring Adventure.

The company is reluctant to become involved in a merger. Adventure started as a closely held, family type business, with investment from outsiders only comprising a small portion of the company's capital. Presently about 55% of the company's outstanding common shares is controlled by the family. The only way that Frontier could obtain control would be through the convertible debt issued by the company in 1983 (see Exhibit 1). If the convertible debt is acquired by Frontier, it would be possible for Frontier to have effective control over Adventure.

To take immediate action to reduce the threat of takeover, Adventure began reacquiring their convertible bonds in the open market. The idea was to hold the bonds for the time being until a decision could be made as to whether or not part of or all of the bonds would be reacquired and retired. By December 31, 1983 the company had purchased $200,000 par value of the bonds at an aggregate cost of $275,000.

---

[*]Adapted from a case prepared by Shring-Wu Wang.

To further reduce the threat of take-over by Frontier, Adventure management began to negotiate the retirement of the remainder of the $1.5 million convertible debt. In February 1984 agreement was reached to retire $1 million of the debt by issuing $2 million of nonconvertible 8% long term debt, an amount that was approximately equal to the $16 per share value of the 125,000 shares into which that portion of original debt was then convertible.

Opinions about the proper treatment of the difference between carrying amount of extinguished debt and the reacquisition price were discussed.

EXHIBIT 1

Adventure Manufacturing Co.
Partial Balance Sheet
December 31, 1983

Long-term Liabilities

First mortgage 9% notes payable in semiannual installment of $50,000	$1,500,000	
Less current maturities	(500,000)	$1,000,000
8% subordinated convertible notes due December 31, 1988		1,500,000

Stockholders' Equities

Common Authorized, 500,000 shares of $2 par value, issued and outstanding	$ 600,000	
Additional paid-in capital	125,000	$ 725,000
Retained Earnings		
Beginning balance, January 1, 1983	$3,250,000	
Dividend	(600,000)	
Net income	2,500,000	$5,150,000

Note A. The 8% subordinated convertible note is subordinated to the 9% mortgage notes payable and short-term bank borrowings. The note is convertible into common stock at $8 a share and 187,500 shares of authorized common stock are reserved for conversion.

INSTRUCTIONS:

1. What are the possible methods that might be used to extinguish convertible debt?
2. Is there a GAAP answer to this problem?
3. What are treasury bonds? Where should treasury bonds be shown on the balance sheet?
4. Should treasury bonds be carried at par or at reacquisition cost?

10-3 Chavez Company

On January 1, 1977, Chavez Company issued for $1,106,775 its 20-year, 8% bonds that have a maturity value of $1,000,000 and pay interest semiannually on January 1, and July 1. Bond-issue costs were not material in amount. Below are three presentations of the long-term liability section of the balance sheet that might be used for these bonds at the issue date:

a. Bonds payable (maturing January 1, 1997) $1,000,000
    Unamortized premium on bonds payable   106,775

  Total bond liability $1,106,775

b. Bonds payable - principal (face value $1,000,000
    maturing January 1, 1997) $ 252,572*
    Bonds payable - interest (semiannual payment $40,000)   854,203**

  Total bond liability $1,106,775

c. Bonds payable - principal (maturing January 1, 1997) $1,000,000
    Bonds payable - interest ($40,000 per period for
    40 periods)   1,600,000

  Total bond liability $2,600,000

*The present value of $1,000,000 due at the end of 40 (six-month) periods at the yield rate of 3 1/2% per period. (Rate adjusted for the premium).
**The present value of $40,000 per period for 40 (six-month) periods at the yield rate of 3 1/2% per period. (Rate adjusted for the premium).

INSTRUCTIONS:

1. Discuss the conceptual merit(s) of each of the date-of-issue balance sheet presentations shown above for these bonds.

2. Explain why investors would pay $1,106,775 for bonds that have a maturity value of only $1,000,000.

3. Assuming that a discount rate is needed to compute the carrying value of the obligations arising from a bond issue at any date during the life of the bonds, discuss the conceptual merit(s) of using for this purpose:

  a. The coupon nominal rate.
  b. The effective or yield rate at date of issue.

4. If the obligations arising from these bonds are to be carried at their present value computed by means of the current market rate of interest, how would the bond valuation at dates subsequent to the date of issue be affected by an increase or a decrease in the market rate of interest?

[AICPA adapted]

10-4 Goodwealth Tire Company

The Goodwealth Tire Company has completed a number of transactions during 1985. In January the company purchased under contract a machine at a total price of $1,000,000, payable over five years with installments of $200,000 per year. The seller has considered the transaction as an installment sale with the title transferring to Goodwealth at the time of the final payment.

On March 1, 1985 Goodwealth issued $10 million of general revenue bonds priced at 99 with a coupon of 10% payable July 1 and January 1 of each of the next ten years. The July 1st interest was paid and on December 30th the company transferred $1,000,000 to the trustee, Country Trust Company, for payment of the January 1, 1986 interest.

Due to the depressed market for the company's stock, Goodwealth purchased $500,000 par value of their 6% convertible bonds for a price of $450,000. They expect to resell the bonds when the price of their stock has recovered.

As the accountant for Goodwealth Tire Company, you have prepared the balance sheet and have presented it to the president of the company. You are asked the following questions about it:

1. Why has depreciation been charged on equipment being purchased under contract? Title has not passed to the company as yet and, therefore, they are not our assets. Why should the company not show on the left side of the balance sheet only the amount paid to date instead of showing the full contract price on the left side and the unpaid portion on the right side? After all the seller considers the transaction an installment sale.

2. What is bond discount? As a debit balance, why is it not classified among the assets?

3. Bond interest payable is shown as a current liability. Did we not pay our trustee, County Trust Company, the full amount of interest due this period?

4. Treasury bonds are shown as a deduction from bonds payable issued. Why should they not be shown as an asset, since they can be sold again? Are they the same as bonds of other companies that we hold as investments?

INSTRUCTIONS:

Outline your answers to these questions by writing a brief paragraph that will justify your treatment.

10-5 Restructuring of Debt

Presented below are a set of situations dealing with restructuring of debt in troubled loan situations:

PART A

National City Bank has a loan outstanding to Hartman Real Estate Trust in the amount of $222 million. Recently, the trust has experienced financial difficulty and has discussed the possibility of restructuring their debt as to make the interest payments less severe over the next few years. The two enterprises decide in late 1985 on the following proposal:

Interest will be set at 130% of prime but only 4% becomes a fixed obligation; the difference to 130% prime is payable as contingent interest and payable out of future recovery on presently nonearning investments. The trust agrees to maintain $50 million net worth at all times.

The auditing firm for National City Bank notes that the interest on the difference between the normal rate (130% of prime) and the fixed rate of 4% should not be accrued as interest revenue. The controller, however, points out that interest is an expense that must be accrued currently on a ratable basis in relationship to the money borrowed. The timing of the payment of interest does not affect the timing of accrual, states the controller.

INSTRUCTIONS:

Do you believe the auditing firm is correct in their analysis?

PART B

At the same time, Hartman Real Estate Trust is having problems with their auditors (a different firm). The auditing firm states that interest expense should be shown at the accrued amount (normal rate) rather than the amount paid. Because of the uncertainty related to this debt restructuring, the auditors want to take a conservative approach and make sure that a full accrual occurs.

The controller for the trust notes that accounting for this transaction should be symmetrical; that is, if the bank is not going to accrue interest revenue, the trust should not be forced to accrue interest expense. The auditors do not have much sympathy with this notion as they are concerned about possible harm to the investment community.

INSTRUCTIONS:

Do you agree with auditing firm or the controller?

PART C

National City Bank also has $100 million in New York Municipal Assistance Corp. (MAC) bonds that pay interest at 11%. Recently they agreed to exchange these $100 million in bonds for new MAC bonds paying only 6%. The auditing firm of National City Bank now wants them to write these bonds down to fair market value. After all, a MAC bond paying 6% isn't worth as much as one paying 11%. In fact, if an 11% bond is worth 11% in the market, a 6% bond is worth $565.80.

However, National City notes that marking these assets down to market value would wipe out massive amounts of bank capital. And, after all, the bank intends to hold the securities until their maturity, when they are expected to be paid in full.

INSTRUCTIONS:

How should the transaction be handled?

PART D

Great American Marketing Trust is a real estate investment trust that has been operating for three years. In 1985, the trust took title to an 80,000 sq. ft. warehouse on which it had made a $1.2 million loan based on a $1.5 million appraisal. It has 20%

rented at $2/sq. ft. The foreclosure took place as the borrower simply could not make the payments for the property financed due to a low rental occupancy. An insurance company appraised the warehouse at $1.2 million and gave the trust a $900,000 loan at 9 5/8% for 25 years. However, the accountants in auditing the trust at year end came up with the following computation:

Mortgage amount	$1,200,000
Add: Rent income for two years under present arrangement	64,000
Expected future rent income	50,000
Less: Cost of money	(204,000)
Estimated sales commission, if sold	(60,000)
Operating expenses (taxes, utilities)	(80,000)
Possible tenant work	(40,000)
Present value	$ 930,000

The accountants, in explaining their rationale for this position, note that the properties have been taken over in a troubled loan situation. The trust is going to have a very difficult time disposing of these assets immediately and therefore the attendant holding costs should be deducted. The president of Great American Marketing argues vehemently that "if we take the accountants' approach to value, management should give the warehouse to the insurance company now." Instead of getting facts, he complains, shareholders will be getting a flood of assumptions about interest costs, estimated holding periods, and many other small details which only confuse investors.

INSTRUCTIONS:

Do you believe the president is right in his statements?

10-6 WLTA Bank*

The balance sheet as of January 1, 1984 of the WLTA Bank has loans receivable of $10,000,000 with an allowance for bad debts of $100,000. Included in the total loans receivable is a loan made to J. M. Brode for $450,000 with an annual interest rate of 6%, dated January 1, 1965 with a maturity date of January 1, 1984. Mr. Brode had always been able to scrape together enough cash so as to meet the annual interest payments of $27,000 for the past 19 years. On January 2, 1984, Mr. Brode went to the loan officer of WLTA Bank, Wes Sutter, and said, "I'm sorry Mr. Sutter, but I just don't have any way of paying off my note at this time, here's the $27,000 for the interest. I know that the current market rate is around 12%, but I just don't have the financial resources to pay that kind of interest, so what I'm willing to do is pay $400,000 three years from now with a 5% annual interest rate."

---

* Adapted from a case by Randy Carson.

Mr. Sutter weighs the situation in light of the fact that it is his responsibility as a loan officer to try and recover as much of the original loan as possible. If Mr. Brode pays $400,000 plus 3 interest payments of $20,000 that will add up to a total of $460,000. That will cover the original loan of $450,000 and yield interest income of an additional $10,000.

"Mr. Brode," he replies, "we'll accept your new offer and draw up the new documents that are required."

INSTRUCTIONS:

1. Does the situation fall under "Accounting for Troubled Debt Restructurings" as defined by FASB 15?
2. Does the additional $10,000 received by WLTA Bank represent income or a reduction of a loss? How would the income or loss be recognized? Would the principal amount of the loan be changed?
3. What are the possible accounting solutions to handle this transaction? Discuss.

10-7 Ross Steel Company

Ross Steel Company has a trade account receivable from International Implements in the amount of $36,000. International is a farm implements manufacturer. During the last 18 months, the farm implements market has sunk to its lowest point in modern times. As a result, International's finished goods inventories are at an all time high. Consequently, International has been unable to meet its obligations on long-term debt, bank notes, or trade accounts payable. Rather than sell its finished goods inventory in the present market, thus sustaining a substantial loss, International's management has advanced a plan to its creditors, the terms of which are:

o   For secured creditors of the Company, it will pay the interest on the debt but will forego principal payments for three years.

o   For all unsecured creditors (including Ross), the Company offers the option of:

-- Acceptance of immediate cash payments of 20% of the balance as payment in full.

-- Exchange of the creditor's receivable for a 5% note receivable for 75% of the balance, principal and interest to be paid as follows:

-- End of third year – 1/3 principal plus previous three years' interest.

-- Fourth year – 1/3 principal plus interest on balance for the year.

-- Fifth year – 1/3 principal plus interest on balance for the year.

The secured creditors have accepted the proposal, contingent upon a significant portion of the unsecured creditors accepting the Company's notes in exchange for their receivables.

INSTRUCTIONS:

1. If Ross accepts the note receivable option, how should the exchange be reported in the financial statements and what disclosures should be made in the accompanying notes?

2. Would the answer to Question 1 be the same if a $10,000 allowance for uncollectible amounts, applicable to the International receivable, had been set up in the prior period? If so, how would it be accounted for?

3. After considering International's proposal, assume that Ross decided to reject both options. As a counter proposal, Ross offered to accept two automatic cattle feeders with a current catalogue price of $20,000 each, as payment in full on the account. International's normal markup on the feeders is approximately 30%, therefore, their management accepted Ross's offer; subsequently, Ross sold the feeders through a broker for $32,000. The brokerage commission was 10%. How should Ross Steel account for the troubled debt restructuring (assume that no allowance for uncollectible accounts existed)?

4. How should the transaction be reflected on International's books?

10-8 The Formerly Troubled Company Inc. (FTC)

FTC's fiscal year end is July 31. The auditor disclaimed an opinion on the financial statements for the year ended July 31, 1984. The disclaimer was based on uncertainties regarding realization of assets (going concern problem) and litigation.

Condensed portions of the financial statements for the years ended July 31, 1985 and 1984 are as follows:

CONSOLIDATED BALANCE SHEET
July 31,

	(000 omitted)	
A S S E T S	1985	1984
Current Assets		
Cash	$1,200	$ 400
Receivables (net) - pledged	3,400	3,500
Inventories - pledged	1,400	1,400
Other	400	700
Total Current Assets	6,400	6,000
Property, Plant and Equipment		
Net pledged	1,700	1,800
Other	2,400	2,400
Total	$10,500	$10,200
LIABILITIES		
Current Liabilities		
Current Installments of long-term debt	$18,429	$15,800
Accounts payable and accrued expenses	2,800	6,600
Total Current Liabilities	21,229	22,400
Long-Term Debt, less current maturities	271	1,100
STOCKHOLDERS' EQUITY (Deficit)		
Common stock	1,000	1,000
Additional paid-in capital	7,600	7,600
Accumulated deficit	(19,600)	(21,900)
Total	$10,500	$10,200

CONSOLIDATED STATEMENT OF EARNINGS
Year Ended July 31

	(000 omitted)	
	1985	1984
Gross profit	$3,000	$3,000
Selling, general and administrative	2,000	2,500
Interest	800	1,300
Total expenses	2,800	3,800
Earnings (loss) from continuing operations before income taxes and extraordinary credits	$ 200	$ (800)

The Company has been in default of its long-term debt to lending institutions for the last five years. As a result, all long-term debt has been classified as current (except for some equipment loans which the Company has been paying to avoid foreclosure). During the previous three years, the Company has been disposing of its losing divisions. The various presidents of the Company have been trying to renegotiate its loan with the banks for the last four years. On September 7 (just prior to the auditor binding the 10K and approving the annual report proofs), the latest president tells the in-charge that a refinancing agreement has been signed on September 6 as described in the following paragraphs:

$18,200,000 of debt ("old debt")(including accrued interest of $3,200,000) was converted into $4,000,000 of "new debt" and 1,000,000 shares of $1.00 par value "preferred stock." The preferred stock has a liquidating value of $6.00 a share and a total fair value of $3,000,000. All assets collateralizing the old debt were released. Simultaneously, $4,000,000 of new short-term financing (collateralized by receivables and inventory) was obtained from a factor ("factor loan"). The proceeds from the factor loan were used to pay off $2,000,000 of the new debt. The remaining balance of the new debt ($2,000,000) bears no interest and requires no principal payment until June 1, 1987. Commencing June 1, 1988, principal is to be repaid in four annual installments of $500,000. From June 1, 1987, interest is payable monthly at 8% per annum. (For purposes of this study, assume total interest to be paid on this debt will total $200,000). The new debt is subordinate to the factor loan.

The preferred stock bears no dividends and is convertible into 25% of the Company's then outstanding common stock from June 1, 1988 through July 31, 1992. Each share may be redeemed by the Company as follows:

After Year Ended July 31	
1986	$3.00
1987	3.50
1988	4.00
1989	4.50
1990	5.00
1991	6.00

If the preferred stock is still outstanding after July 31, 1991, the Company must redeem at least 10% of the outstanding preferred each year at $6.00 a share until all shares are redeemed.

The financing agreement is with reputable lending institutions and is noncancellable. There are no current violations of any negative convenants in the agreement.

The president is anxious to incorporate this good news in the July 31, 1985 financial statements. The auditor tells him that this is a "type two" subsequent event and probably should be disclosed but that the Company cannot give effect to it in the July 31, 1985 statements. The vice president of finance (an ex–Big 8 audit manager) calls you, the account administrator, at home (as you are about to go swimming with your family on your first day off during the summer). He is livid. He insists on giving full effect to FASB Statement No. 15 in the financial statements.

INSTRUCTIONS:

1. Can they?

2. What is the effect of FASB Statement No. 15 (if it were used)?

   a. On the balance sheet?

   b. On the statement of income?

   c. If assets were exchanged, how would fair value be determined?

10-9 Acme Restaurants, Inc.

You have been requested by Acme Restaurants, Inc., a national hotel and motel restauranteur, to evaluate certain accounting treatments proposed by Acme's treasurer regarding a contract for Acme to operate the restaurant and parking facilities of the new Rocklin Hotel over a 30 year period. A condition necessary for securing the contract was that Acme would aid in financing the new hotel by loaning Rocklin $300,000 in addition to paying a normal rental for the facilities. It is estimated that the operations would yield pre-tax profits of $150,000 annually to Acme.

The $300,000 loan will be for 30 years with no payment unless the contract is cancelled by Rocklin. Interest is to accrue at 4% per year compounded annually for the first 20 years and no interest is to accrue during the last 10 years. After 20 years Acme will cancel 10% of the principal and accrued interest each year. If Rocklin should cancel the contract the uncancelled principal and interest would become payable immediately.

The Company's treasurer has proposed accounting for the transaction over the contract life as a loan receivable with interest income accruing at 4% per year for the first 20 years and the unpaid principal plus accrued interest being charged off a 10% per year over the last 10 years. The treasurer's reasoning is that this accounting treatment will be in accordance with the terms of the legal documents and with the accounting treatment that Rocklin plans to employ. Also, the interest income for each of the first 20 years would enhance earnings during an anticipated growth period and the income tax effect for the first 20 years will be offset in the last 10 years of the contract.

Because the amounts involved will be material from the standpoint of both the income statement and the balance sheet, Acme requested your opinion to avoid any statement presentation problems at the end of the year.

INSTRUCTIONS:

1. Does the treasurer's proposed accounting for the contract constitute proper presentation on the financial statements? Support your conclusion by discussing the effects of the proposed treatment on (1) the income statement, and (2) the balance sheet. State any alternatives you believe might be preferable.
2. Discuss the treasurer's suggestions to account for the transaction in accordance with the terms of the legal supporting documents. Discuss the impact that the accounting treatment of the contract by Rocklin Hotel will have in your evaluation of the preferable treatment for Acme.
3. What disclosure, if any, will be necessary in Acme's financial statements in regard to the agreement with Rocklin?

10-10 Chrysis Corporation

Chrysis Corp. has recently fallen into financial difficulties. To help Chrysis avert bankruptcy, two creditors of Chrysis have agreed to restructure the terms of some loans they have made to the company.

First National Bank has agreed to accept 80,000 shares of Chrysis common stock in full payment of a $1,000,000 loan due in 5 years from Chrysis. The interest terms of the loan are 10% per year. Chrysis common stock has recently been trading for $11 per share. Its par value is $10.

Mr. Audrey, controller of First National, intends to record the transaction as follows:

Investment in Chrysis Common	1,000,000	
10% Loan Receivable from Chrysis		1,000,000

This would imply that Chrysis should record the transaction in this manner:

10% Loan payable to First National	1,000,000	
Common Stock		800,000
Paid-In Capital in Excess of Par		200,000

Chrysis, however, has a different view. Lee Cocamocha, controller at Chrysis, is desperate for any sweeteners he can find to improve the financial statements of Chrysis. He would like to record the transaction as follows:

10% Loan payable to First National	1,000,000	
Common Stock		800,000
Paid-In Capital in Excess of Par		80,000
Gain on Restructuring of Loan		120,000

If Mr. Cocamocha's view is correct, this would mean that the bank should record the transaction as below:

Investment in Chrysis stock	880,000	
Loss on Restructuring of Loan	120,000	
10% Loan Receivable from Chrysis		1,000,000

Mr. Cocamocha likes this approach because of the gain it produces. Naturally, Mr. Audrey does not favor this method because of the loss which the bank must show.

Southeast Bank has also given Chrysis a break. Chrysis owes Southeast Bank $2,000,000, payable in 10 years. The interest rate on this loan is 10%. Southeast, wishing to minimize its losses, has agreed to reduce the interest rate to 5% per year.

Mr. Walters, Southeast's controller, sees no need for making any journal entries to record this deal. Since Chrysis still owes $2,000,000 he feels that there is no need for a write-down of this loan and a recognition of a loss. Likewise, he would see no need for a journal entry on the books of Chrysis in recognition of this event.

Mr. Cocamocha, however, would not do it this way. He points out that the present value of Chrysis' restructured obligations to Southeast (discounted at the original 10% interest rate) is considerably less than the present value of the obligation before the interest rate was reduced. He feels that his provides a basis for recognition of a gain by Chrysis. He would record the transaction as follows:

10% Loan Payable to Southeast	2,000,000	
Discount on 5% Loan Payable to Southeast	614,456	
5% Loan Payable to Southeast		2,000,000
Gain on Restructuring of Debt		614,456

Thus he would carry the restructured debt at 1,385,544 (face value less discount). His calculations were as follows:

Present value of principal (2,000,000 received 10 years from now)	771,088
Present value of interest (100,000 per year for 10 years)	614,456
Total present value of loan (using a 10% discount rate above)	1,385,544

If we accept this view, then the bank's entry would look like this:

5% Loan Receivable from Chrysis	2,000,000	
Loss on Restructuring of Loan	614,456	
10% Loan Receivable from Chrysis		2,000,000
Discount on 5% Loan Receivable		614,456

1. What are some arguments that First National and Chrysis would use to support their respective views of the first restructuring? Which is the correct method, according to GAAP?
2. If the cost of issuing the stock to First National was $5,000 and the legal cost of negotiating the restructuring agreement was $10,000 how would these costs be accounted for?
3. What are some of the arguments that you would expect from Southeast and Chrysis to support their respective views of the second restructuring agreement? Which method is correct, according to GAAP?
4. How would the debtor and the creditor present the appropriate gains or losses, if any, in their financial statements?

10-11 In-Substance Defeasance

Following is a footnote prepared by Equimark Corporation in its annual report for December 31, 1983:

"On December 30, 1983, the Bank entered into agreements with a trustee which facilitated in-substance defeasance of the 5% and 5 1/4% capital note issues.

On December 30, 1983, U.S. Government securities costing $10,063,000 were deposited in an irrevocable trust, the principal and interest of which will be sufficient to pay the scheduled principal and interest on the 5% and 5 1/4% capital note issues of the Bank. Proceeds from the sale of certain short-term liquid assets of the Bank were used to purchase these securities. The 5% capital notes require principal payments of $500,000 on January 1 in each of the years 1984 through 1988 and the balance of $7,500,000 in 1989. The 5 1/4% capital notes require principal payments of $262,500 in each of the years 1984 through 1990 and the balance of $1,750,000 due in 1991. Interest on both issues is payable on January 1, and July 1 of each year that the notes remain outstanding. In December 1983, the Bank prepaid the principal and interest payments on both issues due January 1, 1984.

The Corporation recognized a gain calculated as the excess of the current principal outstanding on the note issues over the cost of the securities placed in the defeasance trusts, plus related trustee costs. The gain on the in-substance defeasance of both note issues of $2,732,000 equivalent to a gain of $0.57 per common share, is presented in the Corporation's consolidated statement of income as an extraordinary gain."

1. What is in-substance defeasance?
2. Discuss alternative accounting methods that might be used for this type of transaction.
3. What is the suggested treatment under GAAP?

10-12 Cooperation for Off-Balance Sheet Financing

The Mid-Western Beer Corporation is interested in building its own beer can manufacturing plant adjacent to its brewery in Suds City, Wisconsin. The objective would be to ensure a steady supply of cans at a stable price and to minimize transportation costs. However, the company has been experiencing some financial problems and has been reluctant to borrow any additional cash to fund the project. The company is not concerned with the cash flow problems of making payments, but rather with the impact of adding additional long term debt to their balance sheet.

The president of Mid-Western, Dale Theesfeld, approached the president of the Aluminum Can Company, (ACC) their major supplier to see if some agreement could be reached. ACC was anxious to work out an arrangement, since it seemed inevitable that Mid-Western would begin their own can production. The Aluminum Can Company could not afford to lose the account.

After some discussion a two part plan was worked out. First ACC was to construct the plant on Mid-Western's land adjacent to the brewery. Second, Mid-Western would sign a 20-year purchase agreement. Under the purchase agreement, Mid-Western would express its intention to buy all of its cans from ACC, paying a unit price which at normal capacity would cover labor and material, an operating management fee, and the debt service requirements on the plant. The expected unit price, if transportation costs are taken into consideration, are lower than current market. If Mid-Western did not take enough production in any one year and if the excess cans could not be sold at a high enough price on the open market, Mid-Western agrees to make up any cash shortfall so that ACC could make the payments on its debt. The bank will be willing to make a 20 year loan for the plant, taking the plant and the purchase agreement as collateral. At the end of 20 years the plant is to become the property of Mid-Western.

1. What are project financing arrangements?
2. What are take or pay contracts?
3. What conditions must be met in order for a contractual obligation to be disclosed as an unconditional purchase obligation?
4. Should Mid-Western record the plant as an asset together with the related obligation?
5. If not, should Mid-Western record an asset relating to the future commitment?

CHAPTER 11

☐

STOCKHOLDERS' EQUITY

11-1 "Secret Reserves"

It has been said that the use of the LIFO inventory method during an extended period of rising prices and the expensing of all human-resource costs are among the accepted accounting practices that help create "secret reserves."

Accounting practices in many other countries may also create hidden reserves, as well as, a number of recognized reserves. Following is a portion of the consolidated balance sheet of the Swedish Company, Volvo for the years ending December 31, 1982 and 1981:

	1982	1981
Untaxed Reserves		
General inventory reserves	4,268	3,436
Accumulated extra depreciation	2,278	2,206
Investment reserves	1,002	603
Compulsory investment reserve	54	56
Fixed asset replacement reserve	12	-
Extra appropriation to insurance reserve	130	106
Exchange reserve	102	51
	7,846	6,458
Minority Interest in Capital	732	451
Shareholders' Equity		
Restricted equity		
Share capital	1,698	1,394
Legal reserves	2,257	1,389
	3,955	2,783
Unrestricted Equity		
Retained earnings	858	577
Net income for year	496	453
	1,354	1,030
Total Shareholders' Equity	5,309	3,813

INSTRUCTIONS:

1. What is a "secret reserve"? How can "secret reserves" be created or enlarged?
2. What is the basis for saying that the two specific practices cited above tend to create "secret reserves?"
3. Is it possible to create a "secret reserve" in connection with accounting for a liability? If so, explain or give an example.
4. What are the objections to the creation of "secret reserves"?
5. It has also been said that "watered stock" is the opposite of a "secret reserve." What is "watered stock"?
6. Describe the general circumstances in which "watered stock" can arise.
7. What steps can be taken to eliminate "water" from a capital structure?

11-2 Bush Terminal

A trustee of Bush Terminal Company, appointed in a proceeding under a section of the Bankruptcy Act, sued former directors of that company to recover on its behalf the amount of dividends declared and paid between November 22, 1928, and May 2, 1932, aggregating $3,639,058.06. At the time of the declarations and payments, the company's books showed a surplus which ranged from not less than $4,378,554.83 on December 31, 1927, to not less than $12,199,486.77 on April 30, 1932. The plaintiff claims, however, that in fact there was no surplus, that the capital was actually impaired to an amount greater than the amount of the dividends, and that the directors consequently are personally liable to the corporation for the amount thereof. Defendants claim that there was no impairment of capital and that the surplus was actually greater than the amount which plaintiff concedes as the amount shown by the books.

The facts of the case are as follows:

Until 1915 the company's land was carried upon its books at cost. In 1915 the land was written up to 80% of the amount at which it was then assessed for taxation, and in 1918 it was written up to the exact amount at which it was then so assessed. Those two write-ups totalled $7,211,791.72, and the result was that during the period here in question the land was carried on the books at $8,737,949.02, whereas its actual cost was $1,526,157.30. Plaintiff claims that the entire $7,211,791.72 should be eliminated because it represents merely unrealized appreciation, and dividends cannot be declared or paid on the basis of mere unrealized appreciation in fixed assets irrespective of how sound the estimate thereof may be. That obviously is another way of saying that for dividend purposes fixed assets must be computed at cost, not value, and plaintiff here plants himself upon that position, even to the point of contending that evidence of value is immaterial and not admissible. If that contention be sound, the company indisputably had a deficit at all the times here involved in an amount exceeding the dividends here in question.* * *

The words of the statute, as it existed during the period here involved, are: "No stock corporation shall declare or pay any dividend which shall impair its capital or capital stock, nor while its capital or capital stock is impaired, nor shall any such corporation declare or pay any dividend or make any distribution of assets to any of its stockholders, whether upon a reduction of the number of its shares or of its capital or capital stock, unless the value of its assets remaining after the payment of such dividend, or after such distribution of assets, as the case may be, shall be at least equal to the aggregate amount of its debts and liabilities including capital or capital stock as the case may be."

If the part of the statute containing the words "unless the value of its assets" etc. is to be read as relating back to the beginning of the section, the lack of merit in plaintiff's contention is apparent, for the statute would then read: "No stock corporation shall declare or pay any dividend * * * unless the value of its assets remaining after the payment of such dividend * * * shall be at least equal to the aggregate amount of its debts and liabilities including capital or capital stock as the case may be." I think there is much to be said in support of the view that this is what was intended, but nevertheless the structure of the statute is such as to make that reading grammatically impossible, and I hence prefer to base my decision upon the assumption that the controlling words of the statute are merely there: "No stock corporation shall declare nor pay any dividend which shall impair its capital or capital stock, nor while its capital or capital stock is impaired." * * *

Those statements by our highest court seem to me to make it entirely plain that the terms capital and capital stock in these statutes mean an amount, i.e. a value, of property up to the limit of the number of dollars specified as the par value of paid-up issued shares (or as the stated value of no-par shares), and that when the amount, i.e. the value, of the company's property exceeds that number of dollars the excess, whether "contributed by the stockholders or otherwise obtained" is surplus or surplus profits and may be distributed as dividends until the point is reached where such dividends "deplete the assets," i.e, the value of the assets, "below the sum," i.e. below the number of dollars, specified as the par or stated value of the paid-up issued shares. In other words, the capital or capital stock referred to in these statutes is the sum of the liability of stockholders, and any value which the corporation's property has in addition to that sum is surplus. And I cannot doubt that the words "otherwise obtained" and "accumulated," as used by the court in the cases just mentioned, include an appreciation in the value of property purchased whether realized or unrealized. * * *

I am of the opinion that the same reasons which show that unrealized appreciation must be considered are equally cogent in showing that unrealized depreciation likewise must be considered. In other words, the test being whether or not the value of the assets exceeds the debts and the liability to stockholders, all assets must be taken at their actual value.

I see no cause for alarm over the fact that this view requires directors to make a determination of the value of the assets at each dividend declaration. On the contrary, I think that is exactly what the law always has contemplated that directors should do. That does not mean that the books themselves necessarily must be altered by write-ups or write-downs at each dividend period, or that formal appraisals must be obtained from professional appraisers or even made by the directors themselves. That is obviously impossible in the case of corporations of any considerable size. But it is not impossible nor unfeasible for directors to consider whether the cost of assets continues over a long period of years to reflect their fair value, and the law does require that directors should really direct in the very important matter of really determining at each dividend declaration whether or not the value of the assets is such as to justify a dividend, rather than do what one director has testified that he did, viz. "accept the company's figures." The directors are the ones who should determine the figures by carefully considering values, and it was for the very purpose of compelling them to perform that duty that the statute imposes upon them a personal responsibility for declaring and paying dividends when the value of the assets is not sufficient to justify them. What directors must do is to exercise an informed judgment of their own, and the amount of information which they should obtain, and the sources from which they should obtain it, will of course depend upon the circumstances of each particular case. * * *

INSTRUCTIONS:

1. What was the ruling of the judge in this case?
2. If the appreciated value of the property had not been recorded on the financial statements, would the judge have ruled the same way?
3. What would be the accounting implications of the dividend payment if the appreciation were not recognized?
4. What factors must be considered in a dividend policy?

5. If you were a member of the board of directors of a company that had a large unrealized appreciation on its plant assets, would such a situation have any impact on your dividend policy?

11-3 Ford Motor Company

Presented below is a partial comparative balance sheet of Ford Motor Co. in which they record treasury stock as an asset:

FORD MOTOR COMPANY

	1980	1979
	($ Millions)	
Total current assets............................	$11,559.0	$11,571.3
Equities in Net Assets of Unconsolidated Subsidiaries and Affiliates................	2,142.2	2,041.8
Property		
Land, plant and equipment, at cost..............	15,567.3	14,264.3
Less accumulated depreciation...................	7,992.2	7,215.5
Net land, plant and equipment..............	7,575.1	7,048.8
Unamortized special tools......................	2,450.8	2,178.2
Net property...............................	10,025.9	9,227.0
Other Assets (Note 15).........................	620.5	684.5
Total Assets..............................	$24,347.6	$23,524.6

Note 15 (in part): Capital Stock

At December 31, 1980, there were 300,127 shares of Common Stock of the Company, with a cost of $12 million, included in other assets in the Consolidated Balance Sheet. Such shares were acquired for delivery under the deferred payment provisions of the Company's Supplemental Compensation Plan.

INSTRUCTIONS:

1. Provide conceptual reasons why treasury stock should be reported as an asset.
2. What is the present GAAP requirement for classification of treasury stock in a balance sheet? What is the basis for this classification?
3. How are dividends on treasury stock reported on the income statement?
4. What are some major reasons why corporations purchase their own stock?

11-4 Hawkeye Chemical

Presented below is the balance sheet of Hawkeye Chemical, Inc.

Hawkeye Chemical, Inc.
Balance Sheet
as of December 31, 1985

Current Assets			Current Liabilities		
Cash	$ 800,000		Accounts Payable	$ 600,000	
Accounts Receivable	2,000,000		Notes Payable	300,000	
Inventories	8,100,000			900,000	
	10,900,000		Stockholders' Equity		
Long-Term Assets			Common Stock ($1 par)	20,000,000	
Plant Assets (Net)	12,000,000		Paid-in Capital	3,000,000	
	$22,900,000		Deficit	(1,000,000)	
				$22,900,000	

The company's deficit only recently occurred as a result of five straight quarters of losses caused by a decline in the demand for certain of its chemical products. However, the company is now optimistic because a number of market surveys indicate that the company should be quite successful in the next five to ten years given its present product mix.

However, the company is concerned because it is presently in a deficit position and state law does not permit it to pay a dividend in such a situation. In addition, the company has certain plant assets that are overvalued by $3,000,000 and if it is forced to depreciate the plant over a 10 year period, earnings will be significantly reduced or eliminated. Thus, the company is unable to pay dividends to its existing stockholders and is having difficulty attracting interest in its stock. Other financing alternatives also are not promising, given the poor earnings results provided.

INSTRUCTIONS:

    1. Would a quasi-reorganization be appropriate in this situation?
    2. What conditions must occur before a quasi-reorganization is permitted?
    3. Why are quasi-reorganizations permitted?
    4. Prepare the journal entries necessary to effect a quasi-reogranization in this case.
    5. What other disclosure requirements occur in a quasi-reorganization? Discuss the rationale for these requirements.

11-5 City Utility

City Utility Company has been struggling for a number of years. Its recent cost overruns in building two nuclear facilities have created an enormous need for capital. Unfortunately, interest rates have been unusually high and therefore financing has become a problem. In addition, the state regulatory board has not provided the types of increases needed to offset the increased costs associated with building those nuclear plants, much less to meet the high financing costs that are necessitated under current economic conditions.

The company is therefore in a real dilemma. Debt financing costs have become so expensive that the company can no longer consider this option as feasible. In fact, the two major bond rating agencies have downgraded its existing bonds two levels in the last six months, a situation management considers intolerable. These rating agencies have indicated that the company is too highly levered and more equity capital must be injected into the company. However, the common stock price is severely depressed because of the conditions affecting the company. If stock were sold, it would have to be sold below book value, and it is highly likely that existing stockholders would be unhappy about this arrangement.

In discussing this situation with its investment banker (Morgan Co.), it is decided to issue preferred stock. Because preferred stock will be considered part of stockholders' equity, the company will decrease its debt to equity ratio. Furthermore, a fixed claim related to interest will not have to be paid, if the company has substantial financial difficulties. The terms of the preferred stock are as follows:

> Preferred stock will be issued at $100 per share; (same as par value) and a dividend of $15.80 per share will be paid. The preferred stock will be cumulative and non-participating. To ensure the marketability of the stock, the stock is redeemable in four years at the option of the holder or the issuer at $180 per share.

The investment banker in discussing this plan with the company believes that the issuance of preferred stock of this type has the most advantages of any type of financing plan. First, the company will not be able to pay any dividend in the first year or two and therefore it will have the opportunity to strengthen its cash flow position.

Furthermore, if the company is able to get its nuclear plants on line, it should be able to meet the dividend payments in the later years. In fact, if the company becomes extremely profitable, it may even retire the preferred stock to decrease the cash flow requirements related to the dividend distribution. If, of course, after four years the company is unable to generate any cash flow, then the preferred stockholders can call their stock and receive $180, for a cumulative return of approximately 15.80%.

The plan appears to be a good one and should solve the financing problems experienced by City Utility Company.

1. Where would you classify the preferred stock on the balance sheet? Discuss.

2. At what amount would you report the preferred stock at the date of issue? At the end of the second year? Discuss.

3. Assuming that the preferred stock was callable only by the issuer, would this change your answer to question one?

11-6 Financial Press Statement

The following statements appeared in a financial magazine:

"The question immediately arises: What is the difference in principle between a profits (or income) test and a balance sheet test for dividends? The answer, one essentially of interpretation and not of computation, lies in the difference between the term 'capital,' which to the economist and accountant is a concept roughly dichotomous to income, and the term 'legal capital,' which to the lawyer is a concept specifically defined by statute and having no necessary relationship to income. The economist's concept lies behind the development of the profits or income test, while the concept of 'legal capital' is reflected in the balance sheet test. Conceptually, capital can be thought of as the capital assets themselves, or their value at a specified time. Income then consists of all other assets -- those generated by, and existing in addition to, the capital assets.

On the other hand, capital loses its dichotomous relationship with income when stated capital is defined by statute as the dollar value of assets required to be provided and retained for the protection of creditors -- as though all assets (capital or otherwise) are to be thrown into a grain bin and dividends therefrom to be prohibited when the top surface of the assets falls below a certain level. The classic dividend question illustrates the problem arising from these different approaches."

"If assets equal to balance sheet capital were not actually provided -- if the stock was watered or issued at a discount -- can the fruits of the enterprise, its earnings, nevertheless be deemed available for dividends as income? If assets were contributed to the corporation in excess of the required capital, must they be deemed not available for dividends as not being income? If the assets constituting the economic or contributed capital of the corporation appreciate in value, has there been income or just change in the value of the corporation's capital -- whether or not realized -- with no effect on income? If the corporation's economic or contributed capital has been impaired, or diminished through losses, or has lessened in value, or has been sold at a loss but the earning capacity of the capital remains unaltered, are the fruits thereof still income, or can there be no income until the capital impairment has been repaired by retention of earnings?"

INSTRUCTIONS:

1. What is the distinction that is normally made between economic capital, accounting capital, and legal capital?
2. Answer the questions in the second paragraph.

11-7 Hock Pencil Company

The Hock Pencil Company is a small closely held corporation. Eighty percent of the stock is held by Clay Hock, President; of the remainder, 10% is held by members of his family and 10% by Phyllis Barker, a former officer who is now retired. The balance sheet of the company at June 30, 1985 was substantially as shown below:

Assets		Liabilities and Capital	
Cash	$ 11,000	Current liabilities	$ 75,000
Other Assets	285,000	Capital stock	150,000
		Retained earnings	71,000
	$296,000		$296,000

Additional authorized capital of $150,000 par value had never been issued. To strengthen the cash position of the company, Mr. Hock issued capital stock of a par value of $50,000 to himself at par for cash. At the next stockholders' meeting, Ms. Barker objected and claimed that her interests had been injured.

1. Which stockholders' right was ignored in the issue of shares to Mr. Hock?

2. How may the damage to Ms. Barker's interests be repaired most simply?

3. If Mr. Hock offered Ms. Barker a personal cash settlement and they agreed to employ you as an impartial arbitrator to determine the amount, what settlement would you propose? Present your calculations with sufficient explanation to satisfy both parties.

11-8 Growing Shares of Stock

Bill and Sandy Wall have expanded their greenhouse and silk flower shop to a chain of stores throughout the Midwest. Their strategy was simple: do a good job of researching the potential marketing area by a thorough screening of demographic information, locate in a high traffic strip shopping center, and carry high quality products.

As with many small growing businesses, expansion was limited to a great degree by the availability of financing. Although their profitability was good, retained earnings was insufficent to permit their aggressive expansion plans. The banks were cooperative in providing short term and inventory financing, but it was time to consider other means to raise capital.

The initial capitalization of the firm was provided by a small stock offering of 20,000 shares of $10 par common stock. Bill and Sandy control 51% of the stock, a venture capital firm 35% and the remainder is held in small amounts by approximately twenty other shareholders.

Sandy suggested borrowing additional money from their bank or attempting to privately place a small bond issue. The interest costs could be factored into their pricing structure and if the maturity were at least ten years away, they could plan for eventual repayment.

Bill disagreed. He felt it was time to attract additional equity capital. Common stock dividends were not mandatory and would, therefore, not require any cash payments, as would the debt, for the foreseeable future. All available cash could then be reinvested in the business.

The two consulted an investment banker for some advice. The advisor commented that a common stock issue might be difficult to sell since the company had never paid dividends and had no public market. It seemed that in the near future debt financing would be the only alternative. However, he did advise that the company begin to establish a track record of dividend payments to increase the probability of a successful stock sale sometime in the future.

Bill was depressed. Not only would the company be forced to borrow money and use needed cash for interest payments, but they would also have to start paying cash dividends on the common stock -- another cash drain. To make matters worse, the cash dividends would be taxable to Bill and Sandy and could not be deducted by the corporation for income tax purposes.

When talking with his CPA about the problem, the accountant came up with some additional suggestions. Why not issue stock dividends and also consider a stock split to increase the outstanding shares of stock, potentially broaden the distribution and reward the shareholders, while still maintaining control of the corporation? The Walls have asked you to discuss the proposed action by answering the following questions:

INSTRUCTIONS:

1. What is a stock dividend? How is a stock dividend distinguished from a stock split a) from a legal standpoint? b) from an accounting standpoint?
2. For what reasons does a corporation usually declare a stock dividend? A stock split?
3. Discuss the amount, if any, of retained earnings to be capitalized in connection with a stock dividend. A stock split.
4. Discuss the position against considering the stock dividend as income to the recipient.

11-9 The Value of Treasury Stock

Government and public pressure on the health care industry to contain rising health care costs had begun to have its impact on General Medical Systems. Orders for new equipment had dropped dramatically and the company had a large amount of unsold inventory despite aggressive price cutting.

Medical Equipment Corporation (MEC), a publicly held company, was experiencing problems for the same reason. The price of the company's shares was well below historical trading levels and the company was looking for ways to support the share price.

Despite what they considered a temporary industry problem, MEC continued to upgrade its medical equipment. During 1985 MEC approached General Medical

Systems about purchasing $144,000 worth of equipment for $90,000 cash and a promise to deliver an indeterminate number of treasury shares of its $5 par common stock, with a market value or $15,000 on January 1 of each year for the next four years. Hence $60,000 in "market value" of treasury shares will be required to discharge the $54,000 balance due on the equipment.

MEC had acquired 5,000 of its own stock in the expectation that the market value of the stock would increase substantially before the delivery dates. As a temporary measure the purchase of the 5,000 shares had bolstered the company's stock market price.

General Medical Systems liked the proposal. The $90,000 cash covered their costs and the sale helped alleviate their inventory problem. Since they too were confident in the long run success of the industry, the common stock would allow them to share in its future success. If not, they could always sell the stock and still realize a profit.

INSTRUCTIONS:

1. Discuss the propriety of recording the equipment at:

   a. $90,000 (the cash payment).
   b. $144,000 (the cash price of the equipment).
   c. $150,000 (the $90,000 cash payment + the $60,000 market value of treasury stock that must be transferred to the vendor in order to settle the obligation according to the terms of the agreement).

2. Discuss the arguments for treating the balance due as:

   a. A liability.
   b. Treasury stock subscribed.

3. Assuming that legal requirements do not affect the decision, discuss the arguments for treating the corporation's treasury shares as:
   a. An asset awaiting ultimate disposition.
   b. A capital element awaiting ultimate disposition.
                        (AICPA adapted)

11-10 Microsoft Corporation

Microsoft Corporation reports the following in its stockholders' equity section of its balance sheet as of January 1, 1985.

```
Common Stock, par value $10, 100,000 shares
    authorized, 50,000 shares outstanding          $  500,000
Paid-In Capital in Excess of Par-Common Stock         250,000
Preferred Stock, par value $25, 10,000 shares
    authorized and outstanding                        250,000
Paid-in Capital in Excess of Par-Preferred Stock       50,000
Retained Earnings                                     200,000
    Total Stockholders' Equity                     $1,250,000
```

During the course of 1985, several transactions occurred which had an impact on the stockholders' equity of Microsoft Corporation.

a. The company repurchased 5,000 shares of its common stock on the open market at $20 per share.

b. One of the company's original stockholders died during the year and bequeathed 1,000 of his shares of common stock to the company. At the time of the bequest, the common stock was selling for $18 per share.

c. The company repurchased 3,000 shares of its preferred stock on the open market at $20 per share.

d. The company issued 3,000 shares of its common treasury stock to purchase new machinery for the business. The fair market value of the machinery at time of purchase was $75,000. Assume the average cost method is used to value treasury stock.

e. The company exchanged 3,000 shares of its common treasury stock to repurchase 2,000 shares of its preferred stock. At the time of the exchange, the market price of the common stock was $20 per share and the market price of the preferred stock was $25 per share.

f. The stockholders voted to retire all 5,000 shares of its preferred treasury stock.

g. The average price of the company's common stock for the year was $19; the average price of the preferred stock was $21.

1. Discuss the methods available to account for treasury stock.
2. What accounting treatment for treasury stock is prescribed under current GAAP?
3. How is stockholders' equity affected differently by using the cost method instead of the par value method for treasury stock purchases?
4. Prepare the entries that would be made for the above transactions under both the cost and par value methods.
5. Illustrate the balance sheet presentation of the stockholders' equity section under both the cost and par value methods.

CHAPTER 12

[ ]

DILUTIVE SECURITIES AND EARNINGS PER SHARE

12-1 Summary Indicator

The FASB's 1979 Discussion Memorandum entitled "Reported Earnings" introduced the term summary indicator. A summary indicator exists when considerable information is summarized in such a way that a single item can communicate substantial information about a company's performance or financial position. Examples of summary indicators are the current ratio, debt to equity ratio, return on investment, price earnings ratio, and earnings per share.

Earnings per share ratios are used as one of the indicators of a firm's value (especially as reflected in the price earnings ratio) and as an indicator of future earnings per share and expected dividends per share. The number may also be used to evaluate company performance, management effectiveness, and dividend policy.

Reporting EPS has been commonplace for many years. However, prior to APB Opinion No. 9 management had discretion as to whether or not to report the number, how to calculate it, and where to report it. This opinion recommended but did not require its disclosure on the income statement. Because EPS calculations could be manipulated and be misleading without specific rules, the APB reconsidered the issue and enacted APB No. 15 "Earnings Per Share."

A primary consideration in the review of EPS calculations and requirements was whether earnings per share data should reflect historical information only or whether they should reflect pro forma and predictive information. The final opinion placed more emphasis on usefulness of EPS calculations to evaluate a firm's potential and investment decisions. Thus, APB No. 15 includes the presentation of two earnings per share concepts which are pro forma in nature and are assumed to be predictive in nature.

157

1. One criticism of APB 15 is that it is inconsistent to say that convertible debt should be classified solely as debt in the balance sheet (APB 14) and to classify it entirely as a common stock equivalent in computing earnings per share.
   a. What accounting treatment is required for convertible debt? What accounting treatment is required for debt issued with stock purchase warrants?
   b. What are the arguments for giving separate accounting recognition to the conversion feature of debentures?
   c. Explain how the conversion feature of convertible debt has a value to the issuer and to the purchaser.
   d. Explain how convertible bonds are determined to be common stock equivalents and how those convertible senior securities that are not considered to be common stock equivalents enter into the determinations of earnings per share data.
2. What are some of the other potential criticisms of the earnings per share calculations as required in APB 15?

12-2 Noreen Enterprises

Dan Sanders, Controller for Noreen Enterprises, is discussing the possibility of adding a new type of compensation package for a number of the company executives with a compensation specialist from McKinsey. The company has always had different types of stock option contracts in the past, but because of the volatility in the market, some executives have fared quite well and others not as well, depending on their eligible time to enter these plans.

In addition, a number of questions about the existing stock option plan were raised by stockholders at the last annual meeting. These questions centered on whether any real correlation existed between executive performance and stock market performance. Unfortunately, at the meeting the chairman of the board could provide little in the way of hard evidence, other than to indicate that increases in the market price of the stock must have resulted because the company was successful and the company was successful because of the efficiency of its key executives.

At a later closed session among board members and key executives, a consensus seemed to form that perhaps some other measure than increases in stock price should be used as a basis for its option packages. Thus, the Board instructed the controller to discuss the possibility of utilizing some different or additional types of compensation packages.

The discussion between the controller and compensation specialist is as follows:

Compensation Specialist: Some companies are changing to what is referred to as a restricted stock purchase plan. While individual plans vary somewhat as to specific terms, a typical plan provides for certain specified employees or groups of employees to be awarded the right to purchase a predetermined number of shares at a specified price, generally book value or less. Upon exercise of the option, the individual stockholder would receive dividend and voting rights, and would possess all other rights of a stockholder, except that for a stipulated period the stockholder can sell the shares, at book value, only to the issuing company. Sometimes the stipulated period runs for the entire time the stockholder continues to be an employee. In addition, the company commonly contracts to reacquire the shares at book value upon termination, retirement or death. In some cases, the individual stockholders may elect not to redeem his shares from the company following the end of the stipulated holding or vesting period (or at retirement), at which point the restriction for redemption at book value would lapse.

Controller: What are the objectives of these types of plans?

Compensation Specialist: These restricted stock purchase plans generally have two objectives. The most important objective is to provide certain benefits to the employees. A secondary objective is to provide capital to the issuing company. Thus, these plans differ in fundamental intent from stock purchase plans often used by advertising agencies, brokerage houses, and professional corporations wherein the principal objective is to provide capital for the issuing entity. These latter plans have little, if any, compensatory motivation and the book value repurchase agreement is principally designed to achieve equity upon termination of an employee–stockholder.

Controller: Well, thank you very much. This looks like the type of plan we need. If earnings increase, book value goes up and the key executives will be compensated. Thus, a better correlation with the efficiency of the executive and earnings probably can be achieved.

Compensation Specialist: I will be back later this month to settle the final details (she leaves).

Controller: (to himself) – Well, the Board should like this plan. One thing I still need to check is how this will affect our financial statements. Well, the auditors will be in tomorrow, I can ask them.

INSTRUCTIONS:

What do you think the auditors will say?

12-3 Steel City Gem

As auditor for Steel City Gem Paper, you have been asked about accounting for the following plan.

The plan is a tandem stock option/performance unit plan. Exercise of the performance unit cancels the stock option and vice versa. The stock option portion of the plan is the normal stock option with the exercise price equal to the quoted market price of the underlying stock at the date of grant. The options may continue to be outstanding for a maximum period to overcome a perceived weakness of the straight stock option plan -- performance may not be reflected in the quoted market price of the company's stock.

The existence of the performance unit guarantees to the executive that if certain specific performance goals are achieved over a defined performance period, the executive will receive (in cash or stock) a specific dollar reward. Obviously, if the exercise of the stock option results in a larger reward than exercise of the performance unit, the executive may elect to exercise the stock option.

The characteristics of the performance unit are more specifically described below:

1. A performance unit is assigned a maximum value (say $20 per unit) that is based on the company's assessment of what the appreciation in its stock price "should be" at the end of the performance period (say three years) if its performance (say, in terms of return on equity) averages a specified level (say 18%) over the performance period.

2. If the performance of the company is less than, for example, the 18% average return on equity over the three-year performance period, the executive electing the performance unit would

receive a specified percentage (but less than 100%) of the maximum value of the unit ($20). If performance is less than a specified floor (say 15% average return on equity), the performance unit would have no guaranteed value.

3. At the end of the performance period (three years in our example), the executive may request that the amount earned under the performance unit be paid to him (in cash or stock). The election of the performance unit cancels the stock option.

The individual may also decide to exercise the stock option, in which event the performance unit is cancelled.

Last, the executive may decide to not make either election immediately but rather wait to make an election sometime during the maximum period under the option (ten years). During this waiting period, the value of the performance units the executive has previously earned during the performance period would accrue interest. Prior to expiration of the stock option, the executive may elect either to exercise the stock option or the performance units.

INSTRUCTIONS:

What would you tell the company?

12-4 Epson Company

Epson Company has requested your advice in accounting for the stock options and stock appreciation rights (SARs) it issued during the year ended December 31, 1985. The company provided you with the following information:

The company adopted a stock option plan in 1984 to compensate selected management employees. The plan allows the board of directors to grant options for 10,000 shares of common stock per year. The options are to be granted at the sole discretion of the board of directors. Each option allows the employee to purchase one share of common stock at the quoted market price on the date the option was granted. The options terminate on the earliest of the following date: date of death, date of departure from the company, or 2 years from the date the option was granted.

On July 1, 1984, the company granted 10,000 options when the quoted market price of the stock was $50 per share. As of December 31, 1985, 5,000 of these options had not been exercised and the quoted market price was $80 per share.

The company made the following amendments to the plan on January 2, 1985:

Board of Directors were authorized to issue up to 10,000 stock appreciation rights (SARs) each year in tandem with related stock options. Stock options could still be issued without SARs.

The amendments give the employee the choice of exercising the stock option or the SAR. Exercise of either the SAR or the option automatically terminates the other. The SARs have the same termination provisions as the stock options.

When a SAR is exercised, the employee is given the alternative of receiving cash or shares of stock equal to the excess of the quoted market price of the stock over the exercise price of the related stock option times the number of shares granted under the option plan.

The amendments allowed the board to issue SARs to employees who had not yet exercised the stock options they had received on July 1, 1985. These SARs have the same exercise price as the related 1984 options.

The Company issued 2500 SARs on January 2, 1985 to certain employees who had not exercised their 1984 options. The quoted market price of the stock on January 2, 1985 was also $80 per share.

On July 1, 1985, the company issued another 10,000 stock options including 5,000 with attached SARs. The quoted market price of the stock on July 1, 1985 was $70 per share.

The following stock options and SARs were exercised in 1985:

a) 1,000 of the SARs attached to the 1984 stock options were exercised and employees were paid $25,000.
b) 1,000 of the SARs attached to the 1985 stock options were exercised and employees were paid $5,000.
c) 2,000 of the 1984 stock options to which SARs were not attached were exercised. The quoted market price of the 2,000 shares issued totaled $156,000.
d) 1,000 of the 1985 stock options to which SARs were not attached were exercised.

The quoted market price of the 1,000 shares issued totaled $77,000.

The quoted market price of the common stock at December 31, 1985 was $75 per share. Assume that none of the employees who were issued SARs elected to exercise stock options instead.

INSTRUCTIONS:

1. Determine the compensation expense for financial reporting purposes for the year ended December 31, 1985.
2. Why is the profession so concerned about the proper accounting for these transactions?

12-5 Beam-O-Light Corporation[*]

In 1975, Beam-O-Light Corporation developed and patented a laser beam that could be used in medical surgery. Beam-O-Light had been run since its inception in 1974 by its founder, Hector Beam. Because of the increased demand for this laser beam, Beam-O-Light has recently gone public to provide capital for production expansion. Its balance sheet for 1985 is as follows:

ASSETS		LIABILITIES	
Cash	$ 100,000	Current Liabilities	$ 100,000
Property, plant and		Stockholders' Equity	
equipment	2,000,000	Common Stock	2,000,000
Intangible assets		$10 par, 300,000 shares	
(Patent)	1,000,000	authorized, 200,000 shares outstanding	
		Retained Earnings	1,000,000
	$3,100,000		$3,100,000

Hector is a mechanical engineer by training and has little business acumen. He therefore decided that a production manager was needed to run the plant so that he could devote himself to basic research. Hector hired an executive search firm which came up with an individual named Sam Daniel. Sam is an MBA who had 10 years of experience with Specific Electric in their Medical Products Division.

Sam was interested in coming to work for Beam-O-Light because he was familiar with their laser beam. However, Sam was a top-notch production man and required a substantial salary to quit Specific Electric. Beam-O-Light did not have enough cash to pay Sam since it was spending heavily on capital expansion. Hector called Sam and they had the following conversation over the phone.

Hector: I would really like to have you come to work for us but we just cannot afford your requested salary at this time, which

---

[*]Adapted from a case prepared by Robert A. Greenheck.

I believe you stated was $200,000. The best we could do until our capital expansion gets off the ground is $100,000 cash.

Sam: Well Hector, I really do not have a need for a total cash payment right now since my house is paid for and I am in the 50% tax bracket. Why not issue me some convertible preferred stock so that if the company proceeds as planned, I can share in the growth through conversion.

Hector: Our lawyers just set up our capital structure for a public offering so I am reluctant to issue preferred stock at this time. Let me talk to our accountant and see if he cannot come up with a compensation package that will be suitable to both our needs.

Sam: That sounds good to me Hector, I'll be waiting for your proposal.

Later that day, Hector comes into your office and tells you about the conversation he has just had with Sam. He asks you to come up with a solution. You mention that perhaps that incentive stock options might be issued. You tell Hector that you will check into these and get back to him right away.

INSTRUCTIONS:

1. What are the advantages to an executive of receiving an incentive stock option? Why do some accountants believe that the present accounting for these options is inappropriate?
2. What date or event does the profession believe should be used in determining the value of a stock option? What arguments support this position? What criticism may be brought against the date or event advocated by the profession?
3. What support can be offered for dates other than the date of grant on which to determine the value of a stock option?
4. What is the advantage to an executive of a stock appreciation right (SAR) plan? How is compensation expense measured in an SAR plan?

12-6 Smother Co.

In 1981 Smother Co. adopted a plan to give additional incentive compensation to its dealers to sell its principal product -- fire extinguishers. Under the plan Smother transferred 9,000 shares of its $1.00 par value stock to a trust with the provision that Smother would have to forfeit interest in the trust and no part of the trust fund could ever revert to Smother. Shares were to be distributed to dealers on the basis of their shares of fire extinguisher purchases from Smother (above certain minimum levels) over the three-year period ending June 30, 1984.

In 1981 the stock was closely held. The book value of the stock was $6.90 per share as of June 30, 1981, and in 1981 additional shares were sold to existing stockholders for $7 per share. On the basis of this information, market value of the stock was determined to be $7 per share.

In 1981 when the shares were transferred to the trust, Smother charged prepaid expenses for $63,000 ($7 per share market value) and credited capital stock for $9,000 and additional paid-in capital for $54,000. The prepaid expense was charged to operations over a three-year period ended June 30, 1984.

Smother sold a substantial number of shares of its stock to the public in 1983 at $60 per share.

In July 1984 all shares of the stock in the trust were distributed to the dealers. The market value of the shares at date of distribution of the stock from the trust had risen to $120 per share. Smother obtained a tax deduction equal to that market value for the tax year ended June 30, 1985.

INSTRUCTIONS:

1. How much should be reported as selling expense in each of the years noted above?
2. Smother is also considering other types of option plans. One such plan is a stock appreciation right (SAR) plan. What is a stock appreciation right plan? What is a potential disadvantage of a SAR plan from the viewpoint of the company?

12-7 Earnings Per Share

"Earnings per share" (EPS) is the most featured single financial statistic about modern corporations. Daily published quotations of stock prices have recently been expanded to include for many securities a "times earnings" figure which is based on EPS. Stock analysts often focus their discussions on the EPS of the corporations they study. Trend analysis of earnings on a per share basis is a frequently used measure of performance, which may form a starting point for the valuation of securities.

Unfortunately, the computation of earnings per share is sometimes difficult and the underlying theory is complex. Surveys have found that finance oriented users find difficulty in interpreting the current earnings per share figures. Specifically, users of earnings per share figures may misunderstand the effects of common stock equivalents in primary earnings per share. It is commonly assumed that dilution from convertibles, options and warrants is evident only in fully diluted earnings per share.

INSTRUCTIONS:

1. Discuss the reasons why securities other than common stock may be considered common stock equivalents for the computation of primary earnings per share.

2. Explain how dividends or dividend requirements on any class of preferred stock that may be outstanding affect the computation of EPS.

3. One of the technical procedures applicable in EPS computations is the "treasury-stock method."

   a. Briefly describe the circumstances under which it might be appropriate to apply the treasury-stock method.

   b. There is a limit to the extent to which the treasury-stock method is applicable. Indicate what this limit is and give a succinct summary of the procedures that should be followed beyond the treasury-stock limits.

   c. What is the rationale for this limitation?

4. Under some circumstances, convertible debentures would be considered "common stock equivalents"; under other circumstances they would not.

   a. When is it proper to treat convertible debentures as common stock equivalents? What is the effect on computation of EPS in such cases?

   b. In case convertible debentures are not considered as common stock equivalents, explain how they are handled for purposes of EPS computations.

12-8 Hargrove Manufacturing Company

The "Highlights in Review" section of the 1985 Annual Report of Hargrove Manufacturing Company included these items:

	1985	1984
Net earnings after taxes	$2,100,000	$2,300,000
Net earnings per share of common stock	$6.65	$7.62
Net earnings per share assuming full conversion of convertible notes	$4.76	$5.39

Excerpts from the December 31, 1985 Balance Sheet were as follows:

Long-Term Debt		
5% Note due December 31, 1987		$1,500,000
6% Subordinated Convertible Note due December 31, 1993		2,000,000
Stockholders' Investment		
Common stock ($2 par) shares outstanding - at Jan. 1, 302,000; at Dec. 31, 316,000		632,000
Additional Paid-in Capital		2,000,000
Retained Earnings		
Balance--January 1	$3,500,000	
Dividends	(500,000)	
Net income	2,000,000	$5,000,000

Note A: The 6% subordinated convertible note is subordinated to the 5% note and short term bank borrowings. The note is convertible into common stock at $16 a share and 125,000 shares of authorized common stock are reserved for conversion.

To reduce the threat of a take-over by a larger company, the Hargrove management began to negotiate the retirement of the $2 million convertible note. In February, 1986 agreement was reached to retire $1 million of the note for payment of $3 million, an amount that was approximately equal to the $48 per share market value of the 62,500 shares into which that portion of the original note was then convertible.

Hargrove naturally intended to take the $2 million difference as a tax deduction, claiming the discharge of the liability as a necessary business expense. The company's tax attorney stated, however, that its deductibility was not completely assured, and that treatment of the item as a charge against earnings in the financial statement could prove crucial in any contest with the Internal Revenue Service.

INSTRUCTIONS:

How should the transaction be treated?

12-9 Satellite Services, Inc.

Satellite Services, Inc. (SSI) is a company extensively involved in the telecommunications and cable television markets, both civilian and military. The company was founded and incorporated in Texas in 1978. Although the company initially operated in the satellite communications market alone, they have grown significantly because of their aggressive acquisition program into the field of cable television. Such mergers have often been accomplished with cash payments, but several larger acquisitions involved the use of convertible securities.

SSI made its first public offering in 1980 and its stock was subsequently afforded a price earnings ratio high enough to facilitate the use of a variety of securities convertible directly to common stock or that afforded the opportunity to acquire common stock. However, in early 1983, SSI's stock had fallen substantially in price due to a slowdown and halt to their cable television acquisition program. This was caused primarily by an antitrust consent decree which prevented the firm from making further acquisitions. From that point in time the company has concentrated on internal growth and the consolidation of their existing operations.

Following is some information relating to their operations for the year ending December 31, 1985 and other pertinent information.

A. Income before tax	$6,800,000	
Tax	3,400,000	
Net Income	3,400,000	
Preferred dividends	200,000	
Net Income to common stock	$3,200,000	

B. Common Shares Outstanding (12/31/84)	1,000,000
Common Stock Offering (3/31/85)	400,000
Common Shares Outstanding (12/31/85)	1,400,000

C. Price/share (1/1/85)	$32.75
Average Price/Share for fiscal 1985	$30.00
Price/Share (12/31/85)	$26.25

D. Other Outstanding Securities

1) $1,000,000 5.75% Convertible Debentures due 1998 issued at 98 on 6/1/80. Each bond is convertible into 50 shares.

2) $2,000,000 - $100 Par $6 Convertible Preferred Stock issued at par on 1/1/81. Each share is convertible into 20 shares of common stock.

3) $4,000,000 - $100 Par 2% Cumulative Preferred Stock issued at par on 7/1/81.

4) 1,000,000 Common Stock Warrants issued 9/1/81. Five warrants are convertible into one share of common stock at an exercise price of $60.

5) 300,000 Stock Options issued 2/15/82 to certain executives to buy common stock at $10 per share.

6) AA Bond average yield
   6/1/80   8.75%
   1/1/81   10.00%
   12/31/85   8.00%

INSTRUCTIONS:

1. What is the importance of "earnings per share"?
2. Discuss the history of EPS.
3. Discuss the theoretical basis for computing EPS.
4. Based upon the information in the case, calculate primary and fully diluted earnings per share for 1985.

12-10 Fast Grow Corporation

Fast Grow Corporation, a rapidly expanding conglomerate in the travel field, transportation industry, and insurance business, has engaged you to prepare their 1985 audited financial statements. Fast Grow intends to comply fully with the requirements of APB No. 15 and has elected to determine the classification of all securities under the provisions of the Opinion.

1985 was an active year for Fast Grow. One division, Slow Grow, was sold at a loss and was replaced by the acquisition of Gaming Corporation, an operator of gambling casinos in the Bahamas. In order to finance the 100% acquisition of Gaming Corporation, the company preserved its working capital and omitted the annual dividend. A 5% stock dividend was issued instead. Additional capital was raised by issuing previously unissued stock.

The management, although competent in their own fields, have little knowledge of accounting practices and are somewhat resentful of the increased costs associated with the rather lengthy computations required by APB No. 15. They also fear a reduction in their 1985 earnings per share ratio, a ratio which has shown robust increases in the last seven years.

After a thorough audit, you determine that Fast Grow's balance sheet and the income statement are fairly presented in accordance with generally acceptable accounting principles. However, it is also your responsibility to formulate the information required by APB No. 15 and to reassure management that all is not lost.

INSTRUCTIONS:

A. Management is surprised to learn that the number of shares outstanding at the end of the fiscal year is not used to compute the EPS. After all, the President informs you, "that number is readily available and would require no cost of computation."

   1. Using the information provided below, compute the basic weighted-average number of shares outstanding.

      Additional Information
      a. Shares of common stock outstanding as of 10/31/84 were 975,000.

      b. Fast Grow issued a 5% stock dividend to holders of record on January 31, 1985.

      c. 23,750 shares were purchased for the Treasury on May 15, 1985.

      d. On July 1, 1985, the firm issued 250,000 shares of common stock.

      e. An additional 150,000 shares were sold by private sale on September 1, 1985.

   2. Briefly discuss the weighted average vs. shares outstanding approaches in determining the denominator for EPS.

B. Jim Weston, president of Fast Grow, is totally confused by the plethora of terms and concepts that have arisen in conjunction with APB No. 15. He also is amazed at the complexity of the calculation and the securities considered. He asks you "How much information must we present about earnings per share?"
   1. Briefly explain the following terms for Jim:

      a. Common Stock Equivalents.
      b. Simple Capital Structures.
      c. Complex Capital Structures.
      d. Primary Earnings Per Share.
      e. Fully Diluted Earnings Per Share.

   2. Briefly inform Mr. Weston as to the number of earnings per share computations required and information required in footnotes.

CHAPTER 13

INVESTMENTS

13-1 Business Combinations

Following is a footnote from the 1983 annual report of the Coca-Cola Company:

Acquisitions. In 1983, the Company purchased various bottling operations. The operating results for these companies have been included in the consolidated statement of income from the dates of acquisition and did not have a significant effect on operating results for 1983.

In June 1982, the Company acquired all of the outstanding capital stock of Columbia Pictures Industries, Inc. ("Columbia") in a purchase transaction. The purchase price, consisting of cash and common stock of the Company, was valued at approximately $692 million. The values assigned to assets acquired and liabilities assumed are based on studies conducted to determine their fair values. The excess cost over net fair value is being amortized over forty years using the straight-line method.

The pro forma consolidated results of continuing operations of the Company, as if Columbia had been acquired as of January 1, 1981, are as follows (in millions, except per share data):

	Year Ended December 31,	
	1982	1981
Net operating revenues	$6,374	$6,434
Income from continuing operations	489	449
Income from continuing operations per share	3.60	3.31

The pro forma results include adjustments to reflect interest expense on $333 million of the purchase price assumed to be financed with debt bearing interest at an annual rate of 11%, the amortization of the unallocated excess cost over net assets of Columbia, the income tax effects of pro forma adjustments, and the issuance of the 12.2 million shares of the Company's common stock.

The accounting for business acquisitions continues to be an important issue on the national and international accounting scene. In the business community the "urge to merge" continues at a high level of activity. No company regardless of size seems immune to unfriendly takeover attempts.

One question is whether permissive accounting practices have actually fostered this activity. Is merger accounting so creative that it does not represent economic reality? The Accounting Principles Board when issuing Opinion 16 "Business Combinations" stated that:

"The Board finds merit in both the purchase and pooling of interests methods of accounting for business combinations and accepts neither method to the exclusion of the other."

The controversy continues as to how both of these method can represent economic reality.

INSTRUCTIONS:

1. What is the central accounting issue in a business combination?
2. Compare and contrast the three theoretical approaches of accounting for business combinations.
3. What is the basis for the Accounting Principles Board allowing two different methods of accounting for business combinations?
4. What is the difference between the purchase and pooling methods that makes pooling so attractive?
5. Take a position and defend the use of one method only for accounting for business combinations.

13-2 City Builders Corporation

In 1985, City Builders Corporation experienced financial problems on several projects under construction, all of which were financed by two major lenders. The Company delivered deeds of trust cross-collateralizing the projects and the lenders waived their rights to deficiency judgments and agreed to fund the projects to completion. As a result, the lenders could look only to the projects for their security and the Company's loss was limited to their equity in the project. Reserves were established to reduce the investment in the project to zero.

These agreements allowed the Company to continue operation and avoid bankrupcy.

Their investment in the project was approximately 10% of the projected cost. The loss of that equity would have a significant impact on earnings, but at least the balance of their net worth was protected from losses.

The company determined that an immediate write-off of the investment was necessary. The Controller stated that a reserve should be established to reduce the equity to zero. The President felt that the company should establish a fund to anticipate the eventual losses that would occur.

As auditors for this company, your examination for 1985 was generally limited to a determination that the Company had no equity in the projects and that adequate provisions had been provided for any additional costs to be incurred by the company which would not be financed by the lenders.

The amounts involved were significant and a question arose as to the proper balance sheet presentation.

INSTRUCTIONS:

1. Distinguish between a fund and a reserve.
2. What are two general types of funds? Give three examples of each
3. Which is the proper category for this potential loss, a fund or reserve?
4. Indicate three possible presentations to establish the reserves.
5. Indicate your recommended presentation and justify it.

13-3 Acquisitions, Inc. [*]

Acquisitions Inc. obtained an 80% interest in the common stock of Target Company in 1984. Book values of Target's assets and liabilities were deemed to be equal to their fair market values at that time. On January 2, 1985, Target bought, on the open market, a 10% interest in its parent, Acquisitions. Acquisition's assets and liabilities were also deemed to be equal to their fair values. There have been no other stockholders' equity changes for either company. Each company has 1000 shares of stock outstanding on its separate books. The resulting situation is diagramed below:

Ownership

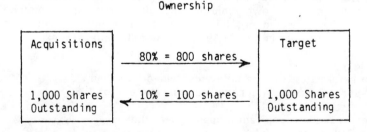

---

[*]Adapted from a case prepared by Jeff A. Hahn.

For 1985, Acquisitions has internally generated net income (excluding complex equity income from its investment in Target) of $50,000. Target has internally generated net income of $20,000.

INSTRUCTIONS:

1. You are a staff accountant for Acquisitions Inc. and are involved with its consolidated financial statements. Determine the controlling and minority interests in consolidated net income by use of the (1) Reciprocal Method, (2) Treasury Stock Method.
2. What are the theoretical justifications of each method?
3. What method is supported by GAAP?
4. Which method is "right"?

13-4 Tanzania Refining Company

Tanzania Refining Company (TRC) has an exclusive right, granted by the Tanzanian Government, to operate an oil refinery located in Tanzania through the year 2,000 (at which time the ownership of the refinery reverts to the Government). As of December 31, 1985, Republic Corporation (REP) owned 32% of TRC, the investment totaling $3,600,000 or 9% of the total consolidated assets of REP. The investment included cash loans and notes accepted for amounts due for interest and for services rendered under a refinery construction contract for which REP served as the prime contractor. REP had a commitment to sell 14% of its 32% ownership to Tanzanian citizens, which would leave it owning 18%.

Through a mix-up of accounting policies and a failure to keep up with professional accounting pronouncements, the company had been reporting this investment on the cost basis, contrary to APB Opinion No. 18.

With the "discovery" of APB No. 18, the question was raised whether or not REP should account for its 32% ownership in TRC using the equity method. REP management felt that it would not be appropriate to adopt the equity method accounting for its investment in TRC in 1985 for the following reasons:

1. It would just be a matter of time until they owned less than 20% of TRC and this could be accomplished by the end of 1986.

2. REP does not excercise significant influence over the operations of TRC since:

a. Absolute control rests in RAD Oil Company by ownership of 67% of TRC and contractual commitments. REP does have two of seven directors, but has agreed to give up one director if requested.

b. REP does not participate in policy-making except for financing arrangements. RAD Oil Company has contracts with TRC to supply the crude oil and to market all of the refinery's products.

c. There are no continuing intercompany transactions except for the repayment of debt to REP and a procurement contract whereby REP buys all material that TRC buys outside of Tanzania. REP is paid $30,000 per year plus the cost of the purchases for this service.

d. There is no interchange of personnel. RAD Oil Company furnishes all technical and marketing personnel.

e. There is no technological dependence. REP is obligated to furnish technical service if requested, but has not been requested to do so to date.

3. Footnote 4 to paragraph 14 of APB No. 18 states that "conclusions in paragraph 14 of this Opinion apply to investments in foreign subsidiaries unless those companies are operating under conditions of exchange restrictions, controls, or other uncertainties of a type that would affect decisions as to consolidation or application of the equity method; if those conditions exist, the cost method should be followed."

4. The Government of Tanzania has jurisdiction over refinery prices, and the concession agreement for TRC commits the Government to maintain a pricing structure which will generate profitable operations for the refinery. The refinery has operated under provisional prices from the start of the operations (1973) and has operated at a loss. TRC was profitable in 1984 because of certain price adjustments granted by the Tanzanian Government during that year.

The corporate controller feels that the use of the cost method is an accounting error and should be changed immediately. The rest of the management disagrees. They have called upon you as their CPA to settle the disagreement.

INSTRUCTIONS:

1. Should the accounting method be changed from cost to the equity method? If so, how should the prior periods be treated?
2. Would you change your conclusion if Republic assigned 14% of the

TRC stock to RAD Oil as an escrow agent to sell the shares at a predetermined price with the voting rights going to RAD Oil in the interim?

13-5 Real Data Systems

Real Data Systems (RDS) and subsidiaries are engaged in the manufacture and sale of data communication equipment. Your firm is engaged to examine the company's consolidated financial statements at March 31, 1985. The company had been previously audited by another national accounting firm. The company's March 31, 1985 financial statements included the following:

Total assets	$7,200,000
Stockholders' investments	3,900,000
Retained earnings	500,000
Net sales	5,600,000
Net income	260,000

During fiscal 1985, a new company, Real Data Leasing Company (RDL), was formed for the purpose of handling the RDS leasing business. The relationship between RDS and RDL is as follows:

(1) The companies have certain common directors, officers and shareholders.

(2) Substantially all of RDL's leases are for equipment purchased from RDS (RDS performs all of the marketing effort relating to finding the lessee, provides all of the administration relating to the lease document, and services the equipment and lease). RDL's full time personnel consists of one individual who is given the title of President.

(3) RDS guarantees the RDL $1,000,000 line of credit with a bank. RDL lease receivables serve as additional collateral on borrowings against the line of credit.

(4) Sales by RDS to RDL during 1985 were $2,900,000 and at March 31, 1985, RDS had a receivable from RDL of $2,300,000. (During the period from March 31, 1985 to September 25, 1985, the date of the auditors' report, RDL had paid RDS approximately $600,000 on account and RDS had made sales to RDL of approximately $700,000.)

The auditors for RDS believe that they should also examine the accounts of RDL. This is to ensure that the receivable from RDL is collectible, leases exist, and that RDS is properly reporting income on sales to RDL. It is their belief that up to $500,000 of RDS sales to RDL during the year was for equipment which was leased to third parties on cancellable lease contracts, and therefore should not be included as income to RDS except to the extent that lease income was realized by RDL.

Also since RDS guaranteed the RDL bank lines (of which $250,000 had been utilzied) they felt that money paid on the receivable to this extent should not be recognized.

RDS company management felt that any additional audit work regarding RDL records was unnecessary after all it was a totally separate company not a subsidiary. Since it was a separate company, the sales to RDL should be recognized immediately, because there was no right of return or additional contingencies. In addition, the receivable should be recognized as paid (the $250,000) since the guarantee of a line of credit is not an uncommon supplier practice in this industry.

The accounting firm is prepared to "go to the mat" with RDS management. In fact, there is a strong feeling by the managing partner that RDL should be consolidated with RDS.

INSTRUCTIONS:

1. Is RDS a separate company?
2. Should the financial statements of RDS and RDL be combined? If so, how?

13-6 Land and Building Planning, Inc.

Land & Building Planning, Inc. (LBP), 25%-owned by Allied Corporation, provides engineering, architecture, land planning and building systems development for housing programs. The remaining 75% of the ownership of LBP is effectively in the hands of certain individuals active in the management of LBP.

To take an aggressive tax position, LBP's management adopted a policy of expensing all costs associated with projects as these costs were incurred with no revenue recognition until the initial loan closing applicable to the project took place. At the initial loan closing 50% of the gross revenue applicable to the project was recognized by LBP; however, approximately 85% of LBP's cost was incurred at this time. The remaining 50% of the revenue was recognized at the rate of 5% a month over the subsequent ten months. LBP's independent accountants had given an unqualified opinion to the financial statements prepared on the basis of the accounting described.

In 1985, at our urging, Allied agreed to equity accounting for LBP; however, Allied management contended that the reported earnings of LBP were not in accordance with acceptable accounting methods and adjusted the reported earnings of LBP for purposes of equity accounting to reflect revenue on the basis of the ratio of costs incurred to total estimated costs with slight modifications. These modifications were to defer 15% of revenue until job completion as a contingency against erroneous cost estimates and to recognize no revenue until a project was at least 20% complete. Basically, all LBP's work was related to Allied construction projects planned or being developed.

You obtained access to LBP records and were able to examine them. You agree with the adjustments made by Allied. The adjustments had the effect of increasing Allied's share of equity by approximately $50,000 as compared to the equity share that would have resulted from the audited LBP financial statements. The necessary entries to reflect the adjusted accounting treatment were made in consolidation and were not booked by LBP as LBP management did not agree with the adjustments.

The adjustment of the LBP audited financials was possible because of our access to the records of LBP and consequent ability to agree with Allied's contention that an alternative accounting method more clearly reflected the results of operation.

In your consideration of this procedure, you recognized the risk that the records of LBP might not be available in subsequent years for your review of the Allied adjustments. The amount of adjustment was relatively immaterial to Allied.

INSTRUCTIONS:

      1. When should LPBs revenue be recognized? Its costs?
      2. Should Allied make the adjustments to the LBP earnings?
      3. What method should Allied use next year?

13-7 Badger Company

In 1978 Yello Company made an investment in Badger Company. The investment consisted of a minority interest in common stock and preferred stock. At a later date Yello Company accepted some long term notes receivable from Badger Company. Badger Company was involved in a new field and was a purchaser of equipment from Yello Company.

The investments were all recorded at cost, and no preferred dividends or interest were received. By 1983, Badger Company had had continuing losses and was in severe financial difficulty. As a result, Yello Company set up a reserve equal to its entire investment in Badger Company and notes receivable through an income statement charge in that year.

By 1985, Badger Company's fortunes had changed. It was very profitable, was able to restructure its capital, and had completed a successful public offering of its common stock. From the proceeds of the offering, Yello Company received payment for its original notes receivable, including the past-due interest, and for the cumulative preferred dividends in arrears. Yello Company, of course, recognized income in 1985 for the entire proceeds received (interest and dividend income and adjustment of the allowance account for the long term note receivable).

The capital restructuring resulted in Yello Company receiving a new class of preferred stock in exchange for its old. Neither the new preferred stock nor the original common stock issued to Yello Company by Badger Co. was marketable. The stock had never been registered.

Yello Company believed that it should restore the original cost basis of the investment in common and preferred stock of Badger Company. The auditor took the position that the write-down in 1983 represented the recognition of a permanent impairment and the establishment of a new cost basis for the common and preferred stock. Thus, no income should be recognized until, and unless, realized.

INSTRUCTIONS:

1. How might Yello Company support its position in this case?
2. How might the auditor support his position in this case?
3. Which position do you feel is appropriate in this case?

13-8 Maniott Corporation

Maniott Corporation is a personal holding company that owns approximately 19,000 acres of land in Alabama from which it receives approximately $2,500,000 per year in oil and gas royalty income. The Board of Directors of Maniott has directed that a portion of this income, the amount not required to be distributed as a dividend under IRS personal holding company regulations, is to be invested on a long-term basis in listed marketable securities.

At March 31, 1985 (the company's fiscal year end), the Company owned investment securities of approximately $3,000,000, consisting of certificates of deposit and blue chip common stocks, the market values of which were approximately $370,000 below cost. At the end of the prior year, investments of approximately $2,700,000 had a market value of approximately $100,000 less than cost. At that time the amount of decline in market value was disclosed, but no reserve for decline in market value was provided since the Company did not feel that the decline was permanent.

At March 31, 1985, the Board of Directors of the Company had instructed management and legal counsel to prepare a tentative plan of liquidation. If such a plan were adopted the investment securities would be sold within a period of approximately one year.

Consideration was given to not recognizing this loss at March 31, 1985, since the Company also owned several tracts of land which were carried on its books at a cost of approximately $100,000 and which had an estimated market value of several million dollars.

INSTRUCTIONS:

1. What are the basic rules for reporting long-term and short-term investments? Are there any differences in the method of reporting these two types of investments?
2. How does an accountant determine whether there has been a permanent decline in the value of an investment?
3. If a permanent decline in the value of the investment is reported, should the investment account be reduced or should an allowance account be established? What should happen if the permanent decline in value later is found to be wrong and that the investment securities appreciate in value?

13-9 Sharp, Inc.

Sharp, Inc. is a medium-sized manufacturer of specialty calculators experiencing financing problems for a proposed production expansion program in 1986. Rather outmoded facilities have led to inefficiencies in production over the last three years resulting in a reported net loss each year. To finance the new expansion program, Mr. Kelly, the President, wishes to obtain financing on a long-term basis. Mr. Rebek, the Treasurer, and you (the Controller) have been asked into the President's office to discuss the proposed financing.

Mr. Rebek notes that due to the reported net losses over the last three years, obtaining a loan would be difficult and Sharp will have to sell some of its securities investments to cover any deficiencies between the amount needed and loaned. Based on his preliminary discussions with the bank, Mr. Rebek believes that Sharp will have to sell one of the three larger noncurrent securities currently owned in addition to the current portfolio of securities. A listing of both the current portfolio and the noncurrent portfolio is attached (see Exhibit I). Mr. Rebek further points out that Sharp's ability to obtain a loan is partially contingent on reported 1985 net income. Since the 1985 financial statements have not yet been published, minimizing any losses reported is imperative.

Mr. Kelly agrees with Mr. Rebek and suggests that he is willing to sell any of the securities classified as current or noncurrent if required to meet the expansion program financing needs. He further states that since the market values of securities

E, F, and G are equal, he is indifferent among them in regards to their sale.

INSTRUCTIONS:

1. Assume that the current valuation allowance at January 1, 1985 is $3,000 and that the noncurrent valuation allowance at January 1, 1985 is $1,000, prepare a recommendation for the 1985 year-end balance sheet presentation of Marketable Equity Securities in accordance with FASB Statement No. 12. Your objective is to minimize the reported 1985 net loss.

2. Prepare the journal entries necessary at December 31, 1985 to record any adjustments to the two valuation allowances given above.

3. What is the net effect on 1985 profitability from the journal entries related to marketable equity securities you need to make in order to close the books for 1985?

EXHIBIT I
Sharp, Inc.
Listing of Securities Owned
As of: December 31, 1985

Security		Cost	Market[7]	Unrealized Gain/(Loss)
Current[1]:	A	$ 10,000	$ 12,000	$ 2,000
	B[2]	5,000	5,000	0
	C	15,000	10,000	(5,000)
	D[3]	20,000	17,000	(3,000)
Totals		$ 50,000	$ 44,000	$ (6,000)
Noncurrent[1]:	E	28,000	30,000	2,000
	F[4]	45,000	30,000	(15,000)
	G[5]	31,000	29,000	(2,000)
	H[6]	11,000	11,000	0
Totals		$115,000	$100,000	$(15,000)

Notes:

1. The current/noncurrent classifications represent December 31, 1984 categorizations.

2. Security B was pledged against a three-year note payable early in 1985. The note prohibits sale of, or substitution for, the pledged security.

3. Security D was a callable preferred stock issue purchased in 1985.

4. It was decided in December that this decline should be considered permanent.

5. Market value at the date of the meeting between Mr. Kelly, Mr. Rebek, and you (in early January) was $30,000.

6. Security H was common stock obtained from a privately-held corporation to replace a current note receivable.

7. Consider all market values as temporary unless there appears a footnote indicating a permanent market value decline.

13-10 Purchase Versus Pooling

Following are a number of situations concerning acquisitions and the use of purchase versus pooling for accounting:

A. Hollett Company proposed to merge with Adam Company on May 31, 1985. Hollett will give 10,000 of its common shares (without voting rights) with an aggregate market value of $10,000 in exchange for 800 of Ace's 1,000 outstanding shares. Adam, formerly a Division of Roderick Corporation, was sold to its present owners in April of 1981.

INSTRUCTIONS:

1. Does this proposed transaction dictate pooling or purchase treatment?
2. List the reasons for your response to (1).

B. Hollett Company proposes to merge with Adam Company on May 31, 1985. Hollett will give 8,000 of its voting common shares at that date (with an aggregate market value of $80,000), plus 1,000 additional shares each at May 31, 1986 and 1987 if Adam meets certain profit targets for calendar years 1985 and 1986. Hollett has also agreed to relieve Adam's five shareholders of their personal guarantees of Company debt, and replace such personal guarantees with the corporate guarantee of Hollett Company. The bank has agreed to such a switch in guarantors.

1. What, if anything, denies pooling treatment of this transaction?
2. What effect, if any, does the switch of guarantees have on your decision -- and why?

C. Hollett Company proposes to merge with Adam Company in a transaction (quite significant to Hollett) which the auditor feels qualifies for pooling treatment. The transaction is to be consummated January 31, 1986. Hollett has indicated to the auditor that since this date is so close to their calendar year ended December 31, 1985, and Adam's 1985 operating results will significantly improve Hollett's income statement, that they will consider the deal to be effective as of December 31, 1985; and accordingly include Adam's 1985 operating results and December 31, 1985 balance sheet in their 1985 Hollett Annual Report to shareholders.

INSTRUCTIONS:

1. Can the auditor consent to Hollett recording the transaction, as outlined above, effective, December 31, 1985?
2. What disclosures should be made relative to the above transaction in Hollett's 1985 Annual Report?
3. Should Adam's 1985 operating results be included in Hollett's 1985 column of their 1986 comparative income statements?

D. Hollett Company (a calendar year company) incurred legal and professional fees of $50,000 (this amount is material) during the calendar year ended 1985 in connection with proposed acquisitions which were each properly accountable for as pooling of interests. One of the two deals was consummated during 1985 and the other fell through, with no expectation of a future potential consummation.

INSTRUCTIONS:

1. With respect to the consummated deal, are the legal and professional fees related to this deal a proper period cost of Hollett in 1985?
2. With respect to the deal which fell through -- may the company defer these expenses since a benefit was derived, and offset against a future unrelated acquisition?

E. Hollett Company merged with Adam Company in what is clearly (per the auditor's review) a "pooling transaction" on December 31, 1985. Because Adam had a very poor year in 1985 (its initial year), and the market value of the stock given by Hollett is equal to book value of Adam at the date of consummation (hence no goodwill to be recorded), Hollett has asked that we consider approving a purchase recording of the transaction.

INSTRUCTIONS:

Would you permit purchase treatment as discussed above -- why or why not?

F. Hollett Company proposes to purchase the net assets (fair market value of $100,000) of Adam for the following alternative amounts of consideration:

a. $125,000 of cash.

b. $125,000 of registered stock (fair market value at consummation of transaction).

c. $95,000 of cash.

d. $105,000 of unregistered stock (fair market value at consummation of transaction) with guaranteed "piggyback" registration rights within the subsequent three years.

INSTRUCTIONS:

What amount of goodwill, if any, would be recorded for each of the above alternatives, and why?

G. Hollett Company proposes to acquire the net assets of Adam company in what is clearly a "purchase transaction." In connection therewith the auditor performed an audit of Adam for Hollett, and rendered a bill to Hollett for $35,000 (such amount is material to Hollett's operating results). Hollett has asked the auditor whether this $35,000 and other indirect and general costs relative to the transaction should be capitalized or expensed.

INSTRUCTIONS:

As the auditor, how would you respond to Hollett's inquiry and why?

H. Hollett Company proposes to merge with Adam Company on May 31, 1985. Hollett will, for all the issued and outstanding common shares of Adam, give 10,000 registered common shares (market value of $10 per share) plus $300,000 at date of consummation, plus –

Situation 1 –– An additional 10,000 shares if Adam is able to secure a proposed $2,000,000 deal with Simpson Photo. Such contract could not be "landed" before June of 1986.

Situation 2 –– An additional 10,000 shares in May of 1986 if Adam is able to achieve a net income of $25,000 in calendar year 1985. Adam's net income for calendar 1984 was $20,000, and unaudited results for the 5 months ended May 31, 1985 report $12,500 net income.

INSTRUCTIONS:

1. Should each of the respective situations be recorded as "poolings" or "purchases?"
2. In each situation above, additional shares might be due to the seller under certain circumstances –– what are these shares called and how are they accounted for, in each of the two cases?

I. Hollett Company proposes to acquire the net assets (FMV = $1,000,000) of Adam for $3,000,000 in what is clearly a purchase transaction. The $2,000,000 premium is being paid primarily because of a significant 10 year aircraft contract just secured by Adam. Hollett has asked that you (the auditor) consider either:

1. The adoption of a 40-year life for amortizing the premium; with a subsequent review of this life at the expiration of the aircraft contract (which has no renewal option), or
2. A charge to Retained Earnings for the premium at the date of consummation.

INSTRUCTIONS:

1. How would you respond to the Company's first suggestion?
2. How would you respond to the Company's second suggestion?

J. Hollett Company proposes to acquire the net assets of Adam Company for cash in

June of 1985. Both companies report a calendar year.

1. What portion, if any, of Adam's operating results will be included in Hollett's 1985 operating statement?
2. Should the 1984 column in Adam's 1985 comparative Annual Report show the combined results of their operations?
3. What financial statement disclosure in connection with the above acquisition would you suggest to your client?

13-11 Boston Corporation

Boston Corporation is involved in a number of real estate ventures. The company has decided to diversify its geographical real estate risk by purchasing the common stock of other real estate investment trusts that have substantial holdings in areas of the United States not covered by the Boston Corporation. In this way company management felt they could avoid the cyclical nature of the business without having to employ company resources to become familiar with and buy real estate in all parts of the country. They would rely on the expertise of other prominent companies to help them diversify their risk.

In 1981, the company began to purchase the stock of Penway Developers and had accumulated 15% of the outstanding stock by the end of the year. Penway was extremely successful and as a result the company purchased an additional 10% of their outstanding stock in 1982. The total cost of their investment at the end of their fiscal year, December 31, 1982, was $1,200,000.

Starting in 1983 and continuing through 1984, Penway began to experience financial problems. The combined losses for the two years was $3,600,000.

In 1985 Boston Corporation was informed that Penway had additional losses, which are expected to be $2,400,000. The company is wondering how this additional loss should be reported and will impact the value of their investment?

INSTRUCTIONS:

1. What method should the company have used to record their investment in Penway in 1981?
2. What method should the company have used to record their investment in Penway in 1982? How should this method be implemented?
3. Distinguish between the cost and equity methods of accounting for long-term investments in stocks subsequent to the date of acquisition.
4. Assume that the investment account according to the equity method was $1,200,000 at the end of 1982. What would be the value of the investment at the end of 1984?
5. Assuming that Boston Corporation is liable for the obligations of Penway, what type of entry would be made at the time that the loss in 1985 is reported?
6. Assuming that Boston Corporation is not liable for the obligations of Penway, what type of entry should be made at the time that the loss in 1985 is reported? Would your answer change if it was highly probable that Penway will be profitable in 1986?

13-12 Temporary Investments

When a company experiences excess cash balances they normally invest the idle funds until they are needed. In order for these investments to be classified as current assets, they must be readily marketable and intended to be converted into cash within an operating cycle or a year, whichever is longer.

In order to provide useful information, the reported value of the temporary investments on the balance sheet should provide the users of financial statements with an indication of the resources that will be available for use in the future. The most useful information is the amount of cash that will be available in the future when the investments are sold. Temporary investments are unlike most other assets in that an objectively determined value is available in the securities market on a day to day basis. The question is what method should be used to value temporary investments.

The accounting for temporary investments was studied by the Financial Accounting Standards Board in 1973 and 1974. This was a period in which stock prices had declined substantially from previous levels and then made a partial recovery. The fall and rise in stock prices during this period had two effects on the reporting for temporary investments:

a. Many companies did not write down their investments to reflect the substantial loss in value. Their costs were above the current market value of those securities.

b. The companies that did write down the value of their investments when the market was at a low point, did not write the value back up when the market recovered. Consequently, the companies were carrying their investments at a value below both their cost and current market.

The volatility of the stock market continues to cause valuation problems for temporary investments. The valuation is to provide useful information.

INSTRUCTIONS:

1. What are the three alternative methods for reporting temporary investments? What are their pros and cons?
2. Did the FASB follow one of these methods? If not, how does FASB 12 differ?
3. Is FASB 12 consistent with the valuation of other current assets? Explain.

13-13 Leather Luggage Company

The president of Leather Luggage Co. is concerned about a proposed accounting change related to investments in marketable securities. The proposal is that all marketable securities be presented at market value on the balance sheet and the changes that occur in market value be reflected in income in the current period. The president agrees that market value on the balance sheet may be more useful to the investor, but he sees no reason why changes in market value should be reflected in income of the current year. Teresa Chavez, controller of Leather Luggage Co., is also unhappy about the proposal and has recommended the following alternatives.

"Recognize realized gains and losses from changes in market value in income, and report unrealized gains and losses in a special balance sheet account on the equity side of the balance sheet."

"Report realized and unrealized gains and losses from market value changes in a statement separate from the income statement or as direct charges and credits to a stockholders' equity account."

"Recognize gains and losses from changes in market value in

income based on long-term yield; for example, use the past
performance of the enterprise over several years (a 10-year
period has been suggested) to determine an average annual rate of
yield because of an increase in value."

These recommendations seem more reasonable to the president of Leather Luggage
Co.

INSTRUCTIONS:

1. Is the use of a market value or fair value basis of accounting for all
marketable securities a desirable and feasible practice? Discuss.
2. Do you believe the president is correct in stating that one of the
alternatives is a better approach to recognition of income in
accounting for marketable securities? Why?

CHAPTER 14

REVENUE RECOGNITION

14-1 Gerscke Enterprises

Gerscke Enterprises, a trucking concern, is considering a public offering of its stock and is carefully examining its financial statements to insure their accuracy and completeness. To determine whether its statements compare favorable to other motor carriers, Gerske's controller is reviewing the financial statements of the competitors. For the most part, they are the same as their functions are practically identical. For example, all the companies appear to be in one of a combination of three types of service.

Pick-up service is the act of picking up the customer's goods (freight) and transporting it to the carrier's terminal (that is, usually within a city or surrounding area).

Line haul service is the act of transporting the customer's goods between carrier terminals (that is, from city to city).

Delivery service is the act of delivering the customer's goods from the terminal to the point of destination (that is, usually within a city or surrounding area).

The controller however in reviewing the revenue recognition methods of its competitors has found the following:

A. Recognize revenue on date freight is picked up.

1. Treatment of costs not disclosed.	9
2. Anticipated costs accrued.	1
3. Costs charged to period incurred.	4
	$\overline{14}$

B. Recognize revenue at date of delivery.   5

C. Recognize revenue on percentage of completion basis $\frac{4}{\underline{\overline{23}}}$

Gerscke Enterprise falls into the second category; that is, it recognizes revenue at the date of delivery.

INSTRUCTIONS:

1. What is revenue? How does its definition relate to the revenue-expense and asset-liability approaches to the determination and definition of accounting income?
2. Distinguish between recognition and realization.
3. What criteria are used for revenue recognition?
4. In general, when can sales and service revenue be recognized?
5. When is revenue conventionally recognized? What conditions should exist for the recognition at date of sale of all or part of the revenue and income of any sale transaction?
6. If you are the controller of Gerscke and considering a public offering, would you consider changing your revenue recognition method? Discuss.

14-2 Real Estate Development, Inc.

Following is a series of real estate transactions consumated by Real Estate Development, Inc. (REDI) during 1985.

A. REDI acquired land and acted as the prime contractor for the construction of an apartment complex on Lake Shore Drive in Chicago. Total land and construction costs to REDI are $3,200,000. Charles Whiggly, a local investor, signs a contract for $3,600,000 on May 1, 1985, makes a down payment of $900,000, and agrees to pay $350,000 a year for 15 years. REDI retains an option to repurchase the complex until May 2, 1995, and guarantees Whiggly the return of the down payment of $900,000, but not the annual payments of $350,000, upon the exercise of the option. The option is included in the contract because Whiggly's financial condition is not highly regarded.

REQUIRED:
INSTRUCTIONS:

How and when should revenue and profit from this transaction be recognized by REDI? Discuss fully. What criteria should be used to make this determination?

B. REDI purchased a 2,000-acre swamp in southern Georgia for $100,000 and has begun an intensified hard-sell marketing program in several northern states. The development is divided into 2,000 one-acre lots having retail prices of $1,500 to $5,000. REDI promises to drain the acreage and make such improvements as access roads, water supply, sewage treatment plant, two lakes, and a club house when sufficient cash is generated. Buyers must make a down payment of $200 upon signing the purchase agreement and promise to pay the balance in 60 equal monthly payments plus interest at 1 1/2% a month on the unpaid balance. During the first year 560 contracts were issued, of which 308 are still in force at year end.

INSTRUCTIONS:

How do you recommend that the company account for the revenues from the development project?

C. In the spring of 1985, REDI had completed an apartment complex near Detroit at a cost of $750,000. In July, REDI was able to sell the property to Edsel Motor Industries for a contract price of $875,000. The terms of the purchase agreement require Edsel Motor to make a down payment of $105,000 and annual payments to REDI of $55,940 (includes a 6% interest factor) for the next 30 years.

INSTRUCTIONS:

1. How and when should revenue and profit be recognized by REDI? Discuss fully.
2. Would you answer change if the down payment was $250,000 with the balance payable over 30 years at a 6% rate of interest?

D. REDI purchased an 18-hole operating golf course near Orlando, Florida for $8,000,000 on September 5, 1984. It planned to reduce this to a 9-hole golf course and sell the remaining acreage as half-acre lots, fully developed exclusive of homes. By February 10, 1985 the improvements (roads, sewers, water, and other amenities) are completed and in place; marketing of the 600 lots at $40,000 each is then begun. No cancellation privileges are granted to the buyers, and down payments of $8,000 per lot are required. For the first year, collections have continued for 96% of the contracts sold.

INSTRUCTIONS:

At what point should sales be recognized and under what accounting method should revenue and profit be recognized?

14-3 Today's Youth[*]

Today's Youth is a monthly magazine that has been on the market for eighteen months. It presently has a circulation of 1.2 million copies. Currently negotiations are underway to obtain a bank loan in order to update their facilities. They are producing close to capacity and expect to grow at an average of 20% per year over the next three years.

After reviewing the financial statements of Today's Youth, George Biggs the bank loan officer, has indicated that a loan could be offered to Today's Youth only if they could increase their current ratio and decrease their debt to equity ratio to a specified level.

Richard Spiel, the marketing manager of Today's Youth, has devised a plan to meet these requirements. Spiel indicates that an advertising campaign can be initiated to immediately increase their circulation. The potential customers would be contacted after the purchase of another magazine's mailing list. The campaign would include:

1. An offer to subscribe to Today's Youth at 3/4 the normal price.
2. A special offer to all new subscribers to receive the most current world atlas whenever requested at a guaranteed price of $1.00.
3. An unconditional guarantee that any subscriber will receive a full refund if dissatisfied with the magazine.

Although the offer of a full refund is risky, Spiel claims that few people will ask for a refund after receiving half of their subscription issues. Spiel notes that other magazine companies have tried this sales promotion technique and experienced great success. Their average cancellation rate prior to the expiration date was 25%. On the average, each company increased their initial circulation three-fold and in the long run had increased circulation to twice that which existed before the promotion. In addition, 70% of the new subscribers are expected to take advantage of the atlas premium. Spiel feels confident that the increased subscriptions from the advertising campaign will increase the current ratio and decrease the debt to equity ratio.

You are the controller of Today's Youth and must give your opinion of the proposed plan.

---

[*]Adapted from a case prepared by Ann Pumpian.

INSTRUCTIONS:

1. How would you account for the new subscriptions?
2. When should revenue from the new subscriptions be recognized?
3. How would you classify the estimated sales returns stemming from the unconditional guarantee?
4. How should the atlas premium be recorded? Is the estimated premium claim a liability? Explain.
5. Does the proposed plan achieve the goals of increasing the current ratio and decreasing the debt to equity ratio?

14-4 Chief Burger*

Chief Burger is a fast food chain run and managed by independent operators. Franchises are sold to these operators for a fee. Portions of the fee are payable upon signing of the contract and upon opening. Chief Burger incurs costs in recruiting and in starting up the franchises. Only a portion of these costs are incurred before the signing of the contract. Credit risks of potential franchisees are evaluated in the recruiting period. Once operations begin, franchisees are charged a fee for advertising and general services performed by Chief Burger. In addition, they are charged a monthly royalty fee based on their gross sales for that month. To insure that the new franchise starts smoothly, Chief Burger assists each in managing operations for the first six months.

J. P. Burger, who has just been appointed president and chief executive officer by his father, has called in his controller, Howard Sharp, to discuss this month's financial statements. J. P. Burger, who is not an expert in accounting matters, is puzzled over the numbers reported on the financial statements. He is concerned with the low figure reported for revenues from franchise fees. He has received reports from his marketing people on the number of new franchises granted, and they indicate that revenues from franchise fees should be on the upswing.

Data relevant to this situation is as follows:

Financial statements being reviewed are for the first month of 1985.

A franchise fee totals $20,000 (implicit interest is ignored in this case, but realistically the principal amount of the note would include an element of interest).

$5,000 is payable at contract signing.

$15,000 is payable when the restaurant opens (6 months after signing).

---

*Adapted from a case by Dianne Schmitt.

Direct costs incurred by Chief Burger in recruiting the franchisees and providing service before and after opening are $16,000.

$4,000 is incurred prior to signing.

The remainder is incurred at $1,000 per month.

The contract term is 10 years from the date of signing.

Advertising and royalty fees are assessed by Chief Burger and are 5% of the franchisee's sales.

Burger and Sharp are discussing operations for the first month since Burger's appointment. Burger told Sharp that 50 new franchise agreements were signed January 2 and that at $20,000 per agreement revenue should be at least $1,000,000, not the reported $250,000. Sharp replies that the entire franchise fee cannot be reported as revenue this month, only the $5,000 paid at the signing of the contract can be recognized. The $15,000 payable upon opening will be recognized as revenue when Chief Burger has substantially performed all the services required under the contract. Burger counters with the statement that they have in hand a legal document which guarantees payment of the full $20,000 and that the credit of each franchisee is carefully evaluated in the recruiting process so payment of the full amount is virtually assured.

INSTRUCTIONS:

1. Discuss the unique features of franchise agreements. Your discussion should include accounting problems that result from these features.
2. Evaluate Sharp's and Burger's contentions as to when revenue should be recognized in light of generally accepted accounting principles.
3. Evaluate other proposals with respect to the timing of revenue recognition as applied to this case.
4. What disclosures relevant to its franchises are required by Chief Burger in its financial statements?

14-5 Southern Fried Shrimp

Southern Fried Shrimp sells franchises to independent operators throughout the southeastern part of the United States. The contract with the franchisee includes the following provisions:

1. The franchisee is charged an initial fee of $25,000. Of this amount $5,000 is payable when the agreement is signed and a $4,000 noninterest-bearing note is payable at the end of each of the five subsequent years.

2. All of the initial franchise fee collected by Southern Fried Shrimp is to be refunded and the remaining obligation canceled if, for any reason, the franchisee fails to open his franchise.

3. In return for the initial franchise fee Southern Fried Shrimp agrees to (a) assist the franchisee in selecting the location for his business, (b) negotiate the lease for the land, (c) obtain financing and assist with building design, (d) supervise construction, (e) establish accounting and tax records, and (f) provide expert advice over a five-year period relating to such matters as employee and management training, quality control, and promotion.

4. In addition to the initial franchise fee the franchisee is required to pay to Southern Fried Shrimp a monthly fee of 2% of sales for menu planning, recipe innovations, and the privilege of purchasing ingredients from Southern Fried Shrimp at or below prevailing market prices.

Management of Southern Fried Shrimp estimates that the value of the services rendered to the franchisee at the time the contract is signed amounts to at least $5,000. All franchisees to date have opened their locations at the scheduled time and none has defaulted on any of the notes receivable.

The credit ratings of all franchisees would entitle them to borrow at the current interest rate of 10%. The present value of an ordinary annuity of five annual receipts of $4,000 each discounted at 10% is $15,163.

INSTRUCTIONS:

1. Discuss the alternatives that Southern Fried Shrimp might use to account for the initial franchise fee. Evaluate each by applying generally accepted accounting principles to this situation, and give illustrative entries for each alternative.
2. Given the nature of Southern Fried Shrimp's agreement with its franchisees, when should revenue be recognized? Discuss the question of revenue recognition for both the initial franchise fee and the additional monthly fee of 2% of sales and give illustrative entries for both types of revenue.
3. Assuming that Southern Fried Shrimp sells some franchises for $35,000, which includes a charge of $10,000 for the rental of equipment

for its useful life of 10 years, that $15,000 of the fee is payable immediately and the balance is payable on noninterest-bearing notes at $4,000 per year, that no portion of the $10,000 rental payment is refundable in case the franchisee goes out of business, and that title to the equipment remains with the franchisor, what would be the preferable method of accounting for the rental portion of the initial franchise fee? Explain.

14-6 Samson, Inc.

Samson, Inc. has engaged an underwriter and decided on a public offering of common shares. Having reviewed the audited statements for the last five years, the underwriter is interested in taking the company public but has said he would not do so unless earnings for the current six months are audited and equal at least $1.00 per share.

Samson has basically two lines of business. It manufactures a large peripheral computer equipment device, which may be either leased or purchased, and it provides computer maintenance services, either on an individual transaction or contract basis. In addition, the equipment division sells computer tapes and drives. The controller is in the process of finalizing the accounts for the six-month period and has prepared the following analysis for discussion:

	Earnings Per Share
Before giving effect to the unrecorded transactions discussed below:	
Equipment sales and leases.	.47
Maintenance.	.43
Unrecorded transactions:	
Sale to Argonne of machines on which installation has been delayed.	.05
Sale to Rotor of machines with maintenance contract.	.05
Sale to Fast-Track of computer tapes with return privilege.	.03
Construction of special machine for Specialty, Inc. (75% complete).	.04
Maintenance contract with Norbert.	.03
Sale of building to Wendell, Inc., a 50% owned subsidiary.	.02
	$1.12

A description of the unrecorded transactions appears below.

Argonne

Samson's normal policy is to sell its machines on an installed basis under a warranty against defects for ninety days after installation. Machines are sold on a FOB shipping point basis, and installation is contracted out to an unrelated party, who assumes all risks in connection with installation. As Samson has been in business for many years, it can reliably predict costs that will be incurred under warranties, so an accrual is made monthly for these costs. In any event, since the machines are installed shortly after delivery and the warranty period is short, there is normally sufficient time before the audit is complete to thoroughly test the warranty reserve.

Two months ago, Samson completed and shipped to Argonne a large order of machines, the largest single contract Samson ever had. Installation has been delayed, however, because of a strike at Argonne. In fact, the machines are sitting in crates, exposed to the elements, on Argonne's unloading dock and have not been taken into the plant, much less installed.

Rotor

Samson sold a large order of machines to Rotor in a package arrangement under which Samson agreed to maintain the machines in working order for a five-year period. While this arrangement was somewhat unusual for Samson, the profit potential was high, and Samson's estimate of the future maintenance cost was relatively minimal (perhaps $.01 per share).

Fast Track

Although Samson generally sells its tape to the ultimate user, to expand its tape business it sold a large order of tapes to Fast Track, a business supply house. Fast Track was a bit reluctant to purchase such a large order but did so on the tacit understanding that Samson would take any unsold tapes back at some future date if so requested. Samson management anticipates no problem on resale.

Specialty, Inc.

Samson is building a special, gigantic machine for Specialty under a long-term contract that should take nine months to complete. Specialty has advanced a 5% down payment. This special purpose machine, 75% complete at June 30, has been constructed under a firm purchase order. Although Samson has not built a machine like it before, it is based on standard models generally sold by Samson. Samson estimates that at this stage, earnings on a percentage basis would be $.04 per share.

Norbert

Samson entered into a one-year maintenance contract on its machines with Norbert, which paid the full cost in advance. Samson regularly provides these services on its machines and can readily estimate future costs. The estimated net income on this contract is $.03 per share.

Wendell, Inc.

Samson has moved out of its old building, which was almost fully depreciated, into newly constructed quarters. Wendell, Inc., a 50% owned subsidiary, has purchased the building with long-term notes at prime interest rates due in annual installments of principal and interest over ten years. Wendell, Inc. intends to lease the building to third parties at a profit.

INSTRUCTIONS:

1. You are the president of Samson. Together with the controller, prepare to discuss the merits of revenue recognition with your auditors in each of these situations. Remember, you need $1.00 per share to complete the underwriting.

2. You are the auditor on the Samson engagement. The controller has given you the above analysis and asked that you and the engagement partner prepare to discuss the merits of revenue recognition in each of these situations with Samson's president.

14-7 Video Station

Video Station Company has developed a video tape library that is continually being updated and further developed. These tapes can be used in connection with several hundred integrated training courses. Video Tape Company rents access to the tape library for a minimum annual fee, plus additional charges for usage above the minimum.

The company provides for the notification to customers of changes to be made to the present library. They also agree to make specialists available to consult with customers who may be having a problem with a training course. Finally they propose that in the future conferences, seminars, and newsletters will be provided to customers free of charge.

Video Station Company proposed that 50% of the profit contribution (defined as total contract revenues less commissions and estimated royalties and servicing costs, all discounted at appropriate interest rates) be recognized at the date the contract is signed and that the remaining 50% be recognized straight-line over the life of the contract.

The principal reasons for proposing this accounting were:

1. The AICPA Motion Picture Films Guide and FASB 53 applied to Video Station Company.

2. The uncertainties with respect to collection of revenues and determination of related costs (as contemplated in the Motion Picture Films Guide and FASB 53) had been substantially removed.

3. The modified operating method (in which profit contribution is recognized as assets are used) did not properly portray current economic conditions. This was especially aggravated when the Company's business made a dramatic swing from sale to rental.

4. The modified operating method did not recognize any contribution by the marketing effort. Such a method resulted in losses at and before rental contract signing.

INSTRUCTIONS:

1. What other alternative might be employed for revenue recognition?
2. What do you believe should be done in this case?

14-8 Modern Investment Services, Inc.

Modern Investment Services Inc. is a relatively new company engaged in servicing loans on mobile homes and home remodeling. By serving as the financing intermediary between the purchaser or home remodeler and a bank, Modern received income from the discounting of the customer notes and insurance commissions. A typical financing example is presented below to facilitate further discussion of the problem.

Example: Assume a customer purchases a mobile home priced at $9,800 and makes a cash down payment of $1,000. Insurance premiums aggregating $1,200 are also financed, making the total principal of the note $10,000. The bank rate to the customer is 7.5% add-on, and the discount rate to Modern is 5.75% add-on.

Cash price	$ 9,800
Down payment	1,000
Unpaid balance	$ 8,800
Insurance premiums:	
Physical damage (five years)	600
Credit life (term of loan)	600
Principal balance	$10,000
Finance charge (7.5% x 10 x $10M)	7,500
Total contract	$17,500

```
Modern's income
   Finance fee (1.75% x 10 x $10M)                          $ 1,750
   Insurance commissions:
      Physical damage (37.5% x $600)                            225
      Credit life (52% x $600)                                  312
                                                             $ 2,287


Dealer participation
   Finance (.5% x 10 x $10M)                                $    500
   Insurance:
      Physical damage (25% of $600)                             150
      Credit life (35% of $600)                                 210
   Credit risk insurance cost
      .80 (.75% x 10 x $10M)                                    600
                                                             $ 1,460

Net to Modern                                                $    827
```

At this point it should be stated that the $827 reflected in the foregoing illustration is received in cash from the lender when the contract is closed. Assuming that the bank's customer makes his payments as prescribed until contract maturity (in this case 10 years), Modern has no further obligations and has fulfilled all of its services and incurred all attendant costs at the contract closing date. If the note becomes delinquent, however, and if preliminary collection efforts by the lender have been to no avail, then Modern is obligated to commence its own collection procedures. This, of course, could necessitate the maintenance of a collection department. Therefore, on a portion of the contracts for which Modern has already received and reported fee income, additional expenses will be incurred in future periods.

In addition to the possibility of future expenses, there are two instances whereby a portion of the fees and commissions already received may have to be refunded to the applicable lender or insurance carrier. First, should the mobile home purchaser prepay his or her note prior to the original contract maturity date, the unearned portion of the finance participation must be returned to the lender. Secondly, should a note subsequently be declared in default thereby resulting in repossession of the mobile home, a portion of the finance fee must again be refunded. The effect in this instance is more severe, however, since the refund is calculated on a pro rata basis.

The percentage of fees refundable varies considerably and is dependent on the following three factors:

1. The reason for premature termination of the loan-voluntary customer prepayment or repossession.
2. The original term of the loan.
3. The year in which payoff occurs.

Modern's management is aggressive and eager to report high income as quickly as possible for their young company. Inasmuch as the income is generally received in cash from the lender upon closing of the contract, the entire amount of the fee is reported as income when received.

1. How would you justify the company's accounting for their service fee income?
2. What other alternatives exist for the accounting for these types of contracts?
3. Which do you feel is the most appropriate accounting method?

14-9 Inexco Oil Company

Following are exerpts from Inexco Oil Company's 1983 annual report:

"Oil and gas properties are accounted for using the full-cost method which provides for the capitalization of all acquisition, exploration and development costs, including nonproductive costs. The costs are amortized on the future gross revenue method by (a) computing an amortization rate by dividing oil and gas sales during each quarter by the sum of current sales and estimated future revenues (both net of windfall profit tax) from proved oil and gas reserves (based on current prices), and (b) applying such rate to the total amortized cost of oil and gas properties, including estimated future development and abandonment costs.

Estimates of Inexco's proved oil and gas reserves and related valuations, as shown in the following tables, were developed pursuant to Statement No. 69 based on existing economic and operating conditions. Substantially all of Inexco's reserves are located in the United States. A substantial portion of the estimates were prepared by Miller and Lents, Ltd., independent petroleum engineers.

Estimated future net cash flow from production or proved reserves and the discounted amount (discounted estimated future net cash flow less discounted estimated future income taxes, or Standardized Measure) were determined by (a) applying prices received at year-end (increased by fixed and determinable contract escalations of gas prices) to the estimated future annual production of proved reserves reduced by (b) estimated future development, abandonment and production costs without consideration of inflation, (c) estimated future income taxes and (d) a discount factor based on an annual rate of 10%.

Future income taxes were determined by applying the statutory income tax rate to the difference between (a) the future pretax cash flow related to proved reserves and (b) deductions of the tax basis in proved properties including net operating loss, depletion and investment tax credit carryovers."

Analysis of Changes in Proved Reserves

	Oil (Thousands of Barrels)		Gas (Million Cubic Feet)	
	1983	1982	1983	1982
Proved Reserves --				
Balance, beginning of year	11,863	9,831	309,442	273,915
Revisions to reserves proved in prior years	1.785	2,671	12,826	145
	13,648	12,502	322,268	274,060
New field discoveries and extensions	1,190	1,715	49,453	58,690
Sales of reserves in place	(190)	-	(8,853)	-
Production	(2,194)	(2,354)	(23,134)	(23,308)
Balance, End of Year	12,454	11,863	339,734	309,442
Proved Developed Reserves --				
Beginning of Year	11,863	9,722	241,624	196,208
End of Year	12,454	11,863	271,913	241,624

Standardized Measures of Discounted Future Net Cash Flow Relating to Proved Oil and Gas Reserves

	December 31	
	1983	1982
	(In Millions)	
Future gross revenue	$1,833.2	$1,837.8
Future production costs --		
Lease operating expenses	(289.1)	(292.9)
Windfall profit tax	(29.3)	(41.7)
Future development and abandonment costs	(11.4)	(14.1)
Future net cash flow before income taxes	1,504.3	1,489.1
Discount for estimated timing of future net cash flows at 10% per annum	(675.6)	(698.3)
Present value of future pretax net cash flow	827.8	790.8
Future income taxes, discounted at 10% per annum	(295.3)	(258.3)
Standardized measure of discounted future net cash flow relating to proved oil and gas reserves	$ 532.5	$ 532.5

INSTRUCTIONS:

1. Describe the current acceptable method for recognizing revenue in the oil and gas industry.
2. How does this method differ from Reserve Recognition Accounting (RRA)?
3. What are the arguments for and against using some form of discovery basis accounting in the extractive industry?

14-10 Satellite Systems Corporation

In 1984 Satellite Systems Corporation became involved with the U.S. Military's "Star Wars" System research project. The company had been involved in the development and production of communication satellites since the early 1970's. The company had experienced rather erratic earnings in their first five years of operation, but since then have experienced continued growth in sales and profits. Most of their growth and stability resulted from a standing order to produce three satellites a year for a consortium of Western governments. Although each satellite takes over a year to complete, the fact that the standing order exists enables them to plan and utilize a stable work force and manufacturing process.

The company receives a down payment at the start of production for each satellite and then six quarterly payments prior to the final payment upon completion. Because of the regularity of the satellite orders, the company has always recognized sales at the time that the satellites were actually delivered.

However, the new Star Wars contract is different. It appears to be a one time contract to build two military satellites over the next three years. The price is to be $10 million each and the estimated costs are $8 million. The higher than average markup involved provides a cushion for what company executives see as high risk associated with potential cost overruns.

The government will provide a 10% down payment at the start of the project, additional payments of 30% at the end of each year and end of the project. The company expects to incur a high proportion of their costs at the start of the project with a lessening degree of cost as the satellites near completion.

Additional risk exists in that the Star Wars System may be cancelled at the end of any fiscal year. Congress may cut off the appropriation for the project prior to the 1988 delivery date. The government is liable only for the payments promised for the current fiscal year.

The president of the company is concerned with how the accounting for the project might be recorded. If they wait for the completion to recognize revenue their earnings may again become volatile. If they don't wait and Congress cancels the appropriation, then they will have even more volatile earnings. This may result from possibly recognizing the revenue in one year and then reversing it in the next.

INSTRUCTIONS:

1. What are the two basic methods of accounting for long-term construction contracts? Indicate the circumstances that determine when one of these methods should be used.
2. For what reasons should the percentage-of-completion method be used over the completed-contract method whenever possible?
3. What methods are used in practice to determine the extent of progress toward completion? Identify some "input measures" and some "output measures" that might be used to determine the extent of progress.
4. What are the two types of losses that can become evident in accounting for long-term contracts? What is the nature of each type of loss? How is each type accounted for?
5. What accounting recommendation, if any, would you make to the company? Why?

CHAPTER 15

ACCOUNTING FOR INCOME TAXES

15-1 Let the Tax Follow the Income

Business income is generally subject to federal and state income taxes. In computing income taxes, businesses must complete tax returns including a statement showing the amount of income subject to tax. In general, the form and content of the tax return income statement are similar to the form and content of the accounting income statement. Taxable income in the tax return, however, is computed in accordance with prescribed tax regulations and rules, while accounting income is measured in accordance with generally accepted accounting principles. And, because the basic objectives of measuring taxable income are different from the objectives of measuring accounting income, tax rules are frequently different from accounting principles. Therefore, differences between taxable income and accounting income exist. The differences between taxable income and accounting income give rise to tax differences, some of which must be recognized in the accounting records and in the resultant financial statements.

Accountants generally view the income tax as an expense that should be matched with the income to which it relates. The process of associating income tax expense with related income is known as tax allocation. Income tax allocation is an integral part of generally accepted accounting principles. The application of intraperiod tax allocation (within a period) and interperiod tax allocation (among periods) are both required. Both intraperiod and interperiod tax allocations are applications of the concept, "Let the tax follow the income."

INSTRUCTIONS:

1. Explain the need for intraperiod tax allocation.

2. Accountants who favor interperiod tax allocation argue that income taxes are an expense rather than a distribution of earnings. Explain the significance of this argument. Do not

explain the definitions of expense or distribution of earnings.

3. Indicate and explain whether each of the following
   independent situations should be treated as a timing difference
   or a permanent difference.

   a. Estimated warranty costs (covering a three-year warranty)
      are expensed for accounting purposes at the time of sale but
      deducted for income tax purposes when incurred.

   b. Depreciation for accounting and income tax purposes differs
      because of different bases of carrying the related property.
      The different bases are a result of a business combination
      treated as a purchase for accounting purposes and as a tax-free
      exchange for income tax purposes.

   c. A company properly uses the equity method to account for
      its 30% investment in another company. The investee pays
      dividends that are about 10% of its annual earnings.

4. Discuss the nature of the deferred income tax accounts and
   possible classifications in a company's statement of financial
   position.

15-2 Personal Financial Statements

Enclosed are a series of letters discussing the accounting treatment of "estimated income taxes on the excess of estimated current values of assets over their tax bases" in the statement of financial condition related to personal financial statements.

Recently the AICPA through its Accounting Standards Executive Committee issued a Statement of Position on Personal Financial Statements in which it recommended that personal financial statements be reported on a current value basis. A question arose as to how the tax effect related to the increase in value should be reported. Their recommendation was that:

"A provision should be made for estimated income taxes on the excess of current values of assets over their tax bases, including consideration of negative tax bases of tax shelters, if any. That excess should be computed as if the current values of the assets had been realized on the statement date, and the provision for estimated income taxes on that amount should be computed using tax laws and operations of tax laws in effect on the statement date, considering recapture provisions and available carryovers. The provision should be shown as one amount subtracted from total gross assets."

The first letter is as follows:

December 29, 1980

To the Committee on
Personal Financial Statements

Steve Rubin and I have telephoned available committee members concerning the placement of "estimated income taxes on the excess of estimated current values of assets over their tax bases" in the statement of financial condition, but no clear choice has emerged. At its recent meeting, the committee decided to place the item as a separate section between liabilities and net worth. In contrast, I believe it is essential to place the item as a deduction from total gross assets, and our chair, Marlin Alt, and several committee members believe my recommendation has merit.

The literature discusses three possible approaches to interperiod income tax allocation:

- Cost savings
- Liability
- Net of tax

Cost Savings Approach

The cost savings approach is used to support present income tax allocation by businesses under APB Opinion 11. The idea is that an enterprise saved tax money by taking larger deductions for tax purposes than corresponding expenses in the income statement. The allocation spreads the savings to the income statement over the periods benefitted. The resulting balance sheet credit is not a liability, but a cost savings awaiting transportation from the balance sheet to the income statement. The cost savings notion is rapidly becoming discredited. For example, APB Opinion 23 introduces indefinite reversal criteria, which does not fit with the idea of spreading a cost savings. Also, in the exposure draft of the proposed Statement of Financial Accounting Concepts on elements of financial statements, the FASB states that the definitions accommodate the liability and net of tax approaches but not the cost savings approach.

Also, the cost savings approach is basically an income statement approach, not suitable for personal financial statements. Our committee does not consider the item to represent past cost savings awaiting future income statement recognition.

Liability Approach

At its recent meeting, the committee decided explicitly that the estimated taxes are not a liability, that the person does not now owe taxes related to them, and would not pay them in the future in the absence of sale or other disposal of the assets in a year or years in which he has taxable income including the gain on the sale.

To buttress its view that it is not a liability, our committee continued to support the computation on the worst case basis, as if all assets had been sold or otherwise disposed of at the date of the statement of financial condition. Were it a liability, the computation should be on the most probable basis rather than on the worst case basis.

Net of Tax Approach

The only remaining approach discussed in the literature is the net of tax approach. So, by process of elimination, our approach is either the net of tax approach or some other approach not yet conceived of, no less considered. I know of no such other approach. However, there are more positive reasons to conclude ours is the net of tax approach. According to AICPA Accounting Research Study 9, Interperiod Allocation of Corporate Income Taxes, (page 52):

> "The underlying assumption [of the net of tax approach is that taxability and tax deductibility are factors in the valuation of assets and liabilities and the amount is measured by the tax effect."

The study goes on to reject the net of tax approach since it is based on values of assets whereas businesses present their assets at unamortized cost.

That objection obviously does not pertain to personal financial statements stated at current value. The whole reason our committee insists the statement of financial condition contain a tax association amount is to warn users, including the person himself, that taxes may have to be paid when the current values are realized, and perhaps only the net amount would be available. The net of tax approach, with the credit deducted from total gross assets is suited for our purpose.

However, how we decide this issue now will likely be the treatment that will be used in personal financial statements for many years to come. Accountants should not be saddled with the complaint by users that personal financial statements are esoteric products of a mysterious art, the complaint that would be lodged if we present an appendage between liabilities and net worth. That treatment might also give the impression that it is a pseudoliability.

Deducting the amount from the total gross assets will portray and impress what we intend: that uncle has to be paid when, as, and if the current values are realized.

I believe this issue is sufficiently important to ask members of the committee to write their views to Steve Rubin with copies to those on the correspondence distribution list.

Sincerely yours,

Paul Rosenfield
Director
Accounting Standards

PR:j-rg

cc: J. T. Ball

The second letter is as follows:

January 8, 1981

To the Accounting Standards
  Executive Committee

The enclosed marked draft indicates changes approved by the Personal Financial
Statements Committee to the May 29, 1980 proposed accounting section of the
personal financial statements guide revision following discussions it had with the
FASB staff. These changes will be discussed at the January AcSEC meeting. The
following highlights the major changes.

Names of Financial Statements

The statement of assets and liabilities will be called the statement of financial
condition. The statement of changes in net assets will be called the statement of
changes in net worth.

Unrealized Appreciation and Related Income Taxes

Estimated income taxes on unrealized appreciation of net assets will be called
estimated income taxes on the excess of estimated current values of assets over their
tax bases. The provision will be shown as one amount deducted from total gross
assets. (See Paul Rosenfield's December 29, 1980 letter attached.) Four of the 12
committee members strongly oppose that presentation. The remaining eight
committee members believe that presentation has considerable merit.

One of the required disclosures will be a note that estimated income taxes on the
excess of estimated current values of assets over their tax bases in the statement of
financial condition will probably differ from the amount of income taxes that might
eventually be paid, because of the timing and method of asset disposal or realization
and the tax laws and operation of tax laws in effect at the time of disposal or
realization.

The guide will point out that significant differences between the current values of
liabilities and their tax bases are rare and seldom result in tax consequences that have
to be accounted for.

Illustrative Financial Statements

Illustrative financial statements have been added as an appendix to the guide.

Accounting Standards Executive Committee
page 2

Computation for Practioners

A simplified illustration will be added as an appendix to demonstrate to practioners how to compute the excess of estimated current values of assets over their tax bases and the related income taxes.

The Next Steps

The Personal Financial Statement Committee intends to resubmit the proposed accounting section to the FASB for review before exposure. After FASB review, the committee will expose the proposed accounting section for comments while it develops compilation and review guidance.

Sincerely,

Marlin P. Alt
Chairman
Personal Financial Statements Committee

mpa/
Enclosures

cc: Personal Financial Statements Committee

The third letter is from the FASB:

January 14, 1981

Mr. Paul Rosenfield
Director, Accounting Standards Division
American Institute of Certified Public Accountants
1211 Avenue of the Americas
New York, NY 10036

Dear Paul:

J.T. Ball, several other members of the FASB staff, and I have discussed your December 29, 1980 letter to the Committee on Personal Financial Statements concerning placement of income taxes on the statement of financial condition of personal financial statements prepared on a current value basis.

We have unanimously concluded that we cannot support the approach proposed in your letter of deducting the "estimated income taxes on the excess of estimated current values of assets over their tax bases" from total gross assets, if a draft of the proposed accounting section recommending that approach is submitted to the FASB.

We do not agree that this item "is not a liability." To the contrary, we believe that it meets the definition of a liability in FASB Concepts Statement No. 3, Elements of Financial Statements of Business Enterprises. The problem is one of measuring the amount of the liability to be recognized, not whether the item is a liability.

We also agree that the net of tax approach could be used but cannot support the variation proposed in your letter that deducts the liability from total gross assets rather than from specific individual assets. Most of the FASB staff contacted regarding this matter agree with the consensus of the Committee on Personal Financial Statements (Committee) that the use of the net of tax method would be confusing to many users of personal financial statements. We can see as many arguments for reducing the net realizable value of appreciated property by liabilities (such as a mortgage) that would have to be paid to realize appreciation as for reducing the net realizable value for tax effect: we favor showing all of those amounts gross rather than as one net number.

If the Committee has concluded not to follow the approach it adopted at our December 15 meeting of placing the estimated income taxes as a separate item between liabilities and net worth with adequate disclosure in the footnotes, we would favor placing the amount in the liability section as the last item. Irrespective of placement, this item would require sufficient explanation by footnote to describe its nature and how the amount was computed.

We would be pleased to discuss this matter further with you or members of the Committee if that would be helpful.

Sincerely,

Tony L. Scott

TLS:370S

cc: Members of the Committee on Personal Financial Statements
     Dennis R. Beresford, Chairman, Accounting Standards Executive Committee
     Steven Rubin, AICPA

The final letter is as follows:

January 19, 1981

To the Accounting Standards
  Executive Committee

Personal Financial Statements File 3830

Tony Scott of the FASB staff sent me the enclosed letter on our draft on personal financial statements, which will be discussed at the AcSEC meeting next week. He states that members of the FASB staff "unanimously concluded that [they] cannot support the approach proposed in [my] letter of deducting the 'estimated income taxes on the excess of estimated current values of assets over their tax bases' from total gross assets," because they "believe that it meets the definition of a liability in FASB Concepts Statement No. 3."

However, the provision for estimated income taxes on the excess of current values of assets over their tax basis does not in my view meet the definition of a liability as that term is defined in SFAC No. 3.

According to paragraph 29 of that Statement:

A liability has three essential characteristics:

(a) It embodies a present duty or responsibility to one or more
    other entities that entails settlement by probable future
    transfer or use of assets at a specified or determinable date,
    on occurrence of a specified event, or on demand,

(b) the duty or responsibility obligates a particular
    enterprise, leaving it little or no discretion to avoid the
    future sacrifice, and

(c) the transaction or other event obligating the
    enterprise has already happened.

The following lead me to my view that it does not meet the definition:

(a) There is no present duty or responsibility to one or more
    other entities that entails settlement by probable future
    transfer or use of assets at a specified or determinable
    date. Income taxes on the excess of estimated current
    values of assets over their tax bases become liabilities
    only when, as, and if the related assets are disposed of
    or otherwise realized.

(b) An individual may avoid future financial sacrifice by giving away the related assets. Similarly, the individual avoids payment of income taxes if he or she dies before the related assets are disposed of or otherwise realized.

(c) No transaction or other event has happened and no condition exists at the financial statement date that obligates an individual to pay income taxes, since he or she has realized no taxable benefit from merely holding the related assets.

The provision for estimated income taxes on the excess of estimated current values of assets over their tax bases more closely meets the criteria of valuation accounts discussed in paragraph 27 of SFAC No. 3: Estimated income taxes on the excess of estimated current values of assets over their tax bases reduce the amounts at which assets are presented in financial statements but are neither assets in their own right nor liabilities.

Further, there is nothing in the net of tax concept that requires a valuation account to be stated piecemeal with each asset. It is not meaningful to use the piecemeal approach in personal financial statements because of the interaction of the various items in taxable income. It is possible that disposing of or otherwise realizing any one asset would not bring taxable income up to zero, while disposing of or otherwise realizing all at once might bring taxable income above zero. Also, the valuation account accumulated depreciation is presented in one amount and not piecemeal for each type of depreciable asset.

Sincerely yours,

Paul Rosenfield
Director
Accounting Standards

PR:en

Enclosure

cc: Personal Financial Statements Committee
Tony Scott

INSTRUCTIONS:

1. Explain the basic issue involved in this controversy.
2. What is the present accounting treatment in accounting for deferred income taxes?
3. Do you believe the method used for determining the amount of deferred income taxes (regardless of where classified) is appropriate?
4. Which of the methods of classifying deferred income taxes do you favor? Justify your position.

15-3 Aetna Life and Casualty

Aetna Life and Casualty is the largest publicly owned insurer in the United States with assets in excess of $40 billion. Its operations include not only property and casualty, but such other areas as life, health and pension markets. In the last five years the company has been actively diversifying, putting substantial monies into several new ventures. Although Aetna had experienced financial difficulty in previous recent years, company executives indicated in their first quarter report for 1982 that the company would "maintain reasonable and improving profits this year."

Some of the financial data for Aetna Life and Casualty for the year 1982 are provided below:

Consolidated Statement of Income
(Millions)

		1982
Revenue:	Previous	$10,654.0
	Net investment and other income	3,510.4
	Total Revenues	14,164.4
Benefits and	Current Fringe Benefits	11,850.8
Expenses:	Operating expenses	1,886.7
	Interest expense	75.4
	Federal income taxes (credits)	
	Current	(10.0)
	Deferred	(135.7)
	Majority interests	6.7
	Total Benefits and Expenses	13,673.9
	Insurance operating earnings	490.5
	International earnings	31.4
Operating Earnings		521.9
Earnings:	Realized Capital Gains (Losses) net of taxes	(94.8)
Net Income		$ 427.1

A portion of footnote number 9 "Federal Income Taxes" is as follows:

Deferred taxes (credits) generated by timing differences were as follows:

	1982
Reserve adjustments	$ 39.4
Special life company deductions	9.1
Deferred policy acquisition costs	11.5
Casualty property underwriting adjustments	(9.9)
Investment income and expenses	10.8
Operating loss carryforwards	(239.2)
Realized capital gains or losses	(12.5)
Investment and foreign tax credits	(0.1)
Tax benefits of operating losses not taken	16.0
Adjustments to prior year's provisions	22.0
Other, net	4.7
Total	$(148.2)

In discussing the recognition of the loss carryforward in the current year, some of the following justifications were provided.

1. Given a fifteen year time span to use the loss carryforward it is virtually certain that it will not be lost.

2. Multi-line insurance companies often may apply operating profits from successful subsidiaries (say a life insurance subsidiary) to other subsidiaries (such as a property and casualty subsidiary).

3. The company can boost taxable income by shifting its property and casualty portfolio away from tax-exempt securities toward the taxable variety, whose higher yields would be tax-sheltered by the carryforwards.

4. When interest rates decline, the selling of property and casualty insurance will become more profitable.

Skeptics, on the other hand, note that

1. Instances in which companies are permitted to anticipate future tax benefits and report them as current income are rare.

2. Losses arising from general economic or industry decline would not normally justify the recognition of future tax benefits in earnings.

3. Although Aetna would increase taxable income by switching its property and casualty portfolio away from tax exempt securities

to taxable securities, the sale of the tax exempt securities (given present market conditions) would result in a loss.

INSTRUCTIONS:

1. What are the general requirements as to when a loss carryforward should be recognized?

2. What appears to be the underlying rationale for the profession's position in this area?

3. Given that the tax law allows the use of loss carryforward for a period of fifteen years, would not any company that will survive not be able to use up the tax losses within a fifteen year period? If so, then should not the carryforward be reported in the current period?

4. In 1982, the company took $239 million into income related to the tax carryforward, an amount accounting for approximately 56% of reported income of $427 million. Do you believe the information presented by Aetna met the requirements of full disclosure?

5. In examining the June 30, 1982 interim report, the tax benefits are displayed on the liability side as negative liabilities. One company executive notes that it was not reported as an asset (future tax benefit) because the amount $144 million was very small in relationship'to all the other asset numbers on the balance sheet. Yet the year end balance sheet displays the tax benefits as an asset of $229.5 million. Where do you believe future tax benefits should be reported?

15-4 Omaha Corp.

The President of Omaha Corp. tried to interpret the company's deferred tax account for the shareholders in the 1985 annual report. Following is an excerpt from the report:

... The required use of deferred taxes has resulted in a serious understatement of our reported earnings. The deferred tax account arises because the new income tax provisions allow us to depreciate our machinery, equipment, and semitrucks at an accelerated rate. Since the accelerated rate will completely depreciate these assets prior to the end of their useful lives, we have chosen to record depreciation for finan-cial statement purposes by use of the straight line method. While the accounting for deferred taxes is somewhat complicated, the understatement of earnings becomes apparent if you refer to our income statement for the year 1985. (See the following pages)

The revenue and expense items represent cash flows either to or from the company that have occurred in 1985 or that will occur in early 1986. The one exception to this statement is deferred taxes which we have deducted in the amount of $10.1 million.

Unlike the other expenses, this $10.1 million will not be paid for an average of ten years. No interest is required to be paid on this amount, but the company is required to show the amount as an expense in 1985 and as a liability for ten years until paid.

We feel that the accounting treatment for this "deferred tax liability" is inconsistent with the accounting for other long term liabilities. Other liabilities without a stated interest rate are to be discounted to reflect the fact that a dollar due in ten years is not worth a dollar today. An obligation to pay $10.1 million in 1996 would not require us to set aside $10.1 million today. In fact, if we were to assume an interest rate of only 6% an investment today of only about one half of that amount would be suffi-cient to accumulate $10.1 million in ten years.

In other words, when a liability is due at some time in the future, simple logic says we should discount the amount to determine what the real liability is today. If that is done in our case, we would deduct substantially less than $10.1 million in determining our 1985 income, and our earnings per share would be materially higher.

Our statement that we will pay the deferred taxes 10 years from now is also quite conservative. There are well known authorities who argue convincingly that the $10.1 million will never be paid as long as the company continues to reinvest in assets. As you might expect reinvestment is critical for the continuation of our business. We have been in operation for over 50 years and plan to continue for at least another 50 years. Our willingness to reinvestment in our asset base has been one of our keys to success. As a result, one might eliminate the entire deferred tax expense from the income statement, since the whole amount may never be paid. . . ."

Omaha Corporation and Subsidiaries
Consolidated Statement of Income
For the Year Ended December 31, 1985
(Dollars in thousands)

	1985
Revenue:	
Net Sales	$35,000
Services	53,900
Net Income from Finance Lease Business	1,200
Net income from 50% Owned Companies	900
Interest Income	1,600
Royalties and Other	1,500
Amortization of Investment Tax Credit	400
	$94,500
Costs and Expenses:	
Cost of Sales	$12,100
Cost of Services	16,000
Selling and Administrative	13,700
Interest Expense	19,600
Minority Interest	300
	$61,700
Net Income Before Taxes	$32,800

```
Provision for Income Taxes:
    Current                                    $ 4,700
    Deferred                                    10,100
    Investment Tax Credit (Deferred)               800
                                               $15,600

Net Income                                     $17,200

Per Share of Common Stock                        $2.61
```

INSTRUCTIONS:

1. What would be the estimated impact on the 1985 financial statement if deferred taxes were discounted assuming an interest rate of 6%? The impact over the next 10 years?
2. Comment on the propriety of discounting deferred income taxes.
3. Comment on the argument that the deferred taxes may never be paid as long as the company continues to reinvest.
4. What would be the impact on the financial statements if the company did stop reinvesting for an extended period of time?
5. How would the partial allocation view handle this problem?

15-5 Subsidy or Stimulant?

Following is a letter mailed by Price Waterhouse & Co. to their clients in November 1971 and a press release issued by the AICPA in December 1971.

November 4, 1971

To our clients:

The accounting profession and the business community are about to be polarized again on an accounting issue that was apparently settled long ago. Present indications are that President Nixon's tax package will include a job development credit against the income taxes of corporations measured by a percentage of their investment in specified assets. Although its name is different, the credit is a revival of the old investment tax credit that was repealed in 1969.

From the time an investment credit was first proposed, the fact that it incorporated two distinct limitations--one based on capital investment and the other on taxes payable -- has generated differences of opinion as to the nature of the credit and its proper accounting. There were some who viewed the credit as a government subsidy against the long-term assets which should be accounted for over the same period as the related assets. There were others who believed it to be a selective tax reduction which Congress intended to use as a stimulant to a section of the economy.

Just as the power to tax involves the power to destroy, the power to ameliorate taxes selectively involves the power to influence the directions in which the economy should go. For example, the contemplated tax package will stimulate consumer expenditures by reductions in the taxes of individuals. It will stimulate the automobile industry by adjustments in excise and import taxes and it will stimulate the capital goods section of our economy by tax credits to taxpayers investing in such goods. Our firm believes, as it has from the very beginning, that when viewed in this light an investment credit is simply a reduction in taxes for those taxpayers who have a part in furthering certain national objectives, particularly when the off-again, on-again nature of this credit is kept in mind.

The advocates of the view that the tax credit is a reduction in the cost of property, however, have renewed their efforts to have the Accounting Principles Board determine there should be only one method of accounting and that should be the "deferral" method. In this they are supported by an indication of a change in attitude by the SEC. The deferral method was the only method permitted by APB Opinion 2 issued in 1962. Because Opinion 2 did not attain the degree of acceptability the Board believed necessary to make it effective, Opinion 4 permitting immediate recognition was issued. Subsequent surveys showed that by far the largest proportion of companies went to the immediate recognition method.

As a firm, we support the view that there should be only one method of accounting for something as simple as an investment tax credit. We deplore the continued controversy that has arisen from the active promotion of differing viewpoints. We believe it would be extremely unfortunate if the accounting profession were to adopt a required form of accounting that again would force a large majority of business taxpayers to reverse their previous accounting practice. Most of all, we believe the presently accepted "flow through" method of current recognition in income to be the proper accounting except in the special circumstances of regulated industries where the effect of the rate-making process should be taken into consideration.

Except in the case of regulated industries the investment credit is both earned and realized by the occurrence of two events: (1) making an investment in newly acquired facilities and (2) the existence of taxable income. The credit realized does not depend on or relate to revenues earned during subsequent periods. Since there is no relation between this element of income tax expense and future revenues, there is no rational and compelling reason for deferral of the investment credit under the matching concept nor is there justification for amortizing it over subsequent accounting periods. It is earned in the same period in which it is realized.

The APB has just issued an exposure draft of a proposed new Opinion on investment tax credits. The terms of this exposure draft are a clear indication that the present Board favors the deferral method. Unless there is a substantial input of views from the business world, the terms of the exposure draft will probably survive.

We believe our clients are entitled to know that, as a firm, we disagree with the accounting proposed in this exposure draft and that the partner of our firm who is a member of the Board intends to vote against any requirement for the use of the deferral method. As long as this credit results in cash in hand in the period it enters into the determination of the final tax bill without restraint for any business purpose that management may elect, and as long as it is clear the the government will use the investment credit as an instrument of short-range fiscal policy, accounting should not obscure its effect on corporate earnings and thus interfere with the government's efforts to create a climate conducive to maximum capital investment.

Statement of the Accounting Principles Board
on Accounting for the Investment Credit
December 9, 1971

The Accounting Principles Board has had to defer its efforts to develop a single uniform method of accounting for the investment credit in view of congressional action permitting taxpayer choice of accounting method of recognizing the benefit of the credit.

The APB had circulated a proposal for public comment with the intent of establishing uniform accounting by year end. This proposal would have required that, for reporting income to shareholders, benefits from the investment credit be spread over the lives of the related assets. This would have ruled out the use of any other method, such as the "flow through" method under which the entire amount of the credit is taken into income in the year in which income taxes are reduced by the credit.

The APB did not discuss further the merits of the accounting methods or the comments received on its proposal, since Congress has stated that no taxpayer shall be required to use any particular method of accounting for the credit in reports subject to the jurisdiction of any federal agency.

The congressional action requires consistency in the use of the accounting method selected, unless the Treasury Department consents to a change. The designation of another agency, the Treasury Department, to approve changes in accounting methods may hamper the APB's efforts to further improve reporting to investors since the APB has recently issued a pronouncement permitting changes in accounting methods only when the new methods are preferable.

The APB unanimously deplores congressional involvement in establishing accounting principles for financial reports to investors, which largely have been the responsibility of the Securities & Exchange Commission and the accounting profession. The APB further deplores congressional endorsement of alternative accounting methods, especially since there has been strong demand by congressmen and others for the elimination of alternative methods which confuse investors.

INSTRUCTIONS:

1. What is the historical background for the two letters presented in this case?
2. Describe the two alternative methods for accounting for investment tax credits and the justification for each.

3. Which method gives the best cash flow for the company? Which method would be preferable or a company?

15-6 American Electric Power Co.

The following court case involved American Electric Power and one of its subsidiaries, Kentucky Power Company. The SEC had certain rules for the amount of debt a public utility company could have in its total capital structure. In this case, questions centered around whether deferred income taxes should be reported as a liability or part of a retained earnings. The AICPA and the SEC had both indicated that a liability presentation was most appropriate.

Excerpts from the case are provided below:

Description of the Companies Involved

American is a registered holding company. The American holding-company system operates an interconnected electric utility system conveying portions of the seven states of Kentucky, Virginia, West Virginia, Indiana, Ohio, Michigan, and Tennessee. At September 30, 1960, the system's consolidated electric utility plant (stated at original cost), less reserves for depreciation, depletion, and amortization totaled some $1,333,000,000. For the 12 months ended September 30, 1960, the system's consolidated electric operating revenues totaled approximately $335,460,000, its consolidated gross income was some $78,851,000, and its consolidated net income for common stock was about $53,963,000.

Kentucky is incorporated under the laws of the Commonwealth of Kentucky and all of its common stock is owned by American. Kentucky is engaged in the purchase, transmission, and distribution of electric power in the eastern section of Kentucky. Its utility assets constitute an integral part of the integrated electric utility system of American. The population in the service area of Kentucky totals approximately 370,000 and it serves some 93,000 customers. At September 30, 1960, Kentucky's electric utility plant (stated at original cost), less reserve for depreciation, totaled some $33,546,000. For the 12 months ended September 30, 1960, Kentucky's electric operating revenues totaled some $15,454,000, its gross income was $2,037,000, and its net income was $1,471,000.

Consolidation of Proceedings

The Division, after a preliminary examination of the application of Kentucky, as amended, under Section 6(b) of the Act, advised us that the balance sheet of Kentucky, as of March 31, 1960, contained an amount of $731,441 identified as "Earned Surplus Restricted for Future Federal Income Taxes"; and that such amount represented the aggregate of the accumulations, as of that date, of balance sheet credits ("accumulated tax reduction") arising from the inclusion in the income statement, as an operating revenue deduction, of items identified as "Provision for Future Federal Income Taxes." The Division, after a preliminary examination of the consolidated balance sheet, as of March 31, 1960, of American and its consolidated subsidiaries, advised us that said consolidated balance sheet contained an accumulated tax reduction, on a consolidated basis, as of that date of $86,976,332 identified as "Earned Surplus Restricted for Future Federal Income Taxes."

The Division indicated, on the basis of its preliminary examination of the financial statements filed with Kentucky's application, that such financial statements of Kentucky and American did not appear to conform with our Statement of Administrative Policy Regarding Balance Sheet Treatment of Credit Equivalent to Reduction in Income Taxes, dated February 29, 1960. In that statement, we discussed the proper treatment of the accumulated credit arising from accounting for reductions in income taxes resulting from deducting costs for income tax purposes at a more rapid rate than for financial statement purposes. We stated that on and after its effective date any financial statement filed with us would be presumed to be misleading or inaccurate: Provided that amounts involved were material, if it designated such accumulated credit as earned surplus (or its equivalent) or in any manner as a part of equity capital, even though such designation was accompanied by words of limitation, such as "restricted" or " appropriated", and even though disclosure was contained in the certificate of the accountant or in footnotes to the statement.

Proposals Regarding Resolution of Issues

Discussions were held between Kentucky and American and the Division with a view to arriving at a mutually acceptable proposal for the disposition of the issues raised in the consolidated proceeding. In such discussions the Division asserted that it could not at this time recommend any disposition which did not involve the filing of supplementary financial statements in a form which, in the view of the division, would eliminate any question which might be raised as to conformity with our Statement of Administrative Policy.

The managements of Kentucky and American were concerned with whether any such supplementary financial statements might affect the terms and conditions which might be imposed with respect to the proposed issuance by Kentucky of its promissory notes and which might adversely affect future financings by American and/or its subsidiaries submitted for our consideration under Sections 6(b) and 7 of the Act. In this connection, officials of American noted that, on the basis of inclusion in the consolidated common stock equity and in total capitalization, including surplus, as of March 31, 1960, of the consolidated accumulated tax reduction of $92,646,873, the system had capitalization ratios consisting of debt of 53.7 percent, preferred stock of 7.6 percent, and common stock equity of 38.7 percent; and that on the basis of exclusion of this item from common stock equity and from total capitalization, including surplus, the respective ratios were 57.7 percent, 8.1 percent, and 34.2 percent. The exclusion of this item, therefore, increased the system's debt ratio by 4.0 percentage points and the preferred stock ratio by 0.5 percentage point, and reduced the common equity ratio by 4.5 percentage points.

American's officials also stated that the 38.7 percent consolidated common equity ratio as of March 31, 1960, which it computed on the basis of inclusion therein of the accumulated tax reduction, was substantially higher than the consolidated common equity ratio, computed on such basis, which the system had in the past generally strived to maintain. It appears that this excess had been occasioned primarily by the fact that American issued and sold, in October 1969, $55,512,000 of additional common stock. American's officials stated it was intended that such consolidated common equity ratio would be substantially reduced from 38.7 percent as a result of normal system debt financing in connection with system construction expenditures effected within the next few years.

For the same reason, they stated, the consolidated common equity ratio, computed without the benefit of the accumulated tax reduction, of 34.2 percent as of March 31, 1960, would necessarily also be substantially reduced after giving effect to the debt financing projected by the system for the next few years.

The officials of American were particularly concerned that, in passing upon future debt or equity financings of its system companies under the Act, we would exclude the accumulated tax reduction from the calculation of common equity ratios and would impose terms and conditions under Section 6(b) or make adverse findings under Section 7(d)(1) which would have the effect of requiring that the common equity ratios of individual system companies or of the system on a consolidated basis exceed, and that the debt ratios be reduced from, the respective ratios which the system has attempted to maintain during the past few years, computed on a basis which included the accumulated tax reduction as a part of common equity and of capitalization, including surplus.

In this connection, American's officials stated that the accumulated tax reduction in the system is expected to grow substantially over the next several years. They testified that if the Commission, by the exclusion of the accumulated tax reduction were in effect to require an increase in common equity and a concomitant decrease in debt, such requirement would result in a substantial increase in the cost of capital and taxes of the American System; that any such increase in cost of capital and taxes would necessarily have an adverse effect on rates charged for its services and would thus impose an unnecessary and unwarranted burden on consumers; and that such a result would be inconsistent with the proper protection of consumers which is one of the primary objectives of the Act.

The Division indicated that it did not believe that any such consequence was intended by, or would result from, the proper application of the provisions of the Statement of Administrative Policy. The Division pointed out that, in our Statement of Administrative Policy, it was indicated in Note 11 thereof that, although we did not intend to consider a company's accumulated tax reduction as a part of common stock equity for analytical purposes, we would nevertheless give consideration to the item as one of a number of relevant factors in appraising the overall financial condition of such company. The Division also correctly pointed out that by our Statement of Administrative Policy we did not intend to and of course could not foreclose rating agencies, financial analysts, investors, and others from regarding the amount of accumulated tax reduction in any manner they deem appropriate for their purposes.

In view of the foregoing, a settlement proposal was developed between the Division and Kentucky and American which the Division is now recommending to us for approval and adoption. The proposal is that (1) supplementary financial statements be filed in the consolidated proceeding which designated the accumulated tax reduction in the manner described below; (2) in any proceeding involving American or any of its system's subsidiary companies under Section 6(b) or 7 of the Act, the Commission will give due weight to the existence of the accumulated tax reduction and its size in determining appropriate capitalization ratios; and (3) so long as the consolidated balance sheet of American and its subsidiary companies or the corporate balance sheet of any public utility subsidiary company of American includes an account, involving a substantial amount, representing an accumulated reduction in Federal income taxes arising from the deduction of accelerated amortization or liberalized depreciation for Federal income tax purposes, the Commission will not impose any terms and conditions under Section 6(b), or make adverse findings under Section 7 of the Act, in respect of capitalization ratios with respect to any proposed financing of the American system where upon completion of the financing:

(a) Common stock equity is not less than 30 percent of total capitalization, including surplus.

(b) Mortgage debt is not in excess of 60 percent of total capitalization, including surplus.

(c) Long-term debt is not in excess of 65 percent of total capitalization, including surplus.

For purposes of these tests:

 (i) The computation of common stock equity, mortgage debt and long-term debt ratios is to be on a system consolidated basis or on a subsidiary corporate basis as is appropriate;

 (ii) The terms "common stock equity" and "total capitalization, including surplus" are not to include any accumulated tax reduction resulting from charges against income as an operating revenue deduction in respect to accelerated amortization or liberalized depreciation for Federal income tax purposes;

(iii) The term "long-term debt" is to include all indebtedness for borrowed money having, at the date of issuance, renewal or the guaranty thereof, a maturity of more than 12 months; and

 (iv) The term "total capitalization, including surplus" is to include long-term debt, the aggregate of the par value of, or stated capital represented by, the outstanding shares of all classes of stock, any premium on stock, and surplus.

The settlement proposal presented to us includes a filing of supplementary financial statements, as at September 30, 1960, in which the accumulated tax reduction is captioned in the corporate balance sheet of Kentucky as "Accumulated Amount Invested in the Business Equivalent to Reduction in Federal Income Taxes Resulting From Accelerated Amortization and Liberalized Depreciation, Which is Recorded as Earned Surplus Restricted for Future Federal Income Taxes in Accounts Maintained Pursuant to State Regulatory Requirements," and in the consolidated balance sheet of American and its consolidated subsidiaries as "Acccumulated Amount Invested in the

Business Equivalent to Reduction in Federal Income Taxes Resulting from Accelerated Amortization and Liberalized Depreciation, Which is Recorded as Earned Surplus Restricted ($94,698,293), or as a Reserve ($6,600,874), for Future Federal Income Taxes in Accounts Maintained Pursuant to State Regulatory Requirements."

We have reviewed the settlement proposal submitted to us and have considered it under the standards of the Act and in light of our Statement of Administrative Policy. We find that the supplementary financial statements do not contravene our Statement of Administrative Policy. It is unnecessary, in view of this finding, for us to consider further the financial statements originally filed with the application of Kentucky under Section 6(b) of the Act.

In appraising the settlement proposal regarding capitalization ratios, with particular reference to the system's consolidated capital structure, we have considered the maximum amount of long-term debt and the minimum amount of common stock equity which American contended the system could issue pursuant to a commitment made by American in a declaration filed with us in 1952, in connection with a financing, as against the respective amounts of securities it could issue under the settlement proposal. Under that commitment long-term debt is limited to a maximum of 60 percent of total capitalization, including surplus, and common stock equity to a minimum of 30 percent thereof.

American estimates, on the basis of its projections as to consolidated capitalization, including surplus, that under the settlement proposal the maximum amount of system debt at the end of 1961, would be $6 million less than that issuable under its 1952 commitment; that at the end of 1965 it would be $24,000,000 less than under the 1952 commitment; and that at the end of 1970, the 2 amounts would be substantially the same.

Accordingly, giving due consideration to the source and the substantial amount of the accumulated tax reductions in American's system companies and having due regard for all of the other circumstances pertaining to the financial condition of the American system, we find that the capitalization ratio tests included in the settlement proposal recommended by the Division are appropriate for that system. Moreover, so long as future financings of American's system companies fall within such limits and the amount of the accumulated tax reduction continues to be substantial, we believe it would be unnecessary for us to impose any terms or conditions under Section 6(b) or to make adverse findings under Section 7 in respect to capitalization ratios.

INSTRUCTIONS:

1. What arguments might be made as to why deferred income taxes should be reported as a part of retained earnings (earned surplus)?
2. Who won this case, the SEC or American Power Company? Comment.
3. Do you believe that special rules should apply to certain industries, say thepublic utilities versus regular manufacturing operations?
4. Why does a utility wish the provision for future income taxes to be reported as a current charge?

15-7 Menlow Engineering

Menlow Engineering (formerly Ro-Stao Engineering) has incurred a deficit from operations of $300,000 from June, 1983 to December 31, 1983, which was comprised solely of expenses in initial operations and product development with no recorded sales. During this period of time, it came to Menlow's attention that Hardent Engineering was in financial difficulty after having spent approximately $5,000,000 on a new engineering design.

Eventually, Hardent entered voluntary liquidation and the liquidator was now ready to accept bids for the company. Menlow decided to submit a bid of $830,390 comprised of $230,390 in cash and 300,000 shares of its stock.

Surprisingly the bid was accepted on November 10, 1983 and the investment in Hardent Engineering was recorded on the books of Menlow at $830,390 which consisted of the $230,390 in cash and the value assigned to the stock of $600,000 or $2.00 a share.

It should be noted that existing stockholders of Menlow paid in .70 a share in June, 1983 to reorganize the old company.

Because there was no ready market for the stock, the book value of the assets received were used to value the assets received from Hardent. Hardent's balance sheet was as follows:

Current Assets	$750,000
Plant Assets	125,000
Total Assets	$875,000
Current Liabilities	45,710
Long Term Liabilities	198,831
Net Worth	630,459
Total Liabilities and Net Worth	$875,000

The purchase looks good from Menlow's perspective because the designs developed by Hardent should be quite useful in retooling much of their existing equipment. In addition, with their expertise, the design may help in supplementing their existing research and development work. The year 1984 therefore was used as a basis for retooling some existing machinery and in 1985 a number of new machines were developed which incorporated some of the design work that had originally been developed by Hardent.

An additional bonus is that Hardent had substantial operating losses prior to acquisition by Menlow and that these losses are available to offset future taxable income for a period of fifteen years. The losses were $2,720,000. In 1983 and 1984, the company did not have any income, but in 1985 the company had income of $200,000.

Assume that your auditing firm has taken over from another auditing firm in 1985, and you are considering the possibilities of how to account for the operating loss carryforwards.

    1. Indicate the possibilities for how the operating loss carryforwards might be reported.
    2. After discussing the possibilities, develop a position as to how these net operating losses should be reported.

15-8 Beck Company

During 1985, the Beck Company incurred an interest cost of $600,000 during construction of a new office building, which was completed on December 31. For tax purposes, the interest cost is deductible in 1985. For accounting purposes, the interest must be capitalized and depreciated over the 15-year life of the building. Based on a 1985 tax rate of 40%, Beck's accountant estimates that the company will enjoy an immediate tax saving of $240,000. He contends that recognition of an immediate deferred tax liability for the full $240,000 will distort the company's debt ratios, since payment of any additional future taxes depends on such uncertain factors as the company's future earnings and tax rates. He believes that use of the deferred method of interperiod tax allocation would be misleading to financial statement users, since the $600,000 timing difference is a "semipermanent difference" which will take 15 years to reverse fully. He believes that the liability method is more appropriate for "semipermanent" differences such as this, and that the tax effect should be discounted to its present value.

INSTRUCTIONS:

    1. Describe the difference between the deferred method and the liability method of interperiod tax allocation.
    2. Assuming pretax accounting income of $2,000,000, prepare the journal entry needed to record income taxes for 1985 under the deferred method.
    3. Assuming annual pretax accounting income of $2,000,000 and a 40% tax rate, prepare the journal entry needed annually to record income taxes during the 15 years subsequent to 1985 under the deferred method.
    4. Assuming that the liability method of interperiod tax allocation was appropriate, what journal entry might be prepared in 1985 to record

income taxes? Assume that a 10% discount factor is used, a 40% tax rate is appropriate, and pretax accounting income is $2,000,000.

15-9 Death and Taxes

Perhaps the single most pervasive influence on the growth of accounting has been the corporate income tax. Individuals, large or small corporations, partnerships, regulated or nonregulated industries are all affected by the surety of taxes.

The corporate income tax is a legal structure, and therefore the solutions to tax problems are legal solutions. To the extent that the tax laws recognize accounting solutions, accounting too becomes part of the law. In some instances accounting has provided the basis for tax laws. Initially net income was defined for income tax purposes as cash receipts minus cash disbursements. The 1913 Revenue Act levied an income tax on corporations using this definition. The accounting profession however promoted and established the eventual acceptability of accrual accounting as the basis for income taxation.

As a result, the initial problem of distinguishing between accounting and taxable income (accrual versus cash) was settled in favor of the accounting profession. However, other distinctions between accounting net income and taxable income have given rise to another set of accounting problems. The general title of tax allocation has been given to an area characterized by timing differences and permanent differences, deferrals and flow throughs, liabilities and deferred credits. Accounting for taxation has strained the ability of accountants to explain the application to them of accounting principles developed in a context different than that developed for taxation.

INSTRUCTIONS:

1. In what basic ways to the objectives of determining taxable income differ from the objectives of measuring accounting income?
2. Explain the accounting rationale for reporting a larger amount of income tax expense than is to be paid to the federal government for income taxes.
3. Describe two items that account for taxable income being higher than accounting income.
4. Describe two items that account for accounting income being higher than taxable income.
5. Explain what a permanent difference is in the interperiod allocation of income taxes.
6. Explain what a timing difference is in the interperiod allocation of income taxes.

15–10 Crop–Keep Corp.

Crop–Keep Corp. manufactures, constructs, and sells huge silos. The company was organized and began operations on January 1, 1982. The silo sells for a gross profit of $75,000. One-third of the total sale is collected in the first year and one-third in each of the following two years. Twelve silos were sold in 1982, 18 in 1983, and 20 in 1984. There have been no bad debts and none are expected. Gross profit is recognized in the year of sale for accounting purposes but is recognized in the year cash is received for tax purposes. Installment accounts receivable are considered a current asset.

The company's plant and equipment, acquired on January 1, 1982, cost $2,250,000. For accounting purposes, straight–line depreciation over a nine–year life is used. For tax purposes, straight–line depreciation over an accelerated cost recovery period of five years is used.

The company owns $125,000 of 10% municipal bonds, the interest on which is nontaxable.

Pretax accounting income for 1984 is $512,000.

INSTRUCTIONS:

1. Prepare the necessary journal entry to record income taxes for 1984 under the deferred method. The tax rate has been 40% since the company was organized.
2. Assume that there was a $720,000 credit balance in the deferred income tax account at December 31, 1983. Of this amount, $480,000 credit relates to the installment sales and the remainder to the depreciation. Compute the balance in deferred income taxes at December 31, 1984, and indicate the section(s) of the balance sheet where it would be shown.
3. Prepare the necessary journal entry to record income taxes for 1984 under the deferred method, assuming that the tax rate changed to 30% for 1984. The gross change method should be used.
4. What is the basic difference between the gross change method and the net change method?
5. In what circumstances is application of the gross change method more desirable than application of the net change method? In what circumstances is it less desirable?

CHAPTER 16

ACCOUNTING FOR PENSION COSTS

16-1 The Pension Obligation

Following is the testimony given by Donald J. Kirk, Chairman of the Financial Accounting Standards Board on "The Health and Future of Private Pension Plans" before the U.S. Senate Subcommittee on Labor on March 21, 1983:

Mr. Kirk: Good morning, Mr. Chairman. I am Donald J. Kirk, Chairman of the Financial Accounting Standards Board. With me is Timothy Lucas, the FASB staff member responsible for the pensions project.

The Subcommittee's hearing today is addressing the health and future of private pension plans. Though the subject encompasses matters far beyond accounting, accounting has a role to play. Assessing the health of pension plans requires measuring financing items, such as the obligation for benefits promised and the amounts of pension assets.   Those measurements bring the discussion into the realm of accounting.

In fact, some have argued that changes in pension accounting might directly affect the health or even the future of pension plans. They believe that the requirement to report certain information could influence decisions on funding or even cause an employer to decide to discontinue his plan. I know members of Congress are receiving copies of letters addressed to me claiming that a recent Board proposal could have those effects.

The Financial Accounting Standards Board is recognized by the Securities and Exchange Commission and the accounting profession as the authoritative body to establish standards for financial reporting. Those standards define the financial statements and other financial information presented in reports, such as corporate annual reports, that are used by investors, creditors, and others outside a business enterprise.

Those who use financial reports simply must have reliable and understandable information about the cost of pensions and the extent of a company's pension obligations.   The significance of pensions for many employers is such that they cannot be ignored. It is difficult to argue, in my view, that the public interest would be served by allowing that information to be withheld from financial statement users.

As you have undoubtedly observed, there is a great deal of complexity, misunderstanding, and more than a little mystery surrounding today's pension arrangements. The FASB has been studying pension accounting questions for almost nine years, searching for improved ways of presenting meaningful and understandable information about the status of pension plans. We believe we have made progress in penetrating the mystery and improving communication of financial information about pensions, but the job is not yet finished.

Progress has been made in providing cost-effective, comparable, and understandable information in the financial statements of pension plans. Progress has also been made in improving pension information disclosed in the notes to employers' financial statements.

Those steps were put in place in 1980. The evidence available at that time, especially that provided by knowledgeable representatives of financial statement users, convinced the Board that the progress to date was not enough. The Board concluded it should also reconsider the accounting rules for measuring and reporting pension cost and pension obligations in employers' financial statements.

It is those rules that are addressed in our current project on employers' accounting for pensions. As the latest step in that project, the Board recently published its "Preliminary Views," a copy of which is included in the material we have submitted.

The Board has expressed the view that some changes in pension accounting are desirable. Those changes include uniform use of a measurement method that is based on the terms of the pension plan. They also include recognition in the employer's balance sheet of the unfunded obligation for benefits based on employee service already rendered. Those changes are discussed in more detail in the summary at the beginning of the "Preliminary View" document.

Those possible changes have already proved controversial, but the Board believes there is a need for improvement in pension accounting. However, no changes will be made without careful consideration of as many views and as much information as the Board can obtain.

Much remains to be done before any change is finally implemented. A document requesting comment on additional issues will be published shortly, and the Board will hold another public hearing this fall. We have also prepared a data bank of pension disclosures by more than 1,200 companies.

An exposure draft of our proposed Statement will be issued for public comment probably in 1984, and after those comments are assessed, a final Statement is expected sometime in 1985.

The Board is working with the Financial Executives Institute in conducting a field test of the proposed changes contained in our "Preliminary Views." All of these procedures are intended to ensure that the Board is aware of all relevant facts and has the opportunity to understand and consider various points of view before making a decision.

We appreciate the interest of the Committee in the work of the Board and we stand ready to assist you in any way we can.

Senator Nickles: Thank you very much, Mr. Kirk. I will certainly agree with you that your proposals caused a lot of controversy. I was snickering to myself, wondering if we should apply the same accountability to government pensions, et cetera, and post those on our annual reports as we tell everybody what a great job we are doing here.

Mr. Kirk: I might comment that the experimental financial statements of the federal government do include information similar in many respects to what we are suggesting. Now, they are not widely disseminated and they are not widely understood, but those experimental financial statements do contain a similar measure of the pension liability. That is, not for the Social Security plan, but for the federal retirement plans.

Senator Nickles: I have had a hard time contrasting the amount of liability that we see hanging over the private sector with what we have in the public sector. I guess now that I am wearing a public sector hat, I see how we ignore what has been going on in that arena, and yet we rightly focus some attention on trying to make some improvements in the private sector.

Some people have discussed possibly trying to cut your initiative off by statutory change. What do you think of such critics of your proposals?

Mr. Kirk: I try to urge them not to foster such a proposal, and I would urge you to think carefully before entertaining it seriously. There is a well-financed private sector effort under way now. We are financed through the private sector. We do have constituents, just as you do, who sometimes oppose what we suggest, but we do think that our process involves a great deal of research. It is an open process, and I think it is the best way to reach a particular conclusion on this subject.

In addition, our process is not complete. I did outline many of the things we have to do yet, and we do intend to assess the validity of many of the assertions that have been made about the effects of our particular proposal.

Senator Nickles: How do you answer that criticism? Some would say that if you did have the financial status of pension funds included with the annual report, those companies that would be in the worst shape pension-wise are also in the worst shape otherwise financially, just making it that much more difficult for them to borrow needed funds, et cetera.

Mr. Kirk: One last comment on your earlier question. We do have a relationship with the SEC, and they are empowered and do exercise oversight on our activities, and so I do think there is adequate governmental oversight under the present arrangement.

Turning to your latter question of how do we respond to some of the assertions regarding the effects of our proposal, it is difficult to assess whether they are valid. I think the first question that needs to be focused on is whether our present proposal is a reasonable reflection of the facts.

It has been stated earlier that one group was trying to determine the true status of pension plans. A little bit later, it was mentioned that, for defined benefit pension plans, it may well be an indeterminable obligation.

What we are attempting to do is present as good a picture as we can as to what the status of plans is. I think the question is, is our proposal a reasonable presentation of the facts? If it is, then I think it is unfair to say that the consequences are necessarily all adverse. Those could well be beneficial consequences resulting from a better portrayal of what the status of pension plans is.

The fact that some people assert they will abandon their defined benefit pension plans, I think, is subject to very careful scrutiny because, as pointed out earlier, defined contribution plans often do not furnish the income security that a defined benefit pension plan may.

Beneficial effects can come about through a better understanding of what the status of plans is, and potentially it might favorably impact decisions made about funding. The level of understanding on pension plans is extremely low and needs to be improved. I do think that better information can help that educational process.

On balance, if there is a reasonable presentation made of the financial status of plans, I think the good consequences would outweigh the adverse consequences.

Senator Nickles: Do you disagree with the critics that you might be the straw that would break the camel's back in a company that was on the verge, say, of bankruptcy and had pension underfunding problems too?

Mr. Kirk: I do not believe so. What we are proposing in no way affects directly the cash flow effects or the obligation that an employer has. It does affect the way in which it is presented and where it is presented, and that can influence some people, but I think the statements of the dire consequences are greatly exaggerated.

We also are proposing a rather gradual transition to a new measurement basis so that the people can get used to a different presentation of what the obligation is under defined benefit pension plans. So, I think we have a way of easing the transition that should help overcome some of the objections to what we are suggesting.

Senator Nickles: Well, I am thinking of a case like a Harvester or a Chrysler a couple of years ago, or something where you had a company that was working aggressively trying to reorganize and refinance. I have countered the argument with the fact that the creditors are probably well aware of that information, but I was wanting to know if --.

Mr. Kirk: Yes, I think the creditors are on top of those particularly troubled situations. I cannot deny that what we are suggesting could change debt-equity ratios in the balance sheet of the corporation.

Much of the same information is availabe now in the footnotes to financial statements. We have in earlier projects been faced with similar arguments that what we are proposing will adversely affect debt-equity ratios; it will cause violation of indentures under bonds. I do think we have been able to cope with those kinds of concerns in the past and I believe we can again here through a reasonable transition to a new standard.

Senator Nickles: Let me ask you a final question. Would there have to be some type of uniformity as far as calculations of unfunded vested liabilities? As pointed out by one of our previous guests, there can be a great disparity based on rates of return, inflation, mortality, et cetera.

Mr. Kirk: This is a very good question. We are proposing that there be a standard measurement of the cost of the pension plan that is charged to income each year. We have already suggested, and are reaffirming, that there should be a consistent way of measuring the unfunded obligation of sponsors.

We have not yet addressed whether certain assumptions should be standardized, and the one referred to earlier was the rate of return on the assets of the pension plan. The present disclosure that is one of our requirements has been criticized by some because it leaves latitude as to the interest rate used. Also, of course, there is latitude in the interest rate used for funding purposes.

We will be looking at that question at our next public hearing as to whether some of the assumptions might be standardized or narrowed. I personally am not optimistic that it makes sense to standardize a rate of return or interest rate.

There is the potential for variation in the actual earnings of pension plan investments, and the rate of return estimate is an attempt, if done properly, to reflect the best estimate of what might be earned. Now, that does require a crystal ball and that is extremely difficult. But if you do not allow some latitude to take into account different situations, you will just end up with certain actuarial gains and losses that will have to be accounted for later.

Senator Nickles: I wonder if you would not have a situation where you would have a firm that would be out trying to hire an actuary who would eventually tell them what they wanted to hear.

Mr. Kirk: Well there are stories that that does exist. It is an area that requires professional judgment and professional responsibility and it is a difficult arena to perform in. But I do think that professional judgment has been the rule in the past. If our standards can help narrow the areas of judgment in the future, we will most certainly take that into account.

Senator Nickles: Thank you very much, Mr. Kirk. We appreciate your appearance before the Committee.

Mr. Kirk: Thank you.

INSTRUCTIONS:

1. Mr. Kirk mentions the "obligation for benefits promised" in the first paragraph and then again later in his testimony. What is the "pension obligation" and what is its importance to accounting?
2. What is the basis for the pension plan accounting controversy?
3. Distinguish between pension costs, expense, and funding. What are vested and non-vested benefits?

4. What is the definition of an accounting liability? Discuss the components of the pension obligation as it relates to accounting liability recognition.

5. What approach revenue-expense or asset-liability is followed by APB 8? Discuss.

6. Discuss potential economic consequences of changes in accounting for pension plans.

16-2 Pretentious Packaging, Inc.

Pretentious Packaging, Inc. is one of the world's leading and most diversified manufacturers of packaging products. Their products include glass, paper, plastic, and metal containers, as well as specialized glass products for home and scientific use, and various lumber products. Sales and earnings have been growing at a steady rate with increases of 7.4% and 4.9% respectively in 1985. Pretentious employs over 50,000 employees in more than 100 United States plants and 30,000 in some 60 plants located in foreign countries. The following are excerpts from the 1985 Annual Report.

Retirement Plans: The Company has retirement plans covering substantially all domestic and certain foreign employees. Retirement costs are computed on the basis of accepted actuarial methods (generally using the entry age normal method) and include current service costs of all plans and the amortization of unfunded prior service cost over periods of 30 years or less. The Company's policy is to pay into trusteed funds each year an amount equal to the charges to earnings for its domestic retirement plans.

Certain foreign subsidiaries have private pension plans which are not separately funded; however, for the most part the actuarial liabilities for future benefits are being accrued in the balance sheet.

Employee Benefit Plans: The Company has benefit plans covering substantially all domestic and certain foreign employees as well as several deferred compensation arrangements. Charges to earnings amount to $48.6 million in 1985 as compared with $42.5 million in 1984. Significant increases in benefits effective in 1984 under the Hourly Retirement Plan, together with changes in actuarial assumptions in 1984 as to retirement age for both Hourly and Salary Retirement Plans had the effect of increasing unfunded prior service cost and resulted in additional current cost. In 1985 benefits in both plans were increased resulting again in increased unfunded prior service costs and additional current cost; however, changes in actuarial assumptions partially offset the total cost of the increased benefits in the two plans. The unfunded prior service cost at January 1, 1985, the latest actuarial valuation of the plan, approximated $293 million. The actuarially computed value of vested benefits under the Hourly and Salary Retirement Plans covering domestic employees at January 1, 1985, exceeded the total value of the pension funds, with their securities adjusted to market value at January 1, 1985, by approximately $153 million. At December 31, 1985, it is estimated that the vested benefits under these plans exceeded the total of the pension funds with their securities adjusted to market value by approximately $120 million.

Other pertinent data from the financial statements is reprinted on the following pages.

INSTRUCTIONS:

1. Discuss the nature of accounting for pension plans in general and define the following relevant terms: Normal Cost, Past Service Cost, Prior Service Cost, Vested Benefits, Fully Funded Plan.
2. What is currently suggested as the appropriate method to attribute benefits earned and their cost to periods of employee service? Why?
3. What assumptions must be made in pension accounting and what impact do they have?
4. Discuss the issues involved in disclosure of pension plans and the adequacy of Pretentious Packaging's disclosure.

Consolidated Earnings
Years Ending December 31, 1985 and 1984
Thousands of Dollars

	1985	1984
Revenues:		
Net sales	$2,273,173	$2,116,436
Dividends	2,068	2,030
Interest	7,506	7,763
Royalties and net technical assistance	14,951	16,714
Equity in earnings of associates	9,502	12,914
Gains on sales of assets	8,638	1,315
Other	14,153	7,009
	2,329,991	2,164,181
Costs and expenses:		
Manufacturing, shipping and delivery	1,895,898	1,741,287
Research and engineering	51,994	52,361
Selling and administrative	193,374	180,223
Interest	43,683	38,018
Other	3,132	5,759
	2,188,081	2,017,648
Gross Income	141,910	146,533
Provision for income taxes	51,000	58,600
	90,910	87,933
Minority shareholders' interests in earnings of subsidiaries	3,754	4,461
Net Earnings	$ 87,336	$ 83,472
Earnings per common share: Primary	$ 6.02	$ 5.74
Fully Diluted	$ 5.51	$ 5.29

Consolidated Balance Sheet
December 31, 1985 and 1984
Thousands of Dollars

	1985	1984
Current Assets:		
Cash and non-equity securities	$ 37,949	$ 47,101
Receivables, less allowances for losses and		
discounts (1985-$12,333; 1984-$12,897)	244,394	232,841
Inventories	341,169	356,772
Prepaid expenses	11,508	11,264
Total Current Assets	635,020	647,978
Investments and Other Assets:		
Listed securities, at cost (quoted market		
value 1985-$83,498; 1984-$49,824)	1,278	1,291
Foreign investments and advances	92,893	91,899
Domestic investments	17,203	15,624
Repair parts inventories	67,889	57,657
Deferred charges	18,578	18,977
Deposits, receivables and other assets	51,151	53,451
	248,992	238,899
Property, Plant and Equipment:		
Land, timberlands and mineral deposits, at		
cost less depletion	90,245	92,372
Buildings and equipment, at cost	1,669,714	1,511,284
	1,759,959	1,603,656
Less accumulated depreciation	696,104	645,250
	1,063,855	958,406
	$1,947,867	$1,845,283

Liabilities and Shareholders' Equity

	1985	1984
Current Liabilities:		
Short-term loans	$ 20,041	$ 20,790
Accounts payable	136,502	147,244
Salaries and wages	60,247	61,558
U.S. and foreign income taxes	28,043	16,435
Other accrued liabilities	65,891	52,601
Long-term debt due within one year	13,878	13,967
Total current liabilities	324,602	312,595
Long-term debt	571,856	553,326

Reserves and Other Credits:		
Reserve for rebuilding furnaces	45,647	35,957
Deferred taxes	76,523	81,549
Obligations under foreign pension plans	36,633	32,276
Other liabilities and reserves	9,254	11,302
	168,057	161,084
Minority shareholders' interests	35,379	28,349
Shareholders' equity:		
Preferred equity	14,198	16,067
Preference shares (liquidation preference, $66,394)	13,279	13,279
Common shares	43,455	43,359
Capital in excess of stated value	71,548	71,424
Retained earnings	705,493	645,800
	847,973	789,929
	$1,947,867	$1,845,283

1985 Employment Compensation
Thousands of Dollars

Wages and salaries	$735,532	81.4%
Social security taxes	58,925	6.5
Insurance benefits	57,864	6.4
Retirement benefits	48,350	5.3
Stock purchase plan benefits	3,200	0.4
TOTAL	$903,871	100.0%

1985 Employment Incentive Compensation
Thousands of Dollars

Plant personnel	$ 17,558	63.2%
Officers and management personnel	7,852	28.3
Sales personnel	1,373	4.9
Miscellaneous	986	3.6
TOTAL	$ 27,769	100.0%

1985 Income Dollar Distribution
Approximate Amounts

Raw Materials, supplies, fuel, etc.	$ .508
Wages, salaries, and benefits	.386
Taxes excluding social security taxes	.033
Depreciation and depletion	.035
Net earnings less cash dividends (retained earnings)	.026
Cash Dividends	.012
TOTAL	$1.000

Report of Retirement Funds (Domestic only)
Thousands of Dollars

	1985	Total Accumulation 1981-1985
Payments into funds by Company	$ 39,049	$292,486
Payments into funds by employees, less refunds	(49)	28,459
Income, including gains and losses, etc.	19,659	169,894
Additons to funds	$ 58,659	$490,839
Benefits paid and admin. expenses, etc.	20,662	129,774
TOTAL	$ 37,997	$361,065

Composition of Funds (Book Value)

Cash and short-term securities	$ 23,047
U.S. Government securities	15,386
Corporate bonds and notes	43,228
Common stocks	241,577
Mortgage notes receivable	2,997
Real estate (net after depreciation)	8,084
Insurance contracts	1,232
Recorded valuation adjustments	25,514
TOTAL	$361,065

16-3 Champion Motors

Marion Frye:, president of Champion Motors, is discussing the possibility of developing a pension plan for its employees with Mark Sullivan, controller and William Strang, Assistant Controller. Their conversation is as follows:

Marion Frye: If we are going to compete with our competitors, we must have a pension plan to attract good talent.

Mark Sullivan: I must warn you, Marion, that a pension plan will take a large bite out of our income. The only reason why we have been so profitable is the lack of a pension cost in our income statement. In some of our competitors cases, pension expense is 60% of pretax income.

William Strang: Why do we have to worry about a pension cost now anyway? Benefits do not vest until after ten years of service. If they do not vest, then we are not liable. We should not have to report an expense until we are legally liable to provide benefits.

Marion Frye: But Bill, the employees would want credit for past service with full vesting ten years after starting service, not ten years after starting the plan. How would we allocate the large past service cost?

William Strang: Well, I believe that the past service cost is a cost of providing a pension plan for employees forever. It is an intangible asset that will not diminish in value because it will increase the morale of our present and future employees and provide us with a competitive edge in acquiring future employees. Therefore, only the interest on the unfunded past service cost should be expensed each year.

Marion Frye: I hate to disagree, but I believe the past service is a benefit only to the present employees, actuarily computed. This past service is directly related to the composition of the employee group at the time the plan is initiated and is in no way related to any intangible benefit received by the company because of the the plans existence. Therefore, I propose that the past service cost be amortized over the remaining lives of the existing employees.

Mark Sullivan: (somewhat perturbed) But what about the income statement? You two are arguing theory without consideration of our income figure.

Marion Frye: Settle down, Mark.

Mark Sullivan: Sorry, perhaps Bill's approach to resolving this approach is the best one. I am just not sure.

INSTRUCTIONS:

1. Assuming that Champion Motors establishes a pension plan, how should their liability for pensions be computed in the first year?
2. How should their liability be computed in subsequent years?
3. How should pension expense be computed each year?
4. Assuming that the pension fund is set up in a trusteed relationship, should the assets of the fund be reported on the books of Champion Motors?
5. What interest rate factor should be used in the present value computations?
6. How should actuarial gains and losses be reported?

16-4 Benevolent Corporation*

On January 1, 1985, the Benevolent Corporation discontinued its informal pension arrangement for hourly-rated employees and adopted a formal plan for retirement. Previously, they were using a "pay-as-you-go" plan in which they charged income with the cost of the annual pension benefits paid to retired employees. Under the new plan the actuarially determined costs of past and current services was to be funded through a qualified pension trust. Management considered a formal plan necessary to increase employee morale and to reduce employee turnover.

---

*Adapted from a case prepared by Willis W. Hagen II.

The Benevolent Corporation has 1,000 employees who have been working for many years, and the independent professional actuaries have determined the present value of the liability for prior service applicable to such employees at $2,000,000. The prior service cost will be funded in 10 equal annual installments of $284,775.01 beginning December 31, 1985. Current (normal) service costs for the 1,000 present employees was actuarially estimated at $200,000 annually and will be funded on December 31 as incurred. A seven percent discount rate was assumed throughout and all interest equivalents are computed as of December 31 of the appropriate year.

Management proposed the following financial reporting for the formal pension plan:

1) Amortize past service cost for present employees over a 20-year period which is the estimated average remaining service life of these employees.

2) Charge expense with current (normal) cost.

INSTRUCTIONS:

1. Compute the pension expense and the deferred pension cost for 1985 (the present value of an ordinary annuity of 20 payments of one at seven percent is 10.594014).

2. Five years after the adoption of the plan, an actuary makes a new study of the assumptions on which the estimated pension costs are based. The study indicates that, due to lower than anticipated interest rates on investments and unfavorable mortality experience, the pension fund balance at the end of the five years was less than the balance originally expected at the end of this period. What treatment (if any) should be given to this fact?

3. Ten years after the adoption of the plan, the Benevolent Corporation acquired Evans Corporation. The acquisition was accounted for as a purchase (not a pooling of interests). At that time, an actuarial study based on Benevolent Corporation's accounting policies indicated that the pension fund balance of Evans Corporation did not exceed the actuarially computed value of its vested benefits. What treatment (if any) should Benevolent Corporation give to these facts?

4. What arguments would you give for either not accruing prior service cost at all or accruing prior service cost only to the extent funded?

5. What are the disclosure requirements regarding the company's pension plan?

16-5 Buying a Pension Plan

Arlan Wilson is the Senior Acquisition Specialist for EYYON, a major oil-producing corporation. EYYON is branching out into the office products industry with a host of companies such as QUYZ, ZARGOX, and RODOT. These subsidiaries need sophisticated electronic components and EYYON has relied on imports and purchases from domestic suppliers to fulfill their needs. However, management has now become more interested in manufacturing these components, and therefore has begun by producing some relatively less sophisticated units. In addition, through merger the company hopes to gain more expertise in this area.

Wilson has therefore been assigned the responsibility to find a company which manufactures circuit boards as EYYON's first acquisition in this area. Wilson believes that he has found two candidates in Morbot, Inc. and Largo Enterprises. Morbot, Inc. has a prime location near a subsidiary assembly plant and has an experienced work force. The acquisition price of $2,500,000 appears reasonable. Largo Enterprises has similar qualifications and if the price was the same, Wilson would be indifferent between the two companies. However, negotiations for Largo have stalled at $2,750,000 and Wilson is focusing his attention on Morbot, Inc.

The condensed financial statements for Morbot, Inc. are presented below:

```
                    Morbot, Inc.
             Statement of Income (Condensed)
                 For the Year Ended 1985

Net Sales                                    $4,000,000
Cost of Goods Sold                            2,600,000

Gross Profit                                  1,400,000
Miscellaneous Expense                           919,000
Interest Expense                                 30,000

Net Income                                   $  451,000
```

```
                    Morbot, Inc.
              Balance Sheet (Condensed)
               As of December 31, 1985

Current Assets   $  700,000   Current Liabilities   $    430,000
Plant Assets      2,000,000   Long-term debt             600,000
                              Common Stock            1,100,000
Total Assets     $2,700,000   Retained Earnings          570,000

                              Total Liabilities and
                                Stockholders' Equity $2,700,000
```

A schedule related to Miscellaneous Expense is as follows:

Miscellaneous Expense

Sales Commissions	$400,000
Administrative Salaries	281,000
Pension Expenses*	20,368
Taxes	217,632
Total	$919,000

*The company has a pension plan which covers all of its full-time employees. Total pension expense for the year was $20,368. The actuarially computed value of the vested benefits of the plan was $203,680, an amount which was fully funded.

Morbot, Inc. employs 120 individuals and sells its product through commission agents. Its owners, Marten and Laurie Morbot, are experiencing financial difficulty and therefore they would be quite happy with the two and half million sales price.

Wilson, however, has an uneasy feeling that something is wrong with the company. He believes the owners are honest, the financial statements have been certified by a "Big 8" CPA firm, and he has all the financial data he needs to make his decision. Yet for what must be the fourteenth time, Wilson analyzes the supporting schedules of the financial statements. He turns to the footnote supporting Miscellaneous Expense and decides that he would like a further examination of Morbot's pension plan. He, therefore, assigns Stuart Jay, EYYON's in-house actuary, to evaluate Morbot's pension plan. He requests that Jay deliver his report within a week.

A week later, the following discussion occurs.

Stuart Jay: Arlan, I've got it, I think. You were right about the pension costs. They're all wrong for EYYON.

Arlan Wilson: OK Stuart. What do you mean?

Stuart Jay: Let me give you some figures. There are 120 employees at Morbot, Inc., with an average age of 35 and ten years of past service cost. Now assume that these individuals will retire with the company and that the pension provides for $75/month ($900 a year) in annual benefits starting at age 65. Based on this and other assumptions the company's actuary uses, that comes to a pension cost of $20,368 this year which is the same number on the financial statements (See schedule A).

Schedule A

General Information

120 Current Employees will retire under the plan. Life expectancy at retirement age of 65--ten years Morbot's plan $75/mo (900/yr); fund can earn 12% per year. EYYON's plan $150/mo ($1800/yr); fund can earn 10% per year.

<u>Normal Costs</u>

Morbot, Inc.: Annual payments on retirement = $900/employee times 120 employees = $108,000/year

Discounted:

Age 65: $108,000 discounted at 12% for 10 years = $610,224
Age 35: $610,224 discounted at 12% for 30 years = $20,368
Normal Costs = <u>$20,368</u>

Arlan Wilson: Stu, I thought you had bad news.

Stuart Jay: I do. Arlan, how familiar are you with actuarial calculations presented in Schedule A?

Arlan Wilson: I had some exposure to them in my Intermediate Accounting course in college.

Stuart Jay: That'll help. From your point of view, its a simple problem of present values.

Arlan Wilson: I suppose I undersand a little more about that plan than most others. That's the same plan we have for our employees here at EYYON except that we pay $1800 a year and the interest rate we use is 10%. What's the catch?

Stuart Jay: The catch is that it is the same plan and it isn't. An actuarial plan depends on many variables. I pretty much agree with Morbot's actuary on some of the ones I've given you; the average employee begins there at age twenty-five, now thirty-five and will retire at age 65. However, we do not agree on two things –the interest rate and the benefit level. First, I use an average interest rate of 10%, whereas Morbot's actuary uses 12%. Doesn't sound like much, does it?

Arlan Wilson: (losing interest in Jay's pedagogical style) Would you be telling me if it wasn't?

Stuart Jay: (ignoring Wilson's sarcasm) The difference, though, is substantial. If we would use our interest rate, I'd figure their normal cost would be much higher than $20,000. The other catch is the benefit level. We have a benefit of $150 per month, and they base their expense on $75 per month.

Arlan Wilson: What is the bottom line in all this?

Stuart Jay: Based on their pension plan, their pension cost was $20,368. If they figure their costs on EYYON's plan, their costs would be substantially higher.

Arlan Wilson: Your findings aren't as earthshaking as you think. They reduce Morbot's profitability, but not enough to make it an unattractive acquisition.

Stuart Jay: That's your decision, of course, but that isn't all you have to consider. If your actuarial assumptions are different, your past service costs and funding requirements are also different. Sure, the company's pension plan is fully funded at $203,680 based on their actuarial computations. But, a comparable EYYON plan would have much more in it. That's your bottom line.

Arlan Wilson: (pensively) I think I know what you are trying to tell me, but can you spell it out?

Stuart Jay: EYYON has two rules in a merger. First all new employees receive identical benefits with existing employees. Second, our pension liabilities are always fully funded. In other words, the merger will cost you more than the price you negotiate with the owners.

Arlan Wilson: Thank you for your time Stu. You've given me a lot to think about.

Before he makes his decision, Arlan Wilson calls Art Young, the company's controller and discovers that this additional amount for underfunded pension liability would be added to the purchase price of Morbot, Inc. for financial reporting purposes and deducted over twenty years for income taxes.

INSTRUCTIONS:

1. What does this case demonstrate about the need for disclosure in pension reporting?
2. Stuart Jay indicated that the normal cost using EYYON's assumptions would be substantially higher. Compute how much higher, considering only the change in interest rate. Compute how much higher considering both the change in interest rate and benefit level.
3. For the Morbot, Inc. to be fully funded using EYYON's assumption, how much more would have to be added to the pension fund?

16-6 Bethlehem Steel Corporation

Following are the partial financial statements for Bethlehem Steel Corporation and related information regarding pension disclosures:

Consolidated Statements of Income and
Income Invested in the Business
(Dollars in Millions)

| | Year Ended December 31, | |
	1977	1976
Revenues:		
Net sales	$5,370.0	$5,248.0
Interest, dividends and other income	40.2	56.7
	$5,410.2	$5,304.7
Costs and Expenses:		
Cost of Sales (Note C)	4,863.2	4,485.9
Depreciation	300.1	275.6
Selling, administrative and general expense	284.6	271.5
Interest and other debt charges	82.5	77.7
	$5,530.4	$5,110.7
Income (Loss) before Non-recurring Items and Provision (Credit) for Taxes on Income	$ (120.2)	$ 194.0
Non-recurring Items:		
Estimated costs of closedown of certain steelmaking and related facilities (Note B)	$ 750.0	--
Flood expense	41.0	--
	$ 791.0	--
Income (Loss) before Provision (Credit) for Taxes on Income	$ (911.2)	$ 194.0
Provision (credit) for Taxes on Income (Note L)	$ (463.0)	$ 26.0
Net Income (Loss) $(10.27) and $3.85 per share	$ (448.2)	$ 168.0
Income Invested in the Business, January 1	2,185.9	2,105.3
	$1,737.7	$2,273.3
Deduct: Dividends ($1.50 and $2.00 per share)	65.5	87.4
Income Invested in the Business, December 31	$1,672.2	$2,185.9

Consolidated Balance Sheets
(Dollars in Millions)

	December 31,	
	1977	1976

A S S E T S

Current Assets:

Cash	$ 55.4	$ 45.6
Marketable securities, at cost (approximating market)	183.4	355.6
Receivables, less allowances of $6,300,000 and $6,100,000	496.7	421.5
Refund of income taxes paid in prior years (Note L)	134.0	38.4
Inventories (Note C)	626.2	834.1
Total Current Assets	$1,495.7	$1,695.2
Investments in Associated Companies Accounted for by Equity Method (Note E)	125.0	116.9
Investments in Other Associated Enterprises	96.7	97.4
Long-term Receivables	36.1	24.8
Property, Plant and Equipment, Less Accumulated Depreciation (Note D)	2,988.3	2,963.4
Deferred Income Taxes (Note L)	80.4	--
Miscellaneous Assets (Note F)	76.7	79.8
Total	$4,898.9	$4,977.5

LIABILITIES AND STOCKHOLDERS' EQUITY

Current Liabilities:

Accounts payable	$ 313.9	$ 274.8
Accrued employment costs	286.6	241.5
Accrued taxes	129.5	165.9
Debt due within one year	3.3	12.9
Current portion of estimated future liability for costs attributable to the closedown of certain steelmaking and related facilities (Note B)	115.1	--
Other Current Liabilities	130.1	127.3
Total Current Liabilities	$ 978.5	$ 822.4
Liabilities Payable after One Year	150.8	140.8
Deferred Income Taxes (Note L)	--	298.6
Estimated Future Liability For Costs Attributable to the Closedown of Certain Steelmaking and Related Facilities (Note B)	435.9	--
Long-Term Debt (Note G)	1,154.8	1,023.1
Total Liabilities	$2,720.0	$2,284.9

	1977	1976
Commitments (Note H)		
Stockholders' Equity (Note I)		
Common Stock - $8 par value -		
Authorized 80,000,000; issued and		
outstanding 45,987,118 shares	$ 576.0	$ 576.0
Income invested in business	1,672.2	2,185.9
	$2,248.2	$2,761.9
Less: 2,322,031 and 2,321,540 shares of Common		
Stock held in treasury, at cost	69.3	69.3
Total Stockholders' Equity	$2,178.9	$2,692.6
Total	$4,898.9	$4,977.5

Footnote B. Closedown of Certain Steelmaking and Related Facilities

On August 18, 1977, the Corporation announced a plan to close down certain steelmaking and related facilities, to reduce capital expenditures and to reduce hourly and salaried work forces. The decision to close down these facilities resulted in a pre-tax charge against income of $750 million. This amount may be summarized as follows (in millions):

Employment related closedown costs	$483
Write-off of facilities, net of estimated salvage	167
Other costs associated with reduction of capacity	100
	$750

The employment related closedown costs include an estimate of the present value of unfunded costs of pensions and of the costs of other benefits accruing to terminated and laid-off employees including, among other things, continued life and other insurance benefits and supplemental unemployment benefits. The write-off of facilities represents the net book value of abandoned plant and equipment adjusted for estimated proceeds of sales or realizable scrap value and losses incurred as a result of the termination of certain in-progress capital projects. Other costs associated with the reduction of capacity include the writedown to scrap value of inventory quantities considered unusable, anticipated operating losses to the date of closedown of certain facilities and estimated losses under certain contracts and agreements whose terms are no longer favorable to Bethlehem following the reduction of capacity.

In the opinion of management, based on available information, the $750 million charge is a reasonable estimate of the costs and expenses associated with the plan to close down these facilities. However, there are uncertainties in estimating amounts payable in future years, and, therefore, it is possible that future adjustments will be made to this charge. The extent to which such adjustments will increase or decrease the charge cannot be determined at this time.

Footnote K. Pensions

Provisions for pension costs were $272.1 million in 1977 and $261.2 million in 1976. Pension costs for 1977 increased nominally to reflect the increases in pension benefits which became effective under the Pension Plan during 1977 and 1976. In addition to the 1977 provision for pension costs, a portion of the estimated costs of the closedown of certain steelmaking and related facilities (see Note B) is attributable to pensions and other employment costs related to terminated and laid-off employees.

The actuarially computed value of vested benefits as of December 31, 1977, exceeded the sum of the market value of the Pension Trust Fund and the pension portion of the estimated future liability for costs attributable to the closedown of certain steelmaking and related facilities (see Note B) by approximately $1,212 million. The unamortized balance of the actuarially computed value of prior service costs, including those related to vested benefits, was approximately $1,120 million at December 31, 1977.

Report of Independent Accountants

To the Board of Directors and Stockholders
of Bethlehem Steel Corporation:

We have examined the Consolidated Balance Sheets of Bethlehem Steel Corporation and its consolidated subsidiaries at December 31, 1977 and 1976 and the related Consolidated Statement of Income and Income Invested in the Business and Changes in Financial Position for the years then ended. Our examinations were made in accordance with generally accepted auditing standards and accordingly included such tests of the accounting records and such other auditing procedures as we considered necessary in the circumstances.

As described in Note B, Bethlehem announced, in August 1977, a plan to close down certain steelmaking and related facilities and accordingly recorded a provision for the estimated costs and expenses to be incurred in connection therewith. Management believes, and we concur, that the provision represents a reasonable estimation of the costs and expenses associated with the closedown. However, the ultimate amount of costs and expenses to be incurred is not presently determinable.

In our opinion, subject to the effect, if any, on the 1977 financial statements of the ultimate determination of the actual costs and expenses associated with the decision referred to in the preceding paragraph, the accompanying financial statements present fairly the financial position of Bethlehem Steel Corporation and consolidated subsidiaries at December 31, 1977 and 1976 and the results of their operations and the changes in their financial position for the years then ended in conformity with generally accepted accounting principles applied on a consistent basis.

153 East 53rd Street   Price Waterhouse & Co.
New York, N.Y. 10022
February 10, 1978

Pension Trust Fund
(Dollars in Millions)

	December 31, 1977	December 31, 1976
Statement of Assets		
Cash, interest and other receivables	$ 5.7	$ 5.3
Contributions receivable from employing companies	51.0	21.7
Investments, at cost:		
Short-term obligations	65.5	64.4
Long-term bonds, notes and other obligations	335.6	283.0
Preferred stocks	1.5	1.5
Common stocks	657.4	588.9
Total, At Cost	$1,116.7	$ 964.8
Approximate Market Value	$1,178.8	$1,119.0

The Pension Trust Fund is not the property of Bethlehem and therefore is not included in the consolidated financial statements.

	1977	1976
Statement of Changes in Fund		
Balance in Fund, January 1, at cost	$ 964.8	$ 815.2
Add:		
Contributions from employing companies	270.0	260.1
Income from investments	54.7	44.3
	$1,289.5	$1,119.6
Deduct:		
Net loss on disposition and write-down of investments	1.7	3.0
Pension payments	171.1	151.8
	$ 172.8	$ 154.8
Balance in Fund, December 31, at cost	$1,116.7	$ 964.8
Pensioners at year end	43,375	40,864

Report of Independent Accountants

To the Investment Committee and Trustees
Pension Trust of Bethlehem Steel Corporation
and Subsidiary Companies:

In our opinion, the accompanying Statement of Assets and Statement of Changes in Fund present fairly the assets of the Pension Fund under the Pension Trust of Bethlehem Steel Corporation and Subsidiary Companies at December 31, 1977 and 1976 and the changes in the Fund during the years, in conformity with generally accepted accounting principles consistently applied. Our examinations of these statements were made in accordance with generally accepted auditing standards and accordingly included such tests of the accounting records and such other auditing procedures as we considered necessary in the circumstances, including confirmation by the custodian of investments owned at December 31, 1977 and 1976.

153 East 53rd Street   Price Waterhouse & Co.
New York, N.Y. 10022
January 25, 1978

INSTRUCTIONS:

1. Would Bethlehem Steel's disclosure be appropriate if financial statements were prepared in 1985? Discuss.
2. What recommendations would you make concerning additional disclosure that should be required in the area of pensions and regarding the impact of ERISA?
3. What has been a reporting problem involving the accounting for pension costs and plant closings?

16-7 Delta & Sigma Phototype, Inc.

Delta & Sigma Phototype, Inc. was organized in 1965 and established a formal pension plan on January 1, 1981, to provide retirement benefits for all employees. The plan is noncontributory and is funded through a trustee, the Corner National Bank, which invests all funds and pays all benefits as they become due. Vesting occurs when the employees retire at age sixty-five. Original prior service cost of $110,000 is being amortized over 15 years and funded over 10 years. The company also funds an amount equal to current normal cost net of actuarial gains and losses. There have been no amendments to the plan since its inception. Portions of the independent actuary's report follows:

Delta & Sigma Phototype, Inc.
Basic Noncontributory Pension Plan
Actuarial Report as of June 30, 1985

I. Current Year's Funding and Pension Cost

Service cost (before adjustment for actuarial gains) computed under the entry-age-normal method		$ 34,150
Actuarial gains:		
Investment gains (losses):		
Excess of expected dividend income over actual dividend income		(350)
Gain on sale of investments		4,050
Gains in actuarial assumptions for:		
Mortality		3,400
Employee turnover		5,050
Reduction in pension cost from closing of plant		8,000
Net actuarial gains		20,150
Service cost (funded currently)	$14,000	14,000
Prior service costs:		
Funding	14,245	
Amortization		10,597
Total funded	$28,245	
Total pension cost for financial statement purposes		$ 24,597

II. Fund Assets

Cash	$ 4,200
Dividends receivable	1,525
Investment in common stock, at cost (market value, $177,800)	162,750
	$168,475

III. Actuarial Liabilities

Number of employees	46
Number of employees retired	0
Yearly earnings of employees	$598,000
Actuarial liability	$145,000

INSTRUCTIONS:

1. What interest rate is being used in the amortization and funding of the past service cost?
2. On the basis of retirements for accounting for the cost of pension plans, evaluate the (a) treatment of actuarial gains and losses and (b) computation of pension cost for financial statement purposes. Ignore income tax considerations.
3. Independently of your answer to part (1), assume that the total amount to be funded is $32,663, the total pension cost for financial statement purposes is $29,015, and all amounts presented in the actuary's report are correct. In accordance with current pension accounting principles, write a footnote for the financial statements of Delta & Sigma Phototype, Inc., for the year ended June 30, 1985.

16-8 Scott Steel Co., Inc.

The steel industry has encountered major problems over the past 10 years. There has been increasing foreign competition and the accusations of "dumping", low domestic demand, low prices, and high costs. The Scott Steel Co., Inc. was hit hard by these conditions and as a result had to dramatically change their operations. The company has experienced heavy financial losses for three years and finally in 1985 adopted a plan of reorganization. The company operated a specialty flat steel division in Cary, Indiana that was to be sold. The decision to sell this segment was made on August 31, 1985. The estimated loss on the disposal of the segment, including the estimated loss from operations was $10.2 million. In connection with the disposal of the segment the company terminated the pension plan and purchased an annuity contract for $2.1 million from an insurance company to pay all projected benefits. The pension plan assets had a current value of $3 million. The management of Scott Steel then entered negotiations with the Steel Workers' Union to reduce the size of the work force and to reduce wages and fringe benefits. The negotiations went on for nearly three months and after a short strike a settlement was reached on December 15, 1985. Pertinent facts concerning the settlement are as follows:

a. The company would permanently lay off 50% of the work force based on seniority. This reduction was in keeping with the 50% reduction of capacity that would result from the reorganization of Scott Steel.

All terminated employees would receive two months salary and an opportunity to enter a one month retraining program sponsored by the company. Projected costs of these programs is $750,000.

b. Wages were to be reduced $2.50 per hour and frozen at that level for two years.

c. The current defined benefit pension plan would be terminated and replaced by a new defined benefit plan with a 25% reduction in projected benefits. The company purchased an annuity contract to guarantee the benefits that the employees had accumulated to date under the old plan. The company had always fully funded the old plan and after purchasing the annuity contract with the plan assets, were still left with a surplus of $5 million in the pension plan fund. These assets would revert to the company.

d. The company would offer an early retirement program to all employees. Under terms of the early retirement agreement, all those employees who elected early retirement would continue to receive health and life insurance benefits for the rest of their lives. The estimated cost is $450,000.

Those employees not electing early retirement had no assurance that postretirement benefits would be available at the time they retired. Those employees placed on permanent layoff were to receive no postretirement benefits. The current yearly cost for health and life insurance benefits for previously retired employees is $45,000.

INSTRUCTIONS:

1. Discuss the appropriate accounting for the pension plan termination related to the proposed sale of the Cary, Indiana flat steel division.
2. Discuss the appropriate accounting for each part of the labor settlement as it pertains to the pension plans, termination benefits, and postretirement benefits.

16-9 Pension Terms

Many business organizations have been concerned with providing for the retirement of employees since the late 1800's. During recent decades a marked increase in this concern has resulted in the establishment of private pension plans in most large companies and in many medium and small-sized ones.

The substantial growth of these plans, both in numbers of employees covered and in amounts of retirement benefits, has increased the significance of pension cost in relation to the financial position and, results of operations of many companies. For example, in 1975 private pension plans covered 27.7 million individuals, paid benefits of $16 billion, and had assets of $21 billion; in 1995 it is estimated that such plans will cover 44.5 million individuals, pay benefits of $106 billion, and have assets in excess of $2.5 trillion.

In examining the costs of pension plans, a CPA encounters certain terms. The elements of pension costs that the terms represent must be dealt with appropriately if generally accepted accounting principles are to be reflected in the financial statements of entities with pension plans.

INSTRUCTIONS:

1. Define a private pension plan. Differentiate between a funded and an unfunded pension plan. How does a contributory pension plan differ from a noncontributory plan?

2. Differentiate between "accounting for the employer" and "accounting for the pension fund".

3. Explain the terms "funded" and "pension liability" as they relate to:

   a. The pension fund.
   b. The employer.

4. a. Discuss the theoretical justification for accrual recognition of pension costs.

   b. Discuss the relative objectivity of the measurement process of accrual versus cash (pay–as–you–go) accounting for annual pension costs.

5. Explain the following terms as they apply to accounting for pension plans:

   a. Actuarial valuations.
   b. Actuarial cost methods.
   c. Vested benefits.

6. Distinguish among the following as they relate to pension plans:

   a. Projected benefit obligation.
   b. Accumulated benefit obligation.
   c. Service cost.
   d. Prior service cost.
   e. Gains and losses.

16-10 Actuarial Services

The actuarial firm of Hickman and Sons has hired a recent accounting graduate to assist them with a number of accounting problems. The firm has decided that they should not only provide actuarial services to their clients but also be able to provide advice as to the financial statement impacts and accounting implications of their pension plans. This approach has been very effective and led to a number of new accounts. Following are some of the situations for which the new accounting graduate is to provide assistance.

A. In April 1984, Morgan Steel terminated approximately 20% of its salaried labor force. These personnel were not associated with any one activity but rather were selectively cut from every level of operations. As a consequence, there was no basic change in the nature of the business or in the activities of the enterprise. As a result of this termination, approximately $800,000 in termination pay was made to these employees. However, the actuary in reviewing the impact of this termination noted that the pension plan was now overfunded by $6,000,000 because the turnover assumption had not considered such a large turnover.

If no changes in pension cost takes place, the pension cost for 1985 would be approximately $2,000,000. The effect of spreading this actuarial gain would be to reduce this cost to $1,500,000.

B. The preliminary actuarial report for Lawrence Co. indicates that its interest rate assumption should be changed from 5% to 6%. The effect of this change is 1985 is as follows:

1985 Pension Expense	
at 5%	$89,452
at 6%	$71,400

The actuary assumes that the above amounts are material, and knows that the effective tax rate is 45%, but wonders what effect this change would have on the footnote prepared by Lawrence Company?

C. Assume that the change that resulted in a decrease in pension expense in (B) above was not caused by a change in the interest rate but that Lawrence Company had changed its amortization of prior service cost from 9 to 17 years. What effect would this change have on the footnote prepared by Lawrence Company?

D. Marty Enterprises has adopted conservative practices in relation to its actuarial assumptions and has experienced above average performance in relationship to its pension fund investment portfolio. As a consequence, at December 31, 1985, it has an excess of $1,000,000 of fund assets over the present value of future benefits. Discussions have ensued in the executive office concerning whether the company should continue to fund the plan and whether a pension expense should be reported. The controller states that he believes it appropriate not to record any pension expense in the current year nor is there any reason to provide financial disclosure in the financial statements.

Annual service cost for the year under the projected unit credit method is $150,000. Prior service costs are fully funded. How should the controller be advised?

INSTRUCTIONS:

1. Over what period(s) should the gain be reported?
2. Should this overfunding be treated as an extraordinary item?
3. Over what period should the termination pay be reported?

CHAPTER 17

☐

ACCOUNTING FOR LEASES

17-1 A Lease is a Lease is a Lease...

Robert O. Whitman the executive vice president, treasurer and chief accounting officer for the American Electric Power Service Corporation made the following comments in an article published in 1975:

"The subject of accounting for leases has been debated for many years. Yet, accounting for leases should not be a complex subject. Basically, a lease is an agreement granting the right to use property for a specified term in consideration for periodic payments of rent. The lessee pays the rent and charges it to expense; the lessor receives the rent and credits it to income. What could be simpler?

Unfortunately, there are some who are not content that a lease should be accounted for as a lease. They have found that if they look at it through their legs, they can perceive a lease as something else -- a sale and a purchase of property!

Now they have something that can get their teeth into -- now, instead of accounting for a lease as it is, they can account for it as if it were something else! This opens new horizons to them. The drudgery of accounting for plain old expenses period after period can be turned into exercises in virtuosity: accounting for assets and liabilities, depreciation, interest, and payments on principal. The liabilities can even by divided into current and noncurrent.

The trouble is that these people will not restrict themselves to their own amusements. They have the zeal of converts. They are like the fox, with his tail cut off in a trap, who devoted himself to persuading the other foxes that they would look much better with bobbed tails. If some people cannot be persuaded, they should be compelled, by a promulgated accounting standard, to present their financial statements from the distorted as if point of view."

INSTRUCTIONS:

1. Discuss the various reasons that have been used to justify the capitalization or noncapitalization of lease contracts. What is the apparent rationale that FASB No. 13 Accounting for Leases is based on?

2. In general, what accounting treatment for leases is desired by the lessee? the lessor? Why?

3. What might be the advantage to a company of leasing assets instead of owning them? What might be the disadvantages of leasing the assets instead of owning them?

4. Discuss the impact that an operating lease will have on financial statements and related financial information as compared to the effect that a capital lease would have.

5. What are the reasons why some managers argue against the capitalization of leases?

17-2 Auto-Lube, Inc.

Auto-Lube, Inc. is a franchisor of oil and lubrication shops. In order to maintain some control over its shop locations, the company enters into sale and leaseback agreements and sublease agreements as described below.

Auto-Lube purchases a shop site and contracts with a construction company to construct an oil and lubrication shop. Upon completion, the land and building are sold to an outside investor at the cost to the company. Auto-Lube leases the shop from the investor, usually for a term of 20 years. The monthly rental is usually 1% of the sales price and the company pays for all insurance, maintenance and taxes. Auto-Lube then subleases the land and building to the franchisee of the shop. The terms of the subleases are similar to the terms of the leases except that Auto-Lube usually receives a markup or slighly higher rental ($25 to $100 per month higher). Neither the leases nor the subleases include a bargain purchase option and title to the land and buildings at the termination of the leases remains with the investor. The fair value of the land portion of these leases normally exceeds 25% of the total fair value. There is no related investment credit involved since only land and buildings are leased.

A typical type of arrangement might be as follows:

Land cost of shop location	$ 75,000	35.2%
Building cost of shop	138,000	64.8
	$213,000	100.0%

Sales price to the investor: $213,000

Lease terms -
  Minimum monthly rental: $2,130
  Inception date: 1-1-86

  Monthly rentals due to the first of each month with
    the first payment due 1-1-86.
  Term: 20 years.

Sublease terms -
  Minimum monthly rental: $2,230
  Inception date: 1-1-86

  Monthly rentals due on same dates as lease payments.
  Term: 20 years.

INSTRUCTIONS:

1. Do the leases require capitalization?
2. Do the subleases meet the requirements to be recorded as direct financing leases?
3. Should the land and building portions of the leases be accounted for separately and, if so, how should the lease rent and sublease rent be allocated?
4. As required by FASB No. 13, should Auto-Lube, as lessee, compute the present value of its minimum lease payments using its incremental borrowing rate if it is lower than the lessor's implicit rate? Should a residual value be attributed to the building in determining the lessor's implicit rate?
5. What are the accounting entries to record the leases and how should the leases be reported by the company?

17-3 Community Hospital*

Community Hospital is a 50-bed general acute-care hospital located in Hamlet, a small rural community. The hospital, owned by the Brown County Hospital Foundation, a not-for-profit corporation, was built in 1960 and was financed by donations from the community of $200,000 and a federal grant of $800,000.

In 1986, oil was discovered near Hamlet and within months thousands of people moved to Hamlet to work for the oil industry. An oil refinery was opened in 1986

---

*Adapted from a case prepared by Steven Thimjon.

providing steady jobs. The hospital facilities became inadequate to meet the demands of the increased population and plans began for a new 70-bed hospital. The Hospital Foundation Board investigated alternatives to pay for a new $10 million hospital. The facility was badly needed but the Foundation was not in any position to borrow that kind of money or to raise it locally from the community.

The Foundation Board asked Health Care Inc. to assist them. Health Care Inc., a tax-exempt nonprofit corporation, is a multi-hospital organization that manages and operates hospitals throughout the country.

After considering several options the Treasurer of Health Care Inc. prepared a proposal for the Foundation to consider.

1. Health Care Inc. would assist the Foundation Board in securing tax-exempt revenue bonds and would assist the community in a fund-raising effort.

2. Tax-exempt revenue bonds for $9 million would be issued by the Hospital Authority of Brown County for the construction of a new 70-bed hospital, Oil Basin Medical Center.

3. The community would be responsible to raise the remaining $1 million from a community fund-raising campaign and from energy impact grants.

4. The Hospital Authority will lease the hospital back to the Brown County Hospital Foundation for rentals equal to the annual principal and interest on the bonds.

5. Health Care Inc. will manage and operate the new hospital under a lease agreement with the Foundation.

6. The lease between the Foundation and Health Care Inc. would be for a term of 30 years, the life of the bond issue, but would be terminable at the option of either Health Care or the Foundation, on six months notice.

7. The agreement obligates Health Care to operate and manage the Oil Basin Medical Center and to pay rental payments to Brown County Hospital Foundation equal to the principal payments and interest expense on the bonds. The rental payments would be reduced by any gifts, grants, or bequests received by the Foundation for the benefit of the hospital.

8. The bonds would be obligations of the Hospital Authority and would be secured by a mortgage on the property, a reserve fund equal to annual debt service payments, and all future revenues of the hospital.

The Foundation Board was very pleased with the proposal and accepted it. Health Care Inc. was also pleased because they were able to lease and manage a profitable hospital in a growing community and were also not guaranteeing the bonds issued to finance the new hospital.

Health Care Inc. accounted for its lease agreement with Brown County Hospital Foundation as an operating lease charging the rental payments to operations.

INSTRUCTIONS:

Do you agree or disagree with Health Care's treatment of the transaction? Explain.

17-4 Amco Company

Amco Company, whose year end is December 31, manufactures large bearings which are used as replacement parts for various types of industrial machinery. During recent years, sales of the bearings have increased substantially and the company is considering leasing additional machines in order to increase production. The company has obtained three proposals for three different pieces of machinery from three different, unrelated companies. The proposals are as follows:

	Kris, Inc.	Tanya Enterprises	Curtis Co.
Monthly rental	$1,350	$4,800	$1,800
Lease term	10 years	5 years	7 years
Noncancelable	Yes	Yes	Yes
Estimated economic life	15 years	15 years	7 years
Purchase option	None	None	None
Fair market value at inception of lease	$100,000	$432,000	$106,000
Renewal option	Yes for $1000/month for 5 years	None	None
Present value of minimun lease payments at the beginning of the lease term	$94,096	$221,587	$106,100

	Kris, Inc.	Tanya Enterprises	Curtis Co.
Implicit interest rate	12.2%	10.8%	10.7%
Investment credit	Lessee	Lessor	Lessee
Incremental borrowing rate	12%	12%	12%
Fair market value at end of lease	$23,000	$288,000	---

Notes:

There are no executory costs included in the lease payments of any of the above leases. There are no lessee guarantees of residual value in any of the above leases. The inception of all leases will be January 1, 1986. All monthly rentals will be paid at the end of the month.

INSTRUCTIONS:

1. How would Amco Company account for each of the leases? Why?
2. What disclosures would be required in the 1986 financial statements of Amco Company relating to each lease?

17-5 Betty Young's Bakery

Due to the growth of its market area, in December 1985 the management of Betty Young's (BY) Bakery decided that it needed an additional delivery truck which could be purchased for $36,000. Previous experience indicated that a new truck would last seven years and could be depreciated under the Company's normal depreciation method, which is straight-line. Management also investigated the possibility of purchasing a used delivery truck and found that a three-year-old truck would cost $21,000 and a five-year old truck would cost $12,000.

BY Bakery has a five-year commitment for financing from the Workman's National Bank at 11% interest. However, since BY Bakery had plans for additional plant expansion in the near future and since the amount available under its commitment was limited, management decided it would be better to lease the truck. Consequently, BY Bakery and Arthur's Auto Center entered into a lease agreement in January 1986. An abstract of the lease terms follows.

LEASE TERMS

Effective Date of Release: January 3, 1986

Arthur's Auto Center Number A–223–6

Pursuant to a Lease Agreement, dated as of <u>January 3, 1986</u>, between Arthur's Auto Center ("Lessor") and <u>B.Y. Bakery</u> ("Lessee"), the terms of which are hereby incorporated herin by reference as if set forth herein in full. Lessor does hereby lease to Lessee, and Lessee does hereby lease from Lessor, the Equipment described herin for the lease term and monthly rent set forth herein.

Type of Equipment: 1986 – 2 ton delivery truck

Manufacturer: General Motors Corporation

Model Number: Serial Number:
  608–2 ton   6M2037P308

Total Acquisition Cost: Thirty-six thousand dollars ($36,000.00)

Location of Equipment: within geographical limits set forth in insurance policy or policies providing coverages specified in Section 8 (a) of Lease Agreement.

Other Details: The lessee shall be responsible for paying all costs for insurance, maintenance and taxes in connection with the equipment. The lessee shall be entitled to any investment tax credit arising from the equipment.

Lease term: –36– months beginning on the Effective Date of Lease specified above.

Renewal: Upon <u>30</u> days written notice prior to the expiration of the lease term, the lessee shall have the option to renew the lease for <u>3</u> periods of <u>12</u> months each.

Monthly Rent:

(a) for each month of the initial lease term: nine hundred dollars ($900.00) per month payable at the end oı each month.

(b) for each month during any extension of the initial lease term: Six hundred dollars ($600.00) per month payable at the end of each month.

Purchase: The lessee may, at his option, purchase the equipment after <u>60</u> months for a purchase price of <u>Six Thousand</u> <u>dollars</u> <u>($6000.00)</u>.

BY Bakery (Lessee)   **Arthur's Auto Center (Lessor)**

By _____   By _____

Title _____   Title _____

INSTRUCTIONS:

Define the following underlined terms and answer the associated questions with respect to BY Bakery's lease agreement.

1. When is the inception of the lease?

2. What is the fair market value of the delivery truck?

3. Is there a bargain purchase option? Why? Or why not?

4. Is there a bargain renewal option? Why? Or why not?

5. What is the lease term?

6. What is the estimated economic life of the delivery truck?

7. What is the estimated residual value of the delivery truck?

8. What are the minimum lease payments?

9. Can the interest rate implicit in the lease be determined? If so, how can it be done?

10. Can you determine the lessee's incremental borrowing rate? If so, what is it?

17-6 The Davids Corporation

The Davids Corporation is a diversified company with nationwide interests in commercial real estate developments, banking, copper mining, and metal fabrication. The company has offices and operating locations in major cities throughout the United States. Corporate headquarters for Davids Corporation is located in a metropolitan area of a midwestern state, and executives connected with various phases of company operations travel extensively. Corporate management is presently evaluating the feasibility of acquiring a business aircraft that can be used by company executives to expedite business travel to areas not adequately served by commercial airlines. Proposals for either leasing or purchasing a suitable aircraft have been analyzed, and the leasing proposal was considered to be more desirable.

The proposed lease agreement involves a twin-engine turboprop Viking that has a fair market value of $900,000. This plane would be leased for a period of 10 years beginning January 1, 1986. The lease agreement is cancelable only upon accidental destruction of the plane. An annual lease payment of $127,600 is due on January 1 of each year; the first payment is to be made on January 1, 1986. Maintenance operations are strictly scheduled by the lessor, and Davids Corporation will pay for these services as they are performed. Estimated annual maintenance costs are $6,200. The lessor will pay all insurance premiums and local property taxes, which amount to a combined total of $3,600 annually and are included in the annual lease payment of $127,600. Upon expiration of the 10-year lease, Davids Corporation can purchase the Viking for $40,000. The estimated useful life of the plane is 15 years, and its salvage value in the used plane market is estimated to be $100,000 after 10 years. The salvage value probably will never be less than $75,000 if the engines are overhauled and maintained as prescribed by the manufacturer. If the purchase option is not exercised, possession of the plane will revert to the lessor, and there is no provision for renewing the lease agreement beyond its termination on December 31, 1995.

Davids Corporation can borrow $900,000 under a 10-year term loan agreement at an annual interest rate of 12%. The lessor's implicit interest rate is not expressly stated in the lease agreement, but this rate appears to be approximately 8% based on ten net rental payments of $124,000 per year and the initial market value of $900,000 for the plane. On January 1, 1986, the present value of all net rental payments and the purchase option of $40,000 is $800,000 using the 12% interest rate. The present value of all net rental payments and the $40,000 purchase option on January 1, 1986 is $920,000 using the 8% interest rate implicit in the lease agreement. The financial vice-president of Davids Corporation has established that this lease agreement is a capital lease as defined in Statement of Financial Accounting Standard No. 13 Accounting for Leases.

INSTRUCTIONS:

1. What is the appropriate amount that Davids Corporation should recognize for the leased aircraft on its balance sheet after the lease is signed?
2. Without prejudice to your answer in part 1, assume that the annual lease payment is $127,600 as stated in the question, that the appropriate capitalized amount for the leased aircraft is $1,000,000 on January 1, 1986, and that the interest rate is 9%. How will the lease be reported in the December 31, 1986 balance sheet and related income statement? (Ignore any income tax considerations)

(CMA adapted)

17-7 Lease Agreement

Presented below are excerpts from a lease agreement:

LESSOR: The Fast Print Machine Co.

LESSEE: The Chattanooga Printing Co.

PROPERTY: A four-color photo-offset printing press
            specially designed per Chattanooga's
            specifications.

TERM: 10 years (January 1, 1985 to December 1994).

RENEWALS: None

RENTALS: $10,000 per year payable annually in advance.

PURCHASE OPTION: Lessee may purchase the machine for $8,000
                at expiration of initial term of lease.

LESSOR TO PAY: Nothing.

LESSEE TO PAY: Taxes, insurance and maintenance.

Additional Information:

● The leased equipment has an economic useful life of 12 years.

● As of January 1, 1985, Chattanooga was borrowing money
   from a local bank at 11%.

● Fast Print built the press at a cost of $66,200.

● Under current market conditions Fast Print's normal gross
   margin on sales of custom equipment is 15%.

● Current estimates indicate that the value of the machine
   at the end of the lease term will be $8,000.

● The lease is designed to yield an 8% return for Fast Print
   (you may assume that Chattanooga is aware of this).

INSTRUCTIONS:

1. How should the lease be classified by the lessee and the lessor?
2. What entries would be required on the books of the two companies to record the lease transaction?
3. In general terms, what disclosures will be required in the financial statements of the companies?

17-8 First City Bank

You are requested by the First City Bank to perform a purchase investigation of Marco Leasing Company, a general equipment lessor (a relatively new company). Marco's leases are accounted for under the finance method for financial statement purposes and, because of a lack of purchase options to the lessees on a large portion of their leases, are treated under the operating method for income tax purposes. Marco follows the flow through method of accounting for investment tax credits. For income tax purposes, Marco claims the investment credit based on the useful lives of the lease equipment and has flowed a similar amount through the income statement. The auditor for Marco has not taken exception to this accounting treatment.

Generally, direct leasing companies, particularly those who lease a large variety of specialized equipment, dispose of the leased equipment at the end of the term of their full-payout lease. In most cases, the useful life of the equipment for income tax depreciation purposes exceeds the initial lease term by a sufficient number of years to result in a greater amount of investment credit being claimed on the income tax return than will ultimately be realized because of the workings of the Internal Revenue Code's investment credit recapture provisions. As a result, in the past you have generally insisted that the amount of investment credit recognized in the financial statements be limited to the amount which the Company may reasonably be expected to realize; that is an amount based on the initial lease term rather than the larger amount computed on the useful life basis.

The auditor for the company and the company both argued that it was the Company's intention not to dispose of the equipment at the end of the original lease but instead re-lease the equipment to the original lessee or to some other lessee. They further argued that in the event that it was not possible to re-lease the equipment, they would opt to place the equipment in storage rather than sell the equipment and be faced with investment credit recapture.

Marco's officers readily admitted that, based on both the economic and business pressures that might be placed upon them at the end of the original lease term, they might very well consider disposing of the equipment at that time. However, they maintain that a decision to sell the equipment would be made based on the facts and circumstances at that time and consequently, any charge to income for investment credit recapture should be a charge of the later period.

What factors might you develop to argue that Marco should not report the entire investment credit immediately?

17-9 Leveraged Leasing

The Board of Directors meeting of Mini-Corp Bank has just been called to order. The first item on the agenda is a proposal to finance a number of oil tankers through a leveraged lease transaction.

The controller explains the basic proposal to the Board members, but there is a great deal of confusion and misunderstanding. The controller anticipated this, and therefore presented the following information:

1. We plan to finance these oil tankers in return for the rental payments and the tax benefits associated with ownership.

2. We (the bank) will borrow a large portion of the money needed to finance the transaction from other long-term lenders.

3. We will purchase the tanker, lease it, and in return collect the rental payments from which we will pay the interest and principal costs to the long-term lender. At the end of the lease we will return the residual value. The key elements of a leveraged lease are illustrated in Exhibit I.

Exhibit I

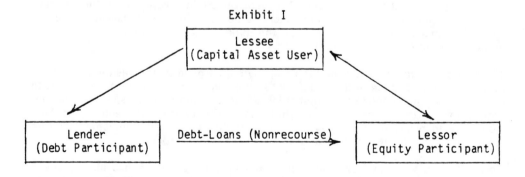

The loan by the debt participants is on a nonrecourse basis and as such the debt participant cannot look to the general credit of the lessor but must satisfy his claim through the lessee.

The controller projects that the after tax yield on this investment should be 18% which he considers excellent. He asks for approval for the project so that the contracts can be finalized.

One of the directors has reservations. She has heard of inherent loss leveraged leases and doesn't understand how this type of lease could return 18% after tax. In addition, she is concerned about the cash flow pattern associated with this type of agreement. Before approval, she wants more information.

INSTRUCTIONS:

1. Assist the controller by explaining:

   a. The general characteristics of leveraged leases.
   b. The general cash flow pattern.
   c. The types of leveraged leases.
   d. The association with taxes.

2. In general, how would the bank account for the leveraged leases?

17-10 St. Francis Hospital*

St. Francis Hospital is a 500 bed institution located in a metropolitan community of 500,000 in the Midwest. St. Francis is a highly regarded hospital and prides itself on its ability to provide the best of medical care. The hospital is also quite cost conscious and dedicated to cost containment measures. The hospital has proven to be financially stable in the past, but a recent cash flow problem has caused concern among its board members.

The finance committee of the board is faced with making a major decision. The hospital is in the need of some new x-ray equipment that costs $400,000. The committee realizes that the hospital does not have the necessary funds and yet, the ever increasing demand for x-ray service dictates a need for this type of equipment. However, the financial market is tight and St. Francis could not withstand the burden of having to take a loan at 18 1/2%.

Henry Jackson, a long time board member, brought up the idea of possibly leasing the equipment from one of the local leasing companies. He points out that a lease would provide 100% financing and that due to the technological changes evident in the health care industry, it may be advantageous to keep the risk of obsolescence with

---

*Adapted from a case prepared by Rodney Nordby.

someone else. The type of equipment St. Francis needs is supposed to have an estimated useful life of 15 years; however, St. Francis' past records indicate that a 10 year life is more realistic.

Paul Brown, another long time board member, further points out that the hospital had leased some laboratory equipment a few years back and had encountered no problems with the quality of service or with obtaining reimbursement for the costs. The reimbursement system is relatively straightforward. The hospital may include approved expenses in determining its rate structure. Paul is asked to check with the leasing company concerning the x-ray equipment and to report back at the next board meeting.

At the next board meeting, Paul Brown reports that leasing companies could have the equipment available if St. Francis so desired. Mr. Brown also reported that the best deal he could find required annual payments of $68,448.54 that includes a built in 15% rate of interest with Sepaka Leasing Company. Further details of the lease with Sepaka Leasing Company are as follows:

> The lease would be a 10 year noncancellable contract for equipment with an estimated useful life of 15 years. St. Francis would have to pay any related executory costs plus the annual payments in the amount of $68,448.54 (15% interest rate) due on January 1 or always one year in advance. The equipment should have a residual value of $20,000 which St. Francis would not have to guarantee. Also, ownership would remain with Sepaka (there is no bargain purchase option.)

The board believes that the hospital would be able to handle the annual fee and therefore is ready to enter into the lease agreement with Sepaka. However, Mike Weaver, a recently appointed board member brings up some important questions concerning the lease which have not yet been discussed. Mike, a recent university graduate, wonders about the accounting treatment of the lease. He remembers from his accounting class that the FASB had released a statement concerning lease accounting and wonders how this might possibly affect the hospital's potential lease. He is asked to do some further checking and report back to the board.

INSTRUCTIONS:

What will he have to report regarding lease accounting and the financial impacts for the hospital?

17-11 BankAmerica Corp.

In September, 1985 BankAmerica Corp. signed a letter of intent of sell its world headquarters complex for $660 million to real estate magnate Walter H. Schorenstein in a transaction expected to yield pretax profits of $580 million.

Daniel W. Costello, executive vice president of BankAmerica's corporate real estate division said the sale would allow the bank holding company to report a "sizable" gain in 1985. An undisclosed portion of the sale price would be paid at the closing and the remainder paid over time with interest. Mr. Costello declined to be more specific about the contract terms and the proposed sale's impact on earnings. He said the earnings and tax implications were still being considered by the finance department.

The complex was built in 1969 for $100 million and has a current book value of $80 million. The tower has 1.5 million square feet and the adjoining buildings have a total of 300,000 square feet.

Real estate industry officials say the 52 story tower and two adjoining buildings, if sold for $660 would command one of the highest prices ever paid for a building complex in the U.S. Some speculate, however that the price was inflated by the terms of the lease-back agreement.

Under the proposed sale, BankAmerica initially will lease back 60% of the tower and all of the adjoining buildings. The bank planned to relocate certain operations to suburban offices over the next seven years and will eventually lease only about 25% of the tower.

Mr. Costello said the bank would pay an average of $37 a square foot for the space. Some local real estate experts say the rent is about 10% higher than the average paid for office space in the city's financial district. Some believe the terms suggest that the bank would get a higher-than-expected price for the complex because it agreed to pay a high rent for office space.

BankAmerica "is paying a premium for the space," said John W. Chamberlain, a vice president of Grubb & Ellis Realty, a San Francisco based real estate brokerage firm. Rents for prime office space "in today's market are closer to the low-to-mid $30s a square foot," he said.

"This deal is made to look a lot better than it really is," said one real estate industry source familiar with the property. "It is obviously an earnings-driven deal and not a cash deal. The gain comes at a time when the bank needs it. In July 1985 they posted a $338 million loss for the third quarter."

INSTRUCTIONS:

1. What is the nature of a sale-leaseback transaction?
2. What are the advantages of such an agreement?
3. Discuss the comment by the industry source who considers the transaction "an earnings-driven deal and not a cash deal."
4. How will BankAmerica account for the expected $580 gain? (ignore taxes).

CHAPTER 18

ACCOUNTING CHANGES AND ERROR ANALYSIS

18-1 The AT&T Divestiture

On August 24, 1982, the final Consent Decree was entered by the U.S. Court for the District of Columbia settling the suit filed by the Department of Justice against AT&T. The terms of the decree required that the company divest itself of certain of its operations. On January 1, 1984 the operating companies were divested by a spin-off to the company's shareholders. The spin-off created dramatic changes for AT&T. Following are exerpts from their notes to the financial statements for 1983:

As a result of the Court-ordered January 1, 1984 divestiture, the Company's integrated telecommunications business has been split up with those portions which operate predominantly under monopoly regulation being assigned to seven regional holding companies ("RHCs") and those portions which face strong and growing competition being assigned to the post-divestiture AT&T. Consequently, certain of the

Company's accounting policies and practices were no longer appropriate after December 31, 1983. Accordingly, the Company adjusted its financial statements on December 31, 1983 to reflect the discontinued use by the post-diversiture AT&T of accounting policies and practices appropriate for rate-regulated enterprises and restated the rate-regulated assets assigned to the post-diverstiture AT&T on a basis appropriate for nonregulated enterprises.

These adjustments, each of which reduces the carrying value of the post-divestiture AT&T's net assets, consist of the following:

(1) Reducing the carrying value of terminal equipment and network facilities from the amounts recognized by regulators in the rate-making process to a lesser amount expected to be recoverable in a competitive environment.

(2) Establishing liability accruals for expenses which in the rate-making process have been accounted for only when paid. These include expenses for future compensated absences and special termination benefits.

(3) Establishing deferred liability accruals for expenses with tax timing differences which regulators in the rate-making process have recognized on a current basis rather than on a deferred basis as is required for nonregulated business.

These adjustments were accounted for as a divestiture-related extraordinary charge on December 31, 1983, reducing Income Applicable to Common Shares by $5.5 billion, net of taxes of $4.5 billion (comprised of $.1 billion of current taxes and $4.4 billion of deferred taxes), or $5.87 per share. Commencing January 1, 1984, the published financial statements of the post-divestiture AT&T will reflect asset values and accounting principles appropriate for a nonregulated enterprise.

Additional accounting changes to be made in 1984 that do not require adjustments to income in 1983 are as follows:

Consolidation – The accounts of all significant subsidiaries controlled by postdivestiture AT&T will be consolidated, including Western Electric and Bell Laboratories which were previously included using the equity method.

Revenue Refunds – Liabilities for probable revenue refunds, if any, will be reflected in current results and, within a year, in the applicable interim periods' results.

Purchases from Western Electric – The profit realized by Western Electric on sales of equipment within the consolidated group will be eliminated. Such profit will not be realized until such equipment either is sold outside the consolidated group or is depreciated.

Lease Commitments – The asset values and related obligations of capital leases will be included in the balance sheet. The amortization of assets under capital leases and the interest cost of capital lease obligations will be included in current results.

Additional changes were also reported in their annual report: In 1982, the Company changed its accounting for certain deferred income taxes (primarily state and local taxes) to record deferred taxes on timing differences only when such deferred taxes are recognized by regulators in the rate-making process. This change was made to achieve greater consistency between financial reporting and the intrastate regulatory rate-making process. The effect of this change increased Income

Applicable to Common Shares in 1982 by $352.7 ($.42 per share),
which include the cumulative effect of the change at the
beginning of 1982 of $286.8 ($.34 per share). See also Note (P)
to Historical Financial Statements.

Pro forma amounts assuming the change in accounting for
deferred income taxes had been applied retroactively are as
follows:

	1982	1981
Income Applicable to Common Shares	$6,850.1	$6,726.3
Earnings per Common Share	$8.06	$8.53

Pension costs as a percent of salaries and wages have decreased
over the past three years. It is management's expectation that
this trend will not continue, but future pension costs as a
percent of salaries and wages will stabilize at about the 1983
level absent future plan amendments and absent deviations between
actual and expected future pension plan experience. The sharp
decrease in pension cost as a percent of salaries and wages from
1982 to 1983 was due primarily to a change in the assumed
investment earnings rate from a flat 5% per year to the varying
rates mentioned above. The effect of this change was to decrease
1983 pension cost by approximately $959.1.

INSTRUCTIONS:

1. What is the basic problem caused by accounting changes?
2. What are the three types of accounting changes that AT&T has
undertaken?
3. What are the three possible approaches that might be used to deal
with AT&T's changes in accounting principles? What is the rationale for
each?
4. Under what conditions are changes in accounting principle
considered appropriate? Evaluate the AT&T changes based on these
conditions.
5. What difficulties arise in applying these conditions?

18-2 Norbert Electrostatics, Inc.*

Norbert Electrostatics, Inc. produces support equipment for nuclear energy research. Its primary markets are governments and large universities. Demand has always been limited because of the high production costs involved. Demand has fallen off considerably in recent years due to increasing public concern over the potential dangers of nuclear waste.

As a result, Norbert began to expand its product line into medical equipment. It hired a large number of highly qualified managers and scientists with experience in the medical products area, offering generous salaries and stock bonuses.

As part of its expansion into medical equipment, Norbert would like to merge with Acme Medical Products Corporation, an established producer of medical equipment. Such a combination would provide Norbert with the immediate availability of production facilities and an existing channel of distribution. Norbert has offered to exchange shares of its own stock to equal Acme's net assets plus $150,000. Pending approval of Acme's stockholders, the merger is to take place February 1, 1986. The present date is December 31, 1985.

Norbert's expansion into medical equipment so far has had a dismal effect on the year's earnings. Increased compensation expenses, research and development costs, and sizable capital equipment purchases have reduced earnings from last year's $207,000 to $155,000, a decrease of more than 25%. This year's income statement, computed using Norbert's traditional accounting methods (LIFO inventory flow assumption, accelerated depreciation, and the deferral method of accounting for investment credit) is as follows:

Sales		$3,000,000
Cost of Sales		(1,800,000)
Gross Profit		1,200,000
Depreciation		(300,000)
Wages and Salaries		(300,000)
Research and Development		(150,000)
Other Expenses		(150,000)
Income Before Taxes		300,000
Income Tax Before Credit	$150,000	
Less Investment Tax Credit	5,000	
Income tax		(145,000)
Net Income		$ 155,000

Norbert's management believes that this large reduction in earnings will cause the market price of its stock to fall substantially. This reduction could have serious consequences. Norbert's management believes that succeeding in the medical products field depends on retaining this department's staff. Since these managers and scientists are highly in demand, they must be well paid by Norbert to assure their

---

*Adapted from a case prepared by Jill Timmerman.

continued employment. Because the compensation plan for these employees depends heavily on increased stock price, a substantial drop in stock prices could cause some (if not all) of these employees to seek other jobs. Secondly, a drop in stock price would require issuance of additional shares to consumate the merger with Acme. Norbert's management would naturally like to issue as few shares as possible to Acme's present shareholders.

Norbert's president has suggested some accounting changes that would yield a higher earnings figure. An income statement using FIFO inventory valuation, straight line depreciation, and the flow-through method of accounting for investment credit appears below.

Sales		$3,000,000
Cost of Sales		(1,500,000)
Gross Profit		1,500,000
Depreciation		(180,000)
Wages and Salaries		(300,000)
Research and Development		(150,000)
Other Expenses		(150,000)
Income Before Taxes		720,000
Income Tax Before Credit	$360,000	
Less Investment Tax Credit	50,000	
Income tax		(310,000)
Net Income		$ 410,000

The president believes that the income figure reported with these accounting changes will support the present stock price and possibly even increase it. After all, it practically doubles last year's reported earnings of $207,000.

INSTRUCTIONS:

    1. Assuming that Norbert Electrostatics, Inc. were permitted to change accounting methods, how would they be reported on the current financial statements?

    2. As auditor for Norbert Electrostatics, would you permit the company to change accounting methods?

    3. Comment on the likelihood that these accounting changes would lead to over valued stock prices.

18-3 Quick-Wash Services, Inc.

Quick-Wash Services, Inc. hired an accounting firm in 1984 for an audit in connection with their plans for a public offering of stock. The company had been operating laundry and dry cleaning stores for a number of years.

At the time of the initial audit, the company increased the estimated salvage values of some of their equipment, thereby increasing income from $.50 to $.54 per share. The increased salvage value was due to some recent changes instituted by the company and part of an overall review of their depreciation policies.

The company had begun to refurbish used washers and dryers at its distribution facility salvaging parts from used machines and therefore had reduced depreciation expense by assigning ten percent of the initial purchase cost of the laundry machines to salvage value. The company initially wanted to restate prior years' earnings to reflect this change in salvage value of the machines. The impact would have been to increase reported earnings by approximately $.04 per share in each of the previous 3 years. The adjusted earnings per share would have been $.46 in 1983, $.48 in 1982 and $.40 in 1981.

There was some discussion with the auditors in 1984 concerning the appropriateness of the accounting for this change. The company argued that they had previously erred in not allowing for salvage value. Their refurbishment policy had started to a limited extent in 1980 and they erred in not adjusting sooner.

The accounting firm suggested this was a change in estimate and, therefore should be dealt with prospectively. Since the company did not want to start off on the wrong foot with their new auditors, they agreed with the accountants. After all, the change would continue to benefit them in future years and it was not as if the expense reduction would be lost.

In 1985, the company revised their estimates of their useful life of their property (other than those changed in 1984). Net income would be increased approximately $.06 per share for each year affected. In 1981, the company had acquired certain machines as a result of the purchase of two competitive laundry operations. The estimated depreciable life of these machines was extended from 5 to 6 years which is the remaining unexpired life of the eight years generally used to depreciate similar machines under their refurbishment program.

Jim Seifert, president of the company, was pleased that the depreciation system was finally straightened out and that he could look forward to a $.06 per share earnings increase both this year and the next. This would be consistent with the prospective treatment given to the change in estimate in 1984. However, the auditors disagreed. They felt that these machines had been overlooked the previous year when the depreciation system was revised. Since this was an error, the previous year should be restated and a footnote provided to disclose the nature of the error. In addition, they reasoned, the 1984 and 1985 results of operations would then be presented on a comparable basis.

Mr. Seifert was furious. He was not pleased with the accounting firm's 1984 demand to treat the revised salvage values prospectively as a change in estimate and now they wanted to treat their 1985 revision as an error! Where was the consistency in application for which the accountants were so famous? Besides, restatement for 1984 would result in an earnings decline for 1985 from a restated $.60 per share in 1984 to $.57 in 1985.

INSTRUCTIONS:

1. Discuss the appropriateness of treating the 1984 revision in salvage values as a change in estimate, change in accounting principle, and change due to an error. How would the accounting treatment differ with each?
2. How should the 1984 change be reported on the financial statements?
3. What is the appropriate accounting for the 1985 change?
4. What is the role of comparability and consistency for the accounting for changes?

18-4 FIFO to LIFO to FIFO

Lebensway Discount Merchandising Co. had been using the LIFO inventory method of accounting for the past four years. At the June 30, 1985 year end, their inventories stated on the last-in, first-out basis were approximately $1,800,000 less than they would be if stated on the first-in, first-out (FIFO) basis. The treasurer, Bruce Leben, is proud of the tax deferral benefits, which he calls tax savings, that have accrued to the company through use of LIFO.

The only problem Bruce has with the use of LIFO is the depressed effect it has had on reported earnings. He understands that lower earnings are the reason for the tax savings, but he really would like to use FIFO for financial statement purposes while using LIFO for tax purposes. He feels this is similar to his use of straight line depreciation for financial statement purposes and accelerated depreciation for the tax return. But unfortunately, accounting principles require the use of LIFO for both, if it is selected for tax reporting.

As a result, each year Bruce prepares a pro forma statement and report for the shareholders showing the impact of LIFO on earnings and the earnings restated on a FIFO basis. He has been able to satisfy the shareholders that they are better off using LIFO because of the tax savings he reports.

Recently, Bruce has heard from a number of sources that there are serious plans for legislation to eliminate the tax rules that for years have required users of LIFO for income tax purposes to conform their financial statements to the same inventory pricing method. If this legislation is enacted, companies previously using FIFO for both financial and income tax reporting will be able to elect the LIFO method for taxes and continue to use FIFO for financial accounting.

This new legislation would be ideal for Lebensway Discount Merchandising. All the company would have to do is change their accounting principle from the LIFO method to the FIFO method for financial reporting; the tax reporting system would remain the same. Bruce remembers, however, that at the time they changed to LIFO the company had to justify the purpose of the switch to the auditors. Bruce isn't sure, but he thinks the reason he disclosed was obvious -- the company would receive tax benefits. The reason for the switch to FIFO would also be obvious -- higher reported earnings.

INSTRUCTIONS:

1. Under the present rules how would a company account for a change from FIFO to LIFO?
2. How would a company account for a change from LIFO to FIFO?
3. Are Bruce's justifications for the switches acceptable?
4. Is there any economic reason for Bruce to change from LIFO to FIFO for financial reporting?

18-5 Harnett, Inc.

Harnett, Inc. is primarily in the business of licensing computer software products which it has developed. Since 1976, the company has followed a policy of recognizing license fee revenue from noncancellable license agreements at the initiation of the license term. In effect, this generally resulted in taking the full amount of revenue from such licenses (after deferral of a sufficient portion to cover maintenance requirements, if any) into income when the license term commenced. The licenses carry terms of from one to five years, and all development and marketing costs were expensed when incurred. Use of this method was based on the view that, since there would be no future costs and since license terms approximated the expected useful lives of the products, the rights to use the software had in fact been "sold" in the same manner that leases for tangible property may be treated as sales. This method was consistent with industry practice.

Late in 1984, Harnett, Inc. became concerned that despite the fact that the license contracts were noncancellable, competition might cause them to incur significant unanticipated costs to maintain contracts currently in effect. Accordingly, early in

1984, Harnett decided to change its policy and recognize all revenue from software licenses pro rata as rentals on a month-to-month basis.

The change to month-to-month revenue recognition was unaccompanied by any change in the method of recognizing costs; development and marketing costs continued to be expensed as incurred. This decision was made because: (1) Harnett is essentially a research and development company with continuing development expenses that may not be readily assignable to one product, and it is therefore most realistic to treat such expenses as period costs; (2) marketing is normally treated as a period cost, and it is an ongoing effort of customer contacts that would be difficult to associate with any one product sale; and, (3) Harnett felt that the unanticipated costs which were leading them to change the revenue recognition method might well result, through the policy of expensing costs as incurred, in a matching of costs and revenues similar to that achieved if all costs had been deferred initially and recognized pro rata with revenue.

The anticipated change created quite a bit of concern within the company. The controller felt that the change might be considered a change in accounting principle and, if so, would require the calculation of the cumulative effect of the change on all contracts currently in force. This would involve a lot of work since the company had a large number of existing contracts. In addition, the cumulative effect would result in a large reduction in income and the company could not afford to take a large loss at the present time.

The controller discussed his concern with the treasurer. The treasurer had always felt the software products were the result of long-term construction type contracts. That is, the development of the products required substantial time for completion. Revenue was then recognized on a completed contract basis -- after the software was "completed" and sold. Following this logic, the large current period loss could be avoided since a change in the method for the accounting for long-term construction-type contracts resulted in a retroactive adjustment to the prior years' financial statements.

The two approached their accounting firm with this proposal. Unfortunately, the auditors did not agree. To them it was a change in estimate. Previously, the company had estimated that no significant costs would be incurred after the sale. Now, however, new information was available that the circumstances surrounding the initial estimate had changed. Competitive pressures changed, so cost estimates changed.

The treasurer and controller were pleased with the work of the accounting firm. Not only could they avoid the costly work of determining the retroactive affect on their old contracts, but they could also avoid the large current period write-off.

INSTRUCTIONS:

    1. Discuss the accounting requirements for each of the proposed treatments of the change in method for revenue recognition.
    2. What is the appropriate method of accounting for this change? Why?

18-6 Interlaken, Inc.

Interlaken, Inc. has recently hired a new independent auditor who says she wants "to get everything straightened out." Consequently, she has proposed the following accounting changes in connection with the client's 1985 financial statements:

a. In the past, the client has spread preproduction costs in its furniture division over 5 years. Because its latest furniture is of the "fad" type, it appears that the largest volume of sales will occur during the first two years after introduction. Consequently, the client proposes to amortize preproduction costs on a per-unit basis, which will result in expensing most of such costs during the first 2 years after the furniture's introduction. If the new accounting method had been used prior to 1985, retained earnings at December 31, 1984, would have been $200,000 less.

b. For the nursery division the client proposes to switch from FIFO to LIFO inventories as it is believed that LIFO will provide a better matching of current costs with revenues. The effect of making this change on 1985 earnings will be an increase of $180,000. The client says that the effect of the change on December 31, 1984, retained earnings cannot be determined.

c. To achieve a better matching of revenues and expenses in its building construction division, the client proposes to switch from the completed-contract method of accounting to the percentage-of-completion method. Had the percentage-of-completion method been employed in all prior years, retained earnings at December 31, 1984, would have been $825,000 greater.

d. At December 31, 1984, the client had a receivable of $525,000 from Harris, Inc. on its balance sheet. Harris, Inc. has gone bankrupt and no recovery is expected. The client proposes to write off the receivable as a prior period item.

e. The client proposes the following changes in depreciation policies:

    (1) For office furniture and fixtures it proposes to change from a 10 year useful life to an 8-year life. If this change had been made in prior years, retained earnings at December 31, 1984 would have been $100,000 less. The effect of the change on 1985 income alone is a reduction of $10,000.

    (2) For its manufacturing assets the client purposes to change from double-declining balance depreciation to straight line. If straight-line depreciation had been used for all prior periods,

retained earnings would have been $190,000 greater at December 31, 1984. The effect of the change on 1985 income alone is an increase of $12,000.

(3) For its equipment in the leasing division the client proposes to adopt the sum-of-the-years'-digits depreciation method. The client had never used SYD before. The first year the client operated a leasing division was 1985. If straight-line depreciation were used, 1985 income would be $40,000 greater.

f. In preparing its 1984 statements, one of the client's bookkeepers overstated ending inventory by $115,000 because of a mathematical error. The client proposes to treat this item as a prior period adjustment.

INSTRUCTIONS:

1. For each of the changes described above decide whether:
   a. The change involves an accounting principle, accounting estimate, or correction of an error.
   b. Restatement of opening retained earnings is required.

2. Do any of the changes require presentation of pro forma amounts?

3. What would be the proper adjustment to the December 31, 1984 retained earnings? What would be the "cumulative effect" shown separately in the 1985 income statement?

18-7 Monte Corp.

Neil Jones, controller of Monte Corp. is aware that APB Opinion No. 20 regarding accounting changes has been issued. After reading the opinion, he is confused and is not sure what action should be taken on the following items related to the Monte Corp. for the year 1985:

1. All equipment sold by Monte is subject to a three-year warranty. It has been estimated that the expense ultimately to be incurred on these machines is 1% of sales. In 1985, because of the production breakthrough, it is now estimated that 1/2 of 1% of sales is sufficient. In 1983 and 1984, warranty expense was computed as $20,000 and $25,000, respectively. The company now believes that these warranty costs should be reduced by 50%.

2. In 1985, the company decided to change its method of inventory pricing from average cost to the FIFO method. The effect of this change on prior years is to increase 1983 income by $30,000 and decrease 1984 income by $10,000.

3. In 1985, Monte decided to change its policy on accounting for certain marketing costs. Previously, the company had chosen to defer and amortize all marketing costs over at least five years because Monte believed that a return on these expenditures did not occur immediately. Recently, however, the time differential has considerably shortened, and Monte is now expensing the marketing costs as incurred.

4. In 1985, the company examined its entire policy relating to the depreciation of plant equipment. Plant equipment had normally been depreciated over a 15-year period, but recent experience has indicated that the company was incorrect in its estimates and that the assets should be depreciated over a 20-year period.

5. One division of Monte Corp., Wigwag, Inc., has consistently shown an increasing net income from period to period. On closer examination of their operating statement, it is noted that bad debt expense and inventory obsolescence charges are much lower than in other divisions. In discussing this with the controller of this division, it has been learned that the controller has increased his net income each period by knowingly making low estimates related to the write-off of receivables and inventory.

6. In 1985, the company purchased new machinery that should increase production dramatically. The company has decided to depreciate this machinery on an accelerated basis, even though other machinery is depreciated on a straight-line basis.

INSTRUCTIONS:

Neil Jones has come to you for advice about the situations above. Indicate the appropriate accounting treatment that should be given each of these situations.

18-8 Restatement for Comparison?

Various types of accounting changes can affect the financial statements of a business enterprise differently. Assume that the following list describes changes that have a material effect on the financial statements for the current year of your business enterprise.

1. Correction of a mathematical error in inventory pricing made in a prior period.

2. A change from prime costing to full absorption costing for inventory valuation.

3. A change from presentation of statements of individual companies to presentation of consolidated statements.

4. A change in the method of accounting for leases for tax purposes to conform with the financial accounting method. As a result, both deferred and current taxes payable changed substantially.

5. A change from the FIFO method of inventory pricing to the LIFO method of inventory pricing.

6. A change from the completed-contract method to the percentage-of-completion method of accounting for long-term construction-type contracts.

7. A change in the estimated useful life of previously recorded fixed assets based on newly acquired information.

8. A change from deferring and amortizing preproduction costs to recording such costs as an expense when incurred because future benefits of the costs have become doubtful. The new accounting method was adopted in recognition of the change in estimated future benefits.

9. A change from including the employer share of FICA taxes to including it with "Retirement benefits" on the income statement.

INSTRUCTIONS:

Identify the type of change that is described in each item above and indicate whether the prior year's financial statements should be restated when presented in comparative form with the current year's statements. Ignore possible pro forma effects.

18-9 The Errors of Naples

The Naples Corporation began operation in December of 1980. The company has been successful selling standardized legal forms, documents, and do-it-yourself wills. In 1985, the company engaged an auditor to perform an audit on its financial statements as requested by their creditors. The books had not yet been closed for 1985. During the course of the audit, the auditor found the following errors:

a. In 1984, the company wrote off $9,000 of inventory considered to be obsolete; this loss was charged directly to Retained Earnings.

b. In 1982 the company purchased a small stationary supplies company and recorded goodwill of $14,000. Although they were aware of the normal requirement to amortize goodwill over a period not to exceed 40 years, they did not amortize it since its value had not diminished.

c. In 1983, accounts payable was debited instead of accounts receivable for the sale of $2,000 of legal forms.

d. In 1983, the sales commission expense of $1,000 was charged to the sales account instead of selling and administrative expense.

e. At the end of 1984, the company failed to accrue wages of $1,500.

f. At the beginning of 1982, the company purchased equipment for $12,000, that had an estimated used straight-line depreciation, but failed to deduct the salvage value in computing the depreciation base.

g. Accrued sales commissions were never recognized at year end. They amounted to $1,200 in 1982, $1,400 in 1983, and $1,700 in 1984.

h. The auditor suggests switching from the specific charge-off accounting method for bad debts to the allowance method. The company's experience with uncollectible accounts is as follows:

	1982	1983	1984	1985	Total
1982 Sales	$600	$ 700	$ 200		$1,500
1983 Sales		700	800	500	2,000
1984 Sales			700	1,800	2,500
	$600	$1,400	$1,700	$2,300	$6,000

Additional allowances for each of the years was estimated to be: $2,000 in 1984, $600 to 1983, and $500 in 1982.

Greg Naples, president of the company, feels that correction of the errors, in general, is unnecessary. Now that the company will have an audit performed each year it is as if the company has a new start. Therefore, the financial statements should basically be presented "as if" 1985 was its first year of operation.

The auditor disagrees and tries to explain that the correction of the errors does not cast any dark cloud over the company in the eyes of the creditors. The correction of the errors may in fact require minimal changes. Following are questions that may help Greg with his understanding of the situation.

INSTRUCTIONS:

1. What is the definition and treatment of errors as described by the accounting profession?
2. What is the meaning of counterbalancing errors? What is its role in the correction of errors?
3. What is the justification for the use of prior period adjustments for the correction of errors?
4. Identify the type of error for each item and indicate whether it is counterbalancing. What adjustments are necessary in 1985, as well as for 1984, if comparative statements are to be presented for the last two years?

18-10 Sturm, Inc.

Sturm, Inc. makes roulette wheels, slot machines, and other gambling equipment and is a wholly owned subsidiary of Kaye Corporation.

A summary of the company's financial statements as of December 31, 1985, prior to an adjustment of accumulated profit (retained earnings), is as follows:

	Half year ended June 30, 1985	Half year ended Dec. 31, 1985	Year ended Dec. 31, 1985
Sales (approximate)	$2,500,000	$3,600,000	$6,100,000
Income (loss) before tax	$ 196,240	($873,870)	($677,630)

	Balance Sheet Dec. 31, 1979
Accounts Receivable	$1,800,000
Inventory	1,200,000
Other assets	500,000
Total Assets	$3,500,000
Liabilities	$3,200,000
Stockholders' equity	300,000
	$3,500,000

A significant amount of the loss in the last half of 1985 was discovered when the physical inventory as of December 31, 1985 disclosed that the book inventory was overstated by approximately $450,000 and that $124,000 of accounts receivable were uncollectible. The remaining loss resulted from a marked increase in manufacturing costs.

The joint effort of the auditor and company to analyze the $450,000 difference between the book and the physical inventory was hampered by a lack of supporting documents for some transactions, lack of accounting control over significant areas of purchasing, manufacturing and sales activity and the resignation of the chief executive, the purchasing agent, and the controller of Sturm, Inc. The three decided to start their own casino operation in Las Vegas. As a result, only $190,000 of the difference could be specifically identified and this amount was found to be a result of errors in the company book inventory as of December 31, 1985.

The company concluded that the remaining difference was probably unrecorded material usage, scrapping and pilferage, etc., in those areas where there was a lack of strong inventory control.

The accounts receivable problems were uncovered when confirmations were mailed to most of the open accounts. Many of the receivables were old and one customer had gone bankrupt nearly three years ago, but the receivable had never been adjusted. This loss was for $45,000. Other accounts were never confirmed. Total adjustments to the accounts receivable were for $79,000.

After this review, an internal auditor from the parent company was assigned to review the audited balance sheet of December 31, 1984 to determine if part of the approximately $678,000 loss for the calendar year 1985 belonged to 1984.

The new chief executive of Sturm and the parent company officers were convinced that the 1984 financial statements were overstated. (The new chief executive related to us that the prior chief executive had admitted to him that the figures at December 31, 1984 and June 30, 1985 had been manipulated.) As a result, management decided to reduce the loss of 1985 by $250,000 and record such amount as an adjustment to the opening retained earnings balance. The reduction of the loss and charge to retained earnings would improve the 1985 consolidated net income. Management admitted that there were no facts to support the adjustment, but this was their best estimate of a loss that they believed did not belong in 1985.

1. As an auditor for Sturm, Inc., do you believe that the Company can charge this loss to a prior period under generally accepted accounting principles?
2. How should the loss be reported for 1985? On a comparative basis if both the results for 1984 and 1985 are presented?

CHAPTER 19

☐

INTERNATIONAL ACCOUNTING

19-1 "The" Accounting Change – 1982

Following is a footnote from the 1982 annual report of IBM:
Accounting Change – Foreign Currency Translation

The company adopted Statement of Financial Accounting Standards
(SFAS) No. 52, "Foreign Currency Translation" in the fourth
quarter of 1982, effective January 1, 1982. The consolidated
financial statements for the years 1981 and 1980 have been
restated to give effect to this change in accounting principle.
Non-U.S. subsidiaries which operate in a local currency
environment account for approximately 85% of the company's
non-U.S. gross income. In applying SFAS No. 52 to financial
statements of these subsidiaries, assets and liabilities are
translated to U.S. dollars at year-end exchange rates. Income and
expense items are translated at average rates of exchange
prevailing during the year. Translation adjustments are
accumulated in a separate component of stockholders' equity.

The remaining 15% of the company's non-U.S. gross income is
derived from subsidiaries and branches which operate in U.S.
dollars or whose economic environment is highly inflationary. In
accordance with SFAS No. 52, inventories and plant, rental
machines and other property, applicable to these operations, are
remeasured in U.S. dollars at approximate rates prevailing when
acquired. Inventories charged to cost of sales and depreciation
are remeasured at historical rates.

Gains and losses which result from measurement are included in
earnings.

The effects of this accounting change on net earnings and
earnings per share are an increase of $449 million and $.75 in
1982, an increase of $302 million and $.51 in 1981 and a decrease
of $165 million and $.28 in 1980. Management interpreted this
change in a section of the "Management Discussion":

IBM's consolidated financial statements have been restated to
reflect the adoption of FASB No. 52. For those non-U.S.
subsidiaries where IBM operates primarily in local currencies,
FASB No. 52 requires that all assets and liabilities are

translated to U.S. dollars at year-end exchange rates. This resulted in a reduction in the reported book value of net assets in the current period of $685 million. The cumulative effect is reflected in the equity section of the Statement of Financial

Position as translation adjustments. If the U.S. dollar continues to strengthen, reported net asset values will be further reduced. Should the dollar weaken in relation to non-U.S. currencies, net assets will increase. The change in net asset values is unrealized. There is no change in the productive capabilities of any of these assets. They continue to serve the needs of IBM's business activities in those countries affected.

It is management's view that the translation adjustment account has significance in a situation where liquidation of the net assets may be anticipated. This is not the case with IBM's operations and, accordingly, the company believes this translation account is not meaningful when evaluating current operations and should be considered only over the longer term of the company's expected continuing operations.

The principal effect on IBM's reported equity, under FASB No. 52, given the dramatic strengthening of the dollar during the past three years, comes from translating rental machines, plant and other property recorded in non-U.S. currencies to U.S. dollars. The cumulative translation adjustment at December 31, 1982 amounts to $1.3 billion. Offsetting this adjustment of net assets is the cumulative positive effect on reported earnings, for 1982 and the two prior years, amounting to $586 million. Thus, the effect on equity of implementing FASB No. 52 is a reduction of $721 million at year-end 1982."

INSTRUCTIONS:

1. Why was the accounting for foreign currency translation changed effective in 1982?
2. What are the two basic problems associated with foreign currency translation?
3. How do FASB Statements No. 8 and 52 handle these problems?
4. What are the two general approaches to accounting for foreign currency translation? Discuss.
5. Trace the history of accounting principles concerning foreign currency translation. How do they relate to the two general approaches cited above. Compare and contrast FASB Statement No. 8 and FASB Statement No. 52.
6. Do you agree with IBM's management assessment of the impact of foreign currency translation? Why or why not?

Northern States Corporation is a leading manufacturer and producer of avionics instruments, electric displays, autopilots for the general aviation market, and data terminal equipment. Since its incorporation in 1965, Northern States Corporation has maintained a strong engineering orientation that has proven instrumental in its recognition and growth, and has been a major influence in the wide acceptance of its products.

Northern States' headquarters and main facilities are in Green River, Wisconsin. The company has another plant in San Diego, California which concentrates on the designing and producing of autopilots. On December 15, 1973, the company organized a wholly-owned subsidiary in the country of Gabon, called Northern States Ltd. This subsidiary engages in the design and production of products comparable to those manufactured in the United States.

Although the subsidiary is operated relatively autonomously, it does have a number of intercompany transactions with the parent. They purchase approximately 50% of their raw materials from Northern States Corporation. Labor, materials not purchased through the parent, and other costs for the subsidiary's products are primarily local costs.

The subsidiary sells 35% of its products locally, with the remainder being sold worldwide. The parent and subsidiary periodically exchange inventory. If production problems exist in one location or the other, or if one manufacturing operation is unable to keep up with demand, the other manufacturing plant will attempt to fill the void. Except for the intercompany sales which are priced at cost, Northern States Ltd. sets their own prices depending upon their own market.

Long-term financing for the operation was done through Swiss banks. Although the subsidiary is directly responsible for the repayment of the loans, the parent was forced to guarantee repayment.

The parent expects the management of the subsidiary to perform, that is they should be profitable enough each year to be able to pay a dividend to the parent to return at least 10% on their investment. This has been difficult to do of late because during the past three years, the inflation rate has been 20%, 35%, and 40%, respectively. The management has been unable to forecast the future inflationary trend in Gabon.

The translation of the foreign subsidiary financial statements under FASB No. 8 had given the parent company some problems. The sizable translation losses were shown in the income statement and were difficult to explain to the shareholders. As a result, they were pleased with the change to FASB No. 52. Any adjustments necessary could now bypass the income statement and instead be shown in stockholders' equity. This had definitely helped their situation and settled their problem. Or had it? During the most recent audit, their accounting firm brought up the topic of functional currency.

1. What is the definition of a functional currency?
2. What is the significance of the functional currency?
3. What is the theory behind the use of a functional currency?
4. What criteria are used to help determine the functional currency?
5. Why does hyperinflation invalidate the functional currency approach? How does remeasurement solve the problem?
6. What is the appropriate functional currency in this case?

19-3 Foreign Inflation

"Inflation! Inflation! Everyone is concerned about it, everyone wants to know how it will impact our company, but no one knows what kind of information they need to assess the impact. It is bad enough to deal with U.S. investors and to try to deal with U.S. inflation, but now we have the international considerations. Ever since we announced our intentions to sell our stock in an international offering, I have been beseiged by inquiries as to the impact of inflation on our British subsidiaries, our investments in South America, our subsidiaries in Mexico it goes on and on!" Bernie Osterkorn, the treasurer of International Affiliated Industries, Inc., was voicing some of his frustration at a meeting with the accounting firm which is working on the proposed international common stock offering.

International Affiliated Industries, Inc. (I.A.I.I.) is a large multinational firm with twenty-five foreign subsidiaries located in twenty different countries. Their sales on a consolidated basis approach $10 billion a year. The company is based in the United States and prior to this year had obtained all necessary financing from domestic sources. This time, however, their investment banking firm suggested forming an international underwriting group and selling their stock in a number of different countries.

The idea seemed attractive. The company could tap previously untapped capital sources, they could gain worldwide recognition of their successes, and promote their foreign subsidiary products in their home markets. That is, the idea seemed attractive until the questions about inflation.

The company had already struggled to prepare consolidated financial statements; being careful to correctly classify the functional currencies of their subsidiaries and to then use the appropriate translation methods. The company had also prepared the required supplementary disclosure concerning inflation, that is, U.S. inflation. Now come the questions regarding foreign inflation.

The accountants suggested preparing supplementary information regarding the impact of each country's rate of inflation on the subsidiaries domiciled in that particular country. For example, supplementary information would be prepared concerning British inflation and its impact on the financial statements of the British subsidiary. The accountants felt that this would be helpful in the countries in which the stock would be sold, especially for those situations in which the subsidiaries themselves were not wholly owned by I.A.I.I.

Bernie was protesting, "Translate the subsidiary financial statements. Restate them for inflation. What does it all mean when we are done? Doesn't translating the financial statements into dollars automatically record the impact of inflation?"

INSTRUCTIONS:

1. Compare and contrast the accounting for inflation and the accounting for foreign currency translation.
2. What is meant by the phrases: "restate-translate" and "translate-restate?"
3. What are the advantages and disadvantages of each?
4. As a potential U.S. investor in a U.S. based multinational firm which construct (restate-translate or translate-restate) would provide you with more relevant information about consolidated operations? Which would be better for share holders of the foreign subsidiary?
5. Do you agree or disagree that translating financial statements automatically reflects the impact of inflation? Why?

19-4 International Consolidation

Morris Equipment Manufacturing Corporation has successfully operated as a producer of specialized construction equipment for over thirty years. Their cranes and material handling equipment are used for constructing high rise buildings. Part of their success has been due to the development of a crane which can "walk up the walls," that is, it easily moves up the building as additional floors are added.

The company established a European sales and distribution operation over fifteen years ago and captured a large share of the building construction equipment market. Their foreign sales had always been denominated in dollars to avoid any foreign currency risks. However, due to the strength of the dollar the company found that they were losing sales by continuing to follow this strategy.

Late in 1984, the company had an opportunity to acquire one of their small competitors located in West Germany. The opportunity seemed ideal; the company could easily convert the German facility to manufacture their product line, their product line would be expanded by the addition of the German construction equipment, they could lower costs of manufacturing and shipping, and over all have an easy way to start production in Europe.

The Germany company was acquired on December 31, 1984. Their first year of operation went smoothly. The subsidiary was profitable and seemed to add to the success of the company. Or did it?

Doris Morris, the controller of the company had been concerned with the selection of the appropriate method for consolidating the subsidiary in their December 31, 1985 financial statements. Doris knew that there had been a recent change in the requirements for translating foreign currency, but was not familiar with the possible methods that could or should be used.

She decided to refer to her accounting textbook. It has been more years than she cared to admit since she had been in college, but she had always kept that book as a reference. Doris turned to the foreign currency chapter for guidance, but was disappointed. The chapter discussed four methods! It described the current rate, current-noncurrent, monetary-nonmonetary, and the temporal methods. She decided to try to understand the methods by applying them to the German subsidiary financial statements. Following are the balance sheet and income statement for the subsidiary.

Deutsch Subsidiary
Balance Sheet
December 31, 1985

Assets	Marks
Cash	2,000,000
Accounts Receivable	4,000,000
Inventory	6,000,000
Fixed Assets (net)	12,000,000
Total	24,000,000

Liabilities and Owners' Equity	
Short Term Payables	6,000,000
Long-Term Debt	8,000,000
Stockholders' Equity	10,000,000
Total	24,000,000

Income Statement
for the Year Ending
12/31/85

	Marks
Sales	30,000,000
Cost of Sales	15,000,000
Depreciation	1,200,000
All Other Expenses	6,000,000
Income Before Tax	7,800,000
Income Tax (30%)	2,340,000
Net Income	5,460,000

The value of the Mark at the time of the acquisition was $.30. The value had declined to $.20 by the end of the year and averaged $.25 for the year. Inventories are carried at lower of cost or market. The owners' equity at the time of acquisition had a translated value of $3,000,000.

INSTRUCTIONS:

1. Explain the difference between the four approaches to foreign currency translation.
2. Translate the given balance sheet and income statement using each of the four methods. Note the different results using each method.
3. What method is required to be used by FASB 52? Is this method consistent with the historical cost accounting model?
4. What method is required to be used by FASB 8? Some feel that the results obtained using FASB 8 do not reflect economic reality, but the results obtained by using FASB 52 do reflect economic reality. Do you agree or disagree? Why?
5. Is it possible to prepare useful consolidated financial statements when foreign subsidiaries are included? Why or why not?

19-5 One or Two Transactions?

The Boulder Corporation is developing plans for an aggressive marketing program to establish their children's furniture product line in the European market. For twenty years the company has been producing bedroom sets, high chairs, wooden chairs, and tables specifically designed for children. The tables and chairs, for example, are smaller than conventional furniture and are targeted for the under ten year old market. The company founded by James Appenzeller had grown to have sales of over $5 million a year.

The company became interested in developing a foreign market almost by accident. Mr. Appenzeller had been negotiating the purchase of some oak lumber for the manufacturing process and, in fact, was engaged in some competitive bidding with a German company. The buyer for Kindercraft AG became interested in Boulder Corporation's product line and placed an order. The first foreign transaction sent them on their way.

Mr. Appenzeller called a meeting for his marketing, finance, and manufacturing vice presidents. "There obviously is a market for our products in Europe. Without any marketing program at all and totally as a result of an unsolicited order, Kindercraft AG has become our highest volume customer. I want to develop a program to take advantage of our opportunities." Mr. Appenzeller was enthusiastic at the meeting.

Mr. Wolf, the finance vice president, commented, "The problem is that the foreign currency transactions are causing losses and if we continue with our current policy of granting 60 days for payment the losses will continue. I think, since the marketing department has requested these terms, that we should adjust the sales dollars to reflect any losses that we incur between the day the sale is made and payment is received."

Joan Hermann, the marketing vice president objected. "The marketing department is not engaging in any foreign currency transactions! We are selling furniture and at prices that include a good markup. We determine our price in dollars and then convert them to Deutchmarks on the day of sale. I don't see how we can be charged with any losses. It is the accounting department's responsibility to collect the bills. If there are losses, they are responsible. Sales and collections are two separate functions."

"I don't agree," continued Joe Wolf. "Here is an example of the problem that exists. On November 30, 1985 we sold some merchandise to Kindercraft, priced it at $12,000, and converted it to Marks using the current rate of $.30, or 40,000 Marks. This is the system Joan explained. By our year end, December 31st, the value of the Mark had already fallen to $.25 and when we collected on January 31st it was worth $.20! We lost $4,000. The sale was really for $8,000."

Mr. Appenzeller needs some help. He doesn't want any problems with his people before the new program is even off the ground. If he could better understand the issues involved perhaps he could solve the problems before they become worse.

INSTRUCTIONS:

1. What is the difference between a foreign transaction and a foreign currency transaction?
2. How do transaction gains and losses arise?
3. Explain the two approaches to the disposition of transaction gains and losses.
4. What are the journal entries that would be appropriate using each approach?
5. What is the appropriate accounting for foreign currency transactions?
6. How does the treatment of transaction gains and losses differ between FASB No. 52 and its predecessor FASB No. 8?

19-6 Hedging

The fiscal year 1985 was a year of mixed blessing for the Cox Pharmaceutical Company (CPC). The domestic operations reported record sales and profits, up 20%

and 27% respectively over the 1984 results. However, their international operations had problems. Foreign currency transaction and translation losses were so dramatic that the company reported an overall operating loss of $500,000.

The company sold its products manufactured in the United States throughout the world and operated a wholly-owned manufacturing and sales subsidiary in Mexico. Because of the competitiveness of the industry, CPC was forced to transact their business in a variety of currencies and to grant rather liberal 60 to 90 day credit terms. These policies differed dramatically from five years ago when the company first started their international sales operation. At that time, they dealt only in dollars and received cash upon delivery. Their sales and marketing strategies had changed with the increasing competition and they had been successful. However, due to the strengthening value of the dollar and their lack of expertise in the foreign currency markets, the company started to incur sizable transaction losses.

Their subsidiary in Mexico seemed to be doing well. The company reported increases in sales and earnings in pesos, but when translated to dollars in the process of consolidating the financial statements these profits suddenly became translation losses. The translation losses appeared on the income statement as required by FASB No. 52, since Mexico was considered a country experiencing hyperinflation.

John Cox, the chief operating officer of CPC, was determined to reverse the losses of the international operations. Early in 1986, he hired International Financial Services Company to suggest ways and, if necessary, to hire and train people to correct these foreign currency problems. John had read articles about hedging and how other companies used these strategies to improve the financial success of their companies. He wanted to start hedging as soon as possible.

After a number of meetings with the consultants, John was anxious to hear their suggestions. "Mr. Cox, you are absolutely correct. What you need is someone to manage your foreign currency problems through hedging. Hedging can eliminate both your foreign currency transaction and foreign currency translation losses. In fact, we suggest that you also start to hedge your future sales commitments. You have a commitment to sell approximately 1,000,000 Swiss francs of pharmaceuticals to a Swiss firm every six months and we think it is to your advantage to hedge these future transactions.

We expect the Mexican peso to continue to be weak and, as a result, suggest that you hedge your subsidiary's asset position to eliminate the translation losses.

Our company will be happy to manage your foreign currency transactions. Certainly our fee is far less than the losses reported last year. You will not have the risk or the worry of foreign currency losses."

This all sounded too good to be true. John still needs some help understanding the basics of hedging. He was confused about the idea of hedging before a sale occurred.

1. What is a foreign exchange contract?
2. Why would a company enter into a foreign exchange contract?
3. What is the difference between hedging of foreign currency transaction and hedging a foreign currency commitment? What is the appropriate accounting for each?
4. Distinguish between hedging a net investment and hedging a net monetary position. What is the appropriate accounting for each? Distinguish between accounting risk and economic risk as they relate to hedging balance sheet positions.
5. Evaluate the consultant's suggestions to hedge their transactions, commitments, and net asset position.

19-7 International Accounting Standards?

Following is an article which appeared in the Wall Street Journal on May 8, 1985:

WHERE BOARDS AND GOVERNMENTS HAVE FAILED,
THE MARKET COULD INTERNATIONALIZE ACCOUNTING

By Paul Hemp - Staff Reporter of the Wall Street Journal

Paris - A French manufacturing company listed recently on the Paris Bourse looks like a promising investment. Its financial statement shows booming international sales and a healthy profit. The company's earnings outshine the disappointing results of a comparable U.S. concern in the same business.

There's only one problem. The two companies used different foreign-currency translation methods during a year of wild exchange-rate fluctuations. Because the concerns took different paths to the bottom line, the figures there could differ by millions of dollars.

Accounting experts warn that this lack of uniformity in financial statements -- the absence of a world-wide accounting language -- threatens the growing internationalization of trade, investment and securities market. If investors and managers of multinational enterprises cannot get understandable financial information about foreign companies and subsidiaries, they are less likely to venture abroad.

Consequently, all kinds of international bodies are trying to harmonize accounting standards. But their success has been limited, and the real changes may come from the companies themselves. As more large European firms seek to raise funds on world markets, especially in the U.S., they have had to upgrade their accounting practices and, in many cases, adopt U.S. accounting standards to attract investors and meet government filing requirements.

Such de facto harmonization could force national governments and accounting bodies to harmonize their standards. "Economics may force something that had been lagging for the last 30 years," says Edmund Coulson, deputy chief accountant of the U.S. Securities and Exchange Commission.

Many groups are working on the problem. The Organization for Economic Cooperation and Development, which monitors developed economies, gathered international business and accounting leaders here recently to discuss the barriers to standardization. The International Accounting Standards Committee, representing accountants in 65 nations, had issued more than 20 nonbinding international accounting standards. The United Nations has a group working on the problem, and the European Common Market has issued several directives requiring European companies to standardize their financial statements.

But widely varying national laws, as well as national pride, still are roadblocks. "Given the complexity of the subject and the weight of the past, the goal of harmonization still seems to be a rather long way off," says Jean-Claude Paye, the OECD's secretary-general. Donald J. Kirk, chairman of the Financial Accounting Standards Board, the professional body that hammers out accounting standards for U.S. companies, says: "Harmonization even within the U.S. is difficult, so I have to be a pessimist about international prospects."

Growing U.S. Influence

But the growing influence of standards issued by Mr. Kirk's group may spur that harmonization. U.S. accounting rules -- the so-called generally accepted accounting principles -- are observed in most audits by large U.S. accounting firms. In addition, the SEC requires all companies seeking a public listing in the U.S. to comply with these principles. Some European companies, anxious to tap the deep pool of funds available in U.S. markets, have adopted the guidelines.

The number of foreign companies seeking listings in the U.S. is growing rapidly. Transactions in the U.S. in stock of foreign companies rose from $2.03 billion in 1970 to nearly $30 billion in 1983. Eighteen companies located outside the U.S. and Canada raised about $1 billion in the U.S. in 1983.

Aside from capital, a U.S. listing "gives the impression that the company is on the move and a major player," says Alfredo Scotti, who helped direct Saipem S.p.A.'s adoption of U.S. accounting standards in anticipation of a New York Stock Exchange offering.

Mr. Scotti says Saipem, the engineering and oil services unit of Ente Nazionale Idrocarburi, Italy's state energy holding company, came out of the process a changed entity. For one thing, earnings increased because of different rules governing the depreciation of fixed assets. (Continental European accounting practices tend to minimize profits, with the aim of minimizing taxes, while U.S. practices tend to maximize profits, with the aim of impressing potential investors.)

Nationalistic Resistence

Some of the differences in accounting practices have a national rationale that causes European accountants to resist the wholesale "imperialistic" imposition of U.S. standards. While countries should seek to promote international harmonization of accounting standards, "each should be free to use the methods best suited to it and its tradition," says French Finance Minister Pierre Beregovoy.

"There's a danger in trying to apply in France standards hammered out for a different country -- that is, America," says Bertrand d'Illiers, chief accountant at the Paris Bourse.

Even the advocates of U.S. standards express concern that they may have become too detailed and rigid. The FASB, in its 12 years of existence, has issued 80 statements refining general accounting principles, a trend Mr. Kirk worries may lead to "standards overload."

In fact, the SEC has modified some of its requirements for offerings by foreign companies. For example companies don't need to report the salaries of individual officers, but only aggregate executive compensation. And differences in national accounting practices are permitted if the required information is provided and a means exists to reconcile it with U.S. standards.

INSTRUCTIONS:

    1. What are some of the advantages and disadvantages of developing international accounting standards?
    2. What are the major forces which support and hinder the development of international reporting standards?
    3. Identify some of the international organizations which have been active in the effort to harmonize international accounting standards. How successful have been their efforts?
    4. What is the role of the large international accounting firms in this area?

5. What means, if any, do you see as the most realistic to attain the goal of international accounting standards? Why?

19-8 Comparative Systems of Accounting

Neil Christiansen was anxious to begin work on his first day in the international capital department of the First West Bank and Trust Company. Neil had almost five years experience in the commerical credit department of the bank and because of his success in that area had recently received a promotion to assistant vice president. Neil wanted to expand his areas of expertise and had requested a transfer to the international group of the bank.

The first assignment sounded interesting. The First West was considering "taking down" a portion of two loans as a member of a syndicate of banks. Each syndicate was headed by a New York City bank which was acting as the lead in the negotiation. Each potential loan was for approximately $20 million dollars and each member bank could participate to the extent of from one to five million dollars.

The vice president of the international department wanted Neil to choose one of the two, if acceptable, and to limit the bank's exposure to $1 million. Neil had considered the potential problems that might exist in analyzing the credit worthiness of foreign companies, but felt confident that the two candidates would not present any particular difficulties. One is a British Company and one is domiciled in India. At least both sets of financial statements would be in English and since India had been a British colony, he expected that this financial reporting would be similar. In addition, the U.S. and British accounting systems should be close, he thought, because of the many economic, political, and historical ties.

Since both companies were in the same industry, he would proceed as he had many times before: simply apply the standard financial analysis, compare them to industry averages, interpret the results using his practical experience, and see which company was in better financial condition.

Neil's optimism soon faded. Both statements were in English, but the Indian statement was expressed in rupees. Next, he had never seen such a confusing format. The balance sheet was organized as sources and applications of funds and nothing seemed to be in the right order. In addition, many of the account titles were different and although there were numerous notes, they generally did not help gain any real insight to his problem.

The British balance sheet was also in a different order, but with some manipulation he felt that he could understand the format. However, he was at a loss with the income statement. The income statement was presented in terms of value added. He had heard of this before, but had really not seen a statement like this. Was turnover the same as sales? What is a gearing adjustment? Replacement costs were used throughout. How were they obtained? Are they verifiable? And of course, the statements were expressed in British pounds. The footnote disclosure were extensive, but they seemed only to add to the confusion.

1. In general, what are some of the kinds of potential problems that may arise when analyzing foreign financial statements?
2. In general, why do you suppose there are such significant differences between each country's financial reports?
3. What are some of the determinants of differences between reporting in different countries?
4. What suggestions do you have for Neil to help him with his problem?

19-9 Adjust to GAAP

You have just completed your preliminary analysis of an Icelandic company that you are interested in acquiring. You have received a convenience translation only for the firm and have computed the following ratios based upon those statements:

	Icelandic Co.	U.S. Industry Average
Current	2.6 to 1	1.9 to 1
Acid-test	1.3 to 1	1.1 to 1
D-bt to Equity	72%	47%
Times Interest Earned	3.9 times	6.5 times
Inventory Turnover	4.3 times	6.8 times
EPS	$50.10	$2.50
Return on Assets	4.7%	7.4%
Return on Equity	5.1%	13.9%
Dividends	$25.00/share	$1.25/share

In addition, the following information is provided in the notes to the financial statements.

1. The company has increased its reserves for additional depreciation above historical cost in compliance with Sec. 12.2 of the Icelandic Revenue Code. Inventory reserves were also increased by approximately 10%.

2. The company has changed to the temporal method of accounting for the consolidation of its foreign subsidiaries.

3. The goodwill created in the company's acquisition of a subsidiary in Greenland was written off directly to retained earnings.

4. The company has applied for listing of its common stock on the New York Stock exchange as no active stock exchange exists in Iceland.

5. The company continues to supply substantial social responsibility reporting to comply with government regulation and to exemplify its part in promoting full employment as a national objective.

6. Deferred taxes are determined on the difference between accelerated depreciation for tax purposes and straight-line depreciation for financial statement purposes for only those assets for which the taxes will eventually be paid.

7. All fixed assets are carried on a net basis on the balance sheet, i.e. no separate totals for the cost and total accumulated depreciation. This has been done to more fully reflect the net realizable value of the assets.

8. The company is engaged in extensive research and development which they expect will provide numerous new products over the next ten years. The company capitalized $500,000 of R&D in 1985.

9. The company leases some of its equipment and expenses the rental payments as they are made. The company has benefitted from these lease agreements in the past since they have purchased the leased assets after the lease agreement expired at prices below their market value.

10. Following is the value added statement for 1984:

	Million Dollars
Turnover	17.3
Brought in materials, services, and depreciation	(9.5)
Value Added	7.8
Investment income	1.0
Extraordinary items	(2.1)
Value added	6.7

Applied as follows:
To employees	2.4
To banks	1.1
To government	1.6
To shareholders	0 6
	5.7

Amount retained   1.0

INSTRUCTIONS:

Identify and discuss items from these abbreviated financial statements that you would consider important when evaluating and comparing the ratios and performance of this company versus U.S. companies as possible acquisitions. What specific adjustments, if any, would you make to the preliminary analysis that had been completed?

19-10 Foreign Disclosure

Steve Harvey has been operating an investment advisory service for over five years. His initial success resulted from his abilities to analyze companies in specific industries. His research services were particularly in demand regarding the brewing and automobile industries.

Steve is a forward thinker and feels that the industry analysis of the future will be done on a worldwide basis. Already numerous foreign multinational companies have applied for listing on the New York Stock Exchange. Thus, U.S. industry analysis will become worldwide industry analysis and investment strategies will include buying and selling common stocks of companies domiciled all over the world.

He decided to get a head start in the automobile industry. The first step was to write for the annual reports of SAAB, Volvo, Volkswagen, BMW, Renault, and the Japanese "Big Three." He became concerned, however, as to the potential value of these statements when he read the following article from the August 1980 Journal of Accountancy:

U.S. annual reports rank best overall in 200-company survey

The quality of corporate annual reports is highest in the United States and the Netherlands and weakest in Switzerland, Japan, Brazil, Belgium, Italy and Spain, according to a survey of 200 large industrial companies in 20 countries by Financial Times Business Information Ltd., a subsidiary of the Financial Times of London.

Besides placing first in the survey's overall assessment, American companies were ranked highest in the quality of accounting and business segment data. However, the survey's authors -- Michael Lafferty, a chartered accountant and banking and accounting correspondent of the Financial Times, and David Cairns, C.A. a partner of the London-based accounting firm of Stoy Hayward & Co. -- criticize the "broad geographical and industrial segments" used by some U.S. companies. Of 30 American companies in the 1980 World Survey of Annual Reports, 7 are given a grade of "A,", 22 "B" and 1 "C". No American company is among the 35 receiving the survey's "F" grade. Shell Oil is rated the best American company in overall reporting and in the areas of accounting and nonfinancial statement data, excluding value-added information.

Among the 21 companies from six countries whose reports received an "A", Philips, the Dutch electronics and electrical multinational company, issued the best annual report, according to the survey. English-speaking Anglo-Saxon nations, the survey notes, are strong in annual financial statements but weak in nonfinancial disclosures, while the reverse is true in the case of Continental European countries. Although many companies view annual reports as general-purpose documents, the orientation of most annual reports in the survey is toward shareholders and investors.

In addition to ranking individual companies and countries according to the quality of information in annual reports, the survey shows how specific companies meet international standards. These standards include proposals and pronouncements of the United Nations, the International Accounting Standards Committee, the Organization for Economic Cooperation and Development and the European Economic Community. Survey gradings were determined by measuring available mid-1979 annual reports against these international "yardsticks."

This article might represent good news for the U.S. investor in U.S. companies, but how does the U.S. investor deal with foreign financial statements? Before Steve became too pessimistic, he anticipated that foreign multinationals must prepare annual reports that he could understand. Since these firms are interested in attracting foreign capital or are involved in international money markets, they must attempt to supply useful information to potential investors. If only he could get some insights as to what he might receive from the companies, then he could prepare himself to analyze the information.

1. What are some of the general problems that Steve may encounter when he receives the foreign financial statements?
2. Describe various types of disclosure formats that might be used in the financial statements he receives.
3. What are some advantages and disadvantages of each type?
4. Which format do you feel is most helpful from a foreign reader's perspective? Why?

CHAPTER 20

**FINANCIAL REPORTING
AND
CHANGING PRICES**

20-1 Accounting for Inflation

Major corporations have responded to the requirement of FASB 33 to provide information on the effects of inflation on financial data in a variety of ways. Following are a number of excerpts from some annual reports which are representative of the controversy surrounding this accounting principle:

General Motors Annual Report 1983

The accompanying schedules display the basic historical cost
financial data adjusted for general inflation (constant dollar)
and also for changes in specific prices (current cost) for use in
the evaluation of comparative financial results. The schedules
are intended to help readers of financial data assess results in
the following specific areas:

a. The erosion of general purchasing power,

b. Enterprise performance,

c. The erosion of operating capability, and

d. Future cash flows.

In reviewing these schedules, the following comments may be of
assistance in understanding the reasons for the different
"income" amounts and the uses of the data.

Under both the constant dollar and the current cost methods, the
net income of General Motors is lower (or the net loss is higher)
than that determined under the historical cost method. This means
that businesses, as well as individuals, are affected by
inflation and that the purchasing power of business dollars has
declined. In addition, the costs of maintaining the productive
capacity, as reflected in the current cost data (and estimate of
future capital expenditures), have increased, and thus management

must seek ways to cope with the effects of inflation through accounting methods such as the LIFO method of inventory valuation, which matches current costs with current revenues, and through accelerated methods of depreciation and amortization.

It must be emphasized that there is a continuing need for national monetary and fiscal policies designed to control inflation and to provide adequate capital for future business growth which, in turn, will mean increased productivity and employment.

Allis-Chalmers Corporation Annual Report 1983

The required Financial Accounting Standards Board disclosure of supplementary inflation adjusted data under the current cost method of acounting is experimental in nature and the result of a variety of methods, assumptions and estimates; it is not necessarily a reliable indicator of the inflation effect on financial statements nor is it comparable to supplementary data disclosed by any other company.

The Coca Cola Company Annual Report 1983

The following unaudited disclosures were prepared in accordance with Statement Nos. 33 and 70 issued by the Financial Accounting Standards Board and are intended to quantify the impact of inflation on earnings and production facilities. The inflation-adjusted data is presented under the specific price change method (current cost). Only those items most affected by inflation have been adjusted; i.e., inventories, property, plant and equipment, the related costs of goods and services sold and depreciation and amortization expense. Although the resulting measurements cannot be used as precise indicators of the effects of inflation, they do provide an indication of the effect of increases in specific prices of the Company's inventories and properties.

The adjustments for specific price changes involve a substantial number of judgments as well as the use of various estimating techniques employed to control the cost of accumulating the data. The data reported should not be thought of as precise measurements of the assets and expenses involved, or of the amount at which the assets could be sold. Rather, they represent reasonable approximations of the price changes that have occurred in the business environment in which the Company operates.

IBM Annual Report 1983

Although inflation rates moderated significantly in the United States, and to a lesser extent in many other countries during 1983, its cumulative effect over the past several years have eroded industry's ability to fund the replacement and expansion of productive capacity. Traditional financial statements may not adequately reflect the effects of changing prices and declines in purchasing power on cash flows required to replace capital assets and provide opportunities for future growth. Therefore, supplemental information, which has been prepared in accordance with standards established by the Financial Accounting Standards Board, is presented to assist users of financial statements in understanding the implications of changing prices on the company's operations.

AT&T Annual Report 1983

Statement No. 33 is based on the incorrect premise that depreciation expense, rather than being a means of allocating asset costs to accounting periods, provides funds to be set aside and used for the replacement of those assets being depreciated. Statement No. 33 also assumes that the cost of new assets acquired to replace retired assets will equal the original cost of the retired assets adjusted for either inflation or specific price increases; obviously, such is not the case in a high technology industry such as ours. Technological advances hold down price increases for new communications equipment and also increase significantly the productive capacity of both new and existing equipment.

INSTRUCTIONS:

1. Are disclosures for inflation necessary? Why?
2. What are the three general approaches to adjust for the affects of inflation? What are the differences between them?
3. What are the advantages and disadvantages of each?
4. Based on the sample of footnote disclosure given above how would you assess the acceptance of the FASB's requirement to provide information on the effects of inflation?
5. How has the FASB responded to some of the criticisms concerning FASB 33?

20-2 Enterprise Building Contractors

Enterprise Building Contractors is a relatively small construction firm. They have been building single family dwellings for over fifteen years. Recently, they decided to get involved in larger building projects and successfully negotiated a contract to construct a fifty unit apartment and condominium project.

A project of this size will substantially increase the company's need for working capital. Tom Mader, the president, had developed a good working relationship with the Independence Bank and although he had discussed the potential need for a $350,000 line of credit, no formal agreement had ever been negotiated.

The company's most recent balance sheet shows a net worth of $250,000, of which $200,000 represents the book value of their construction equipment and inventory. The inventory was acquired from a lumber yard bankrupcy sale a year earlier. The lumber was standard construction grade material and with the increase in lumber prices within the last nine months has a current value almost twice the book value.

The equipment was purchased two to three years earlier from two other contractors who decided to retire. The insurance company has issued a policy on this equipment at 175% of book value.

Tom knows the bank will not give him a $350,000 line of credit on the basis of a balance sheet which shows his net worth at $250,000. However, Tom realizes the current value of his company is much more than that. If only there was some way to adjust his balance sheet to reflect the real value of his business.

INSTRUCTIONS:

1. What is the definition of current value?
2. Discuss the three general approaches to current valuation. Include a description of some of the methods used for each approach.
3. What are the advantages and disadvantages of each approach?
4. How might the company utilize their current value information when making application for the line of credit?

20-3 Hershey Foods Corporation

Following is an exerpt from the Hershey Foods Corporation 1983 annual report:

Supplementary Information Regarding the Effects of Inflation (Unaudited)

The Company's consolidated financial statements are prepared based upon historical costs and prices of transactions. The following supplementary information reflects certain effects of inflation upon the Company's operations in accordance with the requirements of Statement of Financial Accounting Standards No. 33, "Financial Reporting and Changing Prices," issued by the Financial Accounting Standards Board.

The effects of inflation on income have been measured in two ways as described below and presented in the following statements. The first method, "constant dollar," measures the effect of general inflation determined by using the 1983 average Consumer Price Index for all Urban Consumers (CPI–U) to recompute results of operations. The second method, "current cost," is more specific to the Company in that it measures inflation by recomputing results of operations using the current cost of inventory and property, plant and equipment rather than the historical cost of such assets. Current costs of property, plant and equipment were developed from external price indices, quotations or similar measurements. The impact of inflation on translated foreign operations is measured utilizing the CPI–U.

The inflation–adjusted information presented may not necessarily be comparable with other companies within the same industry because of the differences in assumptions and judgments. However, of the two methods required, the Company believes the current cost method is more meaningful because it better measures the effects of inflation on Company operations.

During 1983, specific costs of inventories and property, plant and equipment increased by $31.5 million in excess of general price level increases. This specific cost increase related primarily to cocoa beans and other inventory costs. The increase in cocoa bean costs was a major consideration in implementing an increase in the selling price of the Hershey Chocolate Company's standard chocolate bar product line in December 1983.

Depreciation expense increased under both methods because of inflation. Current cost depreciation exceeds constant dollar depreciation because the cumulative increases in the Company's specific cost of property, plant and equipment have exceeded the general inflation rate. Both amounts are based on costs of property, plant and equpment currently used in operations. However, the Company generally takes advantage of the latest technological improvements when actual replacement occurs.

The gain from decline of purchasing power of net amounts owed set forth in the schedule on page 38 presents the Company's gain from holding more monetary liabilities (required fixed future cash settlements) than monetary assets (right to receive fixed amounts of future cash) during periods of inflation, thereby requiring less purchasing power to satisfy such future obligations. However, since this economic gain will not be realized until the obligations are repaid, it is excluded from inflation–adjusted net income.

1. What is a price index? How does a general price index differ from a specific price index?
2. What is constant dollar accounting? How does constant dollar accounting differ from current cost accounting?
3. Distinguish between monetary and nonmonetary items. What is a purchasing power gain or loss on net monetary items?
4. What are realized and unrealized holding gains and losses?
5. A comprehensive current cost model emphasizes three different income numbers. Explain the rationale for these three income numbers.
6. Do you agree or disagree with the comment in the footnote that "... the current cost method is more meaningful because it better measures the effects of inflation..."? Why?

20-4 Allen, Inc.*

Allen, Inc. (wholesaler of hardwood flooring and wall paneling) has been in business since 1960. The company is closely held, but the stock is relatively widely disbursed among Allen relatives.

In early 1980, Roger Allen became president of the firm. Roger succeeded his father who had run the firm for 20 years. Roger's background was engineering and most believed such training was adequate for this position as the job was technically oriented.

Allen sells its products mostly to area contractors in the housing industry. For the past three years, sales have consistently averaged 80% to contractors and 20% to retail customers.

Because of the increase in demand for its products, Allen, Inc. decided to buy more equipment and expand its existing facilities. Because of its limited amount of capital, Roger decided that the company would have to sell shares to the public.

During the management meeting in February, 1985, the problems of issuing stock were discussed. The following comments were made by certain key personnel of Allen, Inc.

Warren Andrews (Vice-President of Finance) We may not be able to sell our stock at an appropriate price because the conventional financial statements do not report the current value of the net assets. At present the financial statements reflect dollars of mixed purchasing power. We should report assets and

*Adapted from a case prepared by Sonthilakson Soncharden.

liabilities at the present value of expected future cash flows.

James West (Vice-President Chief Operating Officer) The primary purpose of inflation adjusted data is to enable an assessment of how well we are maintaining our capital. I am concerned that these disclosures will uncover some problem areas.

Vern Ceaser (Vice-President of Sales Dept.) – I believe that general price-level adjusted data would yield a balance sheet closely approximating current values.

Norm Rundell (Vice-President of the Personnel Dept.) – Use of price-level adjusted financial statements would result in a departure from the historical cost basis of accounting. Data in financial statements should be prepared on the basis of facts, not estimates. The rate of inflation has been so small from year-to-year that the adjustments would be immaterial. Furthermore the accounting profession has not seriously considered price-level adjusted financial statements.

Unfortunately, Andrew Lars the controller was ill and was unable to attend the meeting. Roger was perplexed by the discussion presented by his vice-presidents. He could not make any decision on this matter, because he did not have an accounting background. However, his intuition was that the general price-level method seemed to be the most appropriate for the company.

Roger therefore decided to wait until Andrew Lars was feeling better before a decision about the financial statements will be made. Roger's instructions to Andrew Lars were to prepare a report answering the following questions:

1. In general, what are the main advantages and disadvantages of using inflation adjusted financial statements?

2. If current value is different from the general price-level statements, what are the main differences? How do they differ from historical cost financial statements?

3. Roger did not quite understand the meaning of the statement made by Warren "...financial statements prepared under the conventional accounting model reflect dollars of mixed purchasing power." He wondered whether the statement had any meaning in relation to the financial statements presented.

4. What are the present accounting requirements for price level accounting?

5. What is the theory of capital maintenance and how does the constant dollar approach differ from the current value (current

cost) approach in this regard?

6. Which method is most appropriate for the company?

<u>INSTRUCTIONS:</u>

Prepare the report that the president has requested.

20-5 Valueland Investment Trust

Valueland Investment Trust was formed in 1981 as a four person partnership. The objective of the investors was to buy, hold, and eventually sell real estate. Each individual invested $250,000 which was immediately used to purchase a piece of commercial land. The land was on the edge of the city and was considered a speculative investment. If the city continued to grow, their property would have great development potential.

Nearly four years later the four partners decided to sell their land. The economy in general, as well as, of their city had experienced short term fluctuations with little apparent growth. On September 30, 1985, they sold the land for $900,000.

At the end of each fiscal year the partners had received an appraisal of the land. The value at those times was determined to be:

September 30, 1982	$1,100,000
September 30, 1983	$1,250,000
September 30, 1984	$ 850,000

The partners had contracted for the appraisals to enable an evaluation of their investment decision. The appraisals might also aid in their prediction of the direction of the real estate market and when to sell. The appraisals were a key factor in their decision to sell because the $900,000 offer was seen as an improvement in value (over the 1984 year end figure) rather than as a decrease in value (from the 1981 purchase price).

However, after contemplating the matter further, one of the partners commented that their evaluations did not take the effects of inflation into consideration. He felt that general economy-wide price changes had occurred during the four year period and that those price changes impacted the purchasing power of their investment dollars. He collected the general price level index numbers and distributed them to his partners:

	Index	% Change
July 31, 1981 (Date of Purchase)	105	
September 30, 1982	126	20% increase
September 30, 1983	98	22% decrease
September 30, 1984	113	15% increase
September 30, 1985	102	10% decrease

One of the other partners stated that what was important was the current value of the investment and that this reflected the impacts of inflation specific to them. A third partner was sure that general inflation was somehow incorporated in the land and appraisal values and, therefore, that the appraisals provided the only necessary indicator for their evaluations.

A concern was voiced by the fourth partner after he examined the data. In 1983 and 1985, the appraised value of the land increased despite a decrease in the general price level, and in 1984, the appraised value declined while the general price level rose. This information added to their confusion, yet they felt that an investigation of the effects of inflation and possible interactive effects would be useful for future investment evaluations. Therefore, they were determined to understand what had happened with their first purchase of land.

INSTRUCTIONS:

1. What are the three general approaches to adjust for the affects of inflation? What are the differences between them?
2. If the partnership had prepared financial statements over the four year period adjusting for: a.) general price level, and b.) current values, what was the investment trust's: (1) gain or loss from price fluctuations for each year and (2) gain or loss on the sale of land?
3. Explain the apparent inconsistent inflationary effects that occurred in 1983, 1984 and 1985. Calculate the value of the land for each year after adjusting for the current value and the general price level. What are the gains or losses from price fluctuations for each year?
4. Why might the use of specific price level adjustments (current value) produce a better indicator of disposable wealth than constant dollar accounting?

20-6 The Fallacies of General Price Level Accounting

The general purchasing power of the dollar has declined considerably in recent years because of inflation. To account for this changing value of the dollar, many accountants suggest that financial statements should be adjusted for general price-level changes. Three independent, unrelated statements regarding general price-level adjusted financial statements follow. Each statement contains some fallacious reasoning.

Statement I

The accounting profession has not seriously considered price-level adjusted financial statements before because the rate of inflation usually has been so small from year-to-year that the adjustments would have been immaterial in amount. Price-level adjusted financial statements represent a departure from the historical-cost basis of accounting. Financial statements should be prepared on the basis of facts, not estimates.

Statement II

If financial statements were adjusted for general price-level changes, depreciation charges in the income statement would permit the recovery of dollars of current purchasing power and, thereby, equal the cost of new assets to replace the old ones. General price-level adjusted data would yield statement of financial position amounts closely approximating current values. Furthermore, management can make better decisions if constant dollar financial statements are published.

Statement III

When adjusting financial data for general price-level changes, a distinction must be made between monetary and nonmonetary assets and liabilities, which, under the historical cost basis of accounting, have been identified as "current" and "noncurrent." When using the historical cost basis of accounting, no purchasing power gain or loss is recognized in the accounting process, but when financial statements are adjusted for general price-level changes, a purchasing power gain or loss will be recognized on monetary and nonmonetary items.

INSTRUCTIONS:

Evaluate each of the independent statements and areas of fallacious reasoning in each and explain why the reasoning is incorrect. Complete your discussion of each statement before proceeding to the next statement.

(AICPA Adapted)

20-7 Inflation Accounting for Nonmonetary Assets

The financial statements of a business entity could be prepared by using historical cost or current value as a basis. In addition, the basis could be stated in terms of unadjusted dollars or dollars restated for changes in purchasing power. The various permutations of these two separate and distinct areas are shown in the following matrix:

	Unadjusted Dollars	Dollars Restated for Changes in Purchasing Power
Historical cost	1	2
Current value	3	4

Block number 1 of the matrix represents the traditional method of accounting for transactions in accounting today, wherein the absolute (unadjusted) amount of dollars given up or received is recorded for the asset or liability obtained (relationship between resources). Amounts recorded in the method described in block number 1 reflect the original cost of the asset or liability and do not give effect to any change in value of the unit of measure (standard of comparison). This method assumes the validity of the accounting concepts of going concern and stable monetary unit. Any gain or loss (including holding and purchasing power gains or losses) resulting from the sale or satisfaction of amounts recorded under this method is deferred in its entirety until sale or satisfaction.

INSTRUCTIONS:

For each of the remaining matrix blocks (2, 3 and 4) respond to the following questions. Limit your discussion to nonmonetary assets only.

1. How will this method of recording assets affect the relationship between resources and the standard of comparison?

2. What is the theoretical justification for using each method?

3. How will each method of asset valuation affect the recognition of gain or loss during the life of the asset and ultimately from the sale or abandonment of the asset? Your response should include a discussion of the timing and magnitude of the gain or loss and conceptual reasons for any difference from the gain or loss computed using the traditional method.

20-8 San-Tan, Inc.

The controller for San-Tan, Inc. has recently hired you as assistant controller. Recognizing that you should be quite familiar with accounting for changing prices, the controller shows you supplementary information that the auditors recommend be reported as supplementary data for the year. Part of the information is as follows:

San-Tan, Inc.
STATEMENT OF INCOME FROM CONTINUING
OPERATIONS ADJUSTED FOR CHANGING PRICES
For the Year Ended December 31, 1985
(In 000s of Average 1985 Dollars)

Income from continuing operations, as reported in income statement		$ 9,000
Adjustments to restate costs for the effect of general inflation		
Cost of goods sold	(7,384)	
Depreciation and amortization expense	(4,130)	(11,514)
Loss from continuing operations adjusted for general inflation		(2,514)
Adjustments to reflect the difference between general inflation and changes in specific prices (current cost)		
Cost of goods sold	(1,024)	
Depreciation and amortization expense	(5,370)	(6,394)
Loss from continuing operations adjusted for changes in specific prices		$(8,908)
Purchasing power of net monetary items		$ 7,729
Increase in specific prices (current cost) of inventories and property, plant, and equipment held during the year*		$24,608
Effect of increase in general price level		18,959
Excess of increase in specific price over increase in general price level		$ 5,649

*At December 31, 1985 current cost of inventory was $65,700 and current cost of property, plant, and equipment, net of accumulated depreciation was $85,100.

INSTRUCTIONS:

The controller is interested in the answer to the following questions:

1. Why is the statement presented in average 1985 dollars?

2. What is meant by general inflation?

3. What is the difference in the two losses from continuing operations?

4. Why are the other expenses such as officers salaries not reported on this statement?

5. What is the purchasing power gain on net monetary items? (Explain.)

6. Why are taxes not allocated to the increase in specific prices of inventories and property, plant and equipment?

7. Must San-Tan, Inc. report this information in this manner, or are there other alternatives available? (Assume that the company is required to present supplementary price-level data.)

20-9 The SEC and ASR190

In 1976 the SEC asked all American listed companies to provide replacement cost data in their financial statements.

Richard Insight, a security analyst presented the following discussion regarding the meaningfulness of the new SEC requirements. Insight stated that many different factors will influence the reactions by investment analysts to the new replacement-cost disclosures, including (a) the analyst's perception of the quality of the data, (b) the extent the data represent new information about the company or merely confirm previously existing information, and (c) the analyst's perception of the effect of the data on future public policy and possible future changes in the basic accounting model.

Insight stated that "whether management gives an endorsement to the replacement cost numbers or not, analysts will try to use them. They will do so for two reasons: first, because the numbers represent a potential new source of information and no one in a business as competitive as security analysis ever ignores a new source of information; secondly, because the historic cost numbers now appearing in company accounts are not that much more meaningful or comparable than the replacement cost numbers currently being developed to comply with ASR 190. Indeed, for purposes of company analysis and comparison the replacement cost numbers will in many ways be superior to conventional balance sheet values despite the absence of strict accounting standards."

As a result of the flexibility in the rules, there was a great deal of initial confusion among analysts about how to interpret the footnote disclosures. Analysts had to begin their evaluation of the numbers by finding out how they were developed. How did management define productive capacity? Were all assets included or were some excluded because of obsolescence and dying product lines? What valuation method did management use to determine replacement cost? Did it simply use a price index or did it use functional pricing to make adjustments for technological change? What does management itself think of the numbers appearing in the footnotes? Does it actually use these numbers in its financial planning?

In addition, Insight believed that the replacement cost numbers would indirectly reveal information about a registrant's assets, its plans for them, and the future financial needs implicit in such plans.

In summarizing, Insight stated, "The initial market response to the SEC disclosures will be highly selective, depending upon perceptions of the quality of the data and the information which it provides that is truly new about companies. The long run market reaction will be a function of what effect replacement cost disclosure has directly or indirectly on public policy affecting business, which is really just another way of saying that it will depend on future trends in the profitability of American industry. For while replacement cost accounts will help to put the economic position of companies in a new perspective, it is changes in the ability of companies to generate profits for distribution to their shareholders rather than the accounts in which this information is presented which will, as always, be of value to the investor."

INSTRUCTIONS:

1. What was the history of the accounting profession's position toward inflationary accounting prior to ASR 190?
2. How did ASR 190 impact the accounting profession?
3. What were the disclosures required by the FASB in Statement No. 33? What might be the rationale for the FASB's required disclosures? How were they changed?
4. Why was data disclosed under ASR 190 suspect?
5. What did he mean when he stated, "For while replacement cost accounts will help to put the economic position of companies in a new perspective, it is the changes in the ability of companies to generate profits for distribution to their shareholders rather than the accounts in which this information is presented which will, as always, be of value to investors."

20-10 Wild Enterprises

Wild Enterprises is a large conglomerate. In 1985, Wild did quite well per its conventional financial statements, but Mr. Washburn (the president) is skeptical about the validity of its historical financial statements. Consequently he is interested in having financial statements prepared using what he considers to be more realistic assumptions. That is, he wants to be able to evaluate the company's performance without the distortion of inflationary pressures.

However, there are some practical concerns. Mr. Washburn is not clear as to what information would be helpful for managerial purposes and if that information would be the same as required by the FASB. In addition, how is the necessary information obtained? What indices? How are current values of assets determined? What do you do about income taxes? Mr. Washburn needs some answers before he can proceed.

INSTRUCTIONS:

1. What are the current GAAP requirements for price level accounting?
2. Discuss ways in which information required by GAAP may be helpful for internal management decisions.
3. Why do you believe the FASB required a dual presentation (constant dollar and current cost) for reporting price level effects?
4. What approches might be utilized to find the current cost for inventories? For noncurrent assets?
5. Should income taxes be allocated to realized or unrealized holding gains if a partial or complete current cost income statement is prepared? What is the FASB's position on this matter?
6. Restate Wild enterprises's financial statements in conformity with general price level accounting. Wild Enterprises' financial statements appear below:

Balance Sheet
December 31, 1985

Cash	$100,000
Accounts Receivable	150,000
Inventory	50,000
Equipment	60,000
Buildings	90,000
Land	100,000
	$550,000
Accounts Payable	$ 40,000
Notes Payable	30,000
Common Stock	200,000
Retained Earnings	280,000
	$550,000

Income Statement
For the Year ended 12/31/85

Sales	$900,000
Cost of Goods Sold	
Beginning Inventory	50,000
Purchases	700,000
Goods Available	750,000
Ending Inventory	50,000
Cost of Goods Sold	700,000
Gross profit	200,000
Administrative Expenses	80,000
Depreciation	20,000
Income Before Tax	100,000
Income Taxes	40,000
Net Income	$ 60,000

Additional information: The company's net monetary position at December 31, 1984 was $130,000. Inventories are priced on a FIFO basis and were purchased evenly throughout the year. The company uses straight line depreciation. The relevant price indexes are as follows.

Beginning of year	102
End of year	110
Average	105
Fixed assets acquired	88
Formation of company	85

7. Wild Enterprises' president, Arnold Murphy, is confused by the entire price-level issue. Mr. Murphy wonders whether there are less drastic proposals, such as modifications of historical statements, as opposed to restatement that would suffice. What might these modifications be?

CHAPTER 21

☐

BASIC FINANCIAL
STATEMENT ANALYSIS

21-1 "Picking Winners"

A recent Fortune magazine article reviewed the ability of security analysts to forecast quarterly earnings and pick stocks that increase in price. Excerpts from the article follow.

"Security analysts are the 'royalty of Wall Street', as one brokerage house executive put it recently, and they still command a lot of respect, not to mention salaries that get as high as $500,000 a year for the star performers. But security analysts have a large career problem these days. It centers on the growing suspicion that they're not really very good at what in principle is their main job -- helping investors identify stocks that will outperform the market.

...Back at the office, analysts face long bouts of number crunching in efforts to come up with earnings estimates.

...So the record would seem to show about what you'd expect: some analysts have been doing well in recent years, some have done poorly, the ones who are most eager to share their records with you generally seem to do quite well, and almost everyone tends to structure the performance record in ways that make the firm look best. All in all, the record doesn't really refute the widespread suspicion that security analysts aren't very good at picking stocks.

That doesn't mean, however, that Wall Street would be a better place without the analysts. If they didn't exist, the market would presumably be much less efficient, and investors would have much less reason to believe that their stocks are reasonably priced. In gathering and disseminating huge gobs of information about companies and stocks that investors wouldn't otherwise have, the analysts over the long run help to ensure that stocks are fairly valued. Maybe that's all we can ask of them."

1. Two viewpoints are presented in this article as basic approaches to investing in common stock. What are they and how do they differ?
2. Define the term "intrinsic value" and explain why an investment analyst would be interested in finding this value.
3. Explain the term "Beta" and its importance to the theory of capital market analysis.
4. Why is a portfolio of stocks necessary in the capital market analysis approach to selection of common stocks?
5. What is the main implication of the efficient market theory for accounting?
6. Evaluate the last paragraph above and the role that accountants might play in an efficient market.

21-2 Financial Statement Analysis

A group of recent graduates from Midwestern University were all employed with companies located in downtown Chicago. Now that they had jobs they all were able to start a savings or investment program. The six individuals decided to form an investment club to pool their funds and buy common stocks. It was a great idea. They could formalize their investment programs, apply some of the concepts learned in college, pool their investment dollars to take advantage of more investment opportunities, lower their total commission expense, and meet for lunch once a month.

Each of the club members was to analyze a company and present their recommendations at the monthly meeting. However, before they could proceed with the recommendations they needed to acquire some information and to do some analysis.

One member suggested contacting a securities broker to acquire some recent research reports. Using those reports the group could then make their investment decisions.

Others felt that the main objective of the club should be to acquire and analyze data and to make their own recommendations. They decided to mail letters to various companies requesting annual reports. Once they received the statements they could begin their analysis.

One member of the group was skeptical of this approach. After all, what practical experience did any of them have in financial statement analysis? In fact, she was not even sure of what it meant let alone how to proceed. In fact, she remembers something about an efficient market hypothesis and the importance of investment risk.

She commented at their planning luncheon that, "The significance of financial statement data is not in the amount alone. We have to somehow consider the risk, at least the risk that we are not experienced in financial analysis and the valuation of common stocks."

<u>INSTRUCTIONS:</u>

1. What is financial statement analysis?
2. What basic understandings should the investors have in order to interpret and evaluate the financial statement data that they will receive?
3. Why are financial statements important to the decision process in financial analysis?
4. What is an approach to financial statement analysis? Identify some devices used in financial statement analysis to bring out the comparative and relative significance of the financial information presented.
5. What are some of the most important limitations to which accounting data are subject?
6. Discuss the meaning of the statement "The significance of financial statement data is not in the amount alone."
7. Discuss the consideration of risk, especially as it relates to the investment club's proposed investment strategy.

21-3 Earnings Analysis

In many cases, the culmination of financial statement analysis by users is the assessment of "earnings power." Earnings power is a concept which focuses on stable and recurring elements of an operation and attempts to assess the probability and level of the future income of the company. Accounting supplies much of the essential information for the computation and evaluation of earnings power. An understanding of accounting principles and methods is necessary to aid the analysis.

Following are five year summaries of the Income Statements for the Uni and Bi Companies.

INSTRUCTIONS:

1. Analyze and compare the stability of earnings and earnings power of these two companies. Be sure to include a review of the accounting methods in your analysis.

2. What is the apparent strategy of each company with regard to stability?

BI COMPANY

Comparative Income Statement (in millions)
For the Five Years Ending Dec. 31, 1985

	1985	1984	1983	1982	1981
Sales	$240.3	$198.6	$175.7	$198.2	$204.6
COGS	127.5	88.1	69.5	126.7	109.8
Gross Margin	112.8	110.5	106.2	71.5	94.8
Selling & Admin.	30.1	27.9	25.8	25.0	20.4
Advertising	3.6	9.4	2.4	7.8	10.3
Maintenance	7.7	1.1	3.1	9.0	5.6
Depreciation	9.3	9.2	9.5	8.6	8.0
Interest	5.1	4.8	0.2	5.0	4.0
Loss on Investment	0.0	0.0	(20.3)	0.0	0.0
Income from Operations	57.0	58.1	44.9	16.1	46.5
Extra. Gain (Loss)	0.0	0.0	0.0	25.4	0.0
Discontinued Operations	0.0	(10.0)	0.0	0.0	0.0
Income Taxes	28.2	23.8	22.0	20.7	22.9
Income After Tax	$ 28.8	$ 24.3	$ 22.9	$ 20.8	$ 23.6

Additional Information

1. Bi Company switched to LIFO in 1985.

2. Bi Company uses the deferred method for investment tax credits.

3. Obsolete inventory of $12.0 milion was written off in 1981.

4. Bi Company reclassified some marketable securities from short-term to long-term investment in 1983.

5. The company capitalized $5.0 million of interest in 1983.

6. The company uses straight-line depreciation for financial statement purposes and accelerated for tax purposes.

7. The company extinguished some bonds in 1982 that were due in 1988. They recognized a gain on the early retirement.

UNI COMPANY

Comparative Income Statement (in millions)
For the Five Years Ending Dec. 31, 1985

	1985	1984	1983	1982	1981
Sales	$120.8	$ 98.7	$ 64.2	$ 75.0	$ 50.3
COGS	61.4	49.7	46.7	37.2	25.6
Gross Margin	59.4	49.0	17.5	37.8	24.7
Selling & Admin.	11.3	10.1	11.4	7.2	5.0
Advertising	2.5	2.0	1.8	1.5	0.8
Maintenance	2.2	1.5	1.7	1.5	1.3
Depreciation	17.2	13.7	10.5	10.2	6.0
Interest	2.1	1.6	1.2	2.4	1.6
Income (Loss) from Operations	24.1	20.1	(9.1)	15.0	10.0
Discontinued Operations	0.0	0.0	(5.0)	0.0	0.0
Income Taxes	10.1	10.5	(5.5)	4.5	3.9
Income (Loss) After Taxes	$ 14.0	$ 9.6	$ (8.6)	$ 10.5	$ 6.1

Additional Information

1. Uni Company switched to LIFO in 1983.

2. Uni Company uses the flow thru method for investment tax
   credits.

3. Uni Company uses accelerated depreciation methods.

4. Uni Company now fully funds the pension expense each year (part
   of selling and administrative expense). The company experienced
   an actuarial loss of $3.0 million on its plan when it re-evaluated
   in 1983.

5. Obsolete inventory of $4.0 million was written off in 1983.

21-4 Loan Evaluation

Following is a three-year summary of the Statement of Changes in Financial Position
and Income Statement for the Growth Co. The company has approached your bank to
borrow $100 million for an expansion program. Growth plans to expand its present
production capabilities to produce 50% more output. You are presently making loans
of this type at an interest rate between 15% and 20%. You are the loan officer
required to analyze this information and to prepare a recommendation based upon
this information only.

INSTRUCTIONS:

Analyze and comment on the significant conclusions which can be derived from these statements.

Growth Company
Statement of Changes in Financial Position
(000 Omitted)

Funds Provided By:	1985	1984	1983
Income from Operations	$ 30,081	$ 45,071	$ 43,022
Adjustments:			
Depreciation (Accelerated)	30,928	41,580	45,022
Deferred Taxes	(2,750)	1,250	7,800
Funds from Operations	58,259	87,901	95,844
Other Funds Provided By:			
Issuance of Debt	25,000	12,000	-0-
Sale of Long-Term Investments	20,000	-0-	-0-
Sale of Assets	5.500	2,000	2,100
Total Funds Provided	$108,759	$101,901	$ 97,944
Funds Applied To:			
Dividends	14,670	13,225	11,520
Plant and Equipment	33,397	43,589	12,240
Repayment of Debt	35,000	30,000	10,500
Purchase of Treasury Stock	-0-	-0-	70,000
Total Funds Applied	$ 83,067	$ 86,814	$104,260
Increase (Decrease) in Working Capital	$ 25,692	$15,087	$ (6,316)

	1985	1984	1983
Net Sales	$838,935	$1,026,600	$1,008,135
COGS (LIFO)	657,492	817,289	804,250
Depreciation (Accelerated)	30,928	41,580	45,022
Selling & Admin. Expenses	67,685	62,702	60,241
Interest Expense	23,720	14,979	17,422
Income Before Tax	$ 59,010	$ 90,050	$ 81,200
Tax Expense	28,929	44,979	38,178
Income After Taxes	$ 30,081	$ 45,071	$ 43,022

21-5 Fundamental Investment Analysis

You have been hired as a security analyst to provide a fundamental analysis of the Ace Manufacturing company, a NYSE-listed company. The company sells heavy machinery that requires high capital investment for the manufacturing process. In addition, a high level of inventory is maintained because of the long production process and the high cost of each unit. Sales have been steady or slightly increasing over the past few years in spite of the 10% inflation rate. The company has been profitable and reinvesting in plant and equipment on a regular basis. The company is conservative and uses FIFO and straight-line depreciation for financial accounting and tax purposes, and a 5% interest rate for their pension plan assumptions. The economy is rebounding and interest rates are falling.

INSTRUCTIONS:

Based on the information above and the following financial statements only, analyze and present specific information which you feel are important factors in the investment analysis. What is your recommendation: buy or sell?

ACE MANUFACTURING, INC.
(000s Omitted)
Balance Sheet as of

	12/31/85	12/31/84
Cash	$ 4,000	$ 3,500
Accounts Receivable (Net)	7,500	6,000
Inventory (FIFO)	6,500	5,000
Total Current Assets	$ 18,000	$ 14,500
Land	$ 2,000	$ 2,000
Building	100,000	100,000
Accumulated Depreciation	(50,000)	(40,000)
Equipment	28,000	17,500
Accumulated Depreciation	(8,000)	(6,000)
Total Assets	$ 90,000	$ 88,000
Accounts Payable	7,500	8,000
Short-Term Debt (13%)	20,000	27,500 (8%)
Long-Term Debt '16%)	40,000	30,000 (16%)
Common Stock	10,000	11,500
Retained Earnings	12,500	11,000
Total Liabilities and Stockholders' Equity	$ 90,000	$ 88,000

ACE MANUFACTURING, INC.
(000's Omitted)
Income Statement for the Years Ending 12/31

	1985	1984	1983	1982	1981
Sales	$100,000	$91,000	$105,000	$83,000	$78,000
COGS (FIFO)	62,000	55,000	60,000	53,000	53,000
Gross Margin	38,000	36,000	45,000	30,000	25,000
Depreciation (Straight line)	12,000	11,000	10,500	9,500	8,000
Selling & Administrative Expense	9,000	10,500	19,000	8,500	6,000
Interest	9,000	7,000	7,000	5,000	5,000
Gross Income	8,000	7,500	8,500	7,000	6,000
Tax Expense	4,000	3,750	4,250	3,500	3,000
Net Income	$ 4,000	$ 3,750	$ 4,250	$ 3,500	$ 3,000
EPS	$ 2.50	$ 1.87	$ 2.12	$ 1.75	$ 1.50
Market Price/Share of Common	$ 25.00	$ 22.50	$ 30.00	$ 26.25	$ 24.00
Dividend/Share	$ 1.20	$ 1.00	$ 1.00	$ .85	$ .75
No. of Common Shares	1.6 mil.	2 mil.	2 mil.	2 mil.	2 mil.

21-6 Schaefer Retailers

The retail department store business has been undergoing a number of changes over the past twenty years. The 1960's were characterized as the beginning for the discount department stores. Imported merchandise, considered at first to be of lower quality than merchandise manufactured in the United States accounted for a high percentage of sales. Customer service oriented and specialty shops saw their market shrink as the discount stores grew rapidly.

Schaefer Retailers was slow to adapt to the changing scene. They had always emphasized high quality products and personalized service. After experiencing problems in the early 1970's, they entered the discount market. By that time, however, the competition had become fierce and some previously dominant discount department stores were actually forced out of business. Shaefer was able to hold its own, but their profitability was definitely hurt.

The 1980's to some degree showed a return of the popularity of the full service department stores and specialty shops. Schaefer again was slow to adapt and experienced some problems.

As the CPA for Schaefer Retailers, you have been requested to develop some key ratios from the comparative financial statements. This information is to be used to convince creditors that Schaefer Retailers is solvent and to support the use of going concern valuation procedures in the financial statements.

The data requested and the computations developed from the financial statements follow:

	1985	1984
Current ratio	2.5 times	2.0 times
Acid-test ratio	0.7 times	1.2 times
Property, plant, and equipment to stockholders' equity	2.6 times	2.3 times
Sales to stockholders' equity	2.5 times	2.8 times
Net income	Up 30%	Down 10%
Earnings per share	$3.12	$2.40
Book value per share	Up 5%	Up 8%

INSTRUCTIONS:

1. Schaefer Retailers asks you to prepare a list of brief comments showing how each of these items supports the solvency and going-concern potential of the business. The company wishes to use these comments as requested, giving the implications and the limitations of each item separately, and then the collective inference that may be drawn from them about Schaefer's solvency and going-concern potential.
2. Having done as the client requested in part 1, prepare a brief listing of additional ratio analysis type data for this client which you think its creditors are going to ask for to supplement the data provided in part 1. Explain why you think the additional data will be helpful to these creditors in evaluating the client's solvency.
3. What warnings should you offer these creditors about the limitations of ratio analysis for the purposes stated here?

21-7 Dividend Policy

Tyson Foods, Inc. went public three years ago. The board of directors will be meeting shortly after the end of the year to decide on a dividend policy. A stock or a cash dividend has never been declared. Presented below is a brief financial summary of Tyson Foods, Inc. operations.

The company has experienced strong growth in sales and earnings over the five year period despite having adopted a relatively conservative operating policy. This policy has been to finance their growth primarily through the retention of earnings. The company has had additional market opportunities over the past five years, but they have been reluctant to over extend themselves.

The president, Robert Tyson, put it this way: "Our success has been our people. We can only go as far as we have people to run the operation. It is best not to push them too hard or stretch them too thin. We have to have people to support our growth and it takes time to train them to handle the responsibilities."

Bruce Tyson, the treasurer, views it from a different perspective: "I don't like to borrow money except in an emergency. If we borrow to finance our growth and then experience a slowdown, our earnings could be hurt severely. It is important to have a strong balance sheet."

| | ($000 omitted) | | | | |
	1985	1984	1983	1982	1981
Sales	$10,000	$8,000	$7,000	$3,000	$2,000
Net Income	$ 1,500	$ 800	$ 400	$ 500	$ 100
Average total assets	$11,000	$9,500	$5,500	$2,100	$1,500
Current assets	$ 4,000	$3,000	$1,500	$ 600	$ 500
Working capital	$ 1,800	$1,600	$ 600	$ 250	$ 200
Common shares:					
Number of shares outstanding (000)	1,000	1,000	1,000	10	10
Average market price	$9	$6	$4	-	-

INSTRUCTIONS:

1. Suggest factors to be considered by the board of directors in establishing a dividend policy.
2. Compute the rate of return on assets, profit margin on sales, earnings per share, and price–earnings ratio for each of the five years for Tyson Foods, Inc.
3. Comment on the appropriateness of declaring a cash dividend at this time, using the ratios computed in part 2, as a major factor in your analysis.

21-8 The Value of Book Value

The owners of R. L. Jefferson Company, a closely held corporation, have offered to sell their 100% interest in the company's common stock at an amount equal to the book value of the common stock. They will retain their interest in the company's preferred stock.

The Jefferson family had been at a loss as to how to value their business. Since the company has no publicly held common stock, therefore, no market value for the stock, they were looking for alternative methods of valuing their company. They know that other companies in their industry have been sold on the basis of dollar sales. Some multiplied the dollar sales by one and a half or two and negotiated the sale on that basis. However, due to the dramatic differences in industry price structures and discounting policies the Jeffersons thought that negotiations would be difficult using that valuation technique.

Someone else had suggested using an industry average price earnings ratio to calculate a per share price. Again this was eliminated as a possibility by the Jeffersons, because the last year's earnings were low. In fact, the company had experienced rather volatile earnings in the past.

At last, someone suggested book value. George Jefferson, the president, liked this idea. "Book value reflects the real value of the company. It is the total of what we have invested and what we have earned. This seems like a fair basis to price our company."

The president of the Heilmut Corporation, your client, would like to combine the operations of the R. L. Jefferson Company with the Metal Products Division, and she is seriously considering having Heilmut Corporation buy the common stock of the R. L. Jefferson Company. She questions the use of "book value" as a basis for sale, however, and has come to you for advice.

INSTRUCTIONS:

Draft a report to your client. Your report should cover the following points:

1. Define book value. Explain its significance in establishing a value for a business that is expected to continue in operation indefinitely.

2. Describe the procedure for computing book values of ownership equities.

3. Why should your client consider the R. L. Jefferson Company's accounting policies and methods in the evaluation of the company's reported book value? List the areas of accounting policy and methods relevant to this evaluation.

4. What factors, other than book value, should your client recognize in determining a basis for sale?

21-9 Acquisition Analysis

Yahr Corporation is considering the acquisition of Alpha Corporation and Omega Corporation. Bob Yahr, the president of the company has decided that his company should expand in an orderly fashion and therefore will consider acquiring only one company. The question is which one?

Bob has asked your advice on what to do and how to do it. His main concern is receiving "value" for his investment. Unfortunately, he has not given any more explicit criteria than that on which you may base your analysis.

Following are the financial statements for Alpha and Omega for the year ending December 31, 1985. Both corporations are in the same industry. The Yahr Corporation has a policy of using five times after tax earnings as a guideline for determining a possible acquisition price. On that basis they will pay approximately $875,000 for either company.

INSTRUCTIONS:

1. Which company would your recommend for acquisition, Alpha or Omega? Why?
2. Discuss the inherent limitations of single-year statements for purposes of analysis and interpretation. Include in your discussion the extent to which these limitations are overcome by the use of comparative statements.
3. Comparative financial statements that show a firm's financial history for each of the last ten years may also be misleading. Discuss the factors or conditions that might contribute to misinterpretations. Include a discussion of additional information and supplementary data that might be included in or provided with the statements to prevent misinterpretations.

ALPHA CORPORATION
Balance Sheet, 12/31/85

Cash	$ 50,000
Marketable Securities	50,000
Accounts Receivable (Net)	200,000
Inventory (FIFO)	200,000
Total Current Assets	500,000
Land	50,000
Building	100,000
Equipment	250,000
Accumulated Depreciation (St. Line)	(275,000)
Goodwill	175,000
Total Assets	$800,000
Accounts Payable	$ 50,000
Long Term Debt (10%)	150,000
Common Stock ($10 Par)	100,000
Retained Earnings	500,000
Total Liabilities and Stockholders' Equity	$800,000

ALPHA CORPORATION
Income Statement for the Year Ending 12/31/85

Sales	$1,000,000
COGS	500,000
Margin on Sales	500,000
Depreciation (St. Line)	25,000
Goodwill Expense	5,000
Selling and Administrative	65,000
Lease Rental	50,000
Interest Expense	5,000
Income Before Taxes	$ 350,000
Tax Expense	175,000
Net Income	$ 175,000

Notes:
Alpha Corp. uses conservative policies relating to the amortization of its goodwill and pension plan prior service cost. The period of amortization for both is 40 years. Alpha Corp. fully funds its pension expense each year. The current unvested prior service cost is $200,000.

OMEGA CORPORATION
Balance Sheet, 12/31/85

Cash	$ 50,000
Accounts Receivable (Net)	100,000
Inventory (LIFO)	100,000
Total Current Assets	250,000
Land	100,000
Building	100,000
Equipment	950,000
Accumulated Depreciation (Accelerated)	(138,500)
Leased Equipment (Net)	238,500
Total Assets	$1,500,000
Accounts Payable	$ 50,000
Capitalized Leases (15% interest)	238,500
Long Term Debt (10%)	200,000
Common Stock ($1 Par)	100,000
Retained Earnings	761,500
Total Liabilities and Stockholders' Equity	$1,500,000

OMEGA CORPORATION
Income Statement for the Year Ending 12/31/85

Sales	$3,000,000
COGS	2,250,000
Margin on Sale	850,000
Depreciation (Accelerated)	105,000
Deprec. of Leased Assets (Accelerated)	45,000
Selling and Administrative	105,000
Research and Development	100,000
Interest Expense	24,000
Interest on Capital Leases	22,500
Income Before Taxes	$ 348,500
Tax Expense	174,250
Net Income	$ 174,250

Notes:
The leases expire within a year, at which time they will be rewritten as operating leases. The expected lease payments will be the same as for 1985, a total of $50,000.

21-10 Trading on Equity

A recent college graduate of a school of journalism was hired by the Milltown Enterprise Newspaper Company. One of the young reporter's first assignments was to write a column highlighting the success of two local businesses: Milltown East and

Milltown West. The companies were separately incorporated and independently managed by two brothers.

The brothers did not get along and had developed quite a rivalry. Despite their independent operation each company had assets totalling $4,200,000. The reporter interviewed both of the brothers, but had received conflicting viewpoints as to which of the two companies was most successful.

The manager of Middletown East claimed to have the best operation. The net income after taxes and return on assets were higher than Middletown West's. The Middletown West brother claimed supremacy because of a higher earnings per share and return on stockholders' equity. The newspaper writer was confused as to the appropriate evaluation criteria and has approached you for help.

Following are the equity sections of the balance sheets and selected income statement information for the two companies for the year ended December 31, 1985.

Milltown West		Milltown East	
Current Liabilities	$ 300,000	Current Liabilities	$ 500,000
Long-Term Debt, 10%	1,500,000		
Common Stock ($30 Par)	1,800,000	Common Stock ($20 Par)	3,000,000
Retained Earnings	600,000	Retained Earnings	700,000
	$4,200,000		$4,200,000

	West	East
Income before interest and taxes	$820,000	$820,000
Interest expense	150,000	-0-
	$670,000	$820,000
Income Taxes (40%)	268,000	328,000
Net Income	$402,000	$492,000

INSTRUCTIONS:

1. Which company is more profitable in terms of return on total assets?
2. Which company is more profitable in terms of return on stockholders' equity?
3. Which company has the greater net income per share of stock? Why?
4. From the point of view of income, is it advantageous to the stockholders of Milltown West to have the long term debt outstanding? Why?
5. What is "trading on the equity"?
6. Explain how a change in income tax rates affects trading on equity.
7. Explain how trading on equity affects earnings per share of common stock.
8. Under what circumstances would a company seek to trade on equity to a substantial degree?

CHAPTER 22

☐

FULL DISCLOSURE
IN FINANCIAL REPORTING

22-1 The Penn Central

On Sunday, June 21, 1970 the Penn Central Railroad filed for bankruptcy. The bankruptcy had far reaching affects in the financial community. The accounting profession was not untouched by the resulting controversies. Following is an excerpt from an article which appeared in <u>Fortune</u> August, 1970.

"The underlying causes of the failure can be traced back to the 1968 merger of the Pennsylvania and New York Central railroads, the biggest corporate marriage in business history. The merger should not have happened, for the personalities of the two roads were so far apart they were incompatible. And the men who ran them found it impossible to work in harmony. The merger was badly executed, and management since has been just as bad. There was chaos out on the road, aggravated by infighting between some of the company's top management.

Worse yet, complex and often hazy financial reporting had cloaked the great losses and the steady hemorrhaging of cash that the chaos had wrought. The blame for this falls on many men, not the least of them the directors who went along blandly -- until it was too late."

The firm's auditors were quick to reply in a "Letter to the Editor" published in <u>Fortune</u> September, 1970.

"Fortune's August issue is so wrong in its criticism of Penn Central's 'bookkeeping' as to border on fantasy. Specifically, it is wrong in charging that Penn Central's financial statements put a 'healthy visage' on a hemorrhaging company, and that the company's auditors 'obviously went along' with this effort to 'obfuscate the true picture.'

The August issue is also destructive to the accounting profession

as a whole.   Granted there is substantial room for improvement
in generally accepted accounting principles by strengthening
their specificity and by the gradual elimination of permissable
alternatives. Constructive criticism in such a vein is both
necessary and helpful as the profession works in that direction.
But it was very unhelpful for Fortune instead to embark on a
sweeping attack on generally accepted accounting principles,
calling them 'an open invitation to distortions and outright
fraud.' To abandon those principles which have been hammered out
over the years on the anvil of experience in favor of an
unexplained concept asserted to be 'more realistic' would leave
American business and its investors in a state of chaos."

INSTRUCTIONS:

1. Fortune refers to "hazy financial reporting." What is the role of
disclosure in financial reporting?
2. What is the full disclosure principle in accounting? What is the
definition of disclosure?
3. What has been the role of the SEC in requiring financial disclosures?
4. What are the methods of disclosure?
5. What is the role of materiality as it relates to disclosure?
6. What is a definition of materiality?
7. Why has disclosure increased substantially in the last ten years?

22-2 Management's Responsibilities

Following are excerpts from Dayton Hudson Corporation's Annual Report for the year
ending February 2, 1985:

Report of Management

Responsibility for Financial Statements and Accounting Controls

The financial statements and related information presented in
this report have been prepared by our management according to
generally accepted accounting principles. Estimates and other
amounts in these statements reflect our best judgments.
Management is responsible for the presentation, integrity and
consistency of the data in the Annual Report.

To discharge this responsibility, we maintain a comprehensive
system of internal controls and organizational arrangements

designed to provide reasonable assurance that assets are safeguarded from unauthorized use or disposition, transactions take place in accordance with management's authorization and are properly recorded, and financial records are adequate for preparation of financial statements and other financial information. The concept of reasonable assurance is based upon a recognition that there are inherent limitations in any system of internal controls because the cost of the controls should not exceed the benefit derived. After judging the cost and benefit factors, we believe our system of internal controls provides this reasonable assurance.

To ensure the ongoing effectiveness of our internal control system, our goal is to recruit and employ highly qualified people, provide comprehensive written guidelines regarding procedural and ethical matters, and conduct effective training programs. We also provide and promote an environment which encourages free and open communication at all levels in our organization.

The Audit Committee of the Board of Directors, consisting of six outside directors recommends independent auditors for appointment by the Board, and reviews their proposed services and their reports. The committee also reviews the internal audit plan and the results of the internal audit effort. Our independent auditors, Ernst & Whinney, our internal auditors, our general counsel and our corporate controller have full and free access to meet with the Audit Committee, with or without the presence of management. The Audit Committee meets regularly to discuss the results of the auditors' examinations and their opinions on the adequacy of internal controls and the quality of financial reporting.

Our financial statements have been audited by Ernst & Whinney, whose report appears on this page. Their report expresses an opinion as to the fair presentation of the financial statements and is based on an independent examination made in accordance with generally accepted auditing standards.

Report of Ernst & Whinney, Independent Auditors
Board of Directors and Shareholders
Dayton Hudson Corporation
Minneapolis, Minnesota

We have examined the consolidated statements of financial position of Dayton Hudson Corporation and subsidiaries as of February 2, 1985 and January 28, 1984, and the related consolidated statements of results of operations, shareholders' investment and changes in financial position for each of the three years in the period ended February 2, 1985. Our examinations were made in accordance with generally accepted auditing standards and, accordingly, included such tests of the accounting records and such other auditing procedures as we considered necessary in the circumstances.

In our opinion, the financial statements referred to above present fairly the consolidated financial position of Dayton Hudson Corporation and subsidiaries at February 2, 1985 and January 28, 1984, and the consolidated results of their operations and changes in their financial position for each of the three years in the period ended February 2, 1985, in conformity with generally accepted accounting principles applied on a consistent basis.

INSTRUCTIONS:

1. Who has primary responsibility for the preparation, integrity, and objectivity of a company's financial statements?
2. What is the primary implication of the placement of the responsibility?
3. Is this the primary "Report of Management" required in the annual report? Discuss.
4. Can the "Report of Management" contain financial forecasts?
5. What are seen as the arguments for and against the presentation of financial forecasts?
6. Is the CPA's opinion qualified or unqualified? What is the difference between these two?
7. When does a CPA render a "subject to" opinion? An adverse opinion?

22-3 Social Responsibilities

Following are examples of various types of information contained in annual reports:

United States Steel December 31, 1982
Environmental and Safety Matters

Many uncertainities continue to exist concerning the capital requirements of and operating costs associated with various laws relating to the environment and safety. In some instances, regulations still have not been issued, performance standards have not been established and equipment requirements have not been defined. In 1982, the Corporation entered into agreements with agencies which helped resolve many of these uncertainties with respect to air emissions from the facilities covered. As

to water discharges, effluent limitation guidelines for the iron
and steel industry were not published until May 21, 1982. These
guidelines are under litigation and it is anticipated that they
will be modified. Although unable to accurately predict water
control requirements, the Corporation is attempting to achieve
compliance within a reasonable period of time after specific
requirements become known.

Predictions beyond 1982 can only be broad-based estimates by the
Corporation, in many cases without any detailed engineering or
other documentary support. Such estimates indicate probable
additional expenditure authorizations for bringing into
compliance with the above-mentioned legislative requirements
those existing facilities which are currently expected to be
economically operational ranging from $570 million to $955
million through 1987 (in 1982 dollars, and includes
capitalization of our own engineering and interest costs). These
estimates assume (a) only minor changes in operating procedures,
(b) no process changes and (c) compliance by all Corporation
facilities with such environmental and safety laws and
regulations as presently enforced. The economics of the required
investment may dictate that certain facilities be closed instead
of modified to comply with the requirements. The substantial
sums required for these non-income generating expenditures will
restrict the ability of the Corporation to continue to modernize
and expand its facilities. To preclude a negative impact upon
the Corporation's earnings in future years, unless there is a
substantial increase in productivity, the costs associated with
compliance with all these regulations will have to be recovered
through cost-covering price increases, market conditions
permitting.

The outcome of pending negotiations and potential administrative
and judicial proceedings, as well as future legislative and
regulatory changes, will be significant factors in determining
the specific amount of expenditures required for this purpose
and the periods of time for achieving legislatively established
goals. Federal laws and regulations provide for the assessment
of substantial civil penalities for noncompliance with
environmental requirements under specified circumstances. It is
not possible at this time to estimate the specific amount of such
penalities that might be assessed against the Corporation or the
outcome of any pending or future proceeding in which penalities
are sought. However, it is not anticipated that the outcome of
such proceedings should result in a material adverse effect on
the Corporation's consolidated financial position. Settlements
of a number of proceedings against the Corporation involving air
and water pollution matters have permitted the Corporation to
offset penalities assessed against the cost of facilities to be
constructed in the future and the Corporation will seek such
penalty offsets in any settlements in the future.

Estimated Provision for Occupational Disease Claims

An estimated accrual of $88 million was provided in 1979 for potential awards to those then retired for pneumoconiosis (black lung) as the result of dramatic increase in claims following 1978 amendments to the Federal Coal Mine Health and Safety Act of 1969. Commencing in 1979, a provision for future claims is being accrued over the remaining service life of present employees. In 1982, the provision was reduced by $64 million as a result of a triennial valuation of the estimated liability for occupational disease claims. The adjustment resulted in a reduction of $33 million to Cost of Sales for present employees, while $31 million was recorded as an unusual item for pre-1979 retirees.

Sperry Corporation March 31, 1984
Social Concern

During fiscal 1984, Sperry, primarily through the Sperry Corporation Foundation, made charitable contributions in the United States totaling $2.1 million, representing 2.1% of the company's pretax domestic earnings. The following categories of recipients shared in the fiscal 1984 program in the percentage indicated: education, 45%, United Way, 27%, health and welfare, 6%, culture, 5%, civic (human services, youth, community improvements, environment, law and justice, the family), 17%. Stockholders may obtain a list of the Foundation's contributions of $5,000 or more by writing to the company.

The Greyhound Corporation December 31, 1984
Pension Plans and Other Employee Benefits:

Pensions are generally funded on the basis of annual actuarial determinations of current service costs plus amortization in level annual amounts of unfunded prior service costs, including interest, over periods of thirty to forty years.

Cost of medical and life insurance benefits under employee group plans, including similar benefits for qualified retirees, generally is charged to income as incurred. The future benefits applicable to the retirees of discontinued operations were provided for on an estimated present value basis at the date of discontinuance.

Originally economists and the public felt that the only responsibility of business was to make a profit. This attitude has changed and management has been under fire from those who feel that business ought to be socially responsible. These excerpts reflect some of the changes which have occurred.

1. What is a definition of socially responsible?
2. In general what have been the reasons for corporations' concern for social responsibility?
3. What are some examples of social responsibility reporting?
4. What are some arguments for social responsibiity accounting?
5. What are some arguments that oppose social responsibility accounting?
6. What are some practical problems associated with social responsibiity accounting?

22-4 Comparable Segmental Information?

Eric Packard is the in charge partner for engagements with two major publicly held corporations. Eric recently completed the audit for Amalgamated Industries, a diversified international company organized into seven profit centers for purposes of internal control. The audit went relatively smooth. Eric was impressed with the attitude of Mr. Bean, the controller of the company. He was very willing to disclose information relating to the various operations of the company.

The seven profit centers were reported as individual reportable segments. In addition, the company provided information segmenting the industries on a worldwide basis. Foreign operations account for thirty percent of total revenue; equally distributed among Mexico, Chile, and Brazil. Due to the close proximity and close economic ties between Mexico and the United States, Mr. Bean separately disclosed information about the operations in Mexico and combined the other two countries under the heading of "South America."

Amalgamated Industries derives eight percent of its total revenue from the Winston Co. and six percent from Salem Industries. Because Winston owns 49% of Salem, Amalgamated disclosed that a single customer was responsible for over ten percent of their revenue.

Since the Amalgamated audit was completed, Eric has been concentrating on his other large account, Ponmye Diverisfied Industries. Ponmye had approximately the same total revenues as Amalgamated and has diversified into many of the same industries. They operate their domestic and foreign operations with six profit centers.

Although the two companies have many similarities and are often considered comparable companies in the investment community, their approach to disclosure varies dramatically. Mary Baer, the controller for Ponmye proposes to disclose two segments: consumer products and manufacturing products. In addition, Mary feels that it is impractical to provide industry segmentation on a worldwide basis.

Foreign operations generate 28% of their revenues and will be grouped together as a "Southern Hemisphere" segment. The three countries in this segment, South Africa, Mexico, and Nicaragua account for approximately equal shares of Ponmye's foreign sales.

Ponmye's two largest single customers, Wales Inc. and Genesee Sales Co., account for nine percent and eight percent, respectively, of their revenues. Wales Inc. owns 40% of Genesee. Since neither of the two companies exceed the 10% limitation, no single customer information is deemed necessary.

Eric is troubled with Ponmye's proposed disclosures. He wonders how the investment community will respond to such different disclosures concerning the operations of two companies considered to be so comparable. Eric feels his firm will definitely lose some credibility, if Ponmye is insistent upon their proposal. He knows that Mary's position will be difficult to change since she already stated that, "If I have to disclose other segments individually, the only people who will gain are our competitors and the only people that will lose are our present stockholders."

INSTRUCTIONS:

1. How are segments defined?
2. How is a segment determined to be reportable?
3. In general, what accounting problems are related to diversified companies?
4. Discuss the impact of generally accepted accounting principles on the two companies' segmental disclosures.
5. Evaluate Mary's comment concerning the disclosure of segmental information.
6. How might security analysts use segmental information?

22-5 Big Sky Ski Company

The Big Sky Ski Company, a publicly held manufacturer of snow skiing equipment, issues quarterly financial information to its shareholders and the press. The following data have been included in the quarterly financial information issued during the current year:

	Quarter		
	1st	2nd	3rd
Revenues	$1,000,000	$3,000,000	$8,000,000
Net Income (loss)	(100,000)	400,000	1,400,000

The Company's fiscal year ends on March 31 and it does not plan to issue separate fourth quarter financial information or to report fourth quarter results separately in its annual report. Annual revenues and net income for the current year are $16,000,000 and $1,700,000, respectively, as compared to $13,000,000 and $1,400,000 last year.

We have been the Company's auditors for several years but we have not been engaged to audit the quarterly financial information.

INSTRUCTIONS:

1. What responsibility does the auditor have regarding the quarterly financial information? Would your answer be different if the client issues separate fourth quarter financial information?

2. Discuss the Company's treatment of the following items as they relate to the quarterly financial information:

a. The Company has followed the practice of accruing due but unpaid property taxes at the end of each year. This year, in order to provide more meaningful quarterly financial information, the Company has accrued one-fourth of the estimated year-end property tax liability each quarter. Although property taxes are not material on an annual basis, they are material in those quarters when sales are low due to the seasonal nature of the business.

b. The Company did not provide for federal income taxes in the first quarter.

c. The Company's president had an unfortunate skiing accident in the second quarter and the proceeds from the insurance policy on his life (net of the related cash surrender value) of $50,000 are included in income for that quarter. The Company did not present this as an extraordinary item in its second quarter's financial information.

3. In connection with the year-end audit, you discover the following. What effect, if any, would these items have on the annual report?

a. Company policy is to record costs incurred in connection with product warranties as an expense when paid. These costs remain fairly constant from year to year. $100,000 of these costs were paid during the fourth quarter.

b. The Company uses an estimated gross profit rate, based on last year's actual rate, to determine cost of sales on a quarterly basis. The Company takes a year-end physical inventory. The physical resulted in a downward inventory adjustment of $400,000.

c. The company assumes that their advertising expenditures primarily benefit the third and fourth quarter. Therefore, the company defers first and second quarter advertising costs and expenses them equally in the third and fourth quarter. Advertising costs in the third and fourth quarter are expensed as incurred.

4. What are the disclosure requirements for interim financial statements?

5. Discuss the discrete and integral approaches to interim information.

6. What are the benefits of interim financial information?

22-6 Atlantic, Inc.

Atlantic, Inc. produces electronic components for sale to manufacturers of radios, television sets, and phonographic systems. Sue Davis, CPA, completed field work two weeks ago in connection with her examination of Atlantic's financial statements for the year ended December 31, 1985. Ms. Davis now is evaluating the significance of the following items prior to preparing her auditor's report. Except as noted, none of these items have been disclosed in the financial statements or footnotes.

Item 1
Recently Atlantic interrupted its policy of paying quarterly cash dividends to its stockholders. Dividends were paid regularly through 1984, discontinued for all 1985 to finance equipment for the company's new plant, and resumed in the first quarter of 1986. In the annual report dividend policy is to be discussed in the president's letter to stockholders.

Item 2
A 10-year loan agreement, which the company entered into three years ago, provides that dividend payments may not exceed net income earned after taxes subsequent to the date of the agreement. The balance of retained earnings at the date of the loan agreement was $298,000. From that date through December 31, 1985, net income after taxes has totaled $360,000

and cash dividends have totaled $130,000. On the basis of these data the staff auditor assigned to this review concluded that there was no retained earnings restriction at December 31, 1985.

Item 3

The company's new manufacturing plant building, which cost $600,000 and has an estimated life of 25 years, is leased from the Sixth National Bank at an annual rental of $100,000. The company is obligated to pay property taxes, insurance, and maintenance. At the conclusion of its 10-year noncancellable lease, the company has the option of purchasing the property for $1.00. In Atlantic's income statement the rental payment is reported on a separate line.

Item 4

A major electronics firm has introduced a line of products that will compete directly with Atlantic's primary line, now being produced in the specially designed new plant. Because of manufacturing innovations, the competitor's line will be of comparable quality but priced 50% below Atlantic's line. The competitor announced its new line during the week following completion of field work. Ms. Davis read the announcement in the newspaper and discussed the situation by telephone with Atlantic executives. Atlantic will meet the lower prices that are high enough to cover variable manufacturing and selling expenses but will permit recovery of only a portion of fixed costs.

INSTRUCTIONS:

For each of the items above discuss any additional disclosures in the financial statements and footnotes that the auditor should recommend to her client. (The cumulative effect of the four items should not be considered.)

22-7 "Safe Harbor" Forecasts

A recent article in Barron's noted:

Okay. Last fall, someone with a long memory and an even longer arm reached into that bureau drawer and came out with a moldy cheese sandwich and the equally moldy notion of corporate forecasts. We tried to find out what happened to the cheese sandwich -- but, rats!, even recourse to the Freedom of Information Act didn't help. However, the forecast proposal was dusted off, polished up and found quite serviceable. The SEC, indeed, lost no time in running it up the old flagpole -- but no one was very eager to salute. Even after some of the more objectionable features -- compulsory corrections and detailed explanations of why the estimates went awry -- were peeled off the original proposal.

Seemingly, despite the Commission's smiles and sweet talk, those craven corporations were still afraid that an honest mistake would lead down the primrose path to consent decrees and class action suits. To lay to rest such qualms, the Commission last week approved a "Safe Harbor" rule, that providing the forecasts were made on a reasonable basis and in good faith, protected corporations from litigation should the projections prove wide of the mark (as only about 99% are apt to do).

INSTRUCTIONS:

1. What are the arguments for preparing profit forecasts?
2. What is the purpose of the "safe harbor" rule?
3. Why are corporations concerned about presenting profit forecasts?

22-8 Harness Corporation

Harness Corporation acquired a large tract of land in a small town approximately 10 miles from Capital city. The company executed a firm contract on November 15, 1984, for the construction of a one-mile race track, together with related facilities. The track and facilities were completed December 15, 1985. On December 31, 1985, a 12% installment note of $100,000 was issued along with other consideration in settlement of the construction contract. Installments of $50,000 fall due on December 31 of each of the next two years. The company planned to pay the notes from cash received from operations and from sale of addition stock.

The company adopted the double-declining balance method of computing depreciation. No depreciation was taken in 1985 because all racing equipment was received in December after the completion of the track and facilities.

The land on which the racing circuit was constructed was acquired at various dates for a total of $43,000, and its approximate market value on December 31, 1985, is $60,000.

Through the sale of tickets to spectators, parking fees, concession income, and income from betting, the company's officials anticipated that approximately $175,000 is taken in during the typical year's racing season. Cash expenses for a racing season were estimated at $123,000.

You have made an examination of the financial condition of Harness Corporation as of December 31, 1985. The balance sheet as of that date and statement of operations follow.

Harness Corporation
Balance Sheet
December 31, 1985

A s s e t s

Cash		$ 14,500
Accounts receivable		1,000
Prepaid expenses		7,500
Property (at cost)		
Land	$ 43,000	
Grading and track improvements	68,200	
Grandstand	100,000	
Buildings	60,000	
Racing equipment	40,000	311,200
Organization costs		300
Total assets		$334,500

Liabilities and Stockholders' Equity

Accounts payable	$ 22,000
Installment note payable - 12%	100,000
Stockholders' equity	
Capital stock, par value $1.00 per share,	
authorized 200,000, issued and outstanding	
47,800 shares	47,800
Capital in excess of par, representing amounts	
paid in over par value of capital stock	174,700
Retained earnings (deficit)	(10,000)
Total liabilities and stockholders' equity	$334,500

Harness Corporation
Statement of Income
For the Period from Inception, December 1, 1982
to December 31, 1985

Income	
Profit on sale of land	$ 5,000
Other	100
	5,100
General and administrative expenses	15,100
Net loss for the period	$ 10,000

On January 15, 1986, legislation that declared betting to be illegal was enacted by the state legislature and was signed by the governor. A discussion with management on January 17 about the effect of the legislation revealed that it is now estimated that revenue will be reduced to approximately $48,000 and cash expenses will be reduced to one-third the original estimate.

INSTRUCTIONS:

(Disregard federal income taximplications.)

1. Prepare the explanatory notes to accompany the balance sheet.

2. What opinion do you believe the auditor should render? Discuss.

(AICPA adapted)

22-9 State Utility

State Utility has enjoyed a number of years of continued growth in earnings. During this period consumer satisfaction has diminished, and a number of environmental lawsuits have been filed related to the emission of large amounts of flyash and sulfur. In addition, the utility has difficulty in attracting minority employees and the company has received adverse publicity related to this matter. State Utility is in the process of preparing its current annual report and the chairman of the board has called a meeting of the top executives of the firm to discuss some of these problems.

At the meeting, the chief engineer notes that the company is already spending large amounts on pollution abatement equipment and that a reduction although not a complete elimination of their pollution problems will occur in the near future. The personnel administrator indicates that some headway is being made in attracting minority applicants, but the situation will not be corrected for a number of years. The controller points out that the company is spending monies in many areas of social concern, and that all these expenditures should be explained to the stockholders in the annual report. The chairman of the board, in examining the annual reports of other public utilities, is intrigued by one utility that is already including information in their annual report related to social responsibility issues. He wonders if their public accounting firm could provide any information related to these matters.

1. If the chairman of the board asked its public accounting firm what types of presentations might be used to present information of this nature, what would they say?
2. Which approach should be used for reporting to the public?

22-10 T. A. Properties

T. A. Properties, is a company engaged in owning and managing residential and office rental property. In 1985, its first year of operations, it shared common general office facilities with Thomas Construction Company, a Company controlled by its major stockholder. In addition, the officers of the Company performed various functions for Thomas Construction and the two companies made frequent intercompany advances without charges for interest.

The existence and extent of the transactions with affiliates are as follows:

TRANSACTIONS WITH AFFILIATES:

a. Of the proceeds of the $5,000,000 second mortgage obtained by the Company in October, 1985, $1,605,704 was applied to payments of notes payable to Thomas Construction Company and others affiliated or related to Thomas which was due in 1987. In addition, the Company obtained a second mortgage on the properties acquired in July, 1985, of which proceeds of $1,600,000 were applied to notes due in 1988 issued to Thomas at the time of acquisition of the properties.

b. In September, 1985, the Company acquired for $200,000 a tract of undeveloped land from Thomas Construction. Subsequently, approximately 74% of the land was sold for $270,000 to companies controlled by a relative of the major stockholder of T. A. Properties, Inc. and Thomas Construction Company.

c. During the year ended July 31, 1985, the Company shared general office space with Thomas Construction, prior to the companies' moving, in April, 1985, into a newly completed office building, owned by the Company. Neither Thomas nor the Company was paid a space rental during the year.

d. Certain officers of the Company perform various functions for Thomas Construction. During fiscal year 1985, the Company was paid $35,000 for such services by Thomas Construction.

e. Throughout 1985, the Company and Thomas Construction made intercompany advances without interest to provide funds for operations. The average monthly balance of such advances was $151,000 owed to the Company.

Early in 1986 Thomas Williams was hired by T. A. Properties, Inc. as controller. Upon examination of the above transactions he immediately stated that a number of retroactive changes must be made in order to conform with GAAP.

1. No profit could be recognized on the sale of the land to a relative. Thomas sold the land at less than fair value at $200,000 and a new price of $270,000 must be paid.

2. An office rental must be paid.

3. An interest charge must be made to account for all intercompany advances.

INSTRUCTIONS

1. Are the suggested changes regarding interest on the intercompany notes necessary to conform with GAAP?
2. For the rent?
3. For the land purchase and sale?
4. What are related party transactions?
5. What is the central issue regarding the above transactions that causes concern for accountants?
6. What are the requirements of GAAP concerning related party transactions?

CHAPTER 23

EMERGING ISSUES

23-1 ADC Loans

Financial institutions, particularly savings and loan associations, increasingly are entering into real estate Acquisition, Development, or Construction transactions structured as ADC loans on which they have virtually the same risks and some of the same potential rewards as those of owners of joint ventures. These loans typically have a number (but not necessarily all) of the following characteristics:

1. The loan is structured, explicitly or implicitly, so that the lender participates in expected residual profit on the ultimate sale or use of the project.

2. The lender commits to provide all or substantially all necessary funds to acquire the property and complete the project. The borrower has title to, but little or no equity in, the underlying property.

3. The lender funds the loan commitment or origination fees, or both, by including them in the amount of the loan.

4. The lender completely funds interest during the term of the loan by adding the interest to the loan balance.

5. The loan is secured only by the ADC project. The lender has no recourse to other assets of the borrower.

6. If the borrower does guarantee the loan, the guarantee is frequently limited in application, and is supported by unaudited personal financial statements with few liquid or unmortgaged or unpledged assets. Valuations of assets are typically the borrower's "estimates," unsupported by appraisals, and other ADC project valuations are included based on build-out or end values.

7. The lender must look for recovery of his advances to the sale of the property to independent third parties, refinancing by another lender, or refinancing by the lender and utilization of the property on a level sufficient to provide adequate cash flow

to service the loan.

8. The loan is structured so that default is highly improbable
because the borrower is not required to fund any payments before
the project is completed and, therefore, the loan cannot become
delinquent. Frequently the lender has agreed in advance to
provide interim or long term financing after completion of the
project.

Although construction and development lending has been common for many years,
the activity level in loans having the typical characteristics described above has
increased significantly in recent years. The financial statements of many financial
institutions indicate that ADC loans have increased significantly in many cases, and
by more than 1000% in some cases. An analysis of income statements of these
institutions indicates that fees and interest from ADC loans frequently constitute a
significant percentage of revenues of the institution, and the ADC fees and interest
funded by adding the amounts to outstanding loans may exceed net income of the
institution by several times. Moreover, since ADC loans typically extend beyond one
year (or are rolled-over), the cumulative dollar impact on the net worth is even
greater than on annual income.

Because ADC loans, by their terms, do not become delinquent before the project is
completed, the typical indicators giving rise to the need for added loan loss
allowances do not exist for ADC loans. Thus loan loss allowances for ADC loans are
frequently small, notwithstanding that significant risk may be involved in this type of
lending on an overall basis. There are increasingly frequent reports of substantial
losses arising on ADC projects and loans because of cost over-runs, overly optimistic
appraisals, overbuilding, and other factors. Investigations by Congress, regulatory
agencies, district attorneys and others have frequently been highly critical of both
lending and accounting practices. Therefore more definitive and authoritative
guidance on accounting for ADC loans is critically needed.

INSTRUCTIONS:

1. Discuss the appropriateness of classifying an ADC loan as a loan and
as an investment.
2. Discuss the appropriate accounting for these loans if considered a
loan or an investment.

23-2 Sale of Securities with a "Put"

First Connecticut Securities Co. has been approaching many of its investment banking clients and institutional accounts with a new financing technique. The purpose of the new type of transaction is to recognize a sale and potential tax savings for tax purposes and a borrowing for financial reporting purposes.

First Connecticut will act as an intermediary in arranging the sale of low yielding, tax exempt municipal bonds at prices significantly higher than current market values, providing that the seller simultaneously grant options to the purchaser to sell the bonds back to the seller at a fixed price in the future (that is, a put option). The put option period is generally substantially shorter than the term of the bond being transferred and is usually not exercisable if the municipality defaults on its obligation. The repurchase price is established to ensure that, at a minimum, the purchaser will receive a higher rate of return than that available on similar quality, short-term municipal bonds.

Carol Ostergaard of First Connecticut has approached the Richfield Bank with this idea. Carol has a buyer for the bank's municipal bond portfolio of $10 million par value. The sale price would be $9,250,000 even through the market value of the portfolio was recently determined to be $8,750,000, however the bank would have to grant the purchaser the option to sell the bonds back any time within the next two years at a price of $9,400,000.

She has explained the benefits to the bank in that they can report a loss for tax purposes for the difference between their original purchase price (par value) and the current market value, while treating the difference between current market value and the sale price as the value of the put.

For accounting purposes, however, the bank would not report a loss, but rather account for the transaction as a borrowing. Carol explains that the existence of the put and the recent passage of FASB No. 77, Reporting by Transferors for Transfers of Receivables with Recourse, qualifies the transfer of the bonds as a loan. She argues that since the securities are in effect receivables from municipalities and that the put is in substance a recourse agreement that the transfer requires borrowing treatment.

The bank is very interested in the proposal. They can use the additional tax losses and the additional cash to improve their year end liquidity position. The bank president approved the deal, subject to review by the controller. The controller has some questions since there appears to be no clear cut accounting pronouncement that applies to this area.

INSTRUCTIONS:

1. Identify the main accounting issues that arise with the proposed transaction. Do you agree or disagree with the accounting method proposed by Carol?

2. If the bank records the transaction as a borrowing, should the bank adjust the value of the bonds? Discuss.

3. Suppose FASB No. 77 is found not to apply in this situation, discuss the accounting for this transaction.

23-3 Recognition of Purchased Losses

S & R, Inc. acquires 100% of the outstanding stock of Sandstone Co. for $45 million in cash. At the date of acquisition, the fair value of Sandstone identifiable net assets is $30 million. (None of the assets acquired would require reduction for any negative goodwill, should it arise in the transaction.) Sandstone also has a net operating loss carryforward of $80 million, the tax benefit of which is estimated to be about $37 million. Th estimated present value of the benefit to S & R, Inc. is approximately $30 million.

Assume that the acquired NOL carryforward may be utilized against the subsequent combined taxable income of S & R and the purchased subsidiary. Also assume that:

1. S & R, Inc. has a very strong, consistent earnings history that, coupled with well-documented, realistic projections of future combined taxable income in the near to medium-term, provides assurance beyond any reasonable doubt that the NOL benefit will be realized during the carryforward period; and

2. Net deferred tax credits of $25 million exist on S & R, Inc.'s balance sheet at the acquisition date. These net credits are expcected to reverse completely during the NOL carryforward period, disregarding timing differences that will likely originate during that time.

INSTRUCTIONS:

1. At the date of acquisition, would it be appropriate for S & R, Inc. to give accounting effect to tax benefits it ultimately expects to realize from the purchased NOL carryforward?

2. In what manner should this transaction be recorded in the company's consolidated financial statements at the acquisition date? Alternatives in this regard would appear to include:

   a. Recognize no NOL benefit at date of acquisition, resulting in the following summarized allocation of the purchase price (in millions):

Tangible assets	$30
Goodwill	15
	$45

b. Recognize the entire amount of the NOL benefit expected to be realized:

Tangible assets	$30
NOL benefit	37
Negative goodwill	(22)
	$45

c. Similar to (b), except that the NOL benefit is recorded at its estimated present value:

Tangible assets	$30
NOL benefit	30
Negative goodwill	(15)
	$45

d. Recognize the NOL benefit only to the extent that goodwill would otherwise be recorded:

Tangible assets	$30
NOL benefit	15
	$45

e. Recognize the NOL benefit only to the extent that net deferred tax credits exist on Company A's balance sheet:

Tangible assets	$30
NOL benefit	25
Negative goodwill	(10)
	$45

23-4 Accounting for Section 83 Stock Purchase/Option Plans

A Section 83 "permanent discount" stock purchase/option plan (hereafter referred to as a Section 83 plan) is designed to address the limitations of Section 83 of the Internal Revenue Code and (a) enable employees to purchase company stock at substantially less than fair market value without the employees incurring taxable compensation and (b) allow any appreciation in the stock's value to be taxed at capital gains rates.

While the provisions of Section 83 plans may vary, most plans have the following characteristics:

1. The company grants to the employee the right to purchase stock at a substantial discount from the stock's fair market value at the time or purchase. For purposes of the following example, assume that the purchase price is $1.00 per share while the fair market value of the stock at the time of purchase is $10.00 per share.

A variation of this feature would be for the company not to require the employee to pay the $1.00 -- it would be a stock award. Under this variation, the $1.00 per share would be taxable compensation to the employee.

2. The shares may vest over a period of time. If vesting is not met, the company can reacquire the stock at the original sales price (in this example, $1.00).

3. The company retains a right of first refusal to purchase the stock from the employee if and when the employee decides to sell the shares. The repurchase price is equal to the difference between the then fair market value (say $15.00) and the excess of the fair market value when the employee purchased the shares ($10.00) over the employee's actual purchase price ($1.00). Thus, if the company elected to exercise its right of first refusal in this example, the company's repurchase price would be $6.00 ($15.00 - ($10.00 - $1.00)).

In Section 83 plans encountered to date and considered below in terms of accounting issues, the employee does not have a "put" (i.e., cannot require the company to repurchase the shares), although this could be a possible variation.

During the period of time the employee holds the stock, he or she enjoys the rights of a shareholder -- dividends and voting.

4. If the company does not elect to exercise its right of first refusal when the employee elects to sell the shares to a third party, the restriction does not lapse. The company retains the right of first refusal, including the discounted repurchase price.

Under a less common variation of this feature, the company's restriction lapses upon the sale to the third party and the employee is obligated to remit to the company the portion of the sales proceeds received upon the sale that equals the original spread ($9.00) between the fair market value and the price paid by the employee. Under this arrangement, the company receives $1.00 when the employee originally purchases the stock and the remaining $9.00 of the original fair market value when the employee sells the stock to a third party.

5. Because of the existence of a "permanent discount" (equal to the spread between fair market value at the date or purchase and the employee's purchase price), the position taken for tax

purposes is that the employee's purchase price equals the fair market value and, thus, there is no taxable compensation.

Both public and nonpublic companies have adopted Section 83 plans, which typically have been attractive to young, high technology enterprises.

INSTRUCTIONS:

Identify various approaches for reporting on Section 83 stock purchase/option plans and discuss the pros and cons of each approach.

23-5 Temporary Control Income

GPE, Inc. has had significant financial difficulties in recent years. At this time it has minimal assets, liabilities and operations, but it has accumulated a very substantial net operating loss carryforward for tax purposes. In order to take advantage of that NOL, the controlling shareholders of GPE, Inc. have recently acquired 80% of Hargrove Co. in a highly leveraged purchase business combination. Under the terms of the purchase agreement, the former owners of Hargrove have the option to repurchase a 60% interest in Hargrove for a fixed price by acquiring unissued common stock of Hargrove.

During the past year, Hargrove has made several acquisitions of companies which are profitable or are expected to be profitable. The acquisitions have been merged in as divisions of Hargrove, and it appears that the taxable income of Hargrove can be offset by the substantial net operating loss carryforwards of GPE, Inc. Under a tax sharing agreement between the parties, Hargrove must reimburse GPE for tax savings which accrue to Hargrove as a result of filing consolidated returns.

GPE is presently accounting for Hargrove as a consolidated subsidiary and is recording a minority interest liability to represent the 20% ownership of Hargrove by the investor group. Because of the existence of the options held by the former owners of Hargrove (which would enable them to assume 60% control of Hargrove), you (as auditors) have become concerned whether GPE's practice of consolidating Hargrove and recording 80% of Hargrove's net income is appropriate in the circumstances.

INSTRUCTIONS:

Discuss the appropriateness of this procedure.

23-6 Contingent Stock Purchase Warrants

There have been a number of instances where companies have issued warrants to customers in conjunction with sales agreements (sales volume discounts). The warrants are normally exercisable in increments, at the option of the customer/warrant holder, at a fixed price, after a specified minimum volume of purchases have been made by the customer. Under some agreements, the warrants are immediately exercisable, however, the exercise price is based on the volume of purchases.

In connection with sales agreements with certain major customers, Bolton Corporation issued "contingent warrants" to purchase shares of its common stock at prices 12 to 15% in excess of the current trading price of the stock. They are known as "contingent warrants" because the agreements provide that they become exercisable only if specified amounts of Bolton Corporation's products are purchased by customers within a three year period. Bolton believes that these contingent warrants provide it with the opportunity to sell products at a higher price than might otherwise by possible or to enter into sales agreements which might not otherwise be available because they afford the customers a chance to benefit from any price appreciation of Bolton's stock. Thus, the warrants represent a contingent cost associated with these sales agreements.

The accounting for these transactions is not specifically addressed in the authoritative accounting literature. Bolton's controller believes it appropriate to account for that cost based on the provisions of APB Opinion No. 14 related to debt issued with detachable stock purchase warrants. She valued the shares represented by the contingent warrants, with the assistance of an investment banker, at the date the sales agreements were executed. Valuation involved making certain assumptions as to: 1) the price of the Company's stock five years hence based on estimates of revenue and earnings growth rates over the next five years and a price/earnings multiple; 2) a computation of the present value of the customers' estimated profits on exercise of the warrants five years after date of issuance; and 3) a factor representing the estimated probability (expressed as a percentage) that the specified sales levels would be achieved. The value thus determined was credited to capital stock along with a deferred charge classified as an offset to equity. The deferred charge is being amortized against revenues as products are sold.

INSTRUCTIONS:

Is Bolton Corporation's method of accounting for contingent warrants appropriate?

23-7 Purchased Lease Residuals

Several lease brokers and leasing companies recently have purchased for cash or are planning to purchase future residual values of assets leased from others. Cash paid or to be paid generally approximates the present value of the estimated future residual values of the leased equipment. These residual values are for assets such as aircraft and computers and were acquired by the original lessor in transactions accounted for as leveraged leases. These purchased future residual values may or may not be guaranteed by the seller and/or a third party.

Lease brokers generally act as intermediaries between lessors and lessees and, in turn, receive fees for their services. The brokers' fees may be paid in cash at closing, the brokers may share in the future residual value of the leased assets, or a combination of both.

Computer Resale Co., Inc. has been in operation since 1978 and has as its principal source of revenue the purchase and sale of used computer systems. They have in the past relied on an informal secondary market to acquire their used equipment. They have faced problems with this system, since the source of supply can be erratic and may not include the types of computers that they want.

Early in 1986, a lease broker approached Computer Resale with the proposal to purchase the residual values of the computers leased by Computer Leasing Co. Computer Leasing deals primarily with the leading brand and most popular models of computers. Since Computer Leasing has been in business for a number of years and has a large number of units in place, Computer Resale would be able to acquire a given supply of computers on a regular basis.

The proposal looks promising to Computer Resale's controller, Sarah Waters. If the expected value of a computer at the end of a five year lease period is $10,000, Sarah would be willing to pay the present value of that amount discounted at a 15% rate of interest or $4,972. Sarah sees a problem with this proposal, however. The performance of the company will suffer until they actually receive and resell the computers. There will be no interest costs of carrying those residual values for the lease term and no income recognized.

The lease broker has an answer, accrete the carrying amount of the residual to the estimated future value of the residual. This will result in income recognition over the life of the lease. The investment in purchased residuals would increase if accretion methodology is followed by accreting income so that at the end of the lease term the estimated residual value in the financial records of the purchaser would approximate the amount expected upon sale of leased asset.

The arguments presented for accretion by the broker include the following:

1. Accretion better reflects the economic substance of the transaction.

2. Accretion is consistent with FASB No. 34, Capitalization of Interest.

3. The purchase of a lease residual is a monetary transaction.

INSTRUCTIONS:

Discuss the appropriateness of accounting for the residuals by accretion by assessing the justifications suggested by the lease broker.

23-8 Debt or Equity?

Bank holding companies increasingly are issuing mandatorily redeemable debt instruments, such as equity commitment notes, which are designed to qualify as primary capital in assessing capital adequacy under requirements of the federal bank regulatory authorities. As part of the debt instrument, the bank holding company undertakes to retire the debt with cash proceeds obtained from the issuance, to other than the debt holders, of common stock or perpetual preferred stock. Regulatory guidelines set a maximum twelve year maturity and require the establishment of a segregated account to be funded periodically from the sale of the aforementioned primary equity securities. At maturity, or prior to maturity provided the funding requirements have been met, the notes are redeemed for cash from the segregated account. Most equity commitment notes have been issued with floating interest rates which approximate current market for debt with a similar term to maturity.

In 1984, the Bank of New England Corporation issued $75,000,000 Floating Rate Subordianted Notes due 1996. The interest rate is equal to 1/8 of 1% plus the average of London interbank offered quotations for three month United States dollar deposits determined at the time of quarterly interest payments. The notes are not redeemable prior to July, 1988 and are unsecured and subordinated obligations of the corporation.

A note fund was established with the trustee to hold amounts representing proceeds from certain sales or issuances of permanent equity securities of the bank. The note fund is not to constitute security for the notes nor will the holders of the notes have any rights with respect to the note fund.

The bond indenture provides for the sale of the preferred or common stock in amounts sufficient to make deposits in the note fund at eight years, four years, and sixty days prior to maturity equal to one-third, two-thirds, and the full amount, respectively, of the original notes.

In the second year Bank of Boston Corporation issued $1,000,000 and First Union Corporation issued $50,000,000 of the same type of notes with the same equity commitments.

INSTRUCTIONS:

What are two accounting issues associated with this new type of securities? Discuss.

23-9 Creative Financing

The high interest rates of the early 1980's caused significant problems for the home building industry. The traditional fixed rate mortgages were at rates approaching 20% and even at these rates mortgage money was less available than in previous periods. Savings and loans and other financial institutions had recorded sizable losses on older fixed rate mortgages and were reluctant to enter new 30 year fixed rate agreements.

One reaction to the potential fixed rate loss problem was to have variable rate mortgages. Interest rates are adjusted every six months or year and are normally tied to the prime rate or U.S. Treasury Bill rates. The variable rates provide additional security for the lenders. However, the variable rates were also very high and many potential home buyers could not afford the high monthly payments. This was especially true for potential first time home buyers.

Another creative financing technique developed to help meet the high monthly payment problem: Negative Amortizing Loans. Negative amortizing loans are loans for which the rate at which interest is contractually earned (contract rate) is greater than the rate at which interest must be paid by the borrower (pay rate). For such loans, the principal balance typically increases during the period of time that the contract exceeds the pay rate. The idea is to limit the current monthly payment to fit more potential homeowner' budgets. At a later time higher payments may be made, lower interest rates may exist to enable some principal amortization, the mortgage may be refinanced at the higher principal amount, or any unpaid principal would be paid at the maturity of the loan.

A feature of a number of these loans is an implicit expectation that the appraised value of collateral supporting the loan will generally increase over the period during which principal is being built up by virtue of the negative amortization feature. Typically, the principal balance of the loan does not exceed 80 to 90 percent of the value of the underlying collateral at the inception of the loan, and it is not uncommon for the lending institution to require mortgage insurance on such loans.

There are no specific professional pronouncements that provide guidance as to the accounting for negative amortizing loans. Common practice is for financial institutions to accrue interest at the contract rate.

Is it appropriate to accure interest at the contract rate on negative amortizing loans?

23-10 The Problem of Duplicate Facilities

The brewing industry was undergoing considerable consolidation during the 1980's. Competition increased as beer consumption leveled off and many companies found that growth could best be experienced through the purchase of other breweries. Considerable cost savings would result through the elimination of duplicate facilities and more economical utilization of the remaining plant capacity.

The Fox Brewing Company decided that it could best survive the 1980's and beyond by expanding its product line and increasing its geographical distribution. Fox's primary markets were in the northeastern and midwestern United States. Their idea was to increase their market in the United States east of the Mississippi River.

The Seifert Brewing Co. Inc. had strong distribution in the southeast and a small brewery and some distribution in the Great Lakes states. The company was a family owned business and although remaining profitable after almost seventy-five years in operation, it too was becoming too small to compete.

Joe Fox, president of Fox Brewing approached Jim Seifert about a possible purchase of the family business. Jim was to become chief operating officer of Fox Brewing and responsible for the operations of the company's breweries. The sales force was to be combined and would begin selling all current brands of the combined company. Joe was to oversee the consolidation of the marketing staffs and to eliminate any duplication of efforts.

Jim agreed to consider the offer and to develop a proposal that might be acceptable to the Seifert family. Jim came up with a plan to consolidate the operations of the two companies by closing two breweries, one of his in Eagle River, Wisconsin and one of Fox's in St. Louis. They would then consolidate their brewing in the most modern plant they owned in Cleveland, Ohio. Jim presented the plan to Joe along with a proposed selling price for the company.

Joe likes the ideas, "The projected cost savings appear to be significant and just what we need to show strong earnings from operations almost immediately after the purchase. This will help us since we need strong earnings to enable us to sell some common stock. We have an interim short term credit agreement to finance the acquisition, but we have to sell stock next year to permanently finance the purchase."

Paula Seifert, controller of the family business, saw a problem with this plan. "If we decide to close the two breweries next year we will likely show significant losses associated with these closings. One potential idea would be to allocate the purchase price in the purchase business combination after including an estimated liability for the plant closings. Then when we close the two plants the losses will be charged against the liabilities rather than affecting income from operations. This accounting would be consistent with APB Opinion No. 11, paragraph 88i which indicates that one of the liabilities to be recorded in a purchase business combination is "plant closing expense incident to the acquisition."

INSTRUCTIONS:

Do you agree with Paula's proposed accounting for the plant closing?